ADULT EDUCATION AND TRAINING IN INDUSTRIALIZED COUNTRIES

The Praeger Special Studies
Series in Comparative Education

Published in Cooperation with the Comparative
Education Center, State University of New York, Buffalo

General Editor: **Philip G. Altbach**

With contributions from:

Pierre Besnard and Bernard Lietard
Ralph J. Clark and Donald H. Brundage
K. Patricia Cross
Helmuth Dolff
Chris Duke
Per Himmelstrup
Seymour M. Rosen
Kjell Rubenson
Arthur Stock

ADULT EDUCATION AND TRAINING IN INDUSTRIALIZED COUNTRIES

Richard E. Peterson
John S. Helmick
John R. Valley

Sally Shake Gaff
Robert A. Feldmesser
H. Dean Nielsen

PRAEGER

PRAEGER SPECIAL STUDIES • PRAEGER SCIENTIFIC

LC
5215
A38

This work was developed under a contract with the Department of Education. However, the contract does not necessarily reflect the position or policy of that agency, and no official endorsement of these materials should be inferred.

Published in 1982 by Praeger Publishers
CBS Educational and Professional Publishing
A Division of CBS Inc.
521 Fifth Avenue, New York, New York 10175 U.S.A.

© 1982 by Praeger Publishers
Copyright is claimed until 5 years from date of publication.
Thereafter all portions of this work covered
by this copyright will be in the public domain.
All rights reserved

Library of Congress Catalog Card Number:81-84672

ISBN: 0-03-061551-8

23456789   145   987654321

Printed in the United States of America

NMU LIBRARY

The Praeger Special Studies Series in
Comparative Education
*General Editor: **Philip G. Altbach***

ACADEMIC POWER: Patterns of Authority
in Seven National Systems of Higher Education
John H. Van de Graaff, Dietrich Goldschmidt, Burton R. Clark,
Donald F. Wheeler, Dorotea Furth

ADAPTATION AND EDUCATION IN JAPAN
Nobuo K. Shimahara

CHANGES IN THE JAPANESE UNIVERSITY:
A Comparative Perspective
edited by: William K. Cummings, Ikuo Amano, Kazuyuki Kitamura

COMPARATIVE PERSPECTIVES ON THE ACADEMIC PROFESSION
edited by: Philip G. Altbach

FUNDING HIGHER EDUCATION: A Six-Nation Analysis
edited by: Lyman A. Glenny

US AND UK EDUCATIONAL POLICY: A Decade of Reform
Edgar Litt, Michael Parkinson

UNIVERSITY AND GOVERNMENT IN MEXICO:
Autonomy in an Authoritarian System
Daniel C. Levy

PUBLISHING IN THE THIRD WORLD: Trend Report and Bibliography
Philip G. Altbach, Eva-Maria Rathgeber

UNIVERSITIES AND THE INTERNATIONAL
DISTRIBUTION OF KNOWLEDGE
edited by: Irving J. Spitzberg, Jr.

STUDYING TEACHING AND LEARNING:
Trends in Soviet and American Research
edited by: B. Robert Tabachnick, Thomas S. Popkewitz,
Beatrice Beach Szekely

INTERNATIONAL BIBLIOGRAPHY OF COMPARATIVE EDUCATION
Philip G. Altbach, Gail P. Kelly, David H. Kelly

SYSTEMS OF HIGHER EDUCATION IN TWELVE COUNTRIES:
A Comparative View
Nell P. Eurich

ADULT EDUCATION AND TRAINING IN INDUSTRIALIZED
COUNTRIES
Richard E. Peterson, John S. Helmick, John R. Valley,
Sally Shake Gaff, Robert A. Feldmesser, H. Dean Nielsen

CONTENTS

ADULT EDUCATION AND TRAINING IN INDUSTRIALIZED COUNTRIES

INTRODUCTION

Active interest in providing opportunities for adult
education, recurrent training, and lifelong learning is
growing throughout the world. While government initiatives
may presently be slowed in some countries--because of inflationary and recessionary pressures--in others they are
expanding: witness the numerous government-sponsored national
literacy campaigns. In most industrialized countries, private
and informal adult learning activities in local settings are
clearly expanding. This is unquestionably the case in the
United States, where adult and part-time enrollments in
colleges and universities have also increased dramatically
in the past decade.

Springing from different traditions and concepts,
policies and programs for adult education take different
forms from one country to another. Nonetheless, it can be
instructive indeed for governments, as well as nongovernmental agencies interested in education policy, to understand
pertinent developments in other countries. Forms of service
judged to be effective in one country most certainly warrant
consideration by other countries. The need for people to know
and understand--for reasons of minimal everyday living--must
be virtually universal. Continuous learning, however, can be
the key, not to minimal lives, but to good lives and good
societies.

Background and Purpose of the Study

The origin of the project dates back to education amendments of 1974. Precisely: "The National Center for Education
Statistics shall review and report on educational activities
in foreign countries" (Title V, Section 406 B4). The general
intent of the legislation was to identify practices in other
nations that may have beneficial application in the U.S.
Staff at NCES determined that, among other studies, a comparative study of adult education opportunities would be
conducted.

Their Request for Proposals (RFP) called for a comprehensive, multifaceted study spanning eight industrialized nations
in addition to the U.S.--eight countries which, among them,
could be expected to have developed policies and programs for
adult education warranting consideration in this country.

1

The nine countries--specified in the RFP--include Australia, Canada, Denmark, the Federal Republic of Germany, France, the Soviet Union, Sweden, the United Kingdom, and the United States.

As conceived under the direction of NCES staff, and detailed in its RFP, the project was to give particular attention to policies and programs directed at five population categories: (1) workers, (2) older persons, (3) women entering the labor force, (4) parents, and (5) undereducated adults.

In addition to describing policies and programs for these five population groups, the study sought also to:

(1) Describe national policies and programs, where they exist, for the education of all adults;

(2) Compile comparative statistical information on: (a) the extent of adult education participation--in the general population and for the five subgroups; and (b) the effectiveness of various adult education programs; and

(3) Set forth implications of foreign practices for adult education policy in the United States.

The RFP, as said, was comprehensively framed. ETS staff chose to try also to conduct as comprehensive a study as possible--within cost and time limitations--rather than, in some fashion, to narrow the project.

In brief, then, the general purpose of the project was to gather together information about major adult education policies and programs in eight developed countries, in order to learn if any of these policies may be usefully adopted in this country.

Definition of Principal Concepts

Definition of key concepts is always a critical matter in social research. The paragraphs below, taken verbatim from a project description used throughout the study in gathering information, summarize the meanings given to six of the principal concepts in the study.

Adult education opportunities: All programs of organized and sustained education, either full- or part-time, other than "regular" secondary or higher education, available for people who are above the age of compulsory school attendance (generally age 15 or 16).

"Regular" is a term used in OECD and UNESCO literature to refer to the conventional or mainstream educational sequences, typically enrolling students age 25 or younger full-time. This study in contrast, is concerned with programs that typically enroll working adults on a part-time basis. Some examples are the British Open University, the Danish Folkschools, Russian evening and extramural programs, industry-sponsored courses, proprietary schools, correspondence schools, programs conducted by libraries or museums, church-sponsored programs, and education in the military services.

Workers: Our definition, which includes white collar as well as blue collar workers, is virtually synonymous with employees (except that we are also interested in training programs for adults seeking employment).

The study seeks information, for example, about worker sabbaticals, paid educational leaves, employer- or union-sponsored training programs or benefits, various opportunities for upgrading skills, cooperative arrangements between schools and industries, and special programs for immigrant workers.

Older persons: The definition is again broad, to include people from midlife through relatively advanced age.

We are requesting information about educational services--including counseling and educational information--for individuals changing jobs or entering the labor force in midcareer, for preparation for retirement, and for people of postretirement age.

Women entering the labor force: Adult women seeking to enter or re-enter the labor force after having been away from education or work.

We are particularly interested in special programs for women entering the labor force in midlife, or after a period of child rearing. Programs may include counseling, information, and childcare, for example, in addition to instructional services.

<u>Parents</u>: Men and women with children up to age 18 in the home.

> Called for here is information about programs
> of parent education (toward effective parenting)
> and strategies for overcoming barriers to
> participation in parent education.

<u>Undereducated adults</u>: This definition is intended to be country-specific; that is, it is expected that each country will have a different conception of "under-educated adult."

> The definition in some countries may specify
> failure to complete the normal sequence of
> compulsory education. In the U.S., on the
> other hand, anyone 18 years or older without
> a secondary school diploma is considered "under-
> educated." Thus we are interested in programs
> through which adults may complete secondary
> or comparable schooling, or earn the normal
> certificate granted at the end of compulsory
> education. We also are seeking information
> about adult literacy and adult functional
> competency programs.

Course of the Study

The project, scheduled for one year, began in August 1979 and was completed in September 1980. The first two months were given over to settling issues concerning the scope of the study, information-gathering strategies, and definitions for key terms. The balance of the study's duration was divided roughly between (1) gathering information and (2) drafting and revising the final report from the project.

Six professional staff participated in the study. The division of labor was along country lines. Richard Peterson took responsibility for material about the United Kingdom; John Helmick, for Denmark and West Germany; John Valley, Australia and Canada; Sally Gaff, France; Robert Feldmesser (having a master's degree in Soviet Studies and fluency in Russian), the Soviet Union; Dean Nielsen (with a PhD. from the University of Stockholm), Sweden; and Peterson and Gaff, the United States.

Since travel to any of the eight foreign countries included in the study was not possible under the terms of the contract, it was necessary to rely heavily on published documents. These were obtained primarily through corre-spondence with provider agencies in the respective countries, but also through other sources, including the eight embassies, UNESCO, the Organization for Economic Co-Operation and Development (OECD) and other international organizations with interests in adult education, numerous Washington-based organizations, several U.S. government agencies, and a number of travelers to the U.S. However, in particular, we relied on the good offices of eight country consultants who participated in the study.

In large part because travel to the eight countries was not possible, an early decision was made to enlist an expert on adult education in each of the countries. We were extremely fortunate to obtain the cooperation of individuals who are widely recognized to be among the top experts in their respective nations. Each was asked (1) to write a paper summarizing the major features of adult education in his country, and (2) to act as a gatherer of and conduit for published materials.

Instructions to the country consultants were quite general. They were asked for an up-to-date overview, to include descriptions of major national policies and programs (if such exist) and special programs for the five selected populations, participation data--in general and for the five groups, evidence of program effectiveness, and critical comments on the general condition of adult education in their respective countries. It was expected that the country reports would differ in approach and content, which they did. Nonetheless, they contain extremely valuable information supplementary to the content of Parts I and II; in a number of instances, notably Rosen's piece on adult education in the Soviet Union and Besnard and Lietard's analysis of "animation" in France, they contain material probably not available elsewhere in English.

Midway in the course of the study, it became apparent that an initial project objective--to compile comparative participation statistics for the five analytic subpopulations --would not prove to be attainable. After scrutiny of the documents made available to us, it was concluded--chiefly because either pertinent data were simply not collected or because data categories differed so greatly among the countries--that assembly of comparative tables was not possible, given accepted standards of research practice. As noted in Part IV, even an effort to obtain informed judgments (from our country consultants) proved abortive, mainly for reasons of nonavailability of data.

As the reader will see in Part IV, however, one comparative table is presented, not without some misgivings. It gives estimates of total adult education participation rates, which were arrived at both through tabulations of country program statistics (given in Part I) and the judgments of the country consultants.

Finally, the early objective of examining program effectiveness (as judged, for example, by retention data) proved entirely unattainable. Only a handful of evaluation studies, or reports containing data that could be construed in an evaluative manner, were uncovered. None were in any sense comparable across countries.

Thus, while this report does not contain numerous comparative tables--impossible because of varying approaches to compilation of educational statistics from country to country--the report does contain a wealth of information about the educational services each of the nine nations is providing for its adults in general, and for the five specified population groups in particular.

Structure of the Report

As outlined below, the report is organized into five parts.

Part I contains brief overviews of adult education in each of the nine nations. Each of these country accounts reviews principal national policies, very briefly describes major programs and providers, and concludes with a table giving participation estimates for the major programs.

Part II is devoted to policies and programs for the five specified population categories: workers, older persons, women entering the labor force, parents, and undereducated adults. The beginning section on WORKERS, for example, consists of country-by-country accounts, each describing in some detail educational and training opportunities for workers (including statistical data where available) in that country.

Part III is comprised of the nine country reports prepared by the aforementioned experts from each of the countries included in the study. (The paper on adult education in the U.S.S.R. was written by a U.S.-based expert on education in that nation.)

Part IV consists of an analytic discussion of issues and implications for U.S. government policy in the area of adult education and lifelong learning, on the basis of policies and practices in the foreign countries studied. Part IV contains the study's only comparative data table--estimates of each country's total adult education participation rate.

Part V lists all the documents gathered and used during the course of the study. These references are organized by country, and at the end there is also a list of the multi-national studies and commentaries that were consulted.

Acknowledgments

Because of the general necessity during the study to request information from a great many sources, we are indebted to a very large number of individuals and organizations--far too many for each to be recognized.

We wish to acknowledge first the excellent and extensive work performed under difficult time constraints by the project's country consultants--both in preparing reports on adult learning opportunities in their respective countries, and in gathering and forwarding pertinent documents to project staff in Princeton and Washington, D.C. This group included:

Australia:	Dr. Chris Duke, Director, Centre for Continuing Education, The Australian National University
Canada:	Mr. Ralph J. Clark and Dr. Donald Brundage, Department of Adult Education, Ontario Institute for Studies in Education
Denmark:	Dr. Per Himmelstrup, Director, Sydjysk Univsitetscenter Dr. Poul-Erik Kandrup, Danish Adult Education Council
Federal Republic of Germany:	Dr. Helmuth Dolff, Director, The German Adult Education Association
France:	M. Pierre Besnard and M. Bernard Lietard, Universite Rene Descartes
Sweden:	Dr. Kjell Rubenson, Stockholm Institute of Education, University of Stockholm
The Soviet Union:	Dr. Seymour Rosen, Comparative Education Branch, United States Department of Education
The United Kingdom:	Mr. Arthur Stock, Director, National Institute of Adult Education (England and Wales)

We wish to thank the numerous officials in Europe-based international organizations with interests in adult learning who provided materials for the project. Particularly valuable aid was given by Paul Bertelsen and H. Ben-Amor of UNESCO, Aida Furtada of UNESCO's International Bureau of Education, John Lowe of OECD, and Helen Hootsmans of the European Bureau of Adult Education.

Scores of individuals from governmental and nongovernmental agencies in Washington, D.C. having information about the foreign countries in the study, or about aspects of adult education in the U.S., generously contributed their personal expertise as well as published materials from their files. Especially helpful were Lloyd Feldman and Karen Campbell from the U.S. Department of Labor, Mary Jane Dillon from the Department of Education, Charlotte Nusberg of the International Federation of Aging, Edward Cohen-Rosenthal at the National Institute for Work and Learning, Carol Eliason from the American Association of Community and Junior Colleges, Sandra Timmermann from the Institute of Lifetime Learning, and staff from the Project on Status and Education of Women (sponsored by the Association of American Colleges). Staff in the embassies of each of the countries also kindly lent materials from their files.

Translation services were provided by Genevieve Noel, Catherine Raphael, and Maryann Morrison.

Within Educational Testing Service, Rosemary Lanes served as Administrative Assistant--coordinator extraordinaire --throughout the project. Typing and proofing of draft sections were carried out by Hedy Nash, Audrey Staats, Jeanette Frantz and Lois Harris. Alice Setteducati and Judith Bonnett Hirabayashi of the ETS office in Berkeley edited most of the final draft. Final production of the text was the work of the Conant Text Processing Center at ETS in Princeton and of Monica Laurens in Berkeley.

To all these capable and generous individuals and their organizations, we express our sincerest thanks.

PART I:

COUNTRY OVERVIEWS

AUSTRALIA

Australia's population of 14 million makes that continent-nation roughly comparable to the State of Texas (13.4 million) or the East-South-Central region (Kentucky, Tennessee, Alabama, and Mississippi) of the United States which has 14.1 million people. However, as the following observations will make clear, gross population comparisons between a state or region of the U.S.A. and Australia provide not the slightest hint of the resemblances or differences between these two countries in their provision of adult education. Texas, for example, has 147 colleges and universities, whereas Australia has 1,060 colleges of technical and further education, including 194 major institutions and 866 branches, annexes and centers, plus 72 colleges of advanced education and 19 universities.

Some particularly noteworthy features of adult education in Australia are the following:

(1) The traditional view of adult education in Australia is undergoing change and this change is relatively recent. Until about 1970 the Australian Association of Adult Education defined adult education as liberal education. However, the Association for its 1978 conference proposed as a working definition "noncredit education for those whose principal activity is no longer education." The more recent perceptions of the domain of adult education do, indeed, overlap the interests of this study. However, they are not completely congruent.

(2) While clearly not concerned solely with adult education, the establishment of the Tertiary Education Commission (TEC) in 1976, incorporating as Councils of TEC the formerly separate Universities Commission, the Commission on Advanced Education and the Technical and Further Education Commission, is one indication of new organizational, administrative and structural changes that will impact adult education. TEC is responsible for advising the federal government on postsecondary education. Another change that bears watching is the emergence of a new kind of postsecondary institution, multilevel and open access in character, and serving a fairly widespread educational community. Darwin Community College is the first institution of this design,

while several existing colleges such as Prahan College of Advanced Education, Hawkesbury Agricultural College, or Darling Downs Institute of Advanced Education, among others, are moving in this direction. Finally, Australia's nineteenth and most recently established university, Deakin, is dedicated to the provision of tertiary education at the university level through external studies programs. Deakin, while based in Geelong, Victoria, will serve students both within and outside its home state.

(3)   While Australia has well defined routes of passage between formal secondary and postsecondary education, a second chance philosophy and various practices and arrangements mollify their limitations. A survey of 91 tertiary institutions revealed that while some institutions had admitted no students of mature age (i.e., over 21), at others the proportion of mature age students was about one out of six and in a few instances even greater (Haines and Collins, 1979). Moreover, within the Technical and Further Education Sector, Stream 5 enrollments (courses which can be described broadly as preparatory, including matriculation and diploma courses) were roughly 110,000 in 1977. Of course, in addition to matriculation and bridge courses the opportunities to pursue diplomas, degrees, and other qualifications as part-time external students are also relevant. Nevertheless, the overall adequacy of second chance provision continues to be a concern in that lower socioeconomic groups are not well represented among adult education students. There is also concern that apprenticeships tend to be limited to people in their late teens and more mature individuals have little chance to enter the skilled trades.

(4)   Two demographic aspects--the Aboriginals and the substantial, continuing, and changing character of immigration to Australia--give rise to special adult education needs. In the case of the Aboriginals, the issues are confounded by a shift in policy from self-determination to self-management of Aboriginal affairs and further complicated because some Aboriginals live in highly urbanized areas; whereas others live in tribal settings and circumstances where their educational preferences and requirements are quite different. The immigrant issues, on the other hand, grow out of the large numbers of immigrants (in 1978 somewhat under 30 percent of the total population were immigrants and their children), the changing character of immigration (falling from 70 percent from Britain and other European countries to 40 percent in the six-year period ending 1978), and its projected continuance at about 50,000 immigrants per year. Moreover, these features carry with them several more general adult education concerns: literacy training, education of the aged, and educational opportunities for women.

(5) External study, a method for gaining college of advanced education or university qualifications, pioneered and advanced substantially in Australia, has features that contrast with correspondence education in the U.S.A. External study courses follow the regular on-campus schedule, and they are not especially prepared courses (Deakin University is an exception). There is no limit on the amount of external study that can be accepted towards the degree, and external students qualify for the same degree as internal students. However, there are additional innovative ways in which Australian adult education has dealt with limitations of time and space: for example, assistance in the organization of discussion groups operated out of homes, residential programs of adult education, classes on commuter trains operating between Geelong and Melbourne, and the operation of radio stations by several universities. Yet certain approaches emerging in the U.S.A. have not surfaced in Australia. One example is the development of courses and their distribution nation-wide by newspapers and television. Second (and here the contrast between the two countries is even sharper), the application of diverse approaches to the assessment and recognition of learning through credit by examination, self-assessment, crediting of courses taught by the military or business and industry, and techniques for assessing the learning acquired through volunteer activities, homemaking, and other forms of experiential learning or education.

(6) Systematic and comprehensive data regarding adult education programs, opportunities and participation are either incomplete or not available. In the absence of such information, data for this report have been culled from reports from diverse sources such as federal inquiry committees, federal and state agencies for education and other areas, individual institutions and from analytic essays by individuals knowledgeable of the Australian adult education scene. Moreover, there is room for error growing out of differences in reporting units, differences in time frames, and the possibility that information from one source may overlap to some degree another source. As will be noted later, for some categories of providers data are largely missing. And, as stated earlier, while a definition of adult education is emerging in Australia that relates quite well to the interests of this study, differences remain. The data for individual programs can be accepted as authoritative. However, because of the limitations indicated above, aggregating data across programs results in what is at best a general order of magnitude estimate.

The Major Providers

The Universities. Australia's 19 universities, five of
which were founded after 1969, are unevenly distributed across
the six states and two territories: New South Wales has
six; Victoria four; Queensland three; West Australia and
South Australia two each; and one each in Tasmania and the
Australian Capital Territory. Universities provide adult
education opportunities in three modes: part-time, external
studies, and continuing or community education programming.
Part-time and external students accounted for 55,510 out of
158,411 university enrollments in 1977. The five universities
with major commitments to external studies are the University
of Queensland, the University of New England, Macquarie
University, Murdoch University, and the fledgling Deakin
University. There is some concern about the attrition rate
among part-time and external students which is higher than
that for full-time students. By 1977, for example, of the
group that started in 1971, 59 percent of the part-time and
external students had discontinued. This compares to roughly
70 to 75 percent of full-timers who are expected to graduate.
While the number of full-time university students remained
relatively stable between 1977 and 78, the number of part-time
students and external students rose by 3 percent and 20 percent respectively.
    Universities also offer professional refresher courses
and more general adult education courses in which enrollments
in 1974 numbered over 32,000 in the first instance and over
40,000 in the second. About half of the universities have
established central units to coordinate or conduct university
activities in continuing and adult education.

    Colleges of Advanced Education. There are some 72
colleges of advanced education (CAEs) including 40 teachers
colleges, 10 regional colleges, 8 central institutes of
technology, and 5 metropolitan multi-purpose institutions.
The remaining CAEs are special-focus institutions (agriculture, paramedical studies, arts, and so on). Most CAEs are
relatively small institutions; 50 had less than 1,500 students
in 1973. Part-time students make up 39 percent of the total
140,000 enrollments in CAE. Part-time enrollments are concentrated in teacher education (42 percent) and commerce and
business studies (19.6 percent). In the latter category,
part-time enrollments exceed full-time enrollments by more
than two to one.
    While no enrollment data were located, there is evidence
of substantial interest among CAEs regarding continuing
education programming. The proceedings of a conference held
in 1975 contain statements furnished by 22 CAEs which affirm
their interest in providing continuing education (Duke,
1976b).

Technical and Further Education Institutions. Collectively, technical and further education institutions are the major suppliers of adult education in Australia. The Tertiary Education Act of 1975 defined technical and further education as "a course of instruction or training...preparatory to, a course...relevant to a trade, technical or...skilled occupation or that...meets education needs...not provided at a university...or college of advanced education...or primary or secondary education by way of a full-time course in a school" (Williams, p. 284). There are 194 major TAFE institutions with 581 annexes, and 285 other TAFE institutions with eight annexes whose educational offerings are grouped into six streams:

1. Professional   4. Other Skilled

2. Paraprofessional   5. Preparatory

3. Trades   6. Adult Education

While enrollments in Stream 6 made up over 229,000 out of over 809,000 TAFE enrollments, the estimate of adult participation in this report was derived from a two-step conversion of total TAFE enrollments based on the following observations. First and foremost, 95 percent of enrollments in TAFE are part-time. Second, the Williams Committee was advised by the Technical and Further Education Council that the number of students in TAFE was 80 percent of the number of enrollments. Thus, the total adult education participation is recorded as slightly over 615,000 for purposes of this report and represents an estimate of the number of part-time students in TAFE programs.

Government Departments Other Than Education. In this category information regarding programs and the extent of participation is quite inadequate. The estimates of participation cited in this report serve mainly to illustrate that substantial adult education provision is to be found in spheres of governmental activity other than education. The Department of Labor is dealing with problems of unemployment, and particularly unemployment among young adults, through education and training. The Department of Immigration and Ethnic Affairs has a substantial on-going program of literacy training, language instruction, and other courses designed to facilitate the absorption of thousands of immigrants into Australian society.

Local Volunteer Groups. Today two Worker Educational Associations (WEA) remain active in adult education; one in New South Wales and one in South Australia. They work closely with various educational resources, including universities and colleges of advanced education, to offer extensive educational programming including classes, weekend and vacation schools, and overseas study tours. Some courses run for periods as long as three years. The WEA in New South Wales had 15,765 enrollments, while the WEA in South Australia had 16,553 enrollments in 1978, including 1,792 enrollments in trade union courses offered by correspondence. At one time, there was a WEA in Victoria which has since been replaced by a statutory board known as the Council of Adult Education. There are statutory boards now in other states as well. The data for WEAs serve merely to illustrate rather than to deal with this category of providers of adult education. Other providers that are part of this category for which it was not possible to locate systematic information are various drama groups, arts councils, YM and YWCAs and so on.

Other Programs and Summary Estimates of Participation. Clearly the limited number of programs for which statistics are reported in this category barely scratch the surface. One indication of the far more extensive provision of adult education is found in the survey of the Wollongong Area of N.S.W. (Hooper, 1978). He catalogs over 100 providers of adult education in a compact coastal strip roughly 80 km long and 14 km wide with a total population of around 211,000 and where the adult population is 67 percent blue collar workers.

Consequently, the estimate of total participation of 13 percent, while very conservative, is higher than two estimates found in Australian literature: one of 10 percent (Finnegan, 1977) and one of something in excess of 5 percent, attributed to the Australian Association of Adult Education in 1974 (ACOTAFE, 1974).

In Part III of this volume, Duke comments at some length on the "Status of Data" for Australia using descriptors such as "incomplete," "rudimentary," "notoriously unsatisfactory," and so on. Moreover, he hints at unknown amounts of duplication in TAFE enrollments.

In Table 1 that follows, there is reason to believe some overcounting occurred because of the possibility of duplication across programs. At the same time, participation data were not obtained for diverse programs of a local or highly specialized character. The summary total in Table 1 should, therefore, be regarded as a general order of magnitude estimate.

TABLE 1. AUSTRALIA: MAJOR PROGRAMS AND ESTIMATES OF PARTICIPATION

Program or Provider	Estimated Number of Participants	Year	Source
Universities:			
Part-Time Internal	45,827	1977	Williams Report, 1977
Part-Time External	9,683	1977	
Continuing Education-A	32,058	1974	Universities Commission, 1975
Continuing Education-B	40,256	1974	
A--Professional Refresher B--Adult Education			
Colleges of Advanced Education:			
Part-Time Internal	44,666	1977	Williams Report, 1977
Part-Time External	10,752	1977	
Technical and Further Education Institutions:			
Part-Time	615,063	1977	Williams Report, 1977
Government Departments Other Than Education:			
Army	5,000		Williams Report, 1977
Dept. of Immigration and Ethnic Affairs	100,000+	1979-80	Dept. I & E Affairs, 1980
Dept. of Labor and Immigration: NEAT	110,000		
EPOY	2,500		Williams Report, 1977
SYEP	30,000	1977	
CYSS	30,000		

Program or Provider	Estimated Number of Participants	Year	Source
Worker Educational Associations	31,318	1978	South Australia, WEA 1979; New South Wales, WEA, 1979
Council of Adult Education-- Victoria	29,355	1978-79	Victoria Council of Adult Education, 1977
Other Programs--Suggestive Listing Only:			
Apprenticeships	126,900	1978	Williams, 1977
Non-Gov't Business College--Part-Time	3,385	1978	Williams, 1977
Trade Union Training Authority	8,517	1977-78	TUTA-77-78
Darwin Community College	9,971	1977	Darwin C.C., 1977
Deakin University	2,100	1978	Deakin, 1980
National Employment and Training System	25,000	1975-76	ACOTAFE, 1975
Aboriginal Adult Education	5,000	1977	Adult Aboriginal Education, 1977
Total adult population:	10,423,000		Estimated total participation rate: 13 percent
Estimated total parti- cipation, all programs:	1,368,000		

CANADA

An adult education anthology (Kidd and Selman, 1978), containing articles and papers published originally in the mid-to-late 1960s, speaks of adult education in Canada as "having arrived" during that decade. Consequently, the present moment is a particularly propitious one in which to look at Canadian adult education. That is, what is the extent and character of adult education some ten to twelve years after the announcement of its coming of age in Canada?

First, data indicate an expansion of opportunity and participation in the 1970s. The participation rate per 1,000 population 15 years and over and not in full-time attendance at an educational institution for part-time credit and formal noncredit courses for Canada increased from 91.0 to 118.0 from 1973-74 to 1976-77 (Statistics Canada, 1979c). Similarly, part-time university enrollments increased from 85,814 (Munroe, 1975) to 216,692 between 1966-67 and 1977-78 (Statistics Canada, 1979d) largely because universities introduced the practice of "mature matriculation" and the offering of degree credit for courses given in the evening or in summer sessions. The Adult Occupational Training Act, the authority for the federal Canada Manpower Training Program, is also providing learning opportunities for several hundred thousand adults annually. More details on these activities are presented later in the report.

Secondly, two new institutional forms began to mature in the 1970s: community colleges and open universities. The Canadian usage of the term community college parallels, only in a general sense, its usage in the United States. Moreover, the functions assigned to community colleges are different across provinces.

Beginning in 1967, Quebec brought into being its first colleges d'enseignement generale et professionel (CEGEPs), and by 1975 there were 36 of these publicly supported tuition-free institutions. They serve as buffers between secondary schools and university. All students going on to postsecondary education, including university, attend CEGEPs. In Ontario, on the other hand, there are 22 Colleges of Applied Arts and Technology (CAATs) which are vocational and general education institutions, but they do not offer the first or second year of university work. In British Columbia, the colleges offer the first two years of university work and other programs, while in Saskatchewan the community colleges have planning-integration functions and offer programs themselves only when other institutions are unable to do so. Statistics Canada includes in its data for community colleges not only the kinds of institutions described above, but also institutions offering instruction in specialized fields of agriculture, fisheries, and marine technology. Student enrollments in continuing education in "community colleges" for the whole of Canada were 219,719 in 72-73 and by 1976-77 they were 450,153 (Statistics Canada, 1978).

Athabasca University in Alberta and Tele-universite in Quebec are open universities. Tele-universite, now a part of the University of Quebec, grew out of TEVEC, a pilot project in the use of television to reach students in one of the more isolated parts of the province. Its early assignment was the management of a distance learning in-service training program for mathematics teachers and the offering of a course on the cooperative movement for the general public. By 1972, the University of Quebec had established Tele-universite as a five-year development program in distance education intended for students who were not within reach of the regular university program. By 1977-78 about 12,000 students, well distributed over Quebec and representing a diversity of backgrounds, took one or more Tele-universite courses. Growing out of its early experience with courses on co-operatives, Tele-universite has become involved with the cooperative movement more generally and in joint ventures with school boards, government departments, and various associations (Daniel and Smith, 1979).

Athabasca University started as the fourth campus-based university in Alberta, but was directed away from this role to become a distance learning institution following the recommendations of a commission on Educational Planning calling for an Alberta Academy to offer courses for credit that all post-secondary institutions would recognize (Munroe, 1975). By 1978, it was offering 14 home study courses to 1,900 enrolled students and the expectation is that it will serve 4,800 students in 1979-80. For courses directly related to Canada such as Canadian Literature or Canadian History, Athabasca develops its own distance learning materials. For the majority of its courses, it turns to resources such as British Open University, University of Mid-America and Coastline Community College. The program makes extensive use of the telephone as the medium of contact between student and tutor. See also Clark and Brundage, Part III of this report, for information regarding a third example of an open educational institution, namely, the Open Learning Institute in British Columbia.

Thirdly, there is now a better sense of the dimensions of participation in adult education. A study in Ontario based on interviews with a carefully selected sample of 1,541 residents not enrolled as full-time students revealed that about 30 percent of the population aged 18 to 69 are or were recently involved in some type of systematic learning activity during the previous twelve months (Waniewicz, 1976). The survey was conducted between the end of October 1974 and early January 1975. The learning activities included credit and noncredit courses, training in business and industry, courses offered by community and cultural organizations, activities of special interest and sports clubs, studies via television and radio, or personal learning on one's own time. Individuals so engaged were classified as "Learners" and were estimated at 1,400,000 people. Another 18 percent of the population, over 800,000 people, constituted a "Would-Be-Learner" group who, while not involved in learning activities, indicated an interest in doing so in the next year or so.

The researcher explained not only the general limitations of his data but also that they applied to the province of Ontario. Therefore, it is with considerable trepidation that any inferences about Canada as a whole are made here particularly since there is evidence that adult education opportunities and participation rates are not uniform across provinces. For example, in formal continuing education provided by school boards, departments of education, community colleges and universities for the years of the Waniewicz study, participation rates ranged from 48.9 in the Yukon and the Northwest Territories to 126.5 in British Columbia (Statistics Canada, 1979c). The rate is the number of persons per 1,000 population 15 years and older. Since the rate for Canada as a whole was 13 percent less than for Ontario, it suggests that the adult learner category for Canada might be overestimated from the Ontario data. If adjusted downward by the difference in participation rates for formal continuing education observed between Ontario and Canada, the estimated learner category would approach 26 percent of the adult population of Canada. How would this estimate relate to the major program estimates that follow? First the major program estimates have some duplication which cannot be unraveled. Furthermore, systematic and comprehensive data were not located for several categories of providers mentioned by learners in the Ontario study such as local community and cultural organizations, interest and sports clubs, radio and television, and self-directed study. Consequently the data of the Ontario study and the major program estimates of this report should be viewed as two different approaches to understanding the general magnitude of the provision for adult education in Canada.

The Major Providers

The Universities.   There are 52 universities in Canada but with their affiliated and associated colleges they number 72.   In 1977-78 there were 212,000 part-time university enrollments of which 183,000 were undergraduate and 29,000 graduate (Statistics Canada, 1979d).   Continuing education enrollments in universities in 1976-77 totaled 574,000 of which 227,000 were in noncredit courses and 347,000 were part-time credit courses.   Universities were asked to report the following kinds of programs under the rubric of continuing education: "activities involving organized and sustained instruction (classes, workshops, seminars, forums, institutes, symposia, public lecture and film news...which are (1) not for credit, (2) recognized as credit toward a diploma or certificate awarded by the extension department (unless reported through the registrar's office), (3) recognized as credit toward a diploma or certificate awarded by a professional association or other organization" (Statistics Canada, 1979d).

The Community Colleges.   The number of community colleges is somewhat in excess of 200.   These institutions reported, as continuing education, their enrollments in general interest courses, professional development or refresher courses, in-school training in industry courses, part-time academic upgrading and language courses, part-time pre-employment courses at the trades level, and owner-manager-supervisory courses of the Department of Manpower and Immigration.   The total enrollment of 450,000 students in 1976-77 is divided into 132,000 part-time credit courses and 318,000 noncredit courses (Statistics Canada, 1978).

Departments of Education and School Boards.   The student enrollments in the courses offered through these agencies break down as follows:

School Board--Part-Time Credit Courses	100,000
School Board--Noncredit Courses	539,000
Dept. of Education Correspondence--Part-Time Credit	84,000
Dept. of Education Correspondence--Noncredit	7,000

The courses cover academic upgrading, high school completion, vocational upgrading, refresher courses and general interest (hobby craft, recreation).

Canada Manpower Training Program.   Since 1967, the Canada Employment and Immigration Commission has spent over $3.5 billion to support training and retraining of over 1 million workers.   The program has two major components: Institutional

Training done under contract using educational institutional resources of the provinces to provide up to 52 weeks of occupational skills training, basic training for skill development, job readiness training, work adjustment training, apprenticeship training, and language training; and Industrial Training contracted with employers after training plans are approved (by provincial authorities). Total enrollment in 1976-77 was 280,000 (CMTP, September 1977). In addition the province of Ontario operates a training program for employees in business and industry (Ontario Training In Business and Industry). Total enrollments in 1977-78 were 15,000 with the majority of the training being in merchandising and sales, medical or dental services, management, and transportation and communication (Statistics Canada, 1979f).

Apprentices, Other Employer Training and Labor Education. Apprenticeships, while involving less than 5 percent of the 15 to 24 year-olds of the labor force in 1978, were the main form of training leading to qualification in skilled trades. There were 106,000 registered apprentices in 1977-78 compared to 77,000 in 1973-74 (Adams, 1979, pp. 89-90). Other employer training would include day release (one to eight hours off from regular working hours to attend courses) and extended leave (full-time attendance at an educational program for periods ranging from three months to a year or more). In 1978 the Commission of Inquiry on Educational Leave and Productivity reported 398,000 employees on day-release which represented 15 percent of the work force in the establishments surveyed. The Commission also reported 10,368 employees on extended leave (Adams, 1979, p. 149 and 173).

The author used data from a paper by Verner (in Pearl 1975) to estimate participation in labor education provided by labor unions. Verner reported that 9.2 percent of the union membership was so involved which included learning opportunities provided through national and international unions, locals, provincial federations, local labor councils, the Canadian Labor Congress, in Quebec through a distinctive structure of labor organization and the Labor College. The College was founded in 1963 in conjunction with Montreal and McGill Universities and the Confederation of National Trade Unions.

Parents and Older Persons. Data in this category are particularly elusive. The New Horizons program started in 1972 by the federal government is directed to retired Canadians and provides support for groups of ten or more who wish to promote physical recreation, crafts, hobbies or historical, cultural and educational programs. By June 1976 $34 million had been allocated to 6,000 projects involving

100,000 people (Statistics Canada, 1979a, p. 30).

Clark and Brundage, in Part III of this report, cite an estimate of 350,000 participants reported in a 1970 survey of parent education programs. More recent data, national in scope, has not been located. However the Ontario Provincial Secretary for Social Development in 1979 reported 142,000 people attended classes in Prenatal Education at 40 health units in Ontario plus an additional 190,000 parents enrolled in classes distinctly identified as parent education (Ontario Provincial Secretariat For Social Development, 1979, p. 28).

Overall Estimate of Participation. While in Table 2 there is no way to pinpoint or untangle any possible double-counting of participants, the total estimated participation for Canada does not seem inflated given the kinds of programs that are listed and inferences that would be reasonable about their target audiences. Furthermore, it is acknowledged that summary data were not located for local community and cultural organizations, interest and sports clubs, radio and television learners, and self-directed study. Therefore, the summary estimate provided in Table 2, interpreted in the light of findings of the Waniewicz (1976) study, would appear to be conservative.

TABLE 2. CANADA: MAJOR PROGRAMS AND ESTIMATES OF PARTICIPATION

Program or Provider	Estimated Number of Participants	Year	Source
University Continuing Education	574,000	1976-77	Statistics Canada, 1979c
University Part-time	211,700	1977-78	Statistics Canada, 1979d
Community Colleges-- Continuing Education	450,000	1976-77	Statistics Canada, 1978
Departments of Education-- Correspondence Courses	91,000	1976-77	Statistics Canada, 1979c
School Boards--credit and noncredit	639,000	1976-77	Statistics Canada, 1979c
Canada Manpower Training Program	280,000	1976-77	CMTP, 1977
Ontario Training In Business and Industry	15,000	1977-78	Statistics Canada, 1979f
Registered Apprentices	106,000	1977-78	Adams, 1979
Employer Day Release Training	398,000	1977-78	Adams, 1979
Employer Extended Leave Training	10,000	1977-78	Adams, 1979
Labor Education	227,000	1975	Pearl, 1975 plus author
New Horizons	100,000	1976	Statistics Canada, 1979a
Parent Education--Ontario	332,000	1978	Secretary For Social Development, 1979

Total adult population:	14,869,000	Estimated total participation rate: 23 percent	
Estimated total participation, all programs:	3,433,700		

NMU LIBRARY

DENMARK

Adult education has a long history in Denmark, particularly as a voluntary, leisure time activity. The principal contributor to this has been the Folk High School, the first of which was founded in 1844. Others followed, originally directed at the education of young farmers, not only as a means of acquiring knowledge, but as a way of inculcating personal and Christian values.

There was a gradual shift in this century to urban workers as well, and since World War II the Folk High Schools have appealed to a wide social spectrum. They are residential schools offering both long-term courses of up to 40 weeks and courses as short as one week. Because of problems of long-term absence from employment, the longer courses are attended primarily by younger students (18-25).

While 85 percent of their support comes from the state under the Act on Leisure Time Instruction, preference is given to private rather than government sponsors. A variety of organizations and groups runs the 80 schools within general guidelines provided by the Act. No examinations are required for entrance and no certificates are awarded for completion. Languages and social science or humanities subjects are the most popular. The mode of instruction has shifted from lectures and traditional teaching to various forms of group work and group directed study. There is little emphasis on vocational subjects. However, the work in the schools may nevertheless provide a useful background for further training or employment.

Another form of leisure time education is the study circle. This is a strictly volunteer activity and a group of five or more can band together to study almost any subject of interest that is not purely recreational. The general sponsors for the study circles are the Organizations for Popular Enlightenment, of which there are three major and 17 minor ones. Many of these are religious, political or popular movements and the study topics tend to reflect, but are by no means limited to, the interest of the sponsors.

Financing of the study circles is equally divided among participant fees, the national government and the local community. Each organization, in order to receive the government subsidy, must submit a plan for a minimum number of sessions with a leader and have an appropriate number of students. It is estimated that there are 700,000 participants annually (Kurland, 1979-80).

Quite different from these leisure time activities are the various Labor Market Training Schemes provided for by the Act on Vocational Training. These are strictly vocational and designed to provide new or upgraded skills for those in the labor force in need of them. These programs are free to the eligible students, and, in some cases, paid leave is provided. Most of the cost is paid by the national government with the remainder by employer groups and local authorities. Some of the courses are residential while others are day courses. Most of them are short, lasting from one to three weeks.

One scheme provides training for semi-skilled workers to improve their employment skills. Another provides retraining for skilled workers to bring their basic training up to date and/or to provide new skills and competencies to apply to new production methods and techniques. There is also reconversion training for those unemployed or returning to the labor market as well as to assist those in need of adjustment to technological or other changes in the labor market. These are described in more detail in Part II.

Various employee organizations also provide training programs. While some programs provide more general education, most of them are concerned directly or indirectly with union affairs and are often for shop stewards to improve their effectiveness in that function.

There is a variety of inservice training schemes provided by individual concerns and trade organizations. These are largely on-the-job programs to renew or upgrade skills.

There are several employer associations that offer courses, mainly short residential ones, to management and supervisory personnel in their member firms on topics related to management.

Employees in most national and local government bodies have a variety of opportunities for job related training provided by or at the expense of the government.

Local authorities run Evening Schools which provide courses for one or two evenings a week in any subject that is appealing to adults in their spare time. These may be general school subjects, cultural or social programs, manual or vocational courses. Except for certain courses that are free, the students pay one-quarter of the teacher's fee and the local authorities pay the remainder and furnish the premises.

For youths 14-18 years of age there are opportunities outside the regular school system to obtain the equivalent training and prepare for the leaving examinations as well as to supplement their education in more general ways. The Youth Schools are provided primarily by local authorities although about five percent are private. Continuation Schools are run by various private groups with substantial state subsidies to the schools and grants to the students.

Distance learning is provided through commercial (private) correspondence colleges, some government institutions and Radio Denmark. In the early 1970's there were 100 twenty-five minute TV broadcasts and 300 twenty-minute radio broadcasts.

Statistics on participation are quite limited. For many programs not even figures for overall participation are available. In only a few cases are there breakdowns by age or sex. In almost no case is there adequate information to answer the questions desired about participation rates for the target groups specified for this report. There is also no way to accurately account for any overlap among the major programs or within them. The same individual may be a participant in more than one program or in different offerings of the same program. A person may participate in different study circles during the same year and so be counted more than once. Some allowance has been made for this in the estimate of total participation along with recognition of a partially compensating effect from programs not included in the listing.

TABLE 3. DENMARK: MAJOR PROGRAMS AND ESTIMATES OF PARTICIPATION

Program or Provider	Estimated Number of Participants	Year	Source
Folk High Schools-- Long courses	9,000	1975	Nordic Council, 1976
Study Circles	700,000	1978	Kurland, 1979-80
Labor Market Training Schemes	46,000	1973	Nordic Council, 1976
Youth Schools	120,000	1973	Nordic Council, 1976
Continuation Schools	9,000	1978	Baunsbak-Jensen, 1979

Total adult population: 5,125,000   Estimated total
                                        participation
                                        rate: 17 percent

Estimated total parti-
cipation, all programs: 850,000

FEDERAL REPUBLIC OF GERMANY

Education in the Federal Republic of Germany is the responsibility of the Lander, or states. The federal government sets certain general policies and provides some financing and services, but most actual operations of the educational system are carried out by the Lander under their separate constitutions and laws. While there are similarities among them and generalizations can be made, these general statements are subject to many modifications and exceptions in the details of their application to any individual Land. This also makes difficult accumulation of meaningful and accurate figures on participation. Nevertheless, keeping all this in mind, it is possible to provide a reasonably accurate overall description of adult education in West Germany.

The Volkshochschule

With the exception of vocational education, the responsibility for adult education in Germany has traditionally been assumed by independent institutions or groups, although often with substantial government financial support. The major institution has been the Volkshochschule (literally, the people's high school, but with a meaning well beyond that of the U.S. "high school"). The law in each Land specifies the framework within which the Volkshochschulen operate, but general responsibility is placed on local authorities who may conduct programs themselves or delegate the operation to some other group. Financing also varies, with some Lander providing most of the funds and in others, local authorities and/or student fees sharing much of the burden.

A wide range of courses and programs is offered. Some are designed to prepare for common federal examinations, and some are based on a common model across regions. Others reflect purely local concerns, often specific to the particular group of participants. Because there is no compulsion for attendance, courses must meet the desires and interests of the students if they are to continue.

Many courses are held in the evenings, but there are also daytime courses, weekend seminars, longer full-time courses and week-long seminars in response to opportunities provided by paid educational leave. Some of the programs are linked to media presentations and some are offered in collaboration with universities or other institutions.

In 1978 there were over 4,000,000 course enrollments (Deutscher Volkshochschul-Verband, 1978). Although there are wide variations by the type of program, over two-thirds of the enrollments are women and almost two-thirds are participants under 35 years of age. Less than four percent are over 65.

The Volkshochschulen are located throughout the country, and almost every local area has its own school.

Vocational Training

The Vocational Training Act sets forth the framework for vocational education which is a shared responsibility of the federal government and the Lander. The latter provide for the in-school portion of the training, and the federal government is responsible for the phase of training that takes place in business and industry. Much of this is considered a part of the "regular" school program, but it continues beyond the compulsory school age and facilities are available to adults and youth who have left and return. The out-of-school training is provided by individual businesses or industries and by their organizations where individual firms are not large enough to provide training. Most of this is organized under procedures for apprenticeships with students alternating between periods of classroom instruction in general subjects and on-the-job work in business and industry. There are joint groups from the Lander and the federal government to coordinate the requirements and see that the training in business and industry is coordinated with the work in school.

Employees in the civil service are entitled to up to two weeks of paid educational leave a year. Most of this is directed to upgrading of job-related skills and tends to concentrate at the middle- and higher-career levels. Courses are organized by the federal government, the Lander, and regional or local groups.

Other Providers

The various Chambers of Industry and Commerce arrange for a variety of courses on vocational, political, and civic matters. The Federal Factory Constitution law provides for training of works council members. The employer covers the salary of the participant and the trade unions cover the cost of instruction. The trade unions also provide educational programs emphasizing trade union studies but also including general education courses. In some cases collective bargaining agreements are the basis for arrangements for training, most often for shop stewards. Programs typically provide courses of two or three weeks' total duration.

Churches are also responsible for a substantial amount of general as well as religious education. A church tax of 8-10 percent of an individual's income tax plus additional subsidies from public funds are furnished to the churches. The churches, however, determine how much of the available funds are to be used for education as opposed to support of other church activities.

There are a variety of forms of distance education available in the Federal Republic of Germany. There is a Distance University which operates entirely by correspondence and has enrolled 24,000 students. Others supply both general and vocational courses, fees for appropriate ones being eligible for reimbursement to the student under the Labor Promotion Act. The Funkkolleg is a consortium offering university level courses by radio with supplementary publications and a written examination required to receive a certificate. A television university also provides courses.

Between 1970 and 1975 five of the Lander enacted legislation providing employees with the right to paid educational leave (CERI 1976). While the other Lander do not have legislative guarantees, there are numerous bargaining agreements which include educational leave as a benefit. Civil service employees and judges throughout the Federal Republic have such rights. While it is estimated that ten percent of the workers are entitled to leave, the number actually exercising the right is considerably smaller (EBAE, 1979).

The following table provides information on participation in the major programs for which data were available. In most cases these are estimates, so the total figure given is an estimate based on estimates. Furthermore, the information is typically in terms of participation course by course so that a person taking courses in three programs would be counted three times. The amount of this multiple counting is unknown. It should be recognized, however, and it has been considered in providing the total figure. The accuracy of the correction may be questionable, however.

TABLE 4. THE FEDERAL REPUBLIC OF GERMANY: MAJOR PROGRAMS AND ESTIMATES
OF PARTICIPATION

Program or Provider	Estimated Number of Participants	Year	Source
Volkshochschule	4,144,000	1978	Deutscher Volkshochschul- Verband, 1978
Federal Labor Promotion Act	233,000	1974	von Moltke and Schneevoight, 1977
Industry-financed In-Service Training	600,000	1971	von Moltke and Schneevoight, 1977
Civil Service Training	619,000	1971	Rudolph, 1979
Chambers of Industry and Commerce	76,365	1971	Unpublished OECD report
Trade Union Education	900,000	1970	Rudolph, 1979
Federal Factory Constitution Law	100,000	1972	Unpublished OECD report
Churches	1,500,000	1970	Rudolph, 1979
Correspondence	250,000	1970	Rudolph, 1979
Total adult population:	61,303,000		Estimated total participation rate: 11 percent
Estimated total parti- cipation, all programs:	7,000,000		

FRANCE

Purposes

Historically, three diverse purposes of adult learning in France may be identified: vocational, "social promotion," and cultural. Early work-related training was exemplified by informal tutoring (compagnonnage) and apprenticeship models (apprenti aupres du maitre) (Caspar, 1979). Today apprenticeships continue, but within the framework of initial rather than further education. On-the-job training was the primary vehicle for vocational education until after World War II. Then economic necessity and an ideological thrust toward greater equity and democracy in the educational system gave rise to the notion that adults deserve a second chance to learn. In 1946, 100 state-financed regional adult training centers were established to accelerate the education of workers and technicians whose skills were needed for reconstruction. A quarter of a century later, under the name Association for Adult Vocational Training (AFPA--Association pour la Formation Professionnelle des Adultes), their activities expanded to include training employees sent by firms under paid educational leave provisions of the Law on Continuing Professional Training (to be discussed later). Corporate sponsorship of education has burgeoned since Renault, Air France, and IBM, among others, set up their own employee training centers in the postwar era.

"Social promotion" represents a second adult education tradition. In order both to advance through the highly stratified French social structure, and to gain access to occupations which provide higher status, wages, and levels of responsibility, adults need opportunities to continue basic general education, to remedy deficiencies in cultural knowledge, and to acquire further career preparation (Pasquier, 1977). Examples of education for social advancement might include improvement of oral and written communication skills, or preparation to sit national examinations for degrees or certificates. Given a rigid national scale of standards and diploma equivalencies relative to occupational and salary structures, documentation of further levels of qualification is critical to individual social mobility, enhancement and progress. Trade unions in particular have been active in organizing social advancement

courses. Since 1794, the federally-assisted National School
of Arts and Crafts or Trades (CNAM--Conservatoire National des
Arts et Metiers) has offered evening, now Saturday, classes
for social promotion purposes. Its broad scope will be
discussed later in this section.

Cultural opportunities define a third purpose of adult
learning. A subtle but important distinction must be made,
however. Cultural activities clearly are set apart from
educational activities, and due to a highly circumscribed
French definition, are not included in national statistics on
adult continuing education. A tradition of popular education
institutions similar to folk high schools flourished for
several centuries in France. Today pursuit of vocational
interests, or cultural activities typical of folk high school
offerings, occurs under the label "action culturelle." Those
socio-cultural activities known as "action animation" and
"cadre or militant action" are less well-defined. Often
under trade union or socio-cultural group auspices, these
opportunities are designed to increase individual effectiveness, participation and leadership within groups; and to
increase personal understandings of the exercise of broad
political rights and privileges. Further description of these
activities also occurs later in this section under popular
education organizations.

Policy

The major French policy on adult education is based on
the concept of paid educational leave as an individual right.
This concept is couched within a philosophical commitment to
lifelong learning and supported by a massive and cumbersome
statutory framework (detailed in Part II). Relevant legal
texts were formulated from the 1950's to the explicit
inter-professional agreements of 1970 (revised, 1976)
between employers and trade unions. The Law of 16 July 1971
"Concerning the Organization of Continuous Vocational Training
Within the Framework of Lifelong Education," enlarged and
applied with greater specificity in July 1978, is the
definitive piece of legislation.

"Formation continue," or continuing adult education,
thereby becomes a national obligation. It applies to all who
now are working, engaged in "la vie active," or who wish to be
(Scheffnecht, 1978). The legislative intent (Article I) is
to provide mechanisms, equity, encouragement and financial
assistance for adults to continue their education during
working hours without loss of social benefits, employment
position, or wages. Individuals may seek further training
for many reasons, among them, to adapt to changes in technology or work conditions, to advance to different social

or cultural levels, and to provide access to better job opportunities.

Continuing education within this framework is perceived as an investment in individual potential, as an instrument of national economic, social and cultural development, and as an extension of federal employment policy. Both State aid and compulsory employer contributions finance it. A competitive market for training opportunities is set in motion with a great many organizational players allowed. Administrative accountability at the national level is vested in a Secretary of State for Vocational Training, attached to the Ministry of Labor. This position is simply a pivotal point in a nexus of interministerial and coordinating committees whose members represent the professions, workers, employers and government. This unique shared authority exists also at the regional level in 27 equally diverse committees that provide coordination, adapt national priorities to local situations, and examine agreements brought by adult training organizations for a determination on appropriateness of financing, equipment, and operation (but not course content).

While the key words "formation continue professionnelle," which appear in the 1971 Law, translate to "continuing vocational or professional training," the French meaning does not dictate a narrow restrictive scope of activities as the English language would seem to imply. Emphasis more accurately is placed on the provision of access, through paid educational leave, to various types of training, both necessary and desirable, which relate to one's working life. This includes broadly conceived social and cultural goals as well as limited vocational objectives. The 1978 legislation and recent implementation bills clearly indicate that individuals may pursue further training identified as general, cultural, or vocational in nature, under paid educational leave.

The free market in training courses created in 1971 is based on a consumer demand-multiple supply model implemented through contractual agreements. It establishes the rights and means of a panoply of groups to strive to provide adult education. Providers may include: existing educational institutions at all levels; publicly funded agencies; private profit and non-profit establishments; firms and enterprises; trade unions, chambers of commerce, industry, trade, or agriculture; popular or socio-cultural movements; federal, local or regional authorities and their agents; and that long-standing French unit of social organization, the "association." (Any group of seven or more persons has the right to form and register as an "association" in accordance with 1901 Law. Legally it then may undertake any venture, including education [Scheffnecht, 1978]). While many of these "suppliers" had organized adult training activities previously, the 1971 legislation established more open competition by enlarging both the pool of financial resources available to expend for adult education and the pool of persons eligible to be trained during the work day. In 1978, 2.9 million employed and unemployed persons of working age received training under the Law on "Formation Continue." Most participation data reflect only adult education undertaken within the framework of this law as paid education leave. While during leisure hours and at individual expense adults may be involved in many of the same or similar offerings, they are counted infrequently. A description of the pluralistic universe of adult education providers is given below.

Sources

Local Education Establishments. Within the French national public education system, failure is endemic; and 16 percent of any particular age group still do not complete primary schooling (von Moltke and Schneevoigt, 1977). A detailed discussion of adult basic education provided by elementary teachers outside of working hours, voluntary associations, and federal initiatives for foreigners, is given in Part II.

Since 1971, administrative groups of secondary level establishments (GRETA's--Groupements d'Etablissements du Second Degre) have been formed to manage further training. Each of the more than 370 GRETAs (Pasquier, 1977) typically includes 10 establishments (comprehensive schools, grammar schools, technical grammar schools, etc.) located in a common geographical area, and offers a range of courses taught by staff employed in existing participating institutions. Each includes "further training advisors," concerned only with adult training, and responsible for the general organization of GRETA-based courses. Every educational district has an academic further training center to provide training for these advisors and for faculty who wish to concentrate on teaching adults. During 1975, 205,000 trainees participated in courses organized in public secondary education establishments (Pasquier, 1977).

Higher Education Institutions. Higher education, organized under a Secretary of State for Universities, may be pursued within "Grandes Ecoles," traditionally prestigious institutions, universities, and University Institutes of Technology (IUTs). The last are relatively new, oriented toward adult needs, and similar to the British polytechnics. Staff of IUTs consists of teachers and practicing professionals, who offer adults chances to improve disciplinary knowledge and to prepare for University Diplomas of Technology (DUT--Diplome Universitaire de Technologie). Many IUT diplomas and courses have been adapted for adults who have work experience but not necessarily the traditional secondary-leaving credential of "baccalaureat" (Besnard and Lietard, 1977). Since the Law of Orientation, 1968, when French universities became administratively and financially autonomous, it has been possible, there as well, to admit older persons (possessing three years of professional experience but lacking traditional prerequisites) to work toward corresponding diplomas. Higher education institutions have been encouraged to tailor teaching methods, course content, and class schedules toward the needs of adults.

After the 1971 training law, the state concluded "mutual assistance contracts" with universities to help them introduce adult continuing education programs. Many universities now have lifelong learning centers designed, as they see fit, to: offer courses at the university; contract with firms and others making specific requests; and consult with external organizations wishing to develop their own training programs. Critics claim that the centers remain on the fringes of university life with 60 to 80 percent of the teaching staff lacking adequate qualifications, and that lifelong education itself is not functionally integrated into the university teaching profession (Rey and Brocard, 1979). Other pessimistic notes sounded are that many "grandes ecoles d'ingenieurs" seem unwilling to create special courses which take into account the professional experience already acquired by adults; and that since IUTs have enjoyed success, many adults with a "bac" degree are applying for admission, thereby edging out those without qualifications, those for whom the program was designed originally.

The only French university with a fully actualized "open admissions policy" is the University of Paris VIII, Vincennes. Out of an enrollment of 32,000, 40 percent work full-time; no "bac" is required at entrance. The campus has come under heavy fire for attracting not serious capable students but drug-users, political agitators and those unable to meet regular standards held at other French universities, such as dropouts, foreigners and "misfits" (Time, 1980). Nonetheless, during 1975 there were 105,155 adults, under the educational leave provisions of the 1971 Law, attending courses at higher education institutions.

Distance Education

Distance education is a preferred mode of learning for many adults in France. Major providers under Ministry of Education auspices are the National Center of Distance Study

(CNTE--Centre National de Tele-Enseignement) and the Radio and Television Service (RTS). CNTE provides home study in both initial education and adult further training, sometimes linking with other organizations to offer courses. Through CNTE centers in 1978, 121,000 persons participated in courses which frequently lead to state diplomas and often are related to the service sector. During the same period an estimated 10,000 additional persons followed non-CNTE correspondence courses, while 23,000 were involved in RTS information programs for adults in 1978 (Annexe, 1980).

CNAM--National Academy of Arts and Trades. Mentioned earlier, CNAM offers conventional advancement courses on Saturdays and in the evenings, most of which are open to the general public at no cost, and are divided into credit units which can be accumulated and may lead to formal qualifications or diplomas. CNAM also provides courses held during working hours for people holding advanced study diplomas who wish to pursue work toward engineering or economics diplomas on a full-time basis. Thirdly, the Academy organizes courses in institutes and schools for persons wishing to prepare for vocational examinations and certification (such as certified accountants, or computer engineers). As of 1978, 34,000 were training under CNAM sponsorship.

AFPA--Association for Adult Vocational Training. As discussed earlier, this government-sponsored organization provides testing of general education and vocational aptitude, occupational guidance, and training for adults, including future "trainers," in its widely distributed national centers. During 1975 AFPA was training 85,000 (1978, 100,000) individuals (within the Law) of which 79 percent were under age 25 and 13 percent were women. Courses, typically offered 40 hours a week, are designed to produce skilled or white collar workers in six months and technicians in nine to 12 months for building and public works jobs, electronics or data processing, and commerce or office work. The teacher-trainee ratio is low; teaching methods emphasize participation and trainee responsibility; representatives of industry help with course planning.

Armed Services. Military service in France is compulsory at age 21 unless deferred. During 1976, 34,000 conscripts and 9,000 regular military personnel participated in social advancement courses either in classrooms or through correspondence, to bolster their academic or vocational knowledge at all levels.

National Employment Fund (FNE--Fonds National de l'Emploi). The FNE was created in 1963 to provide short-term retraining interventions financed by the state to prevent temporary unemployment due to changes in industry. It exemplifies vocational training as an integrated part of employment policy and as a crisis management strategy (von Moltke and Schneevoigt, 1977). It is difficult to distinguish FNE efforts from other state-assisted training through paid educational leave for purposes of adapting to critical labor market conditions. In 1978, 10,000 persons participated in training under FNE auspices, though some courses were contracted out.

Agriculture. On the basis of size, most French farms and their workers were exempt from the basic training provisions of the 1971 Law. To provide equity for farm employees, legislation requires that a proportion of income from para-fiscal charges on agricultural products be used to finance further training in agriculture. This sum is paid into Training Insurance Funds (discussed in the section on workers), one for farmhands and one for farmers and associates. During 1974 it financed 41,000 trainees (1978, 44,000). The Ministry of Agriculture organizes most agricultural training courses. These may lead to an academic degree or to agricultural, vocational or technical certificates; or they may be for specialized training or retraining. Participation has increased recently for persons of nonrural backgrounds interested philosophically in "a return to the land" and practically interested in forestry, horticulture, or raising livestock.

Business, Industry and Trade Organizations. One way that firms may comply with the 1971 Law is to provide vocational or cultural training themselves for their employees. Regulations govern the implementation of such courses, and the Ministry of Education suggests they require a minimum of 20 hours for effective knowledge acquisition and application. During 1975, 119,000 participating firms financed training programs for 17.8 percent of their employees, 1,790,000 (1978, 1,735,000) out of a total of 10,060,000 employees. They did not organize all of the training they financed.

National, regional or local branches of employers' organizations have set up training schools and centers for initial and further training. They also have established nonprofit training associations (ASFO), numbering 250 in 1977, on a regional, occupational or inter-trade basis to help firms implement training policies and programs, and to organize courses for employees of member firms. Employers' organizations and trade unions, on a regional or occupational principle, have formed Training Assurance Funds (FAF) for wage-earners and for nonwage earners as a means to collect and administer training monies. During 1975, over two million employees were covered by Training Insurance Funds and 107,402 participated in training (Pasquier, 1977). In 1978, there were 195,000 participants.

Training and further training provided by Chambers of Commerce and Industry has been traditionally short, aimed at salaried staff, and on language and commercial subjects. Nearly all chambers, even those in small towns and villages, now provide further vocational training in long courses and evening social promotion courses. The chambers also set up Training Assurance Funds and ASFOs. Chambers of Commerce and Industry organized courses for 138,000 persons in 1975.

Popular Education and Socio-Cultural Associations. A paucity of systematic information exists about these long-standing informal providers since their activities are considered to be "cultural" and not "educational," and are hence excluded from national data bases. While eligible to receive resources from firms under the 1971 Law, or special state subventions, they are financed usually by private community groups or local/regional government, as Besnard and Lietard point out in their essay in Part III. Municipalities, depending upon the social and educational conscience of the political party in power, may offer classes, films, or discussion groups in "la maison de la culture" or in the town hall. Such community centers provide crafts, sports, music and arts programs for adults as well as for young people. Within schools, L'Association des Parents d'Eleves, the equivalent of a Parent-Teacher Association (PTA) in the U.S., may sponsor parent education programs. Clubs for older people (Clubs des Anciennes) meet in public buildings when they are not otherwise in use, for lectures, painting or gymnastics, for example; they also organize trips for members. "Universities for the Third Age," structured either through universities or local associations, were organized in 1977 and now enroll an estimated 20,000 older citizens. (They will be discussed further in the section on older people.)

Pactes pour l'Emploi. Special employment-training opportunities are available to young persons between 16 and 25 years of age and to certain categories of women through temporary federal measures entitled Pactes pour l'Emploi. They are designed to aid those most vulnerable to unemployment. During 1978, 69,000 persons received training under these employment-training contracts. More detail is provided in the section on women.

General Statistics

The import of the 1971 Law on Continuing Vocational Education and its subsequent revisions is reflected in the character, organization, and presentation of participation data. National statistics on continuing adult education in France are virtually synonymous with training taken under the educational leave provisions of that code. Emphasis is placed on sources of finance rather than on nature of programs, because the Law does not regulate the content or subject matter of the training itself.

Under the code, the state or employer may organize and deliver training, and either or both may finance it. It is impossible to discern precisely, for example, whether participation data reflect firm-financed and organized training, or one but not the other. Moreover, when training is funded by multiple sources, it is not always so indicated.

Another major problem with the data turns on the French definition of adult education. Many adults enrolled in informal learning activities are not counted in total participation tabulations because they are engaged in "cultural" pursuits not considered "education." Thus what appears to be a large segment of adult learning opportunities and participation remains untallied. Participation in education based locally in a municipality or village appears to be underreported, and education undertaken by persons on their own is underrepresented.

TABLE 5. FRANCE: MAJOR PROGRAMS AND ESTIMATES OF PARTICIPATION

Program or Provider	Estimated Number of Participants	Year	Source
State Secondary Education Establishments	205,200	1975	Pasquier, 1977
Higher Education Establishments	105,155	1975	Besnard et Lietard, 1977
(Grandes Ecoles, Universities, University Institutes of Technology)			
Distance Education	154,000	1978	Annexe to Finance Law for 1980, 1979
(Centre National de Tele-Enseignement; Radio and Television Service (RTS); other correspondence courses)			
National Academy of Arts and Trades	34,000	1978	Annexe to Finance Law for 1980, 1979
(Conservatoire National des Arts et Metiers)			
Association for Adult Vocational Training	100,000	1978	Annexe to Finance Law for 1980, 1979
(Association pour la Formation Professionnelle des Adultes)			
Armed Services	43,000	1976	Pasquier, 1977
National Employment Fund	10,000	1978	Annexe to Finance Law for 1980, 1979
(Fonds National de l'Emploi)			

Program or Provider	Estimated Number of Participants	Year	Source
Agriculture	44,000	1978	Annexe to Finance Law for 1980, 1979
Firm Financed	1,735,000	1978	Annexe to Finance Law for 1980, 1979
Training Assurance Fund Financed	195,000	1978	Annexe to Finance Law for 1980, 1979
(Fonds National d'Assurance Formation)			
Chambers of Commerce and Industry	138,000	1975	Pasquier, 1977
Popular Education and Socio-Cultural Associations	unknown		
Universities for the Third Age	20,000	1977	Multiple sources
(Universities du Troisieme Age)			
Employment-Training Pact Contracts	69,000	1978	Ministre du Travail et de la Participation, 1979
(Contrats Emploi-Formation du Pacte pour l'Emploi)			
Total adult population:	41,245,000		Estimated total participation rate: 7 percent
Estimated total participation, all programs:	2,852,355		

THE SOVIET UNION

In its educational system as in its other institutions, the Soviet Union represents a case of extreme centralization. As an official response to a UNESCO questionnaire put it, "In the USSR there exists a single system of education for children and adults, and correspondingly a single plan, administration, financing, and content of instruction" ("Otvety na Voprosnik," 1972). Local educational authorities are essentially administrative agencies of the national government. Both the national Ministry of (General) Education and the national Ministry of Higher and Secondary Specialized Education, which operate the most important adult education programs, are "union-republic" ministries--i.e., they have counterparts in each of the 15 constituent republics; the former, however, clearly have influence over the latter. And while some adult education programs are conducted by agencies outside the jurisdiction of these ministries and of the economic and other ministries which are in charge of some higher educational institutions, behind all of them lies the unifying and coordinating force of the Communist Party. It would hardly be appropriate to these circumstances to speak of the various "providers" of adult education; we shall instead refer only to different programs.

Despite the high degree of centralization, statistical data on adult education in the Soviet Union are no more adequate than in more pluralistic societies. This is attributable to two other characteristics of the Soviet system: (1) the well-known reticence to provide information freely, and particularly to present it in terms of well-defined categories that might reveal undesired trends or variations among segments of the population; and (2) the low level of Soviet participation in the western culture of the social sciences, which has prevented Soviet researchers from becoming familiar with data-reporting procedures that are customary elsewhere. Requests for assistance from the author of this report, directed to the most likely repositories of data--the Research Institute for the General Education of Adults (Leningrad), founded in 1961, and the Research Institute on Problems of Higher Education (Moscow), founded in 1973--were not answered. In one presumably important sphere of adult education, that of the Communist Party itself, there appears to be no recent published information whatsoever. (For materials of an earlier date, see Mickiewicz, 1967 and the articles in <u>Soviet Education</u>, November 1972.)

The concept of "open admissions" plays relatively little part in the organization of Soviet adult education. This may be observed in several of its features. First, admission into part-time study at the college or university level is by competitive examination, and the examinations are similar to those for entrance into full-time study, albeit the standards are less rigorous. Soviet policy-makers have evidently utilized part-time education chiefly as a way of producing larger numbers of trained specialists without creating further pressure on resources, because existing training facilities could be used rather than having to provide additional ones. This decision was made to seem a virtue by emphasizing the desirability of combining theory and practice; and people were encouraged to embark on part-time study by a variety of devices. Nevertheless, it is notable that when, in the middle 1960s, the demand for specialists with higher education began to diminish, it was ordered that there be no further increase in the number of part-time students, while the number of full-time students would be permitted to increase at a normal rate; it was expected that the proportion of part-time students would decline from more than 50 percent of the student body in higher educational institutions to 40 percent by 1975 and to 30 percent "in subsequent years" (Severtsev, 1976). It has not been difficult to discern, in Soviet statements about the matter, the beliefs that the quality of specialists trained in part-time study was lower than that of those trained in "conventional" ways and that the high proportion of part-time students had been a concession to economic necessity rather than a desirable goal in itself. On the other hand, those adult-education programs which are open to the general public without conditions do not lead to a degree or to a higher work-related classification.

Major Programs

Part-time education for adults began in the Soviet Union soon after the Revolution of October, 1917. (Some of its forms, however, had prerevolutionary roots.) At first it was primarily an instrument for the reduction of widespread illiteracy, and then it was used to give adults access to elementary and later to secondary education. A "complete" secondary education of ten grades is now nominally compulsory, but the last two years may be taken part-time by those who have full-time jobs. In 1938, a national program of extra-mural studies was established at postsecondary institutions (Tymowski and Januszkiewicz, 1976). Following World War II, part-time studies came to assume great importance in higher education, constituting more than half of enrollments at that level during much of the postwar era. Other forms of adult education were introduced after the war.

Elementary and Secondary Schooling. Nearly 11 percent of enrollments in schools of general education are in part-time form, some in extramural ("correspondence") courses but the great majority in "evening (shift) schools." The parenthetical term in the latter type indicates that some of these schools are open during the day to accommodate night-shift workers though they follow the truncated curriculum of the evening schools. The yearly schedule is also adjusted to accommodate persons employed in agriculture and in seasonal industries. Students are expected to enter the course at the grade following the last grade completed; thus, some of these schools have classes as low as the third-grade level. As elementary education has become more common, however, secondary enrollments have come to predominate in the part-time schools. Some secondary-level programs combine general and vocational education. There are also secondary-level evening (shift) schools, or evening or extramural branches of full-time day schools, which are entirely vocational; these are under not the Ministry of Education but the Ministry of Higher and Secondary Specialized Education, and many students enter them after completing their general secondary education.

Degree-oriented Programs of Higher Educational Institutions. Nearly all Soviet higher educational institutions have either an evening or an extramural department, and many have both. In addition, there are at least 14 higher educational institutions which offer extramural programs exclusively, and at least two which have only evening courses. Some large enterprises provide facilities for part-time postsecondary study on their own premises, with the faculty and students being drawn partly or wholly from their staff. Part-time higher education in evening or extramural form is available for about 250 of the 365 specializations recognized in Soviet higher education;* it is unavailable only in those requiring extensive laboratory or clinical work (e.g., medicine) or intensive face-to-face instruction (e.g., performing arts). The curricula, specified by the ministry, are the same, but

---

*All Soviet higher education degree programs lead to qualification in some occupation; there are no "liberal arts" curricula.

part-time study generally takes an additional year to complete. The textbooks are also the same, but much effort goes into the preparation of study aids for extramural students especially, for the purpose of helping them develop good study habits. In all cities and at many large enterprises and construction sites, "consultation points" have been established where extramural students can meet with faculty to get help; for this reason, and others to be seen below, the term "extramural" seems a better translation than the more customary "correspondence" for the Russian word (<u>zaochnyi</u>) used to denote this form of education.

A noteworthy feature of Soviet part-time higher education is the network of connections between study and work--and not merely "work" in general but even the student's specific place of employment. Preference in admission is given to those who want to enroll in a field closely related to their present job, and special priority in admission is granted to those whose employing organization has recommended their enrollment. Whether recommended or not, every part-time student has the right to take study leave, increasing from 20 to 40 days a year, while remaining on full pay, and up to one day a week at half pay besides. In the final year of study, students are entitled to four months' leave, to carry out the "diploma project" required of all students and to prepare for final examinations; however, during this time they receive a stipend from the educational institution rather than their regular pay. Most or all of this leave time, for both evening and extramural students, is spent at the educational institution, consulting with faculty, completing laboratory assignments, and taking examinations. Part-time students cannot be required to perform overtime work if it would interfere with their studies. The diploma project of part-time students is often a task that is part of their job duties. Finally, large enterprises may provide laboratory and study facilities for their employees who are part-time students, and they may also have a special committee which monitors their progress.

There is no age limit for entrance into part-time post-secondary education (students are admitted into full-time higher education only up to the age of 35), but there are no known data on actual age distributions, or on proportions of students by sex or by field of study. A British scholar (Matthews, 1972) has estimated that, as of 1964, about 47 percent of evening students and 67 percent of extramural students were white-collar employees, compared to 41 percent in full-time higher education. Blue-collar workers were represented more heavily in evening programs, but less so in extramural studies, than they were in full-time institutions; collective farmers were even less well represented in both types of part-time study (2 percent evening, 7 percent extramural) than they were in full-time (20 percent).

Most higher educational institutions also have a "preparatory department." First established in 1969, these are programs of full-time study for an academic year, open only to industrial and agricultural workers and ex-servicemen who have been out of school for at least two years and have now been recommended for enrollment by their enterprise or unit, apparently as a reward for outstanding performance (though political activity may also be taken into account). Their purpose is to prepare students for entrance into higher educational institutions proper. During the course of study, preparatory students receive the same stipends and living accommodations as regular students. Those who pass the department's final examinations are admitted to the higher educational institution without further examination. It had been planned that 20 percent of admissions to full-time programs would eventually come from the preparatory departments, but we do not know whether that goal has been reached; in 1975, total enrollments in preparatory departments amounted to 15 percent of admissions to full-time programs in the same year, and a few years earlier, only about three-quarters of enrolled students had qualified for admission (Severtsev, 1976).

Upgrading and Refresher Programs. Every position in the Soviet non-agricultural labor force is designated by a job classification and a skill level, and some formal training is required in order for a worker to advance in either respect. Soviet sources claim that as much as one-fourth of the labor force engages in some form of job-related training every year (Narodnoe Khozyaistvo, 1979). The variety of programs for industrial workers is extremely great, ranging from a few hours of on-the-job or after-work instruction in new methods or materials to courses lasting as long as nine months. Shorter programs tend to be offered at workplaces, longer ones at educational institutions; in 1975, ten times as many workers received the former sort of training--often in the form of apprenticeships or as members of "student brigades"-- as received the latter (Swafford, 1979). With a few exceptions ("Otvety na Voprosnik," 1972), no tuition fees are charged for any vocational training--nor, indeed, are they for most other kinds of education in the Soviet system.

At managerial and professional levels, refresher courses are required of each person every five to six years. It is reported that each year, more than 1.4 million people enroll in these courses. The courses are offered by special departments at more than 100 higher educational institutions, and there are also nine institutes which offer this kind of training exclusively. In 1978, an Academy of the National Economy was established to "build up a reserve force of specialists properly trained for promotion to the highest governmental posts" (Vasilyev, 1979). Typical refresher courses occupy one to two months full time, three to six months part time. The employing enterprise continues to pay normal salary and also reimburses for travel and housing expenses where necessary (Darinsky, 1976a).

People's Universities. The only Soviet program of sustained educational activities designed for adults which has no prerequisities for admission is the "People's University." It is also the only educational program which regularly charges tuition fees, though they are said to be small. The 40,000 People's Universities offer curricula which take one, two, or three or more years to complete; it is not clear, however, what a "curriculum" consists of and whether a student must enroll in all parts of it or may select only certain courses. (For these reasons, it is hard to interpret the statement that about 11,000,000 people "attended" these institutions in 1976.) Most of the People's Universities specialize in one or another "branch of knowledge": about one-quarter of them are "pedagogical universities" (which include both teaching and parenting), and about 10 percent each are devoted to health fields and the arts, and others are devoted to social and political affairs, law, economics, agriculture, etc. A few are universities of "broad profile." The term "university" in this context is an honorific title, not an indication of the academic level of instruction; nor do the People's Universities award diplomas, degrees, or credentials entitling the holder to a job classification or skill level. Yet the People's Universities are not limited to "leisure-time" or "general-information" instruction. Many of them offer highly specific occupational training (Popkov, 1964), and some are organized by or contract with industrial enterprises for the upgrading of their employees. One source (Darinsky, 1974) alludes to the possibility that a student might use the knowledge acquired in a People's University "to pass examinations at a secondary or higher educational establishment which will issue him a corresponding document," but there does not appear to be any regularized mechanism for such "credit by examination."

A People's University can be founded by any organization --industrial, agricultural, artistic, educational, research, governmental, etc.--and this organization usually provides material support and perhaps personnel. But all the People's Universities apparently operate under the aegis of Znanie, the Knowledge Society, which may be the closest counterpart in the Soviet Union to the voluntary societies that are so common in western nations. Znanie, founded in 1947 for the purpose of disseminating information to the general population, is reported now to have more than 2,000,000 members, who offer their administrative and teaching services free of charge.

It is said to receive no government funds but to support itself by membership dues, remuneration for organizing special
lectures and exhibitions, and the proceeds of its publishing
activities. Its Central Council draws up a model academic and
methodological plan for each type of People's University and
sets certain conditions for their operation--e.g., a course
must meet at least once a month for four hours (Feldmesser,
1979). One type of People's University is devoted to training
for the "social occupations"--i.e., volunteer work by individuals in the police and court system, in trade unions, and
in Znanie itself.

Of the nearly 7,000,000 people who "attended" People's
Universities in 1973, about 44 percent were reported to be
less than 30 years old, 46 percent to be between 30 and 49,
and 10 percent to be 50 years old or more. A little less
than one-third were workers, 13 percent collective farmers,
34 percent white-collar employees (including administrators
and professionals), and 22 percent "pensioners and other
persons" (Narodnoe Obrazovanie, 1977).

Znanie is also one of many organizations that engage in
activities that are marginal to the concept of "education"
used in this report. It runs conferences and theme evenings,
operates a library and museum, presents lectures on radio
and television, and publishes books and periodicals. Other
sources, including higher educational institutions, also
originate instructional television programs. There has even
been an allusion ("Otvety na Voprosnik," 1972) to a Central
People's Teleuniversity which began transmissions in 1969,
but no additional information about it has been found. Most
ubiquitous are the nearly 150,000 "club organizations"--
palaces and houses of culture, reading rooms, collective-farm
clubs, etc. These cater more to avocational interests than
any other component of the Soviet educational system, but
even at that, their spirit can perhaps be inferred from the
statement of one authority (Darinski, 1972) that "part of
their job is to organize people's leisure and the correct
use of their spare time."

Summary and Conclusions

Soviet adult education has major accomplishments to its
credit. It has helped eliminate illiteracy, has enabled
millions of people to obtain an elementary and secondary
education, and has produced a substantial proportion of the
nation's technical specialists and professionals. Some
of its problems, noted by Soviet educators themselves, are
those common to adult education everywhere: the fatigue of
students who have put in a full day's work, poor attendance
and high dropout rates, the failure of many students to finish

their studies on schedule, the lower attractiveness of programs to older and less well-educated people. Some problems are peculiar to, or at least are exacerbated by, Soviet conditions--for example, the difficulty of providing adequate facilities in remote and sparsely settled areas and indeed in rural areas generally; and the handicaps of women, nearly all of whom are employed and have domestic duties that are not much eased by modern technical devices or retailing methods and that often are apparently not shared by their husbands, so that participation rates of women are lower than those of men (Kokorev and Liubashevsky, 1970). As a whole, Soviet adult education is probably more job-oriented and work-connected than the other adult-education systems discussed in this study; that may be regarded as a strength or a shortcoming, depending on one's values. But what differentiates it most from these other adult-education systems is its high degree of centralization. To persons who appreciate pluralism, that would seem to be a disadvantage; yet Soviet decision makers may perceive the system as not being centralized enough. It is striking to find a high official of Znanie (Vladislavlev, 1978) writing:

> ...at present we still cannot say that an adult education system exists, since in actual fact we have a conglomerate of various forms and types of education that do not sufficiently coordinate their activities and, consequently, either duplicate one another or leave unfilled voids.

Table 7 gives figures, as reported in Soviet sources, on the numbers of participants in the various adult education programs. Since the programs are so heavily vocational in nature, and since each of the vocational programs is accessible to a more or less distinctive audience in terms of occupational position and previous education, there is likely to be less double-counting in these figures than there may be in the data from other countries.

TABLE 6. THE SOVIET UNION: MAJOR PROGRAMS AND ESTIMATES OF PARTICIPATION

Program or Provider	Estimated Number of Participants	Year	Source
Secondary school completion[a]	4,799,000	1978	Narodnoe Khozyaistvo, 1979
Vocational-technical training			
Evening (shift) programs	535,000	1978	Narodnoe Khozyaistvo, 1979
Extramural programs	1,221,000	1978	Narodnoe Khozyaistvo, 1979
Degree-oriented programs of higher educational institu-tions			
Evening programs	653,000[b]	1978	Narodnoe Khozyaistvo, 1979
Extramural programs	1,596,000[b]	1978	Narodnoe Khozyaistvo, 1979
Preparatory programs	90,000	1975	Severtsev, 1976
Upgrading and refresher programs	39,825,000	1978	Narodnoe Khozyaistvo, 1979
People's Universities	11,000,000	1976	Ek'golm, 1978
Total adult population:	190,824,000		Estimated total participation rate: 31 percent
Estimated total parti-cipation, all programs:	59,719,000		

[a] Includes evening (shift) and extramural programs; the great majority of enrollments are of the former type.

[b] Presumably includes both undergraduate and graduate enrollments. The latter are not more than 2 percent of the total.

SWEDEN

The overriding objective of all public policies in Sweden is the achievement of equality, not only of opportunities but of actual living conditions and resources, including economic, political, social and cultural resources. The extensive reforms in public education in Sweden during the past two decades (starting with the creation of comprehensive primary/secondary education in the early 1960s) have all been directed towards this objective (Rubenson, 1976a, 1976b).

It has been during this reform period that government involvement in adult education has begun to attain significant proportions. Before this, adult education, which has flourished since establishment of the first "folk high schools" in the mid-19th century, had been almost exclusively the domain of Sweden's many popular movements (i.e., labor union, temperance, religious, political and cultural organizations). At present, government outlays for adult education comprise roughly 10 percent of all expenditures in education. These outlays are in the form of government subsidies to programs, study grants to individuals, outreach activities, and research and development. Research and development in adult education has grown enormously in recent years to the point that it now uses one-fifth of the National Board of Education's R&D funds (National Swedish Board of Education, 1977).

In the early 1970s the government was alarmed by the discovery that its subsidies of adult education were actually operating to widen the gap between the educationally advantaged and disadvantaged. Surveys showed that barely one-sixth of those with fewer than nine years of public education were involved in adult education, while nearly one-half of the college educated were so involved (The Swedish Institute, 1979a).

Reaffirming the objective of equalization of resources, the government initiated a number of incentive programs designed to promote the further education of the "under-educated." Experiments in outreach--including house-to-house canvassing and work place recruitment--were initiated; more and better study grants became available for the disadvantaged and a national law guaranteeing unconditional educational leaves of absence was passed. It is too early to assess the overall impact of such compensatory mechanisms, but some indicators (described more fully in Part II) are showing positive results.

The Major Providers

Voluntary Educational Associations. The most pervasive and innovative of all of Sweden's subsidized adult educational institutions is that of the study circle, sponsored by one of the country's many voluntary educational associations. A study circle is defined as "an informal group which meets for the common pursuit of well planned studies of a subject or problem area which has previously been decided upon" (The Swedish Institute, 1979a). The group itself determines how its work is to be planned and carried out. A circle leader has certain coordinating and administrative tasks but does not act as a teacher in the ordinary sense. There are no formal requirements for circle leaders.

There are a total of ten voluntary associations which operate study circles. The largest of these is the Workers' Educational Association (ABF), rooted in the strong Swedish labor movement, which sponsored just over one-third of the total study circle hours qualifying for national government subsidies in 1976/77. Such subsidies have been a major factor in the widespread success of study circles. As long as they meet certain requirements regarding size of membership, duration and frequency of meetings, the circles can receive 75 to 90 percent subsidies from national and local government funds. Those which teach priority topics, such as Swedish to immigrants, can receive subsidies of up to 100 percent (Strawn, 1977). By 1979 it is estimated that at least one million out of about five and one-half million Swedish adults participated in at least one study circle.

The most popular topics in study circles are languages, esthetic subjects (art, music, handicrafts) and civics. In recent years many civics study circles have assumed an activist stance--for example, some circles examined energy issues in preparation for the 1980 referendum on nuclear power; others, in villages threatened by loss of job alternatives, have investigated the possibilities of alternative production schemes.

Municipal Adult Schools. Municipal adult schools primarily provide instruction leading to secondary school certification for adults who have not yet had a chance to obtain the compulsory level of schooling (nine years) or who, for one reason or another, have not received the kind of secondary level training considered sufficient for their social and economic advancement. Operated by the school boards in each municipality and linked with regular comprehensive or upper secondary schools, such schools offer courses at the lower and upper secondary levels, all based upon the current national curriculum.

By the late 1970s over 300,000 students attended such courses annually, of which around 40 percent were students at the upper secondary level (general subjects), 30 percent at the upper secondary level (vocational subjects), and 30 percent at the lower secondary level.

Most students are enrolled in the evening on a part-time basis. However, since 1975-76, when special leaves of absence and study allowances became available, a growing number have been able to study full-time during the day. The provision of counseling services, special tutoring and child-care services has also made study at such schools more attractive and feasible in recent years.

Folk High Schools. Originating in the mid-nineteenth century, the Swedish folk high schools were chartered to provide young rural adults with better opportunities for general (civic) education. Today, these uniquely Scandinavian institutions still offer "winter courses" to boarding students in general subjects, but short course of one week or less in topic areas of special interest to students and organizations have become the norm. Each school determines its own curriculum, very often through student participation, within the general guidelines of the Folk High School Code.

According to the Swedish Institute (1978), "recent reforms have considerably changed the pattern of recruitment to folk high schools. Great and rapidly increasing numbers of students are recruited for short courses which the voluntary associations organize in partnership with these schools. Enrollments have also swelled among the ranks of immigrants and handicapped persons. An extensive pilot scheme for the instruction of handicapped persons is financed with special State funds."

The total enrollment during 1977 in Sweden's 110 folk high schools was approximately 150,000.

Private Companies. Seventy percent of the Swedish workforce is employed by firms that have some kind of employee education plan. By the late 1970s almost all of the companies with 300 or more employees provided direct educational opportunities. Employees of smaller firms were generally eligible for training courses sponsored by the various employer federations and their affiliated trade associations.

In general, employers pay the costs of staff training; there are few national government subsidies to private companies for in-plant training. An exception to the above are the subsidized "intramural company schools," which are formed when a local upper secondary school collaborates with an employer in offering on-the-job training to employees in basic vocational skills.

Trade Unions, Employee Organizations. Most adult
education in this area is provided by the two largest national
employee organizations, the Confederation of Trade Unions (LO)
and the Central Organization of Salaried Employees (TCO). The
education offered by such organizations consists mostly of
teaching union officers and members about union affairs and
labor-related statutes. Most courses are residential and
last one or two weeks. Some, however, including those in
leadership training, last up to six months. The national
government provides subsidies for these programs. As of 1975,
there were approximately 82,000 participants per year in such
programs (SCB, 1978).

Labor Market Training. The National Labor Market Board
(AMS) devotes virtually as many resources to adult education
as the National Board of Education through its extensive
involvement in labor market training (The Swedish Institute,
1979a, Ahlqvist, 1977). Briefly, the system of labor market
training originated in the need to act swiftly against
imbalances in the labor markets, retraining those threatened
by unemployment and providing manpower for so-called "bottle-
neck skills." Four main kinds of courses are sponsored by the
AMS, depending on economic and institutional circumstances:
(1) special courses arranged by the National Board of
Education (over one-half of all labor market training);
(2) training within industry; (3) training within the ordinary
educational system; and (4) courses arranged by private firms
or municipalities.
    The rapid action mentioned above is the result of col-
laboration between labor unions, employers and local school
authorities, who together determine what local "retraining"
needs and resources are.

Other Providers. In addition to the above major providers of adult education in Sweden, there are several others
which together reach more than 100,000 learners annually. For
example, there are educational radio and television programs
produced by a special government-funded corporation. This
corporation often collaborates with other organizations (e.g.,
educational associations or folk high schools) in developing
training programs.
    Correspondence institutes, among which two (Hermods and
Brevskolan) are dominant, also provide learning opportunities,
the former in helping students to fulfill formal requirements
for course completion at all levels and the latter in catering
to the needs of special interest organizations. According to
the Swedish Institute (1978), "in recent years the traditional
type of correspondence course has been increasingly combined
with other forms of instruction, especially study circles
and educational broadcasts. This type of combined course

generally leads to more effective learning than pure correspondence courses."

Finally, there are state schools for adults. These
schools (of which there are only two) offer courses simiar to
those offered by municipal adult schools. Their clientele are
mainly people in rural areas who have no access to municipal
adult schools and are able to learn through correspondence
or a combination of correspondence and relative short and
intensive in-school courses.

Summary

Sweden is determined to use its adult educational
programs to further its goal of social equality. Swedish
educators still feel many reforms are needed before this
becomes a reality. Such reforms are currently under way. It
is likely that in the not-too-distant future adult education
as we presently know it in Sweden will be incorporated into an
authentic system of lifelong learning, turning the phrase
"adult education" into an odd anachronism.

Adult Education Statistics in Sweden

In general, national statistics on adult education and
training in Sweden are quite complete and timely. They are
perhaps the best of any of the countries included in the
study. The participation estimate for the study circles, by
far the largest single adult education program in Sweden, has
been corrected for multiple counting. The estimated 1 million
individuals (Table 7) were enrolled in roughly 3 million
circles during the year (SCB, 1979).

TABLE 7. SWEDEN: MAJOR PROGRAMS AND ESTIMATES OF PARTICIPATION

Program or Provider	Estimated Number of Participants	Year	Source
Voluntary Education Associations (study circles)	1,000,000	1979	Estimated from SCB, 1979
Municipal Adult Schools	310,000	1979	SCB, 1979
Folk High Schools	150,000	1977	Folkbildnings- arbeter, 1977
Private companies	300,000	1975	SCB, 1978
Trade unions, employee organizations	82,000	1975	SCB, 1978
Labour Market Training	78,000	1979	Labour Market Board, 1979
Radio and television	58,800	1975	SCB, 1978
Correspondence institutes	41,200	1975	SCB, 1978
State Schools for Adults	5,000	1975	SCB, 1978
Total adult population:	5,617,000		Estimated total participation rate: 29 percent
Estimated total participation, all programs:	1,650,000		

THE UNITED KINGDOM

General

Adult education in the United Kingdom has been described, not necessarily derogatively, as a "patchwork." Unquestionably it is pluralistic; in part because of its long history, a great many organizations now play active roles. Unquestionably it is decentralized, with the great bulk of adult education arranged by the Local Education Authorities (LEAs). In structure and legal basis, adult education in England and Wales is similar. Scotland and Northern Ireland are different in a number of respects, as Arthur Stock points out in his paper in Part III of this report. (Except where noted, comments in this short overview will apply only to England and Wales.)

While the duty to provide educational programs for adults is universally accepted by the LEAs, there are no statutory definitions or directives (in any of the four nations) for adult education. No minimum level of provision is specified. Local spending for adult education is discretionary, rather than mandatory or categorical. The nature and extent of LEA-sponsored programs thus depend heavily on the attitudes and judgments of local officials and advisory bodies; offerings, accordingly, vary greatly from one locality to another. Likewise immensely varied (and complex to a foreign observer) are the structural or organizational arrangements through which adult education is carried on by the LEAs.

Postcompulsory education in England and Wales is sometimes described as "binary," to distinguish between the universities and the local authority colleges. In fact, it seems to be quarternary. First, there are the 43 universities in Great Britain, quite selective in admissions, centrally funded through the University Grants Committee. Second are the 30 Polytechnics, created in 1966, and LEA-controlled. Third are the over 100 diverse institutions, also LEA-administered, which are generally referred to as Colleges of Further Education--a most unfortunate name given the purposes of this report, since they were designed for (and in fact do mostly enroll) students aged 16 to 19 seeking vocational and technical training. In 1977, there were 280,000 students in the universities (Fowler, 1979); 260,000 in the Polytechnics in 1978 (CDP, 1979); and (in 1976) roughly 1.8 million in the Colleges of Further Education (DES, 1979).

The fourth sector--adult education--overlaps somewhat the others in that the first three sectors all enroll substantial and increasing numbers of "mature" students. Adult education, however, involves numerous providers, the largest of which will be briefly described below. As shown in Table 8, the total number of participants in 1977 was on the order of 6.1 million, with almost all attending part-time. This figure, which represents 15 percent of the adult population, is not high in comparison with other industrialized countries.

Adult education's present difficulty in Britain, as reflected by the somewhat low participation rates, is mainly financial--in the form of increasingly austere national budgets in a period of worsening inflation and recession. Education, least of all adult education and training, is not a current government priority, as evidenced most starkly by the Chancellor of the Exchequer's 1980 budget. One may hope that all this will change, perhaps as the North Sea oil revenues begin to come in. In the meantime, the National Institute of Adult Education and especially the recently established (1977) Advisory Council for Adult & Continuing Education are developing and circulating provocative new perspectives and proposals that could, in time, lead to major reforms in the provision of adult education (e.g., ACACE, 1979a, b, c; Jones and Williams, 1979; McIntosh, 1979a and b).

The Major Providers

The Local Education Authorities. The statutory educational system of England and Wales is operated through local government. The elected county or city council is the education authority. By statute, each council must have an education committee. Some two-thirds of the 104 LEAs have further education subcommittees. These bodies determine how the allocation, provided in block form by the (national) Department of Education and Science (DES), will be used for adult education in the locality (including grants to individual, usually needy, students).

As noted earlier, no common organizational pattern for LEA provision of adult education prevails. Three main types are frequently identified (Small, 1979; Stock, in Part III):

(1) The area adult centre or institute. This could be a "wing" of a local school, usually a secondary school, devoted to adult education. Or the Centre could have its own

premises. Frequently the Centre or Institute has satellite centers throughout the area--in churches, village halls, and the like.

(2) The community school, community college, or village college. The basic concept in this instance is that one comprehensive institution is designed to meet the educational needs of everyone in a given area, regardless of age.

(3) The Adult Studies Department of a College of Further Education. All LEA's have Colleges of FE in their jurisdictions. A relatively recent development is for these institutions to offer special vocational courses--and at some sites, general education courses--for older students. College of FE provision would exist alongside either the area centre or community school arrangement in a given locality.

Residential Colleges. These institutions, which tend to be quite different in their histories and educational objectives, afford adults the chance to pursue a general subject in some depth. Typically there are no special requirements for admission. The seven long-term residential colleges, which are generally older, offer courses of one or two years' duration. DES grants aid both the colleges and some of the students. Most of the 50 short-term colleges are maintained or assisted by LEAs, or by an LEA jointly with a university or one of the voluntary associations. Courses vary in length from college to college, as do policies on LEA grants to students. All the residential colleges tend to be small, having on the average about 50 students in residence at any point in time.

The Universities. Beginning with Cambridge's Extension Lectures in 1873, there are now 25 universities (in England and Wales) with extramural departments or departments of adult education. As a so-called "responsible body," universities can receive from the DES 75 percent of the cost of "liberal adult education" courses; other courses must be either self-supporting or financed from other sources.

All university adult education courses are pitched to a "university standard"--a level of instruction at least that of a first or second year undergraduate course. Student admission, nonetheless, is essentially open. Programs for particular groups of workers or professionals, such as police, social workers, and trade union officials, are often provided (Small, 1979). Frequently there is close cooperation between university extramural departments and the Workers' Educational Association in organizing and conducting programs for workers.

The Polytechnics. In their short history, the Polytechnics give evidence of evolving into important institutions for continuing education (in England and Wales). Students on the average are substantially older than in the universities. Roughly one third attend part-time (CDP, 1979). The Polytechnics are notably comprehensive; offerings include: degree, postgraduate, and subdegree options; full-time, part-time (day or evening), and "sandwich" (alternating work and study) schemes; short courses for professional updating; and, at a number of Polytechnics, general and community education courses in addition to the mainstream vocational and professional programs.

The Open University. The OU must be counted one of the most important--and successful--educational innovations in recent times, anywhere in the world. Based on distance learning and home-study concepts, it is designed expressly for older, working adults. Courses are "taught" through specially prepared texts coordinated with television and radio broadcasts produced for the university by the BBC. For review purposes, students can attend one of the 260 OU study centres throughout the United Kingdom. Beginning in 1971 with 24,000 students, there are currently close to 80,000--in either the undergraduate (by far the largest), graduate, or associate student programs.

The recently established Associate Student Programme is of particular interest for this report. It currently offers 80 nondegree, mostly occupationally-related, courses, each lasting about ten months. The Associate Programme is also developing a series of short (eight-week) Community Education courses; one, for example, is titled Consumer Decisions, and has units on such matters as food, cars, and appliances.

The Workers' Educational Association. Founded in 1903, the WEA is concerned for the totality of education, but especially for the education of adults and workers. It is organized into 21 districts and over 900 branches. As a statutory "responsible body," WEA districts receive funds from the DES. LEAs also often make grants to and generally encourage the work of the WEA districts.

In a decentralized and participatory manner, the branches organize classes on student-selected topics; they also arrange single lectures, day-long or week-end schools, and conferences and exhibitions. A recent study (WEA, 1977) indicated 55 percent of all classes to be in liberal and academic areas; 15 percent in trade union studies, 15 percent in social and political education, and 15 percent in subjects for disadvantaged students. Altogether there were some 120,000 registered students in WEA courses in 1976 (DES, 1977).

Industrial Training. Two programs are of particular interest and will be discussed further in Part II. Both are operated centrally, by the Department of Employment's Manpower Services Commission (MSC).

(1) TOPS (Training Opportunities Scheme) provides grants to individuals over age 19, who are either unemployed or who wish to change jobs, to train for up to one year at special skill centres or at any of the colleges having the needed curriculum. There were 99,000 TOPS trainees in 1978 (Small, 1979).

(2) Through the 23 Industrial Training Boards (Agriculture, Petroleum, etc.), the MSC channels funds and training information to industries for "in-house" training of employees. ITB-supported training, however, accounts for less than half of all employer-based training. Stock (in Part III) estimates that altogether some 2.5 million individuals are currently receiving such training, the majority of which is financed directly by the companies and enterprises.

Other Providers. Because of space limitations, a number of additional providers of adult learning opportunities can be little more than mentioned. The BBC's charter mandates education as a principal purpose; on radio and television its excellent programs (including numerous courses) are experienced daily by millions. Correspondence courses are very popular, with some 500,000 adults in the U.K. reportedly involved (Glatter and Wedell, 1971). (The National Extension College alone offers 76 courses.) Voluntary education is widely facilitated in the HM (Armed) Forces. Every prison has an educational program. There are hundreds of proprietary (for-profit) schools. Local units of the National Federation of Women's Institutes, the National Union of Townswomen's Guilds, and the Young Women's Christian Associations provide settings for women of all ages to study topics of personal, cultural and political interest. The Trades Union Congress, using its Training College, offers programs in labor studies for hundreds of trade unionists each year.

The Literacy Campaign

Aimed at the "two million adults with problems of reading, writing and spelling," a broad range of institutions and individuals cooperated in what may indeed be described as a "campaign." Key participants included (in approximate chronological order) the British Association of Settlements, the BBC, the DES and its three annual (1975-1978) one million-pound grants, the NIAE, the LEAs, some 80,000 volunteer tutors, and close to 125,000 self-referred students. This important and by all odds quite successful adult learning effort will also be described in greater detail in Part II.

Adult Education Statistics in the U.K.

The quality and amount of statistical information on adult education in the U.K., not unlike the situation in other countries, is far from satisfactory. Data collected for the DES by the LEAs do not cover the full range of adult education in the localities, and are based on the numbers of individuals attending as of a single date in November (only). No indicators of the extent of possible multiple counting were found in any of the statistical reports. Available statistics are not comparable among the nations of the U.K., except for England and Wales. And there are other difficulties, as noted by Mee and Wiltshire (1978). Only the Open University seems to collect, analyze, and report statistics in a timely manner and in ways useful to adult educators and educational policy makers.

TABLE 8. THE UNITED KINGDOM: MAJOR PROGRAMS AND ESTIMATES OF PARTICIPATION

Program or Provider	Estimated Number of Participants	Year	Source
Local Education Authorities (LEAs)	1,797,000	1976	DES, 1979
Residential colleges	80,000	1976	DES, 1979
Universities: extra-mural departments	165,000	1976	DES, 1979
Polytechnics: part-time students	83,000	1976	CDP, 1979
The Open University	78,000	1978	The Open University, 1978
The Workers' Educational Association	120,000	1976	DES, 1979
Correspondence schools	500,000	1970	Glatter and Wedell, 1971
Industrial training	2,500,000	1979	Stock, in Part IV
Proprietary schools	681,000	1971	Wiseman, 1977
Training Opportunities Scheme (TOPS)	99,000	1978	Small, 1979
Total adult population:	41,500,000		Estimated total participation rate: 15 percent
Estimated total participation, all programs:	6,100,000		

THE UNITED STATES

Government Policy

It is fair to say that the U.S. government has no comprehensive adult education or occupational training policy. The federal government, however, has numerous laws and programs extending educational opportunities to many categories of adults (Christoffel, 1978); but the sum of these categories is far short of the totality of American adults. Typically, "federal" programs are in fact implemented by state and local agencies; that is federal funds are channeled down, to be used according to rather general federal guidelines (regulations).

Among the most important of the federal programs for the education of adults are the following: student financial aid for military veterans (now minimal); agricultural and related education for farm families through the Cooperative Extension Service; in-service training opportunities for government employees; the Comprehensive Employment and Training Act (CETA), which benefits mostly the marginally employable; funding for adult basic education, carried out through locally designed programs; opportunities for voluntary education in the military services; and two grant programs that function in part to promote innovation in services to adult learners: The Fund for the Improvement of Postsecondary Education, and Title I of the Higher Education Act of 1965 (Continuing Postsecondary Education Program and Planning).

As it has developed in the past 20 years, federal education legislation (including adult-related legislation), taken together, has come to reflect a policy of equity--of seeking to provide equality of opportunity, if not of results. Left to the states and local jurisdictions, as it has been, education provision varies greatly in its quality and quantity --depending in large part on the local economic base. Federal education policy--now quite explicitly--is intended to correct these imbalances.

Providing for education is not a responsibilty of the federal government under the U.S. Constitution. It is instead a jealously guarded responsibility of the 50 states and the thousands of local school districts. Over the decades most states have built up education codes of great length and complexity. Within the broad domain of education, however, adult education has almost never been a topic for major state policy (important exceptions include New York, Texas, Vermont, and the Mississippi Authority for Educational Television). Perhaps the most explicit commitment to adult education has come in the form of funding to supplement the federal funds to the states for adult basic education (ABE).

States of course also provide educational opportunities for adults beyond the conventional college-going age, by supporting state college and university enrollment of older adults. And older students are attending in increasing numbers, mostly part-time. They are charged fees at the four-year institutions, to be sure, but the fees do not cover the full cost of instruction (except in extension or continuing education divisions). At the two-year community colleges--in many states heavily funded by the states--charges tend to be low (in California they are still nonexistent); the education of thousands of older adults enrolled at these institutions is substantially subsidized by state government.

However, it is down in the "localities," at the level of single institutions and organizations, that the real initiative for providing learning opportunities for adults resides. In a majority of states, public community colleges and public school adult schools (in part) are locally financed (from property taxes); thus local jurisdictions are investing in the education of their adults. At the state colleges and universities, extension and continuing education programs are set up in response to local needs, usually following only minimal guidelines from state agencies. In addition, a host of local community organizations--museums, libraries, city recreation departments, churches, business enterprises, for example--are entirely free to offer any programs for which they judge there is an interest; and they are increasingly doing so (Peterson and Associates, 1979).

Thus, in spite of the absence of comprehensive federal or state policies, adult education is indeed flourishing in the U.S. While estimates vary, it is probably safe to say that between 25 and 30 percent of all adults have been involved in some kind of organized and sustained learning activity in the past year.

Many problems remain, however: participation across the broad range of adult education in the U.S. is grossly biased in favor of the affluent and well-educated (Cross, 1979); adult illiteracy persists, with only miniscule efforts to reduce it; diverse "providers," often with questionable motives, are entering the arena of continuing education, increasing the likelihood of low quality--even fraudulent-- offerings; programs to attract rank and file workers have generally not proven effective; and, finally, perhaps most sadly, a wave of fiscal and governmental conservatism in the U.S. (beginning in 1977 with Proposition 13 in California and culminating this past year in the policies of the Reagan Administration) is leading to cutbacks in many public services, including education and often, in particular, adult education.

Major Providers

Some 11 major providers (there are numerous others) are described briefly below and in somewhat greater detail by Cross in Part III. The first three are school-based; the rest are operated by organizations other than schools. Total enrollment of adults in the latter, the non-school organizations, is much larger than in the former (Peterson and Associates, 1979).

The Community Colleges. Though but one part of the formal postsecondary education "system" in the U.S., the over 900 public community colleges at the present time are arguably its most significant component from the standpoint of adult learning. At most of them, and especially at those situated in an urban area, evening students--most are working adults-- now outnumber "regular" day students. Admission is essentially open. They typically offer a wide range of vocational, academic, and avocational courses and programs. Tuition is relatively low.

College and University Extension and Continuing Education. Most four-year colleges and universities operate extension or continuing education programs, particularly if the institution is located in an area of substantial population density where there is a base of adults to draw from. Courses typically are scheduled in the evening, although increasingly there are other arrangements, such as "weekend colleges" and special summer programs. While extension divisions offer a variety of courses--avocational, academic, public affairs--they are frequently extensively involved in providing continuing education for professionals-- doctors, nurses, pharmacists, engineers, teachers, and many others--often in response to state legislation mandating continuing education for purposes of relicensure (see Frandson, 1980).

Public School Adult Schools. Most local public school districts operate adult schools. The range of offerings varies greatly from one locality to another, depending on financial resources and attitudes of administrators and school board members. Roughly two-thirds of all the classes are held at night; about half are conducted in elementary and secondary school buildings, with the other half at special adult education centers or in other non-school facilities. Courses tend to be concentrated in avocational subjects, limited vocational specialties, languages--especially English as a second language, high school equivalency studies geared to passing tests that will mean a high school diploma, and basic literacy and consumer skills (described further in Part II). Typically there are no fees. Funding comes from federal, state, and local sources at a ratio of roughly 1:4:1 nationwide (NAPCAE, 1980).

Private Industry. Virtually all large firms--those employing over 500 people--have training programs for their employees (Lusterman, 1977). Most small firms do not. There are no standard models or accepted guidelines and, until this past year, no government incentives. Training opportunities at a given plant are essentially the result of corporate (management) philosophy. Roughly 10 percent of the private sector work force is participating in education and training at a given time.

Professional Associations. For almost every category of professional (broadly defined), there is a professional organization, usually organized at the state as well as local chapter level. Especially in response to the burgeoning legislation in the states requiring continuing education or competency (which statutes the associations usually helped formulate), the professional associations are increasingly providing learning opportunities in a variety of formats for their members.

Government Service. Government at all levels, with over 16 million civilian employees (Smith, 1979), is easily the largest single employer in the U.S. In general, there are numerous learning opportunities--from basic skills to advanced scientific and professional--continuously available to almost all government workers. At the federal level, about 20 percent are involved in education or training at a given time (OPM, 1980).

Federal Manpower Programs. The principle federal program for occupational training is known as CETA (for Comprehensive Education and Training Act), which is described further in Part II. It is highly decentralized; specific programs and combinations of programs are set by some 460 local "prime sponsors." Chiefly because of limited funds, programs mainly involve, as noted earlier, the poor and marginally employable.

Agriculture Extension. The educational work of the U.S. Department of Agricuture's Cooperative Extension Service is a large and important component of adult education in the U.S. Conducted mainly by the country's Land Grant Universities in a variety of instructional and advisory formats, the Cooperative Extension's four principle programs are: Agriculture and Natural Resources, Home Economics, 4-H Youth, and Community Resource Development.

Community Organizations. This is a catch-all category that includes libraries, Y's, museums, personal improvement groups, senior adult groups, recreation groups, political organizations, social service organizations, civic clubs, and social clubs. Not all of these sponsor organized learning activities, but many do, such as the Y's, museums, Red Cross, League of Women Voters, and health-related organizations. Community issues and personal and family living are the predominant topics for study in the (nonchurch) community oganizations (Kay, 1974).

Churches and Synagogues. Some 40 percent of American adults attend church regularly, according to recent Gallup Polls. Almost all churches, but especially the larger ones, have educational programs that deal with secular as well as religious matters. According to the 1972 NCES survey (Kay, 1974), three-quarters of registrations fell in the content area of religion; 17 percent were in personal and family living; and the rest, in community issues, occupational training, recreation, and general (including basic) education.

City Recreation Departments. Almost all cities in the U.S., except the smallest ones, have recreation and/or park departments which offer courses and other learning activities covering a wide variety of mostly avocational topics. Often they provide special programs for the handicapped, the elderly, and other specified populations. Most activities, however, are open to anyone, and fees are nominal. Unfortunately, during the present tide of fiscal conservatism in the U.S., the budgets of many city recreation departments are being cut.

Other Important Providers. In addition to specialized technical training, all of the military services have voluntary education programs, usually in cooperation with local colleges; total participation is close to 1.5 million (see Carr and Ripley, 1980). Proprietary schools, some 9,000 of them (Kay, 1976), offer full-time occupational training--in return for substantial tuition payments. Labor unions sponsor apprentice training, labor studies for union officials, and,

increasingly, skill training and general education oppor-
tunities--all also frequently in collaboration with nearby
colleges and universities (MacKenzie, 1980). Some 4 million
people are reportedly enrolled in correspondence courses.
Almost all correctional institutions have education or
training programs. Over a million adults use tutors or
private instructors to guide their learning (Boaz, 1980).
Finally, some 150 "free universities" provide learning
opportunities for close to 300,000 people (Calvert and Draves,
1978) whose learning is not oriented toward credentials.

Adult Education Statistics in the U.S.

Somewhat unfortunately, there is a range of national
studies and surveys from which, in a sense, to choose. They
fall into two general types: (1) surveys of national samples
of individual adults, and (2) tabulations of participants in
particular programs. The former tend to yield estimates
markedly lower than the latter.

Two widely cited Type 1 studies, however, also yielded
quite different findings--12 and 31 percent participation
rates, for example, from the Boaz (1980) and Carp, Peterson,
and Roelfs (1974) surveys respectively. In part, the
differences reflect somewhat different definitions of adult
education. The Boaz/NCES survey was fairly well limited to
"organized and sustained" adult education, while the Carp/
Peterson/Roelfs survey also included "independent study."

Raw data for the Type 2 surveys generally come from
program directors at local and/or state levels. There is a
tendency to inflate such enrollment figures, for reasons of
program aggrandizement.

Yet another confounding factor is the fact of multiple-
counting--that is, enrollment (or registration) by one individual in more than one course from the same or a different
provider (in a given year). In the Boaz/NCES survey (1980),
18.2 million individuals reported enrollment in 28.9 million
courses--a 38 percent difference, which may usefully serve
as a rough correction factor for multiple-counting.

Participation in the various programs listed in Table 9
totals to roughly 81 million. Subtract 10 million for inflated enrollment reporting. Subtract 10 million more for all
the people who did not participate in a sustained manner
(Cooperative Extension "contacts," for example). Subtract 23
million more (38 percent of 61 million) as a correction for
multiple enrollments. To this figure, 38 million, add 6
million participants in various study arrangements not
included in the table (trade union programs, private lessons,
community education, free universities, prisoner education,
and numerous other arrangements). Thus our estimate of 44
million, and a 27 percent participation rate.

TABLE 9.   THE UNITED STATES: MAJOR PROGRAMS AND ESTIMATES OF PARTICIPATION

Program or Provider	Estimated Number of Participants	Year	Source
Colleges and universities: part-time students	4,621,000	1978	NCES, 1979b
Community colleges: part-time students	2,475,000	1978	NCES, 1979b
University extension and continuing education	3,356,000	1978	Boaz, 1980
Public school adult schools	18,186,000	1979	NAPCAE, 1980
Proprietary schools	1,043,000	1978	NCES, 1979a
Correspondence schools	4,325,000	1973	NHSC, 1973
Private industry	5,800,000	1975	Lusterman, 1977
Professional associations	6,000,000	1979	Author's estimate
Government service	3,000,000	1979	OPM, 1980; Brown, 1976
Federal manpower programs	5,310,000	1976	Fraser, 1980
Agriculture extension	12,000,000	1975	Estimated from USDA, 1976
Community organizations	7,354,000	1972	Kay, 1974
Churches and synagogues	3,614,000	1972	Kay, 1974
City recreation departments	5,000,000	1970	NRPA, 1971
Military services	1,500,000	1979	Carr and Ripley, 1980
Total adult population:	163,099,000		Estimated total participation rate: 27 percent
Estimated total participation, all programs:	44,000,000		

PART II:

LEARNING OPPORTUNITIES FOR SELECTED POPULATION GROUPS

WORKERS

It is reasonably clear that so far as the countries included in this study are concerned, work-related training is the single most important facet of adult education. In industrialized societies, where rapid technological change is the normal condition, much of this training is necessarily aimed at bringing workers--white-collar as well as blue-collar--up to date in their job skills and knowledge. An important objective, also deriving from the fact of change, is to retrain workers whose skills are no longer in demand or who wish to take advantage of new opportunities. Other kinds of work-related training are designed to develop skills needed for trade union activities, to facilitate the entry of new populations of workers--e.g., women or immigrants--into the labor force, or to raise the level of general education of persons who entered the labor force "prematurely."

A great deal of education and training for workers is offered at the enterprise level, since that is where the needs are most evident and the knowledge required for instruction most readily available, and since the augmented skills make an immediate contribution to productive efficiency. Private employers provide a large proportion of this education in every country except, of course, the Soviet Union. However, in several of the countries this enterprise-level training is subsidized by the national government, while in others it is supported by employer groups of one sort or another. The United States is an exception: private firms receive little external aid for employee training. In several countries private efforts are stimulated, coordinated, or regulated by the national government, and in all of them national as well as lower-level governmental bodies play another role by providing often extensive educational programs for their own employees. In all of the countries, again with the exception of the Soviet Union, work-related adult education is available from many other sources as well, although formal educational institutions sometimes play a surprisingly small part.

Perhaps the greatest range of differences in the work-related adult-education programs of the countries considered here is the extent to which the worker has a right to take leave of absence for educational purposes. Probably the extremes are represented by Australia and the United States, on the one hand, where educational leave, and especially paid leave, is a barely known concept (except for the "sabbaticals" granted to faculty members in higher educational institutions), and on the other hand France, where a worker's right to educational leave has been established in law, subjected to detailed regulation, and frequently paid for. This is probably an area of social and educational policy in which major changes will be seen in the next decade or so.*

Australia

Technical and Further Education. Technical and further education (TAFE) institutions are a major source of training of workers.   TAFE enrollments were distributed as follows in 1977:

Stream 1 (Professional):   Leads to professional status or enables professionals to update their technology or to specialize. Enrollment: 5,521.

Stream 2 (Paraprofessional):   For those entering or progressing within middle-level or technician occupations. Three types of courses: basic technician courses, post certificate courses, and higher or advanced certificate courses. Enrollment: 165,330.

Stream 3 (Trades):   Leads to occupations for which apprenticeship exists, plus post-trade courses for non-technical advanced skills. Enrollment: 144,838.

Stream 4 (Other Skilled):   All other skilled trade and vocational courses, not included in Stream 3. Enrollment: 154,335.

---

*Many complex issues surround the concept of educational leave, as von Moltke and Schneevoight's 1977 report points out.   The Center for Educational Research and Innovation, of the Organization for Economic Cooperation and Development, has given attention to these issues for some time and has published a series of useful reports, some of which include studies of educational leave in several of the countries included in this report. See especially CERI/OECD, 1976 and 1978; the first of these was summarized in a publication from the U.S. National Institute of Education (Levine, 1977).

Stream 5 (Preparatory): Matriculation and diploma entrance courses, remedial and courses with vocational orientation not classified elsewhere. Enrollment: 109,624.

Total enrollments in Streams 1 through 5 were 579,648 (547,334 part-time), of which 56 percent were by individuals age 21 or more. TAFE also includes Stream 6, "adult education," which includes courses in handicrafts, cultural appreciation, and so on. Stream 6 enrollments, while open to workers, are not included in this discussion.

Technical and further education is controlled by State Departments of Education in Queensland, Tasmania, Victoria, and West Australia; in New South Wales by a Department of Technical Education; in South Australia by a Department of Further Education; and in the Northern and Australian Capital Territories by the Australian Department of Education. Total TAFE expenditures in 1977 were $382,000,000, of which $109,200,000 came from the Australian government and the balance from the states.

Apprenticeship Training. Apprenticeships, which account for 126,900 of the total TAFE enrollments in Stream 3, deserve special comment. Apprenticeship entry, training, and education requirements are controlled by state statutory authorities, whose work is supplemented by state and federal industrial awards determining wage rebates and other conditions of employment. Further, the Commonwealth Rebate For Apprenticeship Full Time Training (CRAFT) provides rebates to employers for apprentices to attend technical colleges for full-time basic training and full-time off the job training. In 1979-80, 48,000 apprentices were part of this program. While upper age limits on apprentices are not part of legislation in any state, industrial awards have served to establish age 23 as the completion age for all practical purposes. Upgrading, or the reclassification of workers who have not completed an Australian apprenticeship and are paid as tradesmen provides some relief.

1970-76 Tradesmen Certificates Issued Under
Tradesman's Rights Regulation Act

Migrants	28,455	74.3 percent
Australian Civilians	7,043	18.4 percent
Servicemen	2,788	7.3 percent
Total	38,285	100 percent

(Williams, 1979, p. 348)

The magnitude of upgrading is regarded as indicating that the apprenticeship system has not produced sufficient numbers of qualified tradesmen. It has been estimated that there are 75 to 80,000 tradesmen who are unqualified, some of whom could be qualified if training opportunities were available. Other criticisms of the apprentice system, for example, high wastage rates, needlessly long training, changing technologies demanding new skills, led the Williams Committee to offer several recommendations (Williams, 1979, pp. 323-340). The recommendations included training for informally upgraded tradesmen, short courses in TAFE colleges, accreditation of courses provided in industry, support allowances in part-time courses for those employed, formal initial training followed by on-the-job training to be Commonwealth financed, modular educational programs, subsidies to encourage more general industry-based rather than firm-specific training, and testing of tradesmen seeking upgrading.

The National Employment and Training Program. The National Employment and Training (NEAT) scheme is directed to subpopulations of young adults and adults who either lack entry skills and qualifications for employment, or who require retraining because of changes in structural employment due to government action, technological changes or high unemployment. In 1976-77 a Special Youth Unemployment Program (SYEP) providing six months on-the-job training for 15-19 year-olds had 65,000 enrolled. Similarly, Employment Programs For Unemployed Youth (EPUY) secured vocational training for about 3000. Through the Community Youth Support Scheme (CYSS), young adults secure positive work orientation through community based activities. However, since NEAT was introduced at a time of rising unemployment, the education community tends to perceive it as "unemployment relief rather than education or training" (Duke, 1976a, p. 11).

Trade Union Education. Specific provision for union education became a reality in 1975 with the Trade Union Training Act that established the Australian Trade Union Training Authority. TUTA operates a residential educational facility, Clyde Cameron College, plus other Trade Union Training Centers, and arranges for the provision of trade union training through institutions and other bodies. Councils For Trade Union Training are provided for in each state. Through the Workers' Educational Association of South Australia, TUTA offers postal (correspondence) courses. In 1977-78 TUTA offered 442 courses to 8044 participants, plus 473 who completed at least 5 correspondence lessons through the Trade Union Postal Course Scheme. The 1977-78 program also included courses on basic trade union information in

Italian, Greek, Spanish and Turkish, for nonEnglish speaking migrant unionists at the Victoria Center. TUTA looks forward to serving about 1 percent of the total trade union population (28,000) annually over the next four or five years.

Private Employers. While it was not possible to locate statistics on participation in worker education provided through private employers, the Australian Public Service, community agencies and so on, there are indications it is quite substantial. Some examples are Telecom, which indicated it had 5000 trainees, plus 600 officers who took external short courses and 2700 staff who took longer courses. BHP (an iron-steel manufacturer), in addition to 3400 apprentices, had 1100 other professional and subprofessional trainees. A bank with 27,000 employees had 6000 engaged in formal courses annually. Of course, some of this educational activity was provided to workers through programs offered by educational institutions. Universities, as well as colleges of advanced education, are offering continuing education programming, and many have established centers of continuing education. In 1974, 32,058 enrollments were tallied by universities in professional refresher courses. However, six universities accounted for 80 percent of these enrollments.

Paid educational leave appears to be a concept and an opportunity that still awaits development in Australia. Currently, there is some provision: teacher sabbaticals, public servants (5 hours of part-time study on full pay), and most large employers grant short leaves. In 1976, the Chairman of the TAFE Council of the Tertiary Education Commission indicated that "...paid educational leave was not a major platform of the Union Movement..." (Victoria Council of Adult Education, 1977, p. v.).

Canada

The material that follows has been extracted from the paper prepared by Clark and Brundage which is included in its entirety in Part III of this volume. The major provisions of education for workers are as follows:

Through employers:

(1) Between 27 and 32 percent of enterprises have a policy or plan on training and development during working hours.

(2) Sixty-eight percent of all employees work for an organization with a training plan.

(3) Ninety-nine percent of employees in organizations with a training plan or policy allow time off for job-related training, 25 percent for labor studies, and 40 percent for general and social education.

(4) Of the workers in organizations with training plans, 15.1 percent actually received training in 1978.

(5) Apprenticeship training is limited in its availability. Application-position ratios can run as high as 20 or 30 to 1, and of those 16 to 24 years old in the labor force, only one in 20 trains in a registered apprenticeship.

(6) The major programs of continuing education in the work place are provided by the federal government and by the Ontario government. Through the Canada Manpower Industrial Training Program, 78,936 persons received training in 1978-79.

Through federal and provincial resources:

(1) There were 7,054 persons in training programs for the disabled in 1976-77 provided under the federal Vocational Rehabilitation for Disabled Persons Act.

(2) The federal vocational training initiatives are through the Adult Occupational Training Act of 1967. Training was provided in educational institutions and through employers to 286,494 full- and part-time trainees in 1978-79.

(3) The federal Labor Department beginning in 1977 has provided a grant for the Canadian Labor Congress for the promotion of labor studies for a five year period in the amount of $2 million per year. An amount of $600,000 has also been allocated to labor groups not affiliated with the Congress.

(4) Training in Business and Industry, an Ontario provincial program comparable to the Canadian Manpower Industrial Training Program, provided learning opportunities for 85,283 adults in 1977-78.

Through trade union resources:

(1)   Labor education is provided through weekend institutes, evening courses and one-week schools. Labor
studies programs are available through seven
colleges and universities.

(2)   Eighteen of 118 national and international unions
affiliated with the Canadian Labor Congress had a
recognized education department.

(3)   Twenty-five percent of employees of organizations
with plans or policies were covered by extended
leave arrangements and 30.6 percent were covered by
short-term leave arrangements.

(4)   United Auto Workers have 116 collective agreements
providing for leave for union training.

In addition to the comprehensive statement on adult
education of workers provided by Clark and Brundage, two other
topics deserve comment. First, national and provincial
professional associations are increasing their interest in
sponsoring continuing education for their members. Thirty-
three groups reported they conducted programs in 1979,
and one-third had started courses since 1970 (Swan, 1979,
Appendix A, p. 12).

The Adams Commission. The Adams Commission of Inquiry on
Educational Leave and Productivity (1979) recently offered
several major and innovative recommendations.

(1)   Ratification by Canada of ILO Convention No. 140 on
paid educational leave as national policy;

(2)   A tax uniformly applied to industry to generate
funds for industry-based training;

(3)   A vocational development fund which would provide
stipends to enable individuals to pursue advanced
occupational training;

(4)   A legal right for trade union training for union
representatives;

(5)   Day release for literacy training to be funded by
the federal government;

(6)   A Registered Educational Leave Plan that would allow
individuals to deposit up to $2500 each year to be
tax free in the year of deposit as well as tax free
in the year of withdrawal if used for education;

(7)   A study of the current level of management effec-
      tiveness and the adequacy of management education;
      and

(8)   A national education and training agency to coordi-
      nate provision of information, research, assistance
      to employers, unions, and professional associations
      regarding training and to manage the financing of
      education and training related to employment.

Denmark

There are a number of programs in Denmark aimed specifically at workers in addition to the more general programs for
the overall adult population for which workers are, of course,
eligible.   These latter programs are largely nonvocational
while the former are almost all directed toward developing
skills appropriate for entering employment, maintaining one's
position, or qualifying for advancement or change.   The
Ministry of Labor sponsors a number of programs as do business
and industry, unions and employee groups and others.

Labor Market Training Schemes.   Under the 1960 Act on
Vocational Training, the Ministry of Labor sponsors a number
of programs that are designed to improve conditions in the
labor market.   Programs are also offered by the Ministries of
Commerce and Education.
      Three different sorts of schemes are offered.   One is
aimed at upgrading semi-skilled workers, another at retraining
to update skills, and a third toward reconversion of workers
from skills in decreasing demand to those for which there is a
greater need.
      In general these programs are free to students and in
some cases paid leave is provided.   About 85 percent of the
cost is paid by the national government with the remainder by
employer groups and local authorities.   While financing is
largely centralized the actual training is decentralized with
local organizations or institutions responsible for carrying
out the instruction.   Some of the training is conducted by the
industry on the job.
      Anyone 18 years of age or older who is employed or
seeking employment is eligible to apply for semi-skilled
worker training.   There were about 200 courses offered in
the mid-1970s, most of which were short (about 144 hours).
Courses in a particular skill area are modular and correlated

at various levels. In 1972-73 almost 30,000 men and 5,000 women participated. Of the 35,000 total 60 percent were under 30 years of age and only 7 percent over 50 (Nordic Council, 1976).

The retraining schemes for skilled workers are conducted by employer and employee groups and by Technological Institutes and Commercial and Technical Schools. Courses usually run from one to three weeks and take place during the day. They are technical in content and designed to bring skills up to date as well as to provide skills appropriate for new techniques in business and industry. In 1972, 9,400 men and 600 women participated in retraining (Nordic Council, 1976).

Reconversion training is sponsored by an individual concern, by labor exchanges or labor market organizations. These programs are particularly aimed at conditions in local areas to encourage development by providing an adequate supply of labor. These are also important in meeting problems of technological unemployment. In 1972-73 200 men and 500 women participated. Of the 700 total 46 percent were under age 30 and 9 percent over 50 (Nordic Council, 1976). The programs include the equivalent of about a week of general orientation to the economic and social situation and are usually of longer duration than the semi-skilled or retraining schemes.

Employee Organization Training Schemes. Individual trade unions as well as the National Organization, the Workers' Education Association, the Business and Office Staff Association and the Joint Council for Danish Civil Servants offer training designed to improve the effectiveness of their members in carrying out union and employee activities. They are generally not concerned with job skills as such. The major target group is shop stewards for whom one to two week courses are provided covering union affairs and duties, national and industrial economy, workers' rights, wage policies, etc. Financial support is provided through the Danish Industrial Fund, the Workers' Protection Fund, and the individual trade unions, often with contributions negotiated from the employers. The training is normally free to workers or union members, often with paid leave. There are three labor Folk High Schools which receive the regular government support for the part of their program that qualifies under existing regulations, and this helps to cover the general cost of facilities and administration.

Employer Association Training Schemes. The Danish Employers' Association, the Industrial Council, and the Trades Council all sponsor short residential courses on leadership, management, production, marketing, finance and similar subjects for supervisory and management employees.

Inservice Training Schemes. Industrial concerns and trade organizations provide training to the concern's own personnel to improve their skills and productivity. These programs may be offered by the training departments of larger concerns or by independent organizations hired to carry out the training. Some of this may be on the job; some is conducted separately. Apprentice training as such is no longer a major form of imparting job skills.

Programs for Personnel in Public Administration. There is a variety of programs available to employees in public administration, both at the national and local levels. The National Institute of Administration under the Budget Ministry provides short courses, some residential but most spread over a longer period while occupying only a few hours a week during working time. They are aimed primarily at national civil servants, but local government employees may also apply.

The College of Municipal Administration is sponsored by the National Municipal Association and the County Councils Association. It provides general liberal, nonvocational adult education as well as training and retraining in various aspects of municipal service. The College offers residential courses at its own facility and organizes nonresidential courses at other locations.

Youth and Evening Schools. These institutions are sponsored in most cases by local authorities and provide, among other programs, vocational training for youths up to 18 years of age and past the compulsory attendance level, and also for adults. While they are not targeted primarily for workers as such, they do serve them. They also offer general courses, preparation for examinations, and cultural subjects.

The Federal Republic of Germany

The Vocational Education Act provides for joint adminis-tration of vocational education by the Lander and the federal government. The former provide in-school education, and the latter is responsible for the procedures for training on the job in facilities run by business or industry. Most of the participants are continuing regular education through this track up to age 18, but there are provisions for adults or youth beyond the age of compulsory schooling.

Most of the training for adult workers is offered through the Labor Promotion Act or facilities arranged by the unions and/or employers. The Volkshochschulen are open to workers, but their courses are usually more general and not as directly job-related as those provided by the other agencies.

The Labor Promotion Act of 1969. This well-known legislation* systematized and made explicit a number of policies related to vocational training and the labor market in the Federal Republic. The general purpose was to increase worker mobility by providing opportunities for both skills upgrading and training in entirely new fields (where jobs have been determined to be available). The program is funded through the country's social security system; employers and employees contribute through a payroll tax, and, since 1974, the federal government has also contributed. Courses are provided by the private sector: industries, employee associations, trade unions, and private schools.

Potential trainees do not have to be out of work, although they must have paid into the system for at least six years. Full-time trainees receive 80 percent of their previous net wage (58 percent if they were employed and not threatened by unemployment [Schmid, 1978]). Civil service and self-employed people are not eligible. About half the participants attend full time for an average of seven or eight months. The remainder are in shorter courses of at least 50 hours. Most participants are under age 35, and 83 percent are males. Skilled workers tend to be overrepresented (Rudolph, 1979).

Civil Service Training. Every civil service worker has the right to paid educational leave of up to two weeks a year. These programs are designed for upgrading of the vocational skills of employees of the federal, land, and local governments. Exclusive of the armed forces, there were approximately 600,000 participants in various federal programs. They come mainly from the middle and higher career levels and tend to be in the manager category (Rudolph, 1979).

Federal Factory Constitution Law. This program provides training for works council members. The employer pays the salary for the member while in training and the trade unions are responsible for providing the training. New council members receive four weeks of educational leave and subsequently are entitled to three weeks a year. It was estimated that 100,000 participated during a year in the early 1970s.

---

*Its programs were depicted on American television in June 1981 (National Broadcasting Company, 1981).

Trade Union Education and Collective Bargaining Agreements. Union funds provide a variety of courses covering general education and trade union studies. These range in duration from one day to six weeks with an average of three days. There are individual fees for vocational courses which are reimbursed through the Labor Promotion Act. A variety of collective bargaining agreements separately arrived at provide for general, trade union, or vocational education. Some of these include provision of paid leave in addition to covering the cost of instruction. The participants are largely shop stewards and the training is usually for two or three weeks a year.

Educational Leave. As in other aspects of education, the Lander differ in their policy and procedure for educational leave. As of a September 1979 report, only Berlin, Bremen, Hamburg, Hessen and Lower Saxony had legislation establishing rights to educational leave. The requirements and benefits vary. In one case only employees up to age 21 are eligible and in another, up to 25. In two cases not only employees but vocational students, the self employed, and those engaged in homework are also eligible. The duration varies from five working days a year to ten a year to ten in two years. There are requirements that recognized educational courses be taken and usually for a certain minimum of successive days (CERI, 1976; EBAE, 1979).

Although the other Lander do not provide a general legal right to educational leave there are provisions for trade union leaders and throughout the country civil servants and judges have such rights. Furthermore, various wage agreements or contracts with individual firms make provision for educational leave. Overall, it has been estimated that 10 percent of the employees in the Federal Republic can claim educational leave. It is apparent, however, that not all who have the right are fully aware of it (EBAE, 1979).

Experience to date indicates that not all groups of workers benefit equally. Employees of larger firms are overrepresented, reflecting not only greater efforts to make employees aware of their rights by unions and others, but also the greater difficulty of releasing individuals from firms with a relatively small number of employees. Older workers, foreign workers, women, and in general those with less previous education, are also underrepresented.

In 1974-75 there were an estimated 50,000 participants in the five Lander with legislation providing for educational leave.

France

Educational Leave. The French have a penchant for creating a continuously growing body of legislation designed to anticipate any and all particular situations (Caspar, 1979). Space considerations allow only a partial description of the principal adult vocational training system, organized under the 1971 Law on Continuing Vocational Training (as modified 1976 and 1978). In general, the Law enables each individual of working age, currently employed or wishing to be, to take educational leave for general, cultural, or vocational training. Every person has an autonomous right to initiate a request for the training of his or her own choice.

As of 1978, six types of "conge-formation" (educational leave) could be distinguished (Caspar, 1979). They are:

(1) Leave, usually unpaid, defined by 1970, 1971, 1976, and 1978 laws and agreements for any general, cultural or vocational training related to social and economic activities, or for examination preparation (more firms are contributing toward costs incurred in this type of leave than before, and are continuing to pay employees during their training period);

(2) Paid educational leave for personal or vocational purposes during which trainees retain wages and receive grants, if such training is state-approved by a "commission paritaire de l'emploi" (a joint representative body of employers and trade unions);

(3) Worker educational leave (conge d'education ouvriere), paid under certain conditions, and primarily aimed at trade unionists wanting to take specific union seminars;

(4) Teaching leave (conge-enseignent), designed for those preparing to teach full-time in firms, schools or vocational institutes;

(5) Youth educational leave (conge cadrejeunesse) open to persons under age 25 before they assume responsibilities in youth organizations; and

(6) Leave for the young (conge jeune) available to unqualified workers under age 20 for short-term training of 200 hours or less.

Though employers may postpone granting an educational leave until applicable legal circumstances pertain, they may not deny it. A decision to defer leave may result if the number of employees already absent from a large firm at a given time for educational leave purposes exceeds a stated proportion of the total number employed; or if the total number of hours devoted to training is greater than a fixed percentage of total working hours, in the case of a small enterprise (Caspar, 1979). Further regulations govern the total number of training hours permitted during a given time period, and the required elapsed time since prior leave was taken, last diploma earned, and since employment was begun within a particular firm.

Types of Training

Employees whose requests have been approved, by their employer and their firm's works council, may participate in training activities (actions) and courses (stages) which fall within the revised 1978 code. These include (Caspar, 1979):

(1) Preparatory training (actions de preformation) for anyone without occupational qualifications;

(2) Adaptation training (actions d'adaptation) for persons seeking a first or new job;

(3) Promotion training (actions de promotion) for those wishing to gain higher qualifications;

(4) Refresher training (actions de prevention) to counter skill shortages during times of technological and structural changes in the economy;

(5) Retraining (actions de conversion) for persons wanting a different job after experiencing an interruption in their work contracts; and

(6) General training (actions d'acquisition, d'entretien ou de perfectionnement des connaissances) for people desiring to improve or maintain their knowledge, gain cultural access or assume community responsibilities.

Adult training for workers in France is oriented toward preparation for certificates, diplomas, or degrees equivalent to those offerred initially in the vocational or technical tracks of schools and universities, or through apprenticeships. Access to specific vocations largely is determined through a process of examinations and earned formal "qualifications." Any student may opt out of the initial general education system and into a technical or vocational track after the second (cinquieme), fourth (troisieme), or final year (baccalaureat) of secondary education. With a secondary credential, various higher education programs of short or long duration are available.

France officially recognizes six levels (niveaux) of training, which relate to all jobs: level VI competency permits entrance into jobs which require no training after compulsory schooling; levels I and II relate to training of the university or engineering institute sort. In addition, there is an enormous national nomenclature of occupational specialities and vocations. All vocational education occurs in relation to this matrix of training levels, earned qualifications, and precise occupational descriptions. With appropriate "qualifications," training may be received in any sector of the economy: agriculture, industry, or service.

A variety of "providers" participates in this open competitive market established by the 1971 Law. Training may be taken in a public center founded, subsidizied and regulated by the State, or in schools, or trade associations including Chambers of Commerce, Industry or Agriculture, or Guild Chambers of Trade. It also may occur in the private sphere, in centers run by private companies, associations, professional organizations, or private or community educational establishments, all without public monies. The supplying organization selected, of whatever type, enters into a legal contract that defines the mutually agreed upon financial and operational terms of training. These "agreements" are the primary legal mechanisms relating the various market elements, and the French Law sets their nature, parameters, and regulates them. It does not define the content or subject matter of the training itself. Under certain circumstances a private center may receive guaranteed public funds and the State then may reserve some measure of technical control over that training.

Bilateral agreements between consumer and supplier are written to cover only one course or program for its specified duration. An agreement for each activity demanded must be negotiated separately, on its own merit, in compliance with federal regulations. Therefore, no provider, great university or small association, has any long-term claim on a portion of the training market. This means no training staff have permanent job security in courses organized within the framework of this legislation, and bureaucratization is limited.

Financing

Training for workers on paid leave may be born by either employer or the state. The 1971 code mandated firms of ten or more employees to allocate a fixed percentage of their total annual wages for further adult training. (Recently the percentage was set at 1.1; but the rate may fluctuate year to year. All corporations and enterprises covered by the Law must contribute at that rate.) Since 1978, the principle of paid leave applies regardless of type of training or type of firm, whether more or less than ten people (Caspar, 1979). These obligatory contributions may go toward firm-sponsored training for employees, support of a state-approved training organization, outside public or private organizations or specialists with contracts to provide training, Training Assurance Funds (FAF--Fonds d'Assurance Formation), or into the national treasury.

An invention of the 1971 Law, a Training Assurance Fund may be set up on a geographical or occupational basis for wage-earners or for nonwage-earning workers including farmers, craftsmen, shopkeepers or other independently employed persons. For wage-earners, an FAF is an organization formed by an agreement concluded between one or more employers and one or more trade unions to collect and administer, on a parity basis, all or part of those mandated levies which firms are required to pay for adult training purposes (Pasquier, 1977). When paid into a Fund, these monies then cease to belong to the firms. Such payments thus relieve contributing employers of their obligations, if the FAF has been approved by the Prime Minister. Resources from a variety of firms may be pooled or not within a Fund, but they must benefit employees and may be expended in training, research, or public information. Nonwage-earning workers voluntarily may set up a fund so that they can aggregate monies to cover their own training needs. The largest of this type is the Farmers' Fund.

The state's role in adult education under the 1971 legal code, is to work in conjunction with both employers' and workers' representatives to develop training and guidance policy, to organize the national and regional administrative network to manage and coordinate the system, and to set forth terms of the legal agreements and responsibilities for financial aid accorded trainees. The principle of involvement of those population segments with vested interests in the labor and training market in decision-making, priority-setting, and system-management is both fundamental and unique. Though shared-authority is built into this system, it is not characteristic of traditional French employment or education policies and practices. At national, regional, or corporate levels, "commissions paritaires" are responsible for managing activities related to the training law.

In addition, the state approves some training, assumes direct responsibility for public training centers, and identifies certain population sub-groups needing special attention and funds them accordingly. State monies support state-defined economic and employment priorities, but enterprise levies may not be diverted to finance state priorities. No funds are used to subsidize educational institutions, only to finance particular agreements. Recent target groups have included the unemployed, particularly young people; women seeking to enter or re-enter the labor force, especially female heads of households; migrant workers; handicappped persons; and manual workers specifically participating in social advancement training.

The state has sought the support of firms in special programs to combat youth unemployment. The Pactes National pour l'Emploi during 1977-78 addressed the needs of persons under 26, but in 1978-79 expanded to include, without age limitations, certain categories of women. These pacts set up a combination of formalized training together with learning through temporary employment, a format not unlike apprenticeships. Employers have participated in funding some of these short-term employment contracts, the state others. Hence, unemployed workers being trained receive an allowance or wages which represent a proportion of the federally guaranteed minimum wage (SMIC). (This is further discussed in the section on women entering the labor force.)

While public or civil servants such as federal workers, local government bureaucrats or school teachers are not covered under the 1971 provisions, since public establishments are not bound to contribute to training at the compulsory annual rate, measures have been created which extend educational leave to them. Under certain conditions paid educational leave is possible; otherwise an individual personally must pay training costs, and may or may not continue to receive a partial salary. At cursory glance, those in the public service seem to have a less well-developed training system with narrower options.

Worker Participation

Who participates in these educational opportunities? During 1978 adults training under state aid numbered 993,000; under Training Assurance Fund monies, 195,000; and with employer assistance, 1,735,000 (Annexe to Finances Law for 1980). A total of 2.9 million persons or one out of six workers participated in training under the 1971 Law. (Global statistics count each student only once; if trainees received both state and employer aid, they are counted in each sub-total.) Ministry of Labor statistics reveal that of the 1978 "population active" (those adults who have a job or seek one), one in five men and one in seven women participated (Ministre du Travail et de La Participation, 1979). More than half (57 percent) of the trainees were under 25 years of age, including those enrolled in programs of the "cadre du pacte national pour l'emploi" aimed at young people.

French data on workers are reported in four categories: (1) laborers, semi-skilled and skilled workers; (2) trained workers and employees; (3) technicians and lower level management; and (4) engineers and executives.

Although absolute numbers of trainees from each group are not reported, the first two categories represented 61 percent of trainees participating, while the latter two represented 39 percent (in 1978).

State-aided training courses tend to be longer (averaging nearly 500 hours' duration) than those taken with employer funding. Since 1973, state interventions have been redeployed to concentrate on long-term educational programs for individuals in targeted groups, especially the unemployed. Hence, the total number of participants has declined since 1976. In general, the larger the firm, the greater the rate of participation in training. Courses under contracts between firms and training providers are typically technical in nature. (The 750,000 civil or public servants participating in training are excluded from these statistics.)

Success of the 1971 Law

According to one recent informal assessment (Caspar, 1979), it is difficult for employees in firms to initiate their own training proposals. They feel inhibited to ask for something "special" or "unusual" because it may be interpreted as an expressed desire for mobility--an intent to develop new skills and to take a job elsewhere. Co-workers seem less willing to shoulder temporarily an additional workload for someone who is away on educational leave than they are for someone who is ill or on holiday. Hence, individuals opt for "safer" courses: those offered by the firm (since participation in them may enhance personal status and internal advancement opportunities), correspondence courses, or evening classes.

Because of financial strictures, training within a firm may be paid while education outside may have to be taken without remuneration. Even if the training itself is paid, registration fees, travel to the training site, or living expenses while there, may have to be borne by the trainee. It may be too expensive for many people as well as too risky. Moreover, with 5,000 public and private agencies offering training opportunities (Caspar, 1979), the average person

often lacks necessary information about what is available.
There may not be enough approved courses. Counseling services
are minimal. Many individuals lack confidence in their own
abilities to learn new things and doubt the possibility of
social mobility for themselves. They cannot conceptualize
their goals nor evaluate their skills adequately enough to
plot an educational course for themselves. Data on the
involvement of firms in the training endeavor are supplied by
businesses themselves when they must prove, for tax purposes,
that they have provided their minimum mandatory contribution.
Hence, there seems to be considerable room for error or mis-
interpretation (von Moltke and Schneevoight, 1977).

Reflections on the Law itself, as counterpoint to the
traditional French context, are interesting. Legally, it
represents the adult education counterpart of aftershocks
of reform felt at the initial training levels (la Reforme
Haby, 1975) and in the higher education realm (The Law of
Orientation, 1968) following the "social earthquake" of May
1968. These events shook the system into seeking greater
educational diversity, democracy, decentralization and better
distribution of opportunity. Pedagogically its pieces do not
fit into the puzzle of French education which is generally
viewed as rigorous, elitist, rational, selective, competitive,
formal, uniform, and a system in which teachers decide for
students what is important to learn. The Law positions
professional and vocational training beside cultural knowledge
and heritage; individual aspirations and objectives are
legitimate concerns; opportunities for self-determination of
learning exist. The system is highly codified yet designed
to be educationally open and relevant. How to integrate
national, institutional and personal goals is at issue. How
to make choices among multiple options is critical.

This Law emphasizes decentralized, shared authority and
administrative accountability; yet it was developed in a
country known to rest major decision-making power and fiscal
responsibility in a strong centralized state. It directly
involves management, trade unionists, salaried workers,
laborers cooperatively working in advisory and policy-making
roles within firms and state, local and regional coordinating
bodies. This occurs within a national context where class
struggle rather than consensus politics typically has characterized the process of social change.

Furthermore, it was formulated initially while France was
riding the crest of a wave of economic expansion characterized
by rapid technological change and relatively full employment.
Yet its implementation has occurred during a trough of rising
rates of inflation and levels of unemployment, especially
among women and young people. At the Law's inception, a
dynamic, growing economy was envisaged in which adults would
need continual retooling and frequent injections of new

knowledge. In reality, its provisions are being applied
to many special populations such as the young, migrants,
handicapped, manual workers, and women--many of whom have
never enjoyed even a <u>first</u> chance to engage profitably and
productively in "la vie active." The legal structure and
plurality of training opportunities for the education of
adults is notable. Individual French workers have yet to gain
maximum benefits from the systems.

The Soviet Union

Because the Soviet system of adult education is so
strongly oriented toward vocational training, virtually the
entire system--with the partial exception of the People's
Universities--could be thought of as a set of opportunities
for "workers" (in the sense of gainfully employed persons).
Short-term opportunities range from a few hours of instruction on some innovation in production, arranged in an <u>ad hoc</u>
fashion, to courses lasting as long as nine months which are
intended to help a worker qualify for a higher job classification or skill level. Much of this instruction is available at
the work site, and some of it may be taken during working
hours. A somewhat different kind of training for workers
is the "School for Foremen" which is operated by some enterprises. This school is aimed at workers with considerable
experience and technical skill but who have not completed
elementary or secondary education; by giving them general-
education courses and technical courses of a relatively
"theoretical" kind, they can be enabled to qualify for highly
skilled or supervisory positions. The school may take as long
as three years to complete.
Beyond this, workers are, of course, able to complete
elementary or secondary school through evening or correspondence programs, and they may also compete for entrance
into evening or correspondence higher-education programs.
Workers enrolled in these programs are entitled to periods
of leave at full pay to allow them to consult with faculty,
complete laboratory assignments, prepare for and take examinations, and carry out their diploma projects. Special note
should be taken of the "preparatory departments" of many
higher educational institutions, whose mission is to offer a
nine-month course of full-time instruction to persons seeking
to qualify for admission into the full-time program of
the institution. Enrollment in these preparatory departments
is reserved for workers (and servicemen) who have been out of
school for at least two years and who have a recommendation

from a committee of their fellow-workers, in recognition of their outstanding performance. During the course of study, the students receive the stipend and housing of regular students. Presumably, preparatory department students who do not do well enough on the final examinations to qualify for entrance into the higher educational institution can reclaim their old job (though no confirmation of that has been found).

The content of most of the instruction for workers is highly specific to a job and/or a work skill. One may question whether such specific instruction is economically rational in view of the rapid pace of technological change and what seem to be especially high rates of turnover in the Soviet labor force. Swafford (1979) points out that, ironically, the fact that the individual does not have to pay for vocational training may contribute to the high rate of turnover.

Sweden

There are two ways to look at the adult educational opportunities of workers. First is to determine the extent to which workers as a category participate in all forms of adult education. Second is to describe programs which have been created particularly for workers as a group. In this section both aspects will be covered.

Worker Participation in Adult Education. For this project, workers were considered to be those employed in production/distribution, technicians and office employees (as distinct from those self-employed, including farmers). As of 1974 better than one of every four workers so classified was involved in some form of adult education. Participation among white collar workers was higher (39 percent) than among blue collar workers (21 percent) and participation among women was higher (32 percent) than that among men (26 percent). The most popular adult education alternative for workers was the study circles, followed by employer-arranged and labor union courses in that order.

Worker Education Programs

Employer Provided Courses. The most prominent programs designed specifically for workers are those courses organized by employers. In 1974 such courses involved 4.4 percent of blue collar workers and 14.3 percent of white collar workers. According to recent statistics, 70 percent of the Swedish workforce is employed by firms that have some kind of employee education plan. Almost all of the companies with 500 or more employees provide educational opportunities, whereas only 15 percent of the companies with 20 or fewer employees do so. The cost for this form of education represented about 3 percent of total gross wages in 1975. Of the courses offered that year, 25 percent involved employee introduction and orientation, 50 percent continuing vocational training, and 25 percent management training, languages and general education.

Labor Union Courses. Sweden's two largest employee organizations, the Confederation of Trade Unions (LO) and the Central Organization of Salaried Employees (TCO), have extensive study programs of their own. They are designed to give union members a solid background in union affairs and other social matters. They also supply trained union officials at local, regional and national levels. Most courses are residential and last one or two weeks, but some last up to six months. The national government provides subsidies for these programs.

A vital task for the trade unions as well as for the organized employers is to give all employees information and training on the various labor statutes that have been enacted in recent years. The most important of these from the educational point of view is the Law on Employee Participation in Decision-making, which came into force on January 1, 1977. So far all public employees have been assured of at least two days of information about this law. In addition, information must be desseminated about the law on Security of Employment and the act concerning the Status of Shop Stewards (The Swedish Institute, 1979a).

In 1975 roughly 82,000 workers were involved in this kind of training (SCB, 1978). The participation rate among men was almost twice as high as that among women.

Labor Market Training. The system of labor market training originated in the need to act swiftly against imbalances in the labor market, both by helping under- and unemployed workers to improve their employability and by increasing the supply of skills in industries where there is a shortage of suitably trained personnel. The labor market training system currently has the capacity to deal with roughly 1 percent of the total labor force. With courses lasting for an average length of four to five months, more than 3 percent of the labor force can be reached in the space of one year (The Swedish Institute, 1979c).

The main provisions of this scheme are as follows: Persons unemployed or in precarious employment conditions (working in declining sectors or experiencing personal difficulties) as well as those who are willing to leave their employment (or take educational leave of absence) in order to take training for skills in short supply, can attend training courses arranged by the labor market authorities in cooperation with school authorities and employers. Courses are free of charge and trainees receive subsistence allowances. Compensation to trainees exceeds umemployment benefits, amounting to some 80 percent of an average worker's income.

The courses vary in length, from a few weeks for introductory courses designed to familiarize participants with new working situations, to two years for courses for skilled workers and technicians. Most of the training is carried out either at permanent centers or at temporary (and often rapidly improvised) ones. It is administered jointly by the Labor Market Board and the National Board of Education or by arrangement with vocational schools, which are now integrated within the system of upper secondary education. In 1978-79 about 86,000 people participated in this kind of training (The National Labour Market Board, 1978-79).

Under certain employment conditions (e.g., a recession), the Labor Market Board can pay temporary training grants to private firms and municipalities. Special grants are also available to firms which train handicapped workers. In regions with a limited demand for labor, employers can receive training grants for new hires. A subsidy is also available to employers who arrange training of old or new employees in connection with a net increase in their workforces. Firms abstaining from laying off workers during slack periods and giving them training instead can obtain a special subsidy per hour and trainee up to a maximum of 960 hours. This part of in-plant training expanded rapidly during the recession of the mid-1970s, when the number of participants in 1976-77 rose to more than 100,000 compared with roughly 10,000 in the previous year and 50,000 in 1978-79.

Solution of the administrative problems connected with this policy for "rapid action" against employment variations demands a considerable freedom of decision-making by local employment offices in cooperation with municipal and school authorities, trade unions and employers. It also entails a centrally organized provision of educational material (equipment, books, teacher training) and maintenance of reserve capacity in permanent or temporary training centers during high-employment periods, so that courses can rapidly increase their intake as soon as the employment situation in an area begins to deteriorate.

Educational Leave of Absence, Study Grants and Outreach.
A major break-through in the development of a recurrent
education strategy came in 1975 with the implementation of the
law on educational leaves of absence (CERI, 1976). This law
secures the right of all employees in the public and private
sectors to leave for educational purposes during working
hours. To be eligible for this leave an employee must have
worked for his firm at least six months (or 12 months over the
past two years), except in the case of labor union training
where this stipulation does not apply. The law does not
dictate what kinds of courses are appropriate nor does it
specify minimum or maximum time limits on how many employees
can be absent at the same time. According to the law,
employers have the right to postpone leaves in individual
cases, but they are required to give prior notice to union
leaders who are allowed to review the matter. In cases of
more than six months' postponement, employers must obtain
agreement from the local union. Thus under the current law
many of the specific arrangements are matters of negotiation
between management on the one hand and individual workers and
their labor union on the other.

Although the current law provides for reinstatement on the
job at status and income levels equivalent to those in force
before the leave, there are no provisions for the payment of
salary during the leave. However, special subsidies are
available through hourly and daily study grants and special
study allowances. Funds for these grants are made available
through a payroll contribution by employers in effect since
1976. Special compensation for loss of income is given to
those in the undereducated category (including immigrants)
who want to pursue high priority subjects (Swedish, English,
mathematics, social studies) during relatively long uninterrupted periods.

The above mentioned payroll assessment also finances
various outreach programs for adult education at the work
place. These programs focus primarily on recruiting people
with less than nine years of primary schooling into adult
education courses. Such outreach activity is conducted by
local union representatives who are permitted by virtue of a
1974 law to engage in such activities during working hours
while still on the payroll (Rubenson, 1979).

Program Success

Since adult educational training for workers in Sweden
is complex and multifaceted, there are no simple indicators
of program success. There are, however, two interesting
measures available indicating the extent to which certain
national policies are meeting their objectives. First are

the statistics on the success of outreach activities at the work place and second are data on the occupational placement of labor market trainees.

Rubenson (1979) indicates that of the 4,000 people (mostly workers) contacted within the Fovux outreaching program, 50 percent were interested in some sort of adult education and 40 percent eventually enrolled in a course of study (see also the Committee on Methods Testing in Adult Education, 1974). With respect to labor market training, regular follow-up studies show that of those who took vocational courses and then entered the labor market, some 85 percent obtained jobs within three months of course completion. Approximately 85 percent of these people obtained work within the occupational branch for which they were trained (The Swedish Institute, 1979a).

The United Kingdom*

Training of workers and other employees in the United Kingdom has traditionally been left to individual employers. This general policy was explicit as late, for example, as in the Industrial Training Act of 1964. Government-sponsored training was limited to the relatively small Vocational Training Scheme, which was focused on the unemployed, the disabled and ex-servicemen. A major review of training policy in 1971 and 1972 pointed to the need for improved training opportunities to meet both individual career aspirations and national manpower requirements. This study led in 1972 to creation of the Training Opportunities Scheme, which has since become the centerpiece in what is now termed the "national training system."

The Training Opportunities Scheme (TOPS)

Launching of TOPS in 1972 represented a large new government-sponsored training effort. The stated objective was to provide "training on demand" to enable individual adults to change occupations quickly in the face of industrial changes, and generally to promote the idea of adult retraining

---

*Most of the material in this section applies to England, Wales and Scotland, but not to Northern Ireland.

in both existing skill areas and in new and emerging ones.

Through TOPS, training is available in a wide variety of skills, from craft, technician, clerical and commercial, to management skills. In 1979, major concentrations were in the traditional craft fields (e.g., construction, engineering and automotive) and clerical and commercial occupations, each accounting for about one-third of all trainees. All other skills accounted for the remainder, with computer-related training increasing notably in the past three years.

Courses are held mainly in the 70 Skillcentres operated by the Manpower Services Commission (MSC), in over 700 Colleges of Further Education, and at industrial sites. Disabled people may be trained at any of four Residential Training Colleges. Of the 92,500 who completed TOPS training in 1978, 24,000 were at the Skillcentres; 51,000 at the CFEs; 17,000 at employers' establishments; and 800, at the RTCs (TOPS SP1, 1980b).

TOPS courses are available to people aged 19 or over who are "suitable for the course of training," and who have spent at least two years away from full-time compulsory education. They may be unemployed. If employed, they must agree to give up their present job and be prepared to enter a new field--the one they have received training for. A recent follow-up study (TPFU, 1979) found that 73 percent were employed, and 62 percent were employed in the skill for which they received TOPS training.

Courses are normally full-time and must run at least four weeks, but no longer than one year. Most of the 60 different craft courses last six months. A course is provided only if it has been determined that jobs in the field are available. Not available are courses that lead to employment with a single employer; that is, TOPS does not provide trained manpower for particular firms.

Trainees receive allowances which are set at a level which enables them "to maintain themselves during the course, and which puts them in a better position than if they were in receipt of unemployment benefits" (TOPS, SP1, 1980b, p. 4). Employers who allow use of spare training capacity for TOPS training receive fees.

Enabling, as it does, individual adults to choose to receive training in a field of their choice at any point in their work-life, TOPS represents a very significant government-sponsored instrument through which adults can make career changes in their own interests and to the benefit of the labor market. Regarding the latter, a review of TOPS conducted in 1978 concluded generally that the program should be related "more closely to the needs of the labour market... (to) changing skill needs...(to) the requirements of indus- tries...in which there are continuing skill shortages" (TSD, 1978, p. 2).

Industrial Training Boards (ITBs)

The second major component of the "national training system," and by far the largest in terms of the numbers of people involved, is the employer-sponsored training of employees for which the 23 Industrial Training Boards provide extensive direction and support.

As noted earlier, it has been the long tradition in the U.K. for employers to be responsible for the training of their employees, as through apprenticeships. Dissatisfaction with this situation led finally to the 1964 Industry Training Act and to creation of the Industry Training Board system to implement the Act's goals of relating training to economic needs and technological developments, improving the quality of industrial training, and "spreading its cost more fairly over industry and commerce" (TSD, 1977, p. 14). Continued dissatisfaction led to the 1973 Employment and Training Act and establishment of the Manpower Services Commission to direct and coordinate the country's panoply of manpower training services. The prime responsibility for training remained with industry, but the MSC, through its Training Services Division (TSD), would coordinate the varied and largely independent activities of the ITBs (and also help to improve training in industries not covered by the Boards).

Each of the ITBs is comprised of representatives from firms within a particular sector of the economy. They have names such as: Air Transport and Travel Industry Training Board, Carpet Industry Training Board, and Iron and Steel Industry Training Board. Their general purpose is to assist individual firms to develop their training plans and improve the quality of their training. The ITBs variously provide a range of advisory services, training recommendations and guides, and directly-sponsored courses. They also administer the "Levy, Exemption, and Grant Scheme," under which member employers pay into ITB funds, from which grants are then made back to firms for training activities that adhere to the ITB's guidelines. Employer-sponsored training takes place either at the workplace or, part-time, at a College of Further Education (through "day-release," "block release," or "sandwich" arrangements).

The Manpower Services Commission pays most of the costs of operating the ITBs (40 million pounds in 1978-79) and makes grants to them for special training programs in priority skill areas (58 million pounds in 1978-79) (MSC, 1979).

Statistics on the numbers of workers receiving training from their employers--whether financed through ITBs, or directly by employers--are conspicuously absent from most of the reports from the MSC. Stock, in his Part III overview, puts the total figure at roughly 2.5 million. It is clear, though, that most employer training programs are directed at relatively young employees. A recent report from the MSC, Training for Skills, among other matters, however, affirmed the importance of "encouragement of training and retraining opportunities for adults" and that

> Schemes of training and related further education should take full account of how they are to apply both to young people and to adults, whether they are in employment or not" (TSD, 1977, p. 20).

Direct Training Services

The third principal component of the "national training system," much the smallest, is known as Direct Training Services. Conducted also by the Training Services Division of the MSC, it includes:

(1) Sponsored Training, by which employers send employees to Skillcentres for tailor-made courses to upgrade or broaden skills;

(2) Mobile Instructor Service, which produces and delivers special training programs to meet an individual employer's on-the-job training needs;

(3) Training Within Industry, which consists of courses for supervisors; and

(4) Instructor Training Service, which provides training at two designated colleges for instructors in industry.

Conclusions

"On paper" the MSC-orchestrated "manpower training system"--consisting for the most part of TOPS, the ITBs and member firms, the Colleges of Further Education, and the MSC's Direct Training Services--looks to be a rather comprehensive and workable arrangement. From the documents obtained, however, except for research on TOPS, it is difficult to judge how effective, in fact, the total interlocking system is. With the important exception of TOPS, the system is still essentially "front-loaded" in that it emphasizes initial (youth) training--with relatively little provision for later upgrading or retraining. There are signs--e.g., in official documents--of a change in attitude to a more "continuing" or "recurrent" model; TOPS, as said, already exemplifies this conception.

The United States

It is probably fair to say that there is not now, and never has been, any coherent, comprehensive approach to employee training in America. Certainly there is no comprehensive federal policy, although a 1978 Congressionally-mandated National Commission for Employment Policy is working "to develop a framework for a national policy to insure the full development and utilization of human resources" (DOL and DHEW, 1979). This said, the U.S. Department of Labor does administer the Comprehensive Employment and Training Act, a program which, however, operates largely in behalf of disadvantaged youth and adults. And state and local governments do heavily support public colleges, at which individual adults increasingly find it convenient to enroll for vocational training.

The range of available educational opportunities for workers and other employees in the U.S. can be considered under five headings: private industry, government service, federal manpower programs, educational institutions, and trade unions.

Private Industry

The best available information about the nature and scope of employer-sponsored training comes from a study (Lusterman, 1977), now six years old, conducted by the Conference Board, a nonprofit business research organization. The 1975 survey covered a sample of 610 companies having at least 500 employees. Four categories of education and training were identified:

(1) In-house: during hours. This category is by far the largest of the four; 20 percent of all companies give at least one training course, with 30 percent giving at least one course of 30 hours or more duration. Participation in all such courses was estimated at 3.7 million--11 percent of the total employee force.

(2) In-house: after hours. After-hours training is provided by 39 percent of the firms surveyed, with an estimated total participation of .7 million.

(3) Outside the company: during hours. "Paid education leaves" are provided by nine percent of the firms surveyed; no estimate of participation rate was given (author estimate: .1 million).

(4) Outside the company: after hours. Tuition-aid programs were reportedly in effect at 89 percent of the companies surveyed; an estimated 1.3 million--4 percent of the total employee force--participated.

Lusterman divided the subject matter of education and training into four categories: (1) management development-supervisory (involving 37 percent of all employees who took in-house courses); (2) functional-technical (61 percent); (3) basic-remedial (one percent); and (4) other (one percent).
Total participation, about 5.8 million during the year prior to receipt of the survey, agrees closely with the 1972 survey finding of 5.9 million by the Commission on Nontraditional Study (Carp, Peterson, and Roelfs, 1974).

Government Service

As of 1979, about one-sixth of the national work force--16 million civilian workers--was employed by the government at some level: 60 percent by local government, 22 percent by state government, and 18 percent by the federal government. Extensive training opportunities are available to employees at all three levels.
According to a recent training effort report from the U.S. Office of Personnel Management (1980), 24 percent of federal employees engaged in formal classroom instruction of at least eight hours duration, with the average course lasting 41 hours. Sixty-one percent of the training was provided "in house" by the employee's own agency or department; the balance was provided by interagency training groups, other departments, or nongovernmental organizations (such as colleges, commercial firms, and professional associations). With regard to subject matter, development of the employee's technical specialty accounted for 38 percent of the training, followed by legal and scientific topics (15 percent), administration and analysis (15 percent), supervisory principles (10 percent), executive/management (6 percent), clerical skills (6 percent), trades or crafts (5 percent), orientation to government service (4 percent), and adult basic education (1 percent).
Little information is available about the scope of participation in education and training on the part of state government employees in the U.S., although a recent report (National Governor's Association, 1981) outlines organizational and funding arrangements for training of state employees in 41 states. As for employees of local government, a 1975 national survey (Brown, 1976) found that two-thirds of all the cities surveyed operate training programs. Ninety

percent have on-the-job and specific skill development programs; 79 percent have supervisory training; 40 percent and 31 percent have interpersonal relations and team-building programs, respectively.

Government service, it is clear, affords continuing training and retraining opportunities for great numbers of its employees--an estimated three million altogether across all levels. The proportion of government employees involved in education and training is roughly twice the proportion in private industry.

Federal Manpower Programs

Work and training programs administered by the Department of Labor are an important source of education for both youth and adults. Involving 5.3 million first-time enrollees in FY 1976, they are in general designed to increase the employability of people who are out of work or underemployed. There are four separate programs that have education components: The Comprehensive Employment and Training Act (CETA) program, the Work Incentive (WIN) Program, the Job Corps (a residential program for severely disadvantaged youths), and the recently (1978) enacted Youth Employment and Demonstration Projects Act, which provides work experience for unemployed youths aged 16 to 23 to aid in their "transition from school to work."

CETA, enacted in 1973, consolidated a range of previously existing programs aimed chiefly at youths. Its basic policy premise is that every youth and adult should have an opportunity to work. Program planning and implementation are decentralized, their direction entrusted to some 460 local "prime sponsors" (for example, city or county governments). Its various training activities--vocational (classroom) training, on-the-job training, and combination programs-- enrolled 1.4 million participants in 1978 (DOL and DHEW, 1979).

CETA legislation underwent reauthorization (including substantial modification) in 1978. One new component (Title VII) that deals with training for adults is known as the Private Sector Initiative Program. Its general purpose is to increase the involvement of the business community in training and employment of "CETA eligibles" (unemployed and economically disadvantaged individuals). Under the program, prime sponsors appoint Private Industry Councils (PICs), composed of representatives from local business, labor, community and educational organizations. Each PIC then selects firms and organizations to provide training and job placement services, with funding for this work from the Department of Labor.

The WIN program--now, as modified, WIN II--is operated in cooperation with local welfare agencies. Nearly 194,000 AFDC (Aid to Families with Dependent Children) recipients lacking marketable skills received "training or other employability services" during FY 1978 (Work Incentive Program, 1979).

There are also federal vocational training programs other than those administered by the Department of Labor. For example, in the Department of Health and Human Services, the Rehabilitation Services Administration conducts a relatively large program, with matching state funds, designed to rehabilitate disabled and handicapped people (2.3 million clients during FY 1976).

Educational Institutions

Increasingly postsecondary institutions of all kinds are scheduling courses and programs (leading to degrees or other credentials) in large part for the convenience of employed adults--in the evenings and on weekends, and at main campuses or in outlying centers. Close to five million people currently attend college part-time. Most would be employed full-time. Others, especially women, may be unemployed and preparing to enter the work force. While a small proportion-- perhaps 10 percent--have their educational expenses paid by their employers or the government, the vast majority are paying their own way.

Almost all of the 928 public two-year community colleges and technical institutes have evening (as well as day) programs in a wide range of trade, technical, commercial, and service fields. Tuition or fees, which vary from state to state, are generally quite low. Typically there are no admissions requirements.

The four-year colleges and universities are moving quite rapidly to expand their occupationally-oriented offerings for older adults. Compared to the two-year colleges, fees are higher, especially at private institutions. Curriculums tend to be concentrated in such white collar areas as business and public administration and the human services. Admissions requirements vary, although they are typically more lenient in evening divisions and nonexistent in extension divisions.

Proprietary schools are another training avenue for people interested in a trade or a technical career. Numbering some 9,000 (Kay, 1976), most of which are owned for profit by individual entrepreneurs, they enroll altogether about a million students, almost all attending full-time. Their programs are short--typically one or two years--and narrowly focused on particular occupations; they seldom have entrance requirements; tuition is quite high, although at the accredited proprietaries students can use federal financial aid; and they usually "promise" (but do not always made good on) job placement.

Trade Unions

Generally speaking, educational activities in most trade unions are not extensive, certainly not in comparison with the educational activities sponsored by industry and government. There are some 20 million organized workers in the U.S.; on the order of one million, about five percent, are estimated to be involved in education and training, through four general types of programs.

Roughly 500,000 workers are in apprenticeship programs operated jointly, under contract, by management and labor. Close to 300,000 are in programs, covering some 425 apprenticeable occupations, registered with the Bureau of Apprenticeship and Training in the Department of Labor (DOL and DHEW, 1979); their courses are federally funded. Apprentice training typically involves both on-the-job practice and classroom work (a minimum of 144 hours), which in many localities is conducted in cooperation with community colleges. Apprentices are guaranteed jobs before they begin their 2,000 hours of training.

A second type of program, involving as many as 75,000 trade unionists a year, is the labor education sponsored by the education departments of individual unions. The emphasis here tends to be on "tool" courses--shop steward training and grievance handling, for example.

A third type of program is what is now commonly called "labor studies," a special curriculum for union leaders currently available at over 40 universities (Turner, 1977), and at numerous community colleges. In contrast to "labor education," labor studies is more broadly conceived to include topics from all the social sciences that may be relevant to modern collective bargaining.

A fourth type of educational opportunity for trade union members consists of partial or total tuition payment for college courses, an arrangement negotiated currently by over 200 local chapters as a fringe benefit. Many of these plans stipulate that courses be job related, although increasingly there are no such strings attached. Only 3 to 5 percent of the five to ten million eligible employees, however, take advantage of this opportunity (Charner, 1979).

OLDER PERSONS

One is impressed by the diversity of educational programs for older persons across the nine countries studied. (See also UNESCO, 1980.) In part this diversity mirrors the absence of comprehensive national policies; in part it reflects differences among older adults themselves in their interests, requirements and expectations; and in part it grows out of substantial demographic differences. Regarding the latter, it seems clear that resources will be directed differently in Canada where 8.7 percent of the population is over age 65, as compared to France (13.6 percent), the United Kingdom (14.2 percent), or Sweden (15.1 percent). In part it is also a matter of scale: France's over-age-50 population is as large as the entire population of Australia.

While acknowledging the diversity of the nine countries, general themes are apparent also. First: acceptance of the realities that adults without traditional credentials and qualifications are nonetheless interested in further education, and that they are capable of meeting--in many instances exceeding--the requirements of formal programs of postsecondary education. Acceptance of this view seems true of most, if not all, of the countries. Second: increased attention to preretirement planning through education; this is seen particularly in the reports for France, the United Kingdom and the U.S.A. Third: new roles and relationships for the formal educational sector such as in Universities for the Third Age in France and the Elderhostels and Institutes for Retired Professionals in the U.S.A. Fourth: multi-purpose programming directed not just to educational needs but to other requirements as well; illustrative is the first University for the Third Age to be established with objectives to raise students' standard of living, aid both the public and private sectors in providing services to older persons, preretirement planning, research on aging, and publication and dissemination of information. Fifth: a "do it ourselves" orientation reflected in organizations for older persons such as the Danish and Swedish Pensioners Associations, and the retired persons clubs and organizations in France and the U.S.

Educational opportunities for older persons is an emerging policy area in the nine countries. The countries are ranged at different points on a continuum from few initiatives to substantial developments. None of the nine countries has a comprehensive policy or program.

Australia

Information regarding provision of educational opportunities and services for older persons and data regarding their participation in such programs is best characterized as sparse. It has been necessary to take a very broad view of older persons in order to develop even the following discussion.

One effort to widen access to tertiary education commands attention simply by its name--"mature age entry." In most institutions, and in most reports, mature age refers to students roughly age 21 to 23 or older. Mature age entry, consequently, means assisting individuals to qualify for admission who are slightly older than normal matriculants. Mature age entry also implies that the student traveling this route did not possess the credentials required for matriculation by the end of Year 12 in secondary school. An example is the program begun in 1974 at Mount Lawley College, a college of advanced education. Applicants over age 21 were given an intelligence test and asked to write an essay on an assigned topic. The college reports that students admitted under the program are performing at higher levels than the normal student population, particularly in advanced courses. In 1977, of 17 Diplomas in Teaching (with Distinction), 15 were mature age entrants (Haines and Collins, 1979). The successful experience reported by Mount Lawley College is confirmed at other institutions and for even older adult students. For example, a 1978 study of students over age 60 at selected TAFE institutions showed that while such students were not strongly represented in terms of numbers, they were observed to have a low attrition rate (Brougham, 1978, p. 20). With such evidence, one suspects strongly that mature age entry, while an alternate route, is also a more rigorous one. If true, this fact may account for the observed better than normal achievement of older students who follow this route.

In 1977, students age 23 years and over made up a substantial proportion of the enrollments in universities and colleges for advanced education (42.4 percent and 41.3 percent respectively) and made up the majority (60.3 percent) of TAFE enrollments (Williams, p. 508). These proportions are roughly cut in half at age 30 and over (universities, 19 percent; colleges of advanced education, 18 percent; and TAFE, 32 percent) (Williams, 1979, p. 23). It is also of interest to note that roughly one of four enrollments in TAFE Stream 5, (matriculation and diploma entrance courses, remedial courses, etc.) are persons age 30 and over. In terms of actual numbers, 26,000 students age 30 and over are in what is recognized as a second chance program (Williams, 1979, p. 297).

Yet it is puzzling not to find greater concern for educational provision for older persons when one notes that the proportion of workers 25 to 34 years of age with degrees is more than double that in the age group 55 years and older. Moreover, only 26 percent of workers age 55-plus have any post-school qualification, whereas, 42 percent of those 25 to 34 have them. The greatest area of growth among the young age groups has been in the attainment of degrees, qualifications as technicians and in the trades (Job Markets, Economic and Statistical, 1979, p. 13). At a later point in this report, it is noted that illiteracy is more prevalent among older adults than among younger people. Consequently, evidence of educational disadvantage among older persons is neither hard to find nor ambiguous in its message. Perhaps as the population of Australia matures, and the political influence of older persons increases, provision for their continued education will be enhanced.

Canada

In their discussion of education of older adults, Clark and Brundage in their paper in Part III describe the area as in urgent need of policy development and one that has been inadequately researched. Furthermore, there is only one organization in Canada with a primary concern for the continuing education of older adults.

What references are to be found in the literature are mainly tangential indicators of educational issues; information about programs is practically nonexistent. Some observations, while they are completely inadequate as a basis for rationalizing this situation, may throw some light on the matter.

According to 1976 Census data, 8.7 percent of the Canadian population was over 65 years. This percentage is decidedly less than in France (13.6 percent), United Kingdom (14.2 percent), Sweden (15.1 percent) or even the United States with 10.7 percent (Statistics Canada, March 1979). Furthermore, the aged population is concentrated in only three of the provinces, namely Ontario (36.9 percent), Quebec (24.0 percent), and British Columbia (12.1 percent). With close to three-quarters of these persons residing in three provinces, the problem takes on the appearance of being a provincial rather than national concern. These data suggest two reasons which contribute to Canada's inattention to this area of adult education. That is, the issues have yet to blossom in full and when they do, some parts of Canada will be more concerned than others.

While a major characterization of the problem is the disparity in educational attainment between the young (better educated) and the old (less well educated), this is not the complete picture. In one segment of the adult population, older adults are better qualified and trained than younger adults. Eighty-seven percent of the skilled labor force is over age 40; only 2.6 percent are under age 35 (Adams Commission, 1979, p. 91). In twenty-five years, 87 percent of the skilled labor force will have retired and only 45 percent will have been replaced.

Furthermore, the older segment of the population is quite unevenly balanced between the sexes. Statistics Canada (March, 1979) indicated that the over 65 age group is divided between 875,000 males and 1,126,940 females. Thus, among older adults there are not only more women, but older Canadians reflect the disparities of formal educational opportunities of their earlier years. With one-third of 45 to 64 year-olds having had less than a ninth grade education, the consequence of an earlier lack of educational opportunity will increasingly fall on older women. Therefore, the challenge of education for older adults in Canada is not merely a matter of seeking to meet their needs as a group but to respond sensitively to the individuality of those who are in these age brackets.

The New Horizons Program started in 1972 represents a federal initiative directed to retired Canadians. Its objective is to help the elderly deal with loneliness by encouraging participation in community activities such as physical recreation, hobbies and crafts, and historical-cultural-educational programs. The New Horizons Program makes grants to groups of ten or more retired persons to assist them in promoting activities for the elderly of the community. By June 1976, 6000 projects involving about 100,000 people had been funded in the amount of $34 million.

Denmark

Little information could be found on educational programs specifically for older persons in Denmark. Pensioners'

Associations have taken the initiative to develop Pensioners' Folk High Schools, and four were in existence in the mid-1970's. They are subsidized by local authorities. Each year roughly 20,000 retirees attend the courses, which are generally one to two weeks long.

Considering leisure-time instruction in general, in 1973-74, 22 percent of the students were 46 to 65 years of age and 9 percent were over 65. In labor market training, as one might expect, few older persons were involved. Less than one percent of participants in courses for semi-skilled workers and in reconversion training schemes were over age 60.

Federal Republic of Germany

Educational opportunities specifically designed for older persons in the Federal Republic of Germany seem not to be common. Various reports note that participation is lower for older persons, and a number of programs are known to have upper age limits. As mentioned earlier, two of the Lander with provisions for educational leave set the upper age at 21 or 25. The programs of vocational education are generally directed to youth or to persons not beyond the midcareer stage.

Annual statistics for the Volkshochschulen provide detailed breakdowns by age group for the various categories of courses offered throughout the country (DVV, 1978). There is no specification, however, of the extent to which courses are developed primarily or exclusively for the older age group. In 1978 there were 145,000 enrollments by participants over 65 years of age and 344,000 by those between 50 and 65. These represented 3.5 percent and 8.3 percent respectively of all enrollments for the year. As can be seen, by whichever definition of "older" is used, Volkshochschule courses are taken predominantly by younger persons.

There are, however, substantial differences for different categories of courses in the proportions of enrollment by age groups. Older persons are overrepresented in regional and environmental studies, in the arts, and in politics and society. They are heavily represented in the "special" category, which may indicate that there are a number of programs aimed specifically at them.

In terms of the proportion of age groups taking courses in the various categories, the picture is somewhat different. One-fourth of the enrollments of those over 65 and one-third of those between 50 and 65 are in language courses--foreign or German. One-fifth of the enrollments for each of the two age groups are in health and hygiene, including exercise. About one-sixth are in manual work and leisure occupations. None of the other categories (e.g., philosophy and psychology, mathematics, science and technology, business management, domestic science, courses leading to diplomas, as well as those mentioned earlier) has as many as 10 percent of the age group.

France

Attention at the federal level in France is given to the entire organization of working life, of which retirement is regarded as a segment! Social integration of the elderly is a priority action item in the recent five-year National Economic and Social Development Plan (1976-1980). Persons over age 50 are seen as able to learn, create, inquire, work, exercise, remain healthy, and lead productive lives. While national policy on education for older persons is still minimal, several programs and trends are worth noting.

Preparation for Retirement

Preparation for retirement is one area of educational emphasis for older persons in France. The intent of retirement planning has been clearly specified: to help adults anticipate the consequences of this major reorganization in their lives, to discover multiple options, to develop new personal and socio-cultural interests, and to make realistic decisions. Mass media campaigns have been conducted to raise the level of general awareness by the widely-read magazine Notre Temps, various associations concerned with the elderly such as CLEIRPPA (Centre de Liaison, d'Etude, d'Information et de Recherches sur les Problemes des Personnes Agees), company newsletters, and in 1975 by the Fondation de France aided by the broadcasting industry. At the conclusion of the latter effort, the Foundation offered a "Fellowship for the Golden Age" to retired or nearly retired persons to allow them to undertake a project or pursue an interest developed during their working years, or to be trained for personal or community activities, or to reduce the generation gap (Council of Europe, 1977).

Preretirement courses have been widely organized by firms, works councils, associations, local or regional government agencies, and trade unions. Married couples are encouraged to attend together, and costs are low.

Preretirement courses are included under the 1971 Law on
Continuing Vocational Training, which means that individuals
may take such classes on a paid educational leave basis
underwritten by the state or employers.

Characteristically, preretirement courses may include
information on physical and mental health, finance, nutrition, housing, leisure, work, and community resources and
activities.   The National Institute for Active Retirement
(INRAC--Institut National pour la Retraite Active) assists
organizations wishing to develop preretirement planning
programs to do so.   It also sponsors intensive courses of from
one to five days duration in various towns, upon request.
These classes are designed to prepare retired people for roles
as leaders of cultural, social or sports activities.

The GERSPPA (Research and Study Group for the Solving of
the Problems of the Aged, or Groupe d'Etudes et de Recherches
pour des Solutions aux Problemes des Personnes Agees) holds
preretirement courses organized in a different format.   Their
classes last six to eight weeks, distributed in one-half day
weekly sessions.   The GERSPPA uses this form because its
enrollees seem to prefer morning over evening classes, and
shorter sessions to longer ones.   Instructors are physicians
and specialists in "third age" problems.

Programs meeting with success have been held at the
neighborhood or community level through old people's clubs
(clubs des anciennes), "Universities" for the Third Age,
lifelong learning centers, and even mobile units in areas
away from population centers.   There usually are multiple
instructors in preretirement programs, often social workers,
trade unionists, medical doctors, housing or budget specialists; not uncommonly these leaders also are retired.
Preretirement planning courses in firms often are organized
according to employee category; the assumption is that
grouping by occupation improves discussion because of the
greater homogeneity of problems, projected retirement incomes,
and styles of life represented.

Some firms are devising gradual or phased retirement
schemes for older workers to allow individuals a chance
to ease into this life transition.   The extent to which
part-time work with scaled retirement benefits provides an
early retirement incentive, or allows economic viability
at later ages, is yet to be determined.   These options,
however, provide time for older persons to use for educational
purposes.

Universities for the Third Age

The "University for the Third Age" concept was developed
to help older people achieve such goals as personal growth,

autonomy and self-worth, and to counteract passivity, boredom, and physical deterioration.

The first Universite du Troisieme Age was conceived and organized in 1973 by Pierre Vellas--a professor of international law at the University of Toulouse--within the walls of his own university. Individuals were eligible only if they were at least 65 years of age.

Overall objectives of the Toulouse program have been to help raise the standard of living for older people, to improve their living conditions, and to aid the public and private sectors in providing services for older persons. Ancillary services offered at Toulouse, as elsewhere, include pre-retirement training for individuals and representatives of groups seeking to organize such programs, seminars on problems related to old age with those responsible for services to the elderly, research projects dealing with aging, and preparation of publications and dissemination of information.

The primary focus of Universities for the Third Age is on providing a program of classes and activities for older people themselves. Activities related to physical health are emphasized. At Toulouse, free annual medical checkups are given to enrollees; classes include nutrition or preventive health care; and sports, gymnastics, and group walks (called "oxygenization sessions") are available.

There are intellectual, social, and cultural activities as well. Courses in history, language, current events, evolution of women, psychology are common; handicrafts and studio classes such as restoration of antiques also are provided. Reading groups, panel discussions, and conferences are organized, along with guided tours to museums or archeological sites. Some enrollees assist professors with research; others are educated for new social roles and responsibilities such as group leadership of clubs and community organizations in the voluntary sector; a few are trained as technical experts and sent on a paid basis to developing countries as part of technical cooperation programs.

Each program organized under the University for the Third Age framework is free-standing and independent. No single "Troisieme Age" structure has been adopted. Some are related to an existing university department within an education and research unit; some are part of a university institute or attached to a lifelong education center; others are structured as an "association" quite outside any other organization. In Grenoble, the "Interage University," as it is called, was developed by an association of retired people and is managed by retired persons; financial support comes from various community groups, retirement insurance organizations and city government.

Despite the diversity, there are several common threads. Regardless of structure, little federal financial support goes to Universities for the Third Age, although on occasion a small subsidy from the Ministry of Health, or Continuing Education budget, may be provided. A variety of people is required to organize, administer, and teach. Dependence on volunteers is heavy; retired people themselves, students, and community leaders all help. In university-based programs, some faculty are paid while others contribute their services. Classes may be organized around any topic when there is sufficient interest. Fees are charged, but they are minimal and a sliding scale is usually adopted. Those who cannot pay an average estimated tuition of 30F ($6) or a 70F ($14) registration fee, do not pay (Ageing International, 1975).

While each Troisieme Age program is unique, it is typical in university settings that people of all ages enrolled in the program may take regular university courses as auditors, special students, or candidates for degrees. Adults may attend regular university classes and/or those developed especially for the Troisieme Age "university." Recently, greater efforts have been made to integrate the elderly into the total student population.

Encouragement of interaction among the generations has become so important that programs organized originally for the elderly are now being called "Universities for All," "Everyman's University," or "Interage University." People of all ages and social backgrounds, without certificates and with advanced degrees, are attending together. At Paris University X, Nanterre, officials note (Aging, III[2], 1978) that traditional-age students have a number of characteristics in common with the elderly: for example, they are not engaged in productive activities, with few exceptions they have no family liabilities (dependent children), and their relationship to money is not based on wage-earning. When the "third age" is based on a campus, participants are eligible for all university services including libraries, cafeterias, sports facilities, and teachers.

Each "University for the Third Age" seeks to be responsive to the needs of individuals and local communities in its area. Many programs try to preserve local traditions and regional history. For example, there have been projects to collect folklore known to the indigenous elderly (Orleans) and to develop oral histories (Dijon).

In 1978 there were 30 Universites du Troisieme Age in France (Troisieme Age, 1978). Total enrollment is estimated to be 20,000. The movement has expanded to other nations as well. Some 60 "Universities" in several countries have joined together in the "International Association for Universities of the Third Age;" they meet at an annual conference.

Other Sponsors.   Other clubs and organizations for
retired persons, or those concerned more generally with adult
education, also sponsor educational activities for older
persons.   For example, the Retired Club of the Mutuelle
Generale de L'Education Nationale (retired teachers in
the national education system) in Paris, with more than 2,600
participants, offers a variety of courses and activities for
its members.   These range from physical education and photography to genealogy and astronomy.   In addition to seminars,
trips and conferences, these retired teachers perform needed
social services.   They teach literacy classes for migrants
and instruct handicapped, hospitalized or homebound young
people.   At times these groups work cooperatively with the
"Troisieme Age" programs.

Soviet Union

Perhaps because of its dominant work orientation, the
Soviet adult education system seems to make little special
provision for the needs or interests of older persons.   On
the other hand, there may be relatively little demand for
education from this segment of the population. Having been of
school age during the years of revolution, civil war, and
agricultural collectivization, or perhaps during World War II,
the older group contains a large proportion of people
whose education was interrupted and never resumed, and
experience elsewhere suggests that less educated adults are
less interested in obtaining additional education.   However,
some 22 percent of the people who attended People's Universities in 1973 were identified as "pensioners and other persons"
(Narodnoe Obrazovanie, 1977).   Several People's Universities
are named "Universities of Health and Longevity," and they
"hold weekly courses with older population groups," presenting
"the latest ideas in gerontology and preventive medicine..."
(Chebotarev and Sachuk, 1979).

Sweden

Within this category in Sweden are found two main sub-
categories, those who are economically active (or potentially
so) and those who are retired.   These two subgroups differ
substantially with respect to both the level and nature of

their participation in adult education. They will be treated separately.

Older Persons Who Are Economically Active. The age group breakdowns used in reporting educational participation include the category 45 to 64. Since the regular retirement age is 65, the vast majority of people in the category are active economically, many at the height of their careers. The category also includes, however, relatively small numbers of housewives, who are not technically in the workforce, handicapped individuals and those who are unemployed. Almost one-quarter of those in this age group (22.3 percent) were engaged in some form of adult education in 1974. Over half of these were engaged in study association activities and about one-quarter in employer-arranged courses.

For those workers over 50 years old who face unemployment or who have difficulty keeping a job, there are special provisions. The Labour Market Board can pay temporary training grants to companies who hire workers in this category. In addition, there is a special set of "adjustment" courses available at Labour Market Training Centers for older persons who are seeking employment.

Retired Older Persons. The age group breakdowns mentioned above also include a category for those aged 65 to 74. This category does not include all retired people, because retirement at age 65 is not mandatory and because some of the people in the category never were in the workforce. In addition, this category does not include all Swedes (pensioners or not) over the age of 64, since, of course, many live beyond 74 (the average life expectancy for women in Sweden is 77!). Nevertheless, the category does include most of the elderly above age 65 and most of them are pensioners.

The participation rate of those in this older age group is far below that of the economically active. In 1974 slightly over 8 percent of adults in this category participated in some form of adult education--seven-eighths of them in study circles. Recent trends have been for rapid growth in the participation of pensioners in adult education, however. By 1977 the participation rate of pensioners had reached nearly 17 percent (Eckberg, 1978). The participation rate of women pensioners has consistently been almost twice as high as that of men.

Two national pensioners' organizations, Pensioners' National Organization of Sweden (PRO) and the Swedish National Federation of Pensioners (SFRF), whose combined memberships include roughly one-third of all pensioners, channel most of these educational activities. PRO collaborates with the Worker's Educational Association (ABF) in sponsoring a wide variety of study circles, including those in languages, handicrafts, literature, administration and social sciences. Especially popular are those courses that link group travel with learning a new language or studying another culture. According to Eckberg (1978), in 1976 PRO sponsored 8,763 study circles in all, with over 90,000 participants. In addition to the above, PRO sponsors other educational activities for pensioners. At its own training center at Gysinge Mansion near the town of Sandviken, PRO offers "orienting" courses for new pensioners, trains study and leisure activity organizers, provides instruction in inter- national and consumer affairs and operates a two-week residential folk high school.

SFRF has developed similar course offerings in con- junction with the Adults' School Association. In addition, the State Civil Service pension organization provides various courses and leisure activities for former employees.

With the decline of the birth rate in Sweden to below zero population growth, pensioners comprise an increasingly large proportion of the population (currently 20 percent). Swedish policy is aimed at promoting active retirement life- styles in which further education is a central feature.

The United Kingdom*

No national policies or programs exist concerning educational opportunities for older people in the U.K. Many people older than, say, age 50 are of course enrolled in all the programs of adult education and training described thus far. Just how many, however, cannot be determined since neither the DES nor the MSC provide participation data for the older age groups. In the latest statistical compendium on further education from the DES (1979), the uppermost age breakdowns are limited to the following: "30 and over" at the CFEs; "30 and over" at the Polytechnics; and "40 and over" for U.K. students "following courses of initial teacher training" (3,053 of them--3 percent of all students in teacher training).

---

*Material in this section is mostly from a report from the Council of Europe (1977).

Preparation for Retirement

Pioneering work in the area of preparation for retirement has been made in the U.K. where preretirement classes have been held since 1954. Much of the stimulus has come from the Pre-Retirement Association of Great Britain and Northern Ireland. Though its financial base is slim, the Association has been instrumental in encouraging local authorities and employers to organize preretirement courses. It also conducts its own specialized seminars for company employees, supplies advice and instructional material for organizers and tutors, and exerts a considerable influence through its monthly magazine, Choice, which is sold widely throughout the country. It has long had good working relations with both the Trades Union Congress and the employer federations.

There is no standard preretirement course; they vary in duration and frequency of meetings, usually lasting up to a maximum of six to eight weeks. The Glasgow Retirement Council, for example, has been holding day-release courses since 1958 in six of the city's educational institutions; each course lasts for seven weeks, meeting for one full day each week.

Despite the relative progress of preretirement education in the U.K., it is estimated (Council of Europe, 1977) that only five percent of workers receive any form of preparation for retirement. "We are very far from the massive action which is needed" (p. 29).

The United States

Federal Programs

Older persons may participate in scores of federal programs which provide education and training for adults, although few have explicit requirements to serve the elderly. Many of the programs which will be cited unfortunately are currently in danger of serious cutback or elimination by the Reagan Administration.

The Division of Adult Education in the U.S. Department of Education provides funding for locally administered educational programs for adults of all ages. Under the Adult Education Act, as amended, adult basic education in particular is available, and classes may be held in senior centers, nursing homes, and elsewhere in the community, as well as in schools.

The Older Americans Act established the Administration on Aging (AoA) as a federal focal point for programs to serve older citizens. The AoA administers and coordinates programs, conducts research on aging, and serves as an information clearinghouse on problems of the aged (Administration on Aging, 1978). State and area agencies on aging were established by 1973 amendments to work toward comprehensive and coordinated systems of services for older Americans. The Office of Education (now defunct) and the AoA have worked together as advocates for lifelong learning and related services for mature persons. The Fund for the Improvement of Postsecondary Education, the National Endowment for the Humanities, and the National Endowment for the Arts have all funded educational or cultural programs for older people. Moreover, older individuals may participate in federally-funded career education, vocational education, or continuing education opportunities in their states.

Under the 1973 Rehabilitation Act, training is available to the physically or mentally handicapped, including the elderly blind and arthritic. State and community programs under the Older Americans Act, as amended, establish a range of social services for the elderly including legal services, home-health/homemaking services, information and referral services, and multipurpose senior centers. The senior centers, particularly, serve as a nexus for social and instructional services of many sorts, often in coordination with other available community services. Under OAA Model Projects, grants are available to support the development and demonstration of new strategies to serve the elderly and to increase the participation of older citizens in community life (Schecter, 1980). Through Community Education Programs (Title VIII, PL 95-561, Education Amendments, 1978) all age groups in a community are to be served. While administrative costs rather than actual education program costs are borne under this legislation, programs in local schools, educational or cultural centers may benefit older people. Grants for meeting the needs of the elderly for consumer education have been made under the Federal Consumer Education Program. Title I of the Higher Education Act of 1965 provides funds, through the states, to support continuing education projects in colleges and universities; numerous of these innovative efforts have been designed especially for older students.

Providing library services and information to aging persons is a priority of the Library Services and Construction Act. At the state and local levels special information services are provided to senior centers, nursing homes and the homebound. The Brooklyn Public Library's Project SAGE (Service to the Aging), for example, provides books (including large print volumes) and films. Senior centers and branch libraries use senior aides to work with elderly patrons and also with the homebound. Many of libraries provide bookmobile services to nursing homes or to isolated rural areas. Some also provide special information and referral services for the elderly.

The federal government also administers a number of employment and job-related training programs for older citizens. During 1976, 250,000 persons aged 60 or more participated in the following federally-funded programs: Retired Senior Volunteer Program (ACTION), Foster Grandparent Program (ACTION), Peace Corps (ACTION), Volunteers in Service to America (ACTION), Head Start (Office of Education), Service Corps of Retired Executives (Small Business Administration), Green Thumb (National Farmers Union), and several Senior Aides Programs operated by diverse organizations under contract with the Department of Labor (Murphy and Florio, 1978). While some of these programs involve paid work and others volunteering, all older participants are involved in learning.

In the Foster Grandparent Program, with 14,000 mostly female enrollees during 1976 (Murphy and Florio, 1978), 40 hours of orientation and training are provided. Individuals at least 60 years old devote attention to physically or mentally handicapped youngsters up to five days a week. Working, for example, with two children for two hours each, these elderly people receive a tax-free stipend, plus meals while working, transportation allowance, annual physical examinations, and accident insurance. The Retired Senior Volunteers (RSVP), numbering 210,000 in 1976 (Murphy and Florio, 1978), receive an orientation but less training than do the Foster Grandparents. They perform a wide variety of activities in schools, libraries, hospitals, courts, nursing homes, government agencies, and correctional institutions.

A large employment program for older citizens is Green Thumb, sponsored by the National Farmers Union under Department of Labor auspices. Low-income persons of at least 55 years carry out conservation and community improvement projects. Most participants come from rural areas, work 20-24 hours a week, and are paid. Informal training occurs among the 15,000 member current work force (Jones, 1979) while they work, for example, as library aides, in day-care centers, or in jobs insulating homes. Under the Senior Community Service Employment Program authorized under Title IX of the OAA, administered by the Department of Labor, employment for low-income older people is provided in community service projects. Contractors have included the National Farmers Union, the U.S. Forest Service, National Council of Senior Citizens, National Council on the Aging, and the National Retired Teachers Association/ American Association of Retired Persons. Individuals under the poverty income level who are retired or chronically unemployed, and who are at least 55, work about 20 hours a week as paid aides. Local offices in

which these seniors work provide on-the-job training.   Once
trained in these community and public-service agencies,
some are hired permanently either in those agencies or
others.

Schools and Colleges

Of course, older people can and do take adult education
courses in public schools to earn high school diplomas or
simply for their own enjoyment.   They also attend two-year
community and junior colleges and four-year institutions
of higher education on a credit or non-credit basis.   An
estimated 1.7 million Americans over age 55 were pursuing
higher education in 1979 (Jones, 1979).

Of the 50 states and the District of Columbia in 1979,
22 had enacted legislation allowing older students a reduction
or waiver of tuition in colleges and universities (Timmermann
and Chelsvig, 1980).   Of the 29 states with no legislation,
13 have non-legislatively mandated policies of tuition waiver
or reduction for the aged; thus only 16 had no law or policy
at the state level regarding access to higher education by
older people.   Even in these states, individual colleges and
universities have implemented reductions.   Thus in every state
there are higher education institutions which offer tuition
reductions to mature citizens, though the applicable age
varies from 60 up.   As of 1979, 1,449 higher education
institutions have a policy of reduction or waiver of tuition
for older persons; 747 are two-year colleges (Timmermann and
Chelsvig, 1980).

It is not uncommon to find colleges for older citizens
within higher education institutions.   These units, usually
organized and administered by older people, provide a variety
of non-credit courses although the aged can usually take
regular university courses as well, for credit or not.   Their
curricula tends to be interdisciplinary, and teaching methods
tend to be participatory as favored by many older people.
Older students have access to the usual support services
as well as opportunities for both age-segregated and age-
integrated activities.   Some centers place older persons in
part-time jobs or train them in community organization
and administration; others offer retirement planning courses
to corporations or other organizations.

At Fairhaven College (at Western Washington State
College, in Bellingham), older adults may live in "Bridge
House," a dormitory, for up to two years while attending
classes.   They may audit courses or work for degrees, and
tuition is free for Washington state residents of at least
60 of age (Cross and Florio, 1978).

In addition to the various general institutes for learning in the retirement years, there are specialized programs for professionals. The Institute for Retired Professionals at the New School for Social Research in New York City, begun in 1962, is planned and administered by older people. Its curricula are available to those aged 55 or older who have an appropriate educational background and who have recently retired from professional or executive careers. An annual fee is paid to sustain membership. Similar professional institutes have been established at the San Francisco and San Diego campuses of the University of California, as well as at Temple University in Philadelphia.

A variation on the special program for older adults on college campuses is the Elderhostel movement. Martin Knowlton began this effort in 1975 in several New Hampshire colleges. It enables persons over age 60 to spend a week during the summer living in dorms and auditing a variety of courses. Usually individuals take three different courses, each 1-1/2 hours daily, given by regular university professors. During 1979 the cost for one week on a campus was $95 (due to foundation and government grants); in 1980 the national cost will average about $130. In 1979 Elderhostel had 12,000 participants on 235 college campuses (Shoup, 1980). (Alumni associations of many institutions have organized similar short-term, non-credit programs, also usually offered in the summer.)

Other Opportunities

Other informal learning opportunities exist in the form of national networks of discussion groups; particularly well-known are the "great decisions in foreign policy" program organized by the Foreign Policy Association and the Great Books Foundation's discussion groups on classic and modern literature or philosophy. Study guides are provided and individuals may organize their own groups. Museums, libraries, and community centers may also have special programs for mature individuals.

Mini-courses designed for home study by the American Association of Retired Persons have attracted thousands of students: over 20,000 enrolled in the AARP home study art course (Timmermann, 1978); 10,000 requested copies of the self-study booklet on metrics; and 30,000 asked for copies of the self-study course on the Bible. Many older people, preferring self-paced instruction, are enrolled in correspondence courses, television classes, and courses offered in local newspapers.

In some localities, courses are taken to the homebound-- older adults who cannot leave home unaccompanied because of health problems, lack of transportation, or fear of crime (Delaloye, 1980). For example, in a program begun by New York City Community College in collaboration with United Neighborhood Houses (a coalition of 36 settlement houses), "Senior Companions" were taught one course in sociology and one in gardening, in classes of about 15 to 20 persons. Learning companions then took the class to at least one homebound student, teaching the material and engaging in discussion with the student. Feedback was given to the prime teacher, and teaching methods and strategies were individualized. During 1978-79 the program was launched statewide in New York, using television programs periodically as the instructional base. Since 1978, 40 courses have been taught to 428 homebound elderly in New York (Delaloye, 1980).

Retirement Planning

Retirement planning and preretirement courses are other types of adult education for people in their later years. In a survey sponsored by the Corporate Committee for Retirement Planning (New York City) and the National Council on the Aging, Inc. (Washington, D.C.), a slowing of early retirement was noted (World of Work, 1980). Chief executive officers and personnel directors of Fortune 1,000 companies were queried. It was found that a narrow program of printed materials and a personal interview about social security, medicare and pension benefits typified the preretirement activities of small firms. Larger companies had broader programs, with guidance available five to ten years before retirement. Participants in these programs generally spent at least 15 hours on questions relating to financial matters, housing, health, leisure, legal matters, postretirement options, and community resources. Usually the retirement planning program was purchased outside the company and adapted to firm needs. Only a third of responding companies reported a participation rate of at least 75 percent; another third revealed participation rates of 50 percent or lower (World of Work, 1980). The American Association of Retired Persons operates a very active pre-retirement planning program for people aged 50-65 called Action for Independent Maturity (AIM).

WOMEN ENTERING THE LABOR FORCE

Considering their numbers in the population at large, and their representation in the labor and educational marketplaces of the nine countries in this study, women generally find few programs especially designed to help them enter or reenter the work force. Many of these nations have enacted legislation aimed at ending discrimination or facilitating access of women to training and employment opportunities. However, in several of the countries the enabling legislation has not been enacted, and women tend not to have recourse to the law when they have experienced discrimination (Bureau of International Labor Affairs, 1980).

The International Labor Organization supports the concept of equal pay for equal work and encourages its members to embrace that notion. The European Community in 1976 issued an Equal Treatment Directive which called for abolition of all laws contrary to equal treatment of men and women in access to employment, vocational training and work conditions (Bureau ILA, 1980).

At a November 1978 multinational conference on "Facilitating the Re-Entry of Women to the Labor Force" cosponsored by the French Ministry of Labor and the German Marshall Fund, certain themes in common were noted, though social values and approaches differed. Women of all ages, levels of skill, and types of family responsibilities, it was said, seek to enter the work force, and the shift toward more service sector jobs has facilitated this influx. Women throughout the world have been socialized as primary care-givers to children; hence quality child care is necessary if they are to participate fully in education and work. Bridging the gap between men's and women's earnings, implementing existing legislation, making employment and training policies permanent rather than hinging them on economic conditions, providing part-time work with appropriate social benefits, reducing occupational segregation, and establishing information and counseling networks and enabling women to gain access to them were all said to have potential for increasing participation of women in the labor force.

Many of these same themes were set forth earlier during a ten-nation conference convened in 1973 by the Organization for Economic Co-Operation and Development, which was followed up by an OECD Working Party on the Role of Women in the Economy (OECD, 1979a).

In a more recent OECD conference on the employment of women, member nations were urged to develop curricula free of sex-role stereotyping; to provide a full range of choices in education for men and women; to review labor legislation to ensure provisions consistent with equal opportunity in employment; and, since governments are major employers, to eliminate occupational segregation and discriminatory practices in employment conditions in the public sector (Chronicle of Higher Education, May 19, 1980).

Sweden, with its active recruitment of married women into the labor force, higher education study grants for those 25 or older with four years work experience--including work in the home, and a cabinet-level Committee on Equality between Men and Women--currently has a participation rate of 70 percent for women in the labor force. American legislative initiatives to end discrimination in education and employment are notable. Also impressive are the hundreds of women's centers in educational institutions and community agencies throughout the country that provide counseling, guidance and training. Various programs in the U. S. are training women for nontraditional jobs and are providing aid to so-called "displaced homemakers."

Soviet women participate in the labor force at the same rate as men of the same age. German and Danish women participate heavily in leisure time instruction or Volkshochschule courses, but little is known about programs for reentry women. In the United Kingdom the Manpower Services Commission operates a special program entitled Wider Opportunities for Women--a job-exploration and counseling program.

In France, women seeking to enter or reenter the labor force may participate in educational leaves of absence under national law, but their rate of participation is lower than that for males. Temporary Pacts for Employment favor widowed, divorced, and separated women and single mothers in training and employment. The existing information centers for women in France tend to focus on employment and education rights, rather than on personal assessment, counseling, training or placement.

Australia

Very little material is available on the specific matter of education for women in Australia seeking to enter the labor force. There are some data that relate to the participation of women in education generally, as well as in adult education. This information can be of value in understanding the educational context for women, many of whom, of course, are studying in order to enter the work force.

Women in the Labor Force. The labor force of Australia in 1978 consisted of 4,265,600 males and 2,659,900 females, 1,707,100 of whom were married (Australian Bureau of Statistics, 1979). The situation has been summarized succinctly in the Williams Report (1979): "For some time to come, mature women seeking to reenter employment will, on average, have received less education than men or than younger workers, and they will face the added difficulties and anxieties of refreshing out-of-date skills, or of learning anew" (p. 631).

From 1964 to 70 married women who came into the labor force in Australia made up about 90 percent of the increased number of persons employed part-time. Between 1974 and 78 the female labor force increased 11.1 percent when the male labor force increased 3.5 percent. However, the range of women's occupations has not increased. For women, 63 percent are in clerical, service, sports and recreation, and sales jobs, whereas only 20 percent of males are in these occupations. There are further restrictions within these occupations. Of women engaged in service occupations, 44 percent were housekeepers, cooks, maids, and the like.

Women in Higher Education. A 1973-74 survey showed that 73 percent of full-time female workers had no post-school qualifications, compared to 64.2 percent of males. Two percent of the women had trade qualifications, as compared to 18.4 percent of the men (Department of Employment and Youth Affairs, 1979). However, these statistics need to be viewed in the light of changing circumstances. For example, by 1977:

(1)   Secondary school retention rates were higher for females than for males, whereas ten years earlier they were 50 percent less.

(2)   Females constituted 39 percent of university enrollments, whereas in 1951 they were 20 percent. Further, females constituted 42.7 percent of new university students in 1977.

(3)   In colleges of advanced education, females were 47 percent of the total enrollments and 50 percent of FTEs. Also, female full-time enrollment was nearly twice as great as their part-time enrollment.

(4)   In TAFE programs women made up 45 percent of the enrollments.

While these statistics suggest that change is underway, substantial data point to a long road ahead. In TAFE Stream 2 (Paraprofessional Programs), female enrollment is 25 percent and in Stream 3 (Trades) less than 10 percent. While Stream 4 female enrollments were 60 percent, this category includes preparation for hair-dressing jobs, which accounted for most of the enrollments. Also, women account for more than two-thirds of the enrollments in Stream 6, which is devoted to home handicrafts, hobbies and self-expression.

Similarly in universities, female enrollments across programs are very uneven and low, as shown in the following enrollment figures: Agriculture, 21 percent; Architecture, 19 percent; Dentistry, 20 percent; Economics, 21 percent; and Engineering, 2 percent.

In colleges of advanced education, enrollments of women were low in the following programs: Applied Sciences, 22 percent; Business, 18 percent; Agriculture, 17 percent; and Building and Surveying and Architecture, 12 percent.

While not of great significance in itself, an event in 1975 offers a general suggestion of the climate. The proceedings of the National Conference of the Australian Association of Adult Education for that year indicate that a session entitled "Education For Social Change--Women" was canceled prior to the start of the Conference because it was undersubscribed.

In addition to mature age and early school leavers' entry schemes to universities and access and bridging courses to colleges of advanced education and TAFE, authorities have identified other needs that require attention. These include assistance in assessing skills, counseling, and techniques of job search; information regarding jobs, training, assistance available, and careers; smaller decentralized learning facilities with particular attention to rural residents; and child care, flexible schedules, and cooperation of employers in adopting training and recruitment strategies to facilitate the reentry of women to employment.

A few examples of specific responses to these needs can be cited. Of the 25,000 persons approved for training under the National Employment and Training (NEAT) scheme in 1975-76, 51 percent were in clerical and administration occupational groups which are mainly serving jobs filled by mature women. Since 1976, NEAT has operated a two-tier allowance schedule, one for full-time training and one for part-time training. The latter serves mainly to assist married women with family responsibilities. Some NEAT courses have been developed and offered especially for women. These are not widely available, however, and have occurred because of initiatives taken by local women's organizations (Williams, 1979).

Other Programs.   For immigrant women having to contend
with learning a language and other aspects of a new culture,
help is available through the Home-Tutor scheme administered
by the Good Neighbor movement in behalf of the Australian
government.

Some colleges of advanced education are providing mathematics courses for women "who think they can't." Among the
courses offered by the Workers' Educational Association of
South Australia in 1978 was "How to Cope as a Working Housewife." (There were only six participants!)

Women unionists are being encouraged to take courses run
by the Trade Union Training Authority. Only 17 percent of the
participants in 1977-78 were women (TUTA, 1978). Lovering
(1978) summarized the situation as follows: "Concern for
women workers is beginning. Discrimination is starting to be
tackled at school and in the work force. Governments are
providing maternity leaves (of different degrees), paternity
leave, part-time work (in South Australia) and flexitime. The
Commonwealth Government is providing funds for childcare
centers and training. Unionists are beginning to consider the
problems" (p. 10).

Canada

The 1976 Ontario study of demand for part-time learning
illuminates aspects of participation by women in adult
education in Canada (Waniewicz, 1976). Following are the more
noteworthy findings regarding women "Learners:"

(1) Forty percent of the estimated 1,400,000 Learners in
     Ontario are women.

(2) In the 18-24 year age bracket there are more
     Learners among men than women, while there are more
     women Learners than men age 45 and over.

(3) Women Learners tend to be slightly older than men
     Learners.

Regarding "Would-Be-Learners:"

(4) Sixty percent of women are Would-Be-Learners.

(5) There are more women than men Would-Be-Learners in
     each age bracket.

(6)   At age 18-20 women exceed men Would-Be-Learners by 2 1/2 times.

(7)   At age 18-20 and 25-34 one of every three women is a Would-Be-Learner.

(8)   Some 125,000 women age 18-24 are interested in learning compared to 64,000 men.

(9)   Some 221,000 women age 30-49 are Would-Be-Learners compared to 126,000 men.

Systematic data for women entering the Canadian work force are available for three categories of providers of adult education: universities, employers, and the federal government. Community colleges, local boards and departments of education and universities are all major suppliers of adult education. Statistical breakdowns by sex, however, are available only for the universities.

University Enrollments. In 1972-73 full-time undergraduate male enrollment (175,161) exceeded female enrollment (109,736) by 66,425 (Statistics Canada, 1979d). After five years the gap had narrowed substantially. In 1977-78 male enrollments numbered 185,437 vs. females 148,063, a difference of 37,374. Full-time graduate enrollment moved in the same general direction but not forcefully. In 1972-73 male graduate enrollment stood at 28,387 vs. female enrollment of 9,120 for a difference of 19,267. In 1977-78 the difference in male vs. female graduate enrollments was 14,741 (males 27,713 and females 12,972). Admittedly these comparisons do not concern adult education specifically. Most of these students are traditional students moving directly from secondary school to university. However, as future cohorts of traditional students achieve an equalization of male-female university enrollments, the necessity for women to catch up to men in terms of university education will be eased. Yet it may be harder to achieve than we might think. Full-time enrollment patterns for women are related to their prime childbearing period. We note, for example, that in 1976-77 the only age group for which male full-time undergraduate university enrollments exceeded those of women is between ages 19 to 32. Female enrollments exceed that of males among students younger than age 18, at age 18, and at all age brackets beyond age 32. It is of special interest to note that in 1976-77 there were 89 women over age 65 enrolled as full-time undergraduate students.

Female part-time undergraduate enrollments for all age levels from age 18 to 60 plus exceed those of men, and the differences increased from 1971-72 to 1977-78. Male part-time graduate enrollments continue to exceed those of women although the gap has narrowed somewhat.

Part-Time Undergraduate and Graduate Enrollment

		1971-72	1977-78
Undergraduate	Female	69,981	106,095
	Male	62,519	76,966
	Difference	7,462	29,129
Graduate	Female	5,316	9,973
	Male	15,165	18,658
	Difference	-9,849	-8,685

Employer-Sponsored Training. Employers can contribute to educational opportunities for women through the provision of daycare, flexitime work schedules, and programs of release time for training. An OECD report (1979a) cited estimates by the Women's Bureau of the Canadian Ministry of Labor that in 1976 there were 1,282,000 mothers in the work force with 2,614,000 children under age 16. Only 7,000 daycare spaces were available at that time. Outside of universities, community colleges and some hospitals, few employers were providing daycare facilities. Access to daycare not only increases female employment prospects but it also indirectly expands access to training that employers provide. Similarly, flexitime, or flexible work schedules, were being considered in Canada in the early 1970s particularly in certain departments of the federal public service.

The Adams Commission (1979) reported 398,336 employees were engaged in training and development activities in 1978 in the form of day release, block release, and extended leaves. While it is anticipated that women could be involved in some of the half-dozen or so particularly innovative block release programs, the single major application of block release is in apprenticeship programs where the number of women is practically nil. In 1975-76, for example, only three percent of apprentices were women (Employment and Immigration Canada, 1977). The data below compare men and women in employer day release and extended leave training programs in 1978 (Adams Commission, 1979).

	Executive, Professional and Managerial		Office		Non-Office		All	
	No.	%	No.	%	No.	%	No.	%

Day Release Programs

| Male | 68,072 | 73 | 42,062 | 46 | 130,079 | 74 | 240,213 | 67 |
| Female | 24,792 | 27 | 49,626 | 54 | 45,640 | 26 | 120,058 | 33 |

Extended Leave Programs

| Male | 2,032 | 54 | 1,792 | 65 | 2,106 | 68 | 5,930 | 62 |
| Female | 1,740 | 46 | 970 | 35 | 972 | 32 | 3,682 | 38 |

In general, men have access to twice as much short-term training as women, and the situation is not materially different in extended leave programs except among executive, professional and managerial employees.

Government-Sponsored Training. The federal government in Canada has been a major provider of opportunities to facilitate the reentry of women into the work force. "With the exception of Sweden, the federal government allocates a greater share of gross domestic product to training than any other OECD government" (Employment and Immigration Canada, 1977, p. v).

The efforts are not confined to training, but also consist of counseling and advisory services, consciousness raising efforts, and programs directed to subsets of the women's work force such as single parent heads of households, women on family benefits, immigrant women, and so on. The Canada Manpower Training Program (CMTP) is the major federal vehicle through which such services are made available. Clark and Brundage in their paper call attention to the special features of several of these services and discuss in detail the provision of training opportunities available through CMTP. The reader is referred to their paper for this information.

There are data that show the training opportunities available to women through CMTP are different than for men. Cook (1976) cited data indicating women tended to be referred to institutional training while men were referred to training in industry or training on-the-job. In 1973-74 there were

56 females per 100 males in institutional programs of CMTP, whereas in in-industry and on-the-job training there were 39 females per 100 males. The overall enrollments for men and women in Canada Manpower Industrial Training were 49,997 and 19,701 respectively in 1977-78 (Statistics Canada, 1979f). Of close to three dozen different training categories, women exceeded men in only five (arts; fabricating, assembly and repair of textiles, fur and leather; medical and health services; service occupations; stenographic and clerical trades). Of course one must remember that men and women are equally represented neither in the labor force nor among the unemployed. The CMTP is particularly targeted to the latter group. In 1975-76 the percentage distribution of men and women among the major program areas of CMTP was as follows (Employment and Immigration Canada, 1977):

CMTP Program Enrollments: 1975-76

	1	2	3	4	5	Labor Force	Unem- ployed
Male	61.6	45.8	47.7	96.9	76.5	65.0	68.3
Female	38.4	54.2	52.3	3.1	23.5	35.0	31.7

1. Occupational Skills Training

2. Basic Training for Skill Development

3. Language Training

4. Apprenticeship

5. Canada Manpower Industrial Training Program--1974-75 data

Employment and Immigration Canada (1977) has undertaken extensive evaluations of CMTP revealing gains and benefits to trainees, but with differential effects for men and women. For example, a comparison of men and women 27 months after training with a group not trained revealed the following weekly wage differentials:

Average Weekly Wage

	With Training	Without Training
Men	$ 217	$ 187
Women	$ 138	$ 113
Total	$ 187	$ 159

Benefit-cost analyses have been calculated for various component programs of CMTP. The following is an illustration using data for Occupational Skills Training for three different years:

Benefit-Cost Ratios

	Men	Women	Total
1973	4.4	1.5	3.5
1974	4.4	1.5	3.4
1975	3.3	1.2	2.5

It can be seen from the two sets of illustrative data regarding gains from training that while benefits for women are documented, they are of a lower magnitude than those for men, suggesting that the underlying problems are more pervasive than can be handled through adult education alone.

Denmark

There is little information available on programs organized specifically for women in Denmark seeking to enter or return to the labor force. Several programs provide statistics by sex, but they are generally in such broad categories that it is impossible to distinguish personal and recreational activities from more vocational ones.

Overall figures for leisure time instruction for 1973-74 show 370,000 women participating, making up 69 percent of the total group. The percentage of women in successive total age groups increases progressively from 51 percent for those under 18 years of age to 76 percent for 46 to 65 years and 81 percent for those over 65. Most of the programs included in these statistics would not be primarily in preparation for entering the labor force.

For the most recent year available (early 1970's), the percent of women in voluntary adult education in the various residential colleges was: 63 percent in the Folk High Schools, 5 percent in Agricultural Colleges, 99 percent in Domestic Science Colleges, 46 percent in Continuation Schools, and 46 percent in Youth Residential Colleges.

More to the point are figures for participation in Labor Market Schemes for 1972-73. Women accounted for 15 percent (5,400) of the participants in training for semi-skilled work,

6 percent (630) of those in retraining for skilled workers, and 71 percent (490) of those in reconversion training.

The Federal Republic of Germany

Seemingly there are also a few programs designed expressly for women entering or reentering the labor force in the Federal Republic. In only a few cases were educational statistics available separately for men and women. There was little indication that programs were not open to both sexes, but the implication was often that programs reflected stereotypes of who is a worker and who is a housewife.

In 1970, 64 percent of the apprentices in training were male and 36 percent were female. When categorized by the economic sector involved, 41 percent of the apprentices in industry and commerce, 20 percent of those in the trades, 24 percent in agriculture and 71 percent of those in "other" were female. The last two categories were small--2 percent and 14 percent of the total female group respectively (Rudolph, 1979).

Other 1970 figures show that 17 percent of the participants in different types of vocational education grant-aided under the Labor Promotion Act were female. The actual number involved is 16,600. Sixty-one percent of these women were in training for adaptation or upgrading, 28 percent were in retraining and 11 percent in job instruction (Rudolph, 1979). For total participation under the Labor Promotion Act the figures for women are higher, and in 1973, 22 percent of the participants were women. In 1978, 69 percent of the enrollments in Volkshochschule courses were women (DVV, 1978).

France

Full equity for women in France has yet to be achieved in the educational arena, the labor market, and in the larger society. Consider that French women did not receive the right to vote or run for public office until 1945; that equal and joint parental authority was not established by law until 1970; that the law on equal remuneration was put on the books only in 1972; and that the law on equality of access to jobs was not codified until 1975. Discrepancies still exist, however, between policy formulation and actual implementation of these and more recent laws.

Equity of access to many higher education institutions is a recently acquired right for French women. The legal right to compete for higher education's top level diplomas and degrees in all disciplines was acquired by women in a 1974 law which took effect in 1976. This included access to the prestigious and elite "grandes ecoles."

Young women in France are better educated today than 20 years ago, but they tend to follow general rather than technical training. Many avoid the baccalaureat "C" course of study which emphasizes mathematics and physical science. When they do choose to enter a technical program, women tend to select short rather than long-term training. Thus, they tend to be generally well-prepared but not highly skilled in technical areas, and not trained as top level experts, specialists or engineers.

Participation in the Labor Force

Female participation in the labor force in 1977 accounted for 39 percent of the total working population (Ministere du Travail et de la Participation, 1979). Women are far from evenly distributed throughout the occupational structure, however. Only 0.3 percent of working women hold positions designated as "liberal professions" such as physicians, lawyers or university professors; and when those are grouped with mid-level and top management positions the proportion reaches only 14 to 18 percent. While nearly 50 percent of French public servants are women, they tend to be employed in bureaucratic ranks, not in top administrative or decision-making roles.

To fewer jobs being open to women than to men (MTP, 1979), to the tendency for women to have less education and lower levels of qualifications than men, is added the fact that women earn less pay for the same or equal work, despite statutory protection against such inequitable practice. An annual salary variation of between 20 and 30 percent was noted in 1971 between men and women with the same qualifications (Callet et Granrut, 1973). Salaries have continued to be lower for women than men, with a greater difference in the top echelons of the occupational structure. Moreover, though public sector administration or teaching jobs tend to be among the best potentially available for women with higher education, salaries for females are 20 percent lower than those for males in the same jobs (MTP, 1979).

Programs

The French government has given support in a number of ways to women seeking to enter the labor market. Since the post of Secretary of State for the Feminine Condition was created in 1974 to look at aspects of the life of women in French society, several federal initiatives were taken. In 1976 a new delegation for the condition of women was established reporting directly to the Prime Minister, followed in 1978 by establishment of an Assistant Secretary of Labor for Women's Employment. The latter assists with all matters related to the education, training, work and vocational advancement of women. Broad goals are to promote equality of treatment in the working world; to give women in their daily lives the means to realize that equity; and to help women handle successfully both family and work responsibilities.

The Centre d'Information Feminin is a private association (under the 1901 law), recognized by the government. It is presided over by Madame le Ministre Delegue Charge de la Condition Feminine (a delegate appointed by the Prime Minister and charged with responsibility for the condition of women). The C.I.F. works with the hundreds of women's associations and family associations around the country as well as with public organizations such as the national training association, family allocations agency and social security office, in behalf of women. It operates as a free, direct, public information service with about 30 centers set up throughout the country. It studies and produces publications on topics of importance to women, works with the media, serves as a sounding board and formulates ideas for consideration by state ministeries, and coordinates activities and diffuses information among regional and private groups. Originally its exclusive focus was on helping women, and C.I.F. sought to look at their problems and related issues--professional life, family life, social legislation--in very pragmatic ways. Currently, it still helps women to learn about available "recyclage" opportunities (recycling training), for instance, but it also serves men and deals with issues of general interest to young and old alike.

Family Support Services. Day care centers and preschools are available, and are widely used--especially since children of working mothers are given priority or exclusive rights to participation in some of them. Children are cared for in public and private centers (creches collectives, les garderies, jardins enfants); in private homes under some government regulation (creches familiales); and in Ministry of Education preschool (les ecoles maternelles) and kindergarten programs for children. In 1975, more than 61,500 children were cared for in creches (Comite du Travail Feminin, 1977). The demand, however, still far exceeds the supply.

After-school care (la garderie extra scolaire) was provided for almost 10.5 million children and adolescents in 1975, and of that total 5 to 6 million were offspring of working women (CTF, 1977). Local governments sponsor youth activities at sports and cultural centers, while associations, clubs, or sports federations also organize events to help fill the void. During the summer, under federal, local, and private auspices, there are children's vacation colonies, vacation villages, and family vacation houses to provide room, board and leisure activities designed especially for low to moderate income families. Public social and health services are available in most communities, both urban and rural, and also in many firms. Thus, there is a basic network of support services for women in France who want to work.

Training Programs. If women manage to garner information, few counseling centers exist to help them sort it out. Even if they are able to arrange their family lives satisfactorily, they still do not participate heavily in training activities. Since the 1971 Law on Continuing Vocational Training was passed, women have been equally eligible under its provisions. However, out of 2.9 million persons participating in training within this framework during 1978, only 29 percent were women (MTP, 1979). That represents only 13 percent of women actually working or seeking employment as against 19 percent of the male "active population." Often those who organize training, or employers who finance it, incorrectly assume that women cannot travel to a training site, attend evening classes, or function competently in widely diverse jobs.

The "Pactes pour l'Emploi" represent a second national training effort. To combat unemployment concentrated among the young, the state initiated the First National Pact for Employment. This 1977 measure provided special employment and training programs for a minimum period of six months for persons 16 to 25 years of age. These programs included a mixture of theoretical and practical training and were similar in principle to apprenticeships. They were implemented under "employment contracts" negotiated with firms, to allow young people to take courses (within those firms) usually reserved only for employees--or "without contracts" under state auspices. Trainees were paid a low wage while training or received a percentage of the guaranteed minimum wage (SMIC).

In subsequent "pactes" (including those in force until the end of 1981), certain new categories of women became eligible, including widows and divorcees who have not remarried, legally separated women, and unmarried mothers

(Centre d'information Feminin, 1979). Each "pacte" redefines eligibility, duration, and the relative proportions of training and employment, as well as the remuneration to be received. The Third Pact removes the age limitations on all administrative competitions for women who are widows, mothers of at least three children, divorced and not remarried, legally separated, or unmarried mothers. The age limits for access to permanent full-time employment in local communities is set at 40 years, and at 45 for certain categories of examinations in state administrations and local collectivities. With an infant or a handicapped person to care for, age limits are extended by one year.

Women as well as men registered with the National Employment Agency are eligible to receive training through a local agency office. Mothers, widows, divorcees, legally separated women and unmarried mothers may be paid 90 percent of the SMIC, while others receive only 25 percent of the minimum wage during the training period. Another permanent federal measure gives priority of training access to widows, women alone with at least one child, and mothers who have a child at least three years old. A further measure provides that women may conclude an employment-training contract without age conditions if they are widows, divorcees, unmarried mothers, legally separated, or mothers seeking to reenter the labor force after being away from two to five years after the birth or adoption of a child (C.I.F., 1979).

The Soviet Union

It is a characteristic of Soviet society that women, regardless of marital status or domestic responsibilities, participate in the labor force at virtually the same rate as men of the same age. Thus, the problems of women entering the labor force are not different from those of men, except for sex stereotyping and sex discrimination, which apparently do exist. Although little systematic data on these subjects are available, the vice-rector of the National Polytechnical Extramural Institute (one of those which offers only extramural education) has said that men tend to "dominate" in the mining, metallurgical, and construction specializations at his institute, while "engineering economics and some of the chemistry specializations are largely female" (Feldmesser, 1979). The special problems of women "reentering" the labor force hardly arise at all in the Soviet context.

On the other hand, by all testimony women continue to carry most of the burden of household duties, and they have not been provided in abundance with the labor-saving devices that are common elsewhere. Thus, even with some help from child-care institutions (see Rosen's comments in Part III), women apparently participate in adult education at lower rates than men. Again, systematic data are lacking. However, one Soviet source (Kashin and Chekharin, 1970) has stated that women constitute only about one-third of the students in evening (shift) and extramural general-education schools; a study of the time budgets of a sample of adults in the city of Pskov showed that one-quarter of the employed males but only 14 percent of the employed females were engaged in part-time study (cited in Matthews, 1979); and an American student of the condition of Soviet women has said that "the enrollment of women in evening programs virtually ceases with the birth of a child" (Lapidus, 1979).

Sweden

Since none of the official agencies record statistics specifically for women planning to enter the labor force, it is difficult to assess precisely the extent of adult education participation for this group. It is, however, possible to describe occupationally-oriented educational opportunities available to women who were not previously active in the work force and to present a general notion of the extent of their participation.

In 1978, 71 percent of all Swedish women between the ages of 16 and 64 were gainfully employed (Gustafsson, 1979). The same percentage (71 percent) of all married women were working at least half-time outside of the home. Thus the proportion of those outside of the labor force (and planning to enter) is rather small compared with that of other industrialized countries. Nevertheless there are obstacles encountered by Swedish women who have been absent from education or work force participation because of childrearing and other responsibilities. Swedish authorities have recognized these problems and have instigated various measures to deal with them.

One unique Swedish law in the area of higher education provides study grants for those who are over 25 years of age and who have had at least four years of work experience, including work inside the home. This has attracted many women to universities where they have often chosen part-time vocationally-oriented courses. According to an OECD report (1979a), this type of the recurrent education was designed, at least in part, to help women join or reenter the labor market after childbearing years.

Another form of postsecondary education designed to reach women who have inadequate child care facilities is "distance education," which can be used in the home.

Labor market training is a vehicle through which women are receiving training directly related to labor force entrance. The various programs of labor market training were described in general terms in the section on workers. Of special interest here is the fact that over 50 percent of the participants in labor market training are women. In addition, those who previously had no income are offered training grants. Recent revisions in the regulations have eliminated the need to adjust such grants in accordance with spouse's income (The National Labour Market Board, 1979).

Finally, as was mentioned earlier, labor market training includes orientation in general subjects (Swedish, math, civics, etc.) for those whose general education has been deficient, in order to strengthen their labor market position in the long run. As women constitute a high proportion of those who did not receive a complete comprehensive education, these courses are of particular value for them.

Recruitment to other forms of adult education has also been part of the Swedish policy on women's opportunities. Much of the recent outreaching activity subsidized by pay-roll taxes and local government supports has taken place in residential areas. Outreach activity in these areas is managed by local branches of voluntary educational associations. Priority is given to establishing contact with immigrants, the handicapped, housewives, and others working in the home. Study grants and child-care support are available to potential participants whose previous education is considered incomplete.

Since 1974 a special equality grant has been made available to employers who train men and women for jobs dominated by the opposite sex. A similar program stipulates that in order to receive a state subsidy toward plant construction, a firm must hire at least 40 percent women if a "male" industry is involved, and vice versa (The Swedish Institute, 1979b).

Overall, Swedish authorities agree that training and related programs have increased females' chances of being accepted or reintegrated into the labor market. However, in recent years no great changes have occurred in the traditional patterns of the labor market. Most female adult education participants "train for traditionallly female" occupations, and, like their daughters in school, they often choose courses that are shorter than the ones males pick (The Swedish Institute, 1979b).

To consider this and other issues related to sex equality, the Swedish government has established a cabinet level Committee on Equality between Men and Women. In 1979 the committee examined the problems of women who work inside the home, considering their circumstances regarding reentry to the labor market, child care and education. The committee's report should be available sometime during the current year (1981).

The United Kingdom

Government policy at present calls for no special training programs for women. There is, however, a small program sponsored by the Manpower Service Commission entitled "WOW"--Wider Opportunities for Women (involving occupational information and counseling)--that has been judged successful and is currently being expanded. Women, of course, may obtain occupational training through the Training Opportunities Scheme, described earlier, which is open to essentially all adults over age 19. Women are also enrolled in large numbers in the Colleges of Further Education and in the Polytechnics. Finally, women outnumber men in most of the other categories of adult education provision in the U.K.

Wider Opportunities for Women Courses. Designed by the MSC (TOPS staff, more precisely), "WOW" courses are intended to "help women considering going back to work after being at home for some time, who are not sure what sort of work they want to do or how to go about getting a job. The focus...(is on)...women likely to enter unskilled or semiskilled employment" (Fairbairns, 1979, p. 1). The courses aim to:

(1) Provide information on opportunities for employment, training, and further education;

(2) help women make realistic occupational plans; and

(3) help women acquire the necessary confidence and skills to "take the next step forward."

Students in WOW courses assess their personal capacities in relation to working life in general and to particular jobs. They try a variety of job and training "samples," including jobs that are traditionally for males (e.g., construction and engineering trades).

During 1978 and 1979 five WOW courses, ranging from four to 12 weeks in length, were offered at colleges in Birmingham and Cardiff. Full-time and part-time versions were tried at each site. Average class size was ten students. An evaluation by the MSC (Fairbairns, 1979) gave a number of suggestions for improvements and made the general recommendation that the program be expanded.

TOPS reports that a "modest expansion of WOW courses is planned for 1980/81...the MSC hopes that courses will be running at 18 colleges by the end of this year (1980) which will provide up to 500 places in a full financial year" (TOPS SP1, 1980a, p. 3).

(One may assume, in the absence of direct information, that courses similar to WOW are offered through other organizations, such as the YWCA, Women's Institutes, and Townswomen's Guilds.)

The Training Opportunities Scheme. In TOPS courses, which do provide direct job training, women are enrolled in almost the same numbers as men: 42,000 of 99,000 completers in 1978 (Small, 1979). Three-quarters were in clerical and commercial occupations. Eighteen percent (in 1977) were management or higher level trainees (Training Services Division, 1978). On the other hand, only 3 percent of the students at the Skillcentres, where the bulk of the craft training is carried out, are women.

Colleges of Further Education. Fifty-seven percent-- 850,000--of the 1.5 million students enrolled at the CFEs (in 1976) are women (DES, 1979). Twenty-nine percent of these women are full-time students, many presumably aiming toward entry into the work force. Over half are in initial teacher training. There is a substantial age range: 11 percent (26,000) of the full-time students are age 30 and older (compared to 8 percent of full-time males in the CFEs).

Polytechnics. Again using 1976 data (DES, 1979), of the 190,000 total enrollment, 30 percent are women. Sixty-two percent of them are enrolled full-time. By selected general subject area, 36 percent of the full-time enrollees are in education; less than 1 percent in engineering; 6 percent in science; 26 percent in "social, administrative and business studies;" and 5 percent in (other) professional and vocational subjects. Thirteen percent are age 30 and over (the comparable figure for men is 10 percent).

Other Adult Education Programs. Women predominate in LEA "evening institutes" (adult education centres): approximately 1.4 million women compared to 624,000 men in England and Wales in 1975 (Small, 1979). All are enrolled very much in part-time fashion, and very few of the courses would be directly job-related.

In courses sponsored by the "responsible bodies"--chiefly the universities (their extramural programs) and the Workers' Educational Association--roughly twice as many women are enrolled as men in all four countries of the U.K. (Small, 1979). Some 1,677 of the 168,000 registered women students (in 1976) were studying law (DES, 1979). Eleven percent were in the physical or biological sciences. The remainder were in various general or liberal arts courses.

The United States

More women entered or reentered the labor force in the U.S. during the decade of the seventies than in any other decade in this century; by the first half of 1979 approximately 43 million women, 51 percent of all women 16 years old or more, were in the work force (U.S. Bureau of Labor Statistics, 1979b). The gain in 1978 alone was 1.9 million women--a record number.

Women seeking to enter or reenter the labor force encounter harsh realities. Women's earnings on the average are considerably below men's; median earnings of women working full-time in May 1978·were about 60 percent of the median earnings of men--just as in May 1967 (U.S. Bureau of Labor Statistics, 1979b). In June 1979 only about two percent of apprentices were women (Harrison, 1979). Eighty percent of working women hold blue and pink collar (service work) jobs--mostly low paying and low status positions (Harrison, 1979). Though 455,000 women joined labor unions between 1976 and 1978, they represented only 27.4 percent of all organized workers in 1978 (World of Work, 1979).

According to the latest NCES survey of participation in adult education (Boaz, 1980), 662,000 women were full-time students in occupational programs of six months or more duration sometime during the year ending in May, 1978. During that same year, the NCES survey found that 2.7 million women reportedly were looking for work, and of female participants in adult education, 358,000 were seeking employment.

In 1975, "latch key" children (those who care for themselves without supervision after school until a parent comes home from work) between the ages of 7 and 13 were estimated at 2 million (DOL/DHEW, 1979). Need for quality childcare is voiced by the majority of mothers who wish to return to school or work. The U.S. has never had a national childcare policy. Only a handful, relatively speaking, of businesses, industries, and government agencies provide free or low cost day care facilities for employees (DOL/DHEW, 1979). Surveys of campus childcare centers indicate a shortage. A 1971 Department of Labor survey of 1100 four-year higher education institutions found 25 percent had some kind of preschool program; a 1977 survey of 1,200 community colleges and technical institutions conducted by the Center for Women's Opportunities of the American Association of Community and Junior Colleges found 132 had child care facilities on campus; and a more recent survey of four-year colleges and universities under the auspices of the National Council on Campus Child Care revealed only 750 childcare programs in those institutions (Creange, 1980).

Federal Statutes

Several federal measures have been designed to overcome sex and age biases which entry and reentry women have faced in education and employment. Under the Equal Pay Act of 1963 (section 6d of the Fair Labor Standards Act of 1938 as amended) it is required that male and female employees in the same establishment performing equal work in jobs requiring equal skill, effort and responsibility, and which are performed under similar working conditions, be paid equal wages. With extensions in 1972 and 1974, other categories of workers became covered, including executive, administrative and professional employees, outside salespersons, and federal, state, and local government employees. The comparability of work and its value remains at issue, especially regarding traditionally female occupations (DOL/DHEW, 1979).

Title VII of the Civil Rights Act of 1964 as amended by the Equal Employment Opportunity Act of 1972 prohibits job descrimination on the basis of sex (and race, color, religion, national origin) and applies to training, retraining and apprenticeships as well as to hiring, firing and the like. As amended, coverage is extended to employees of state and local governments, educational institutions and employers with 15 or more employees. It specifically does not apply to elected officials, their staffs, and policy-making appointees.

Executive Order 11246 (1965) as amended in 1968 prohibits employment discrimination based on sex (as well as race, color, religion, and national origin) by employers with federal contracts or subcontracts over $10,000 and requires affirmative action be taken to ensure equality of employment opportunities. Regulations as of 1978 provide for further actions by construction contractors with federal contracts or subcontracts to meet affirmative action standards to insure equal employment opportunities for women and minorities.

Title IX of the Education Amendments of 1972, as amended, prohibits discrimination on the basis of sex in educational

programs or activities receiving federal funds, and 1975
regulations extend the employment provisions of the act to
include recruitment, hiring, promotion, consideration for and
award of tenure, job assignment, compensation and other
job-related activities.

    Federal Programs. Some entering or returning women bene-
fit from federally-assisted employment and training programs,
although continuation at present levels of several of these
programs is doubtful under the new Republican Administration.
The Work Incentive Program (WIN) helps applicants for and
recipients of Aid to Families with Dependent Children (AFDC)
to find jobs and provides support services, including childcare and coaching in job-search and interview skills. The
Department of Labor also sponsors high quality skill training
in structured work environments for AFDC recipients, enabling
them to become eligible for nontraditional jobs (DOL/DHEW,
1979). The U.S. Employment Service has emphasized counseling,
testing, job development, referral to jobs or training, and
placement for women because of the barriers they often face
when entering or reentering the workplace.

    The Bureau of Apprenticeship and Training seeks to
promote equity in apprenticeship programs registered with the
Department of Labor, as do other groups with or without
federal support. The National Urban League's Project LEAP
(Labor Education Advancement Program) seeks to involve more
women in apprenticeships and has been successful in placing
women as bricklayers, sheet metal workers, electricians, and
welders, among others. Advocates for Women, in San Francisco,
also places women in construction training apprenticeships.
Another DOL program is designed to identify qualified minority
women for managerial, professional and technical jobs in the
private and public sectors, especially where few minority
women are employed. During 1978, 1,650 women, after receiving
help with interview and resume preparation, were placed by the
Minority Women's Employment Program (DOL/DHEW, 1979).

    Support Services. Personal guidance, vocational counsel-
ing and skill assessment are needed by most women seeking
to enter or reenter the labor force. The State of Maryland,
for example, has sought to achieve greater equity in vocational counseling by establishing skill assessment labs in
various locations throughout the state to help women with
career choices. Women's centers for continuing education,
counseling, awareness and information, personal support,
academic and occupational exploration, and training exist
throughout the United States. Not all centers offer all
services; some are sponsored with public monies and others by
private funds. Some are attached to an existing educational
institution or community agency; others are free-standing.

More than 120 established centers providing educational and career counseling are members of the Catalyst National Network of Local Resource Centers (Catalyst, 1979). The American Association of Community and Junior Colleges reports that over 300 member institutions have some type of women's center. A survey conducted by the National Woman's Center Training Project of Everywoman's Center, University of Massachusetts, funded under the Women's Educational Equity Act, elicited responses from 99 campus-based centers: while such centers are diverse, they were typically five years old, offered an average of nine different types of services, and served 2,363 clients on the average with a median budget of $3950 in 1978 (Project on the Status and Education of Women, 1979).

Various community college-based women's centers offer counseling and testing programs, learning skills programs including tutorial assistance, literacy or catch-up programs, job placement services, child care services, and opportunities to study women's issues (Eliason, 1977b).

For example, the George Washington University Continuing Education for Women Center, begun in 1963, is based in a four-year institution and has provided comprehensive services to women aged 18 to 78--to 7,000 of them between 1964 and 1977 (Grosgebauer, 1977). While helping women reestablish confidence, gain new direction and purpose and objectively evaluate interests and abilities, this center provides counseling, job training and referral services, as well as credit and noncredit courses and degree programs. The GWU one-year (or more) career certificate programs for graduate-level women who wish to obtain career skills in fields identified as employment growth areas have focused on landscape architecture, publications, fund-raising, psychometry and legal-assistant work. The Center helps in job placement as well.

Another four-year institution, Purdue University (Indiana), offers a "Span Plan Program" to returning adult undergraduate students or those wishing to reassess life and/or career goals for future reentry (Purdue University, 1979). In addition to services already discussed at other centers, Purdue makes Student Spouse Grants available to encourage, among married students, more two-student families to further their education; usually husbands are enrolled and wives are employed or caring for small children at home. Mature Student Grants are available to assist adults over 25 wishing to pursue undergraduate study to do so. Other educational institutions and private and public organizations provide a limited number of scholarships or fellowships for reentry women.

Training for Nontraditional Jobs. Two additional trends deserve note. Since women tend to study for and work in traditionally female-intensive professions, attempts are being made in the U.S. to train women for nontraditional occupations with favorable employment prospects. The National Science Foundation has supported retraining programs for women scientists who are trained but not employed in their fields of interest, to help them return to the labor market. Trainees are able to update their knowledge and are helped to find science-related jobs. Programs for women at other skill levels in nontraditional fields have been described earlier.

Accommodating Geographical Mobility. With high levels of geographical mobility in this country, women often follow where a spouse's career or their own takes them. There are a number of innovative programs which address this need. In the educational arena, residency requirements may be adjusted to accomodate women who move often or attend part-time. American University, for example, has "mobility clause contracts" which may be negotiated by students seeking a Bachelor in General Studies. If accepted into this program with an approved course of study, an individual receives a "permit to study" which may be used to begin, continue or complete a program at another institution, though 30 hours must be taken at AU.

Credit for prior learning experience and independent study such as that permitted by the Illinois Board of Governors Bachelors of Arts Program (Fisher-Thompson, 1980) aids women wishing to enter or return to college. Because women often attend part-time, transfer policies and time limitations on completion of graduate work are crucial; it takes longer to get a certificate or degree that way, and it may not be possible to stay in one location.

Displaced Homemakers. A displaced homemaker is defined as:

> an individual aged 35 or more (many states set lower age limits), usually female, who has been performing unpaid work at home for substantial numbers of years for family members; has had or would have difficulty in securing paid employment; is unemployed or under-employed; has been dependent on the income of another family member but no longer is supported by that income; or is receiving time-limited spousal support or government assistance as a parent of minor children (Watfish, 1979).

The Comprehensive Employment and Training Act, particularly Title III as amended, targets women, single parents and displaced homemakers--because of their relative disadvantage in the labor market--for special programs. The Vocational Education Act provides funds to states to meet the needs of displaced homemakers, single heads of household, part-time workers wishing full-time jobs, and men and women seeking employment traditionally dominated by the opposite sex. Legislation to aid displaced homemakers now exists in 31 states.

Displaced homemakers are ineligible for unemployment insurance because they have been doing unpaid work at home, usually are too young to qualify for social security, and are increasing in numbers. In 1980, $5 million were earmarked for CETA demonstration projects in their behalf. The Washington-based National Displaced Homemakers Network reports an estimated 300 programs, with various means of support, throughout the nation. These multiservice centers provide counseling, skill and needs assessment, support services, educational and skill exploration, employment training, and placement. They also give women hands-on career exploration and training, and in some instances mobile units bring services to rural women.

PARENTS

Specific references to adult education aimed strictly at parents and the problems of parenting are relatively in-frequent in the materials reviewed for this project. In most of the countries studied one may infer, however, that in the general range of programs available, particularly where the offerings are governed by demand, courses or programs on parenting are available. The subject is undoubtedly covered, at least tangentially, in a number of activities where the reference to parent education is not made explicit. For example, health services and well-baby clinics are treated primarily from the medical perspective, but certainly provide some education in parenting as well. The equivalents of parent-teacher associations include topics in their programs that touch on problems of parents. Study circles or their equivalents may be arranged to deal with parenting issues and problems.

As the reports that follow point out, there are, in fact, a variety of programs that can be identified in the nine countries that clearly cover some aspects of parent education, directly or indirectly. In many cases they are local or regional efforts or the product of organizations not ordinarily identified with adult education. This variety of agencies concerned with family problems also militates against within-country summary reporting on participation, and thus tends to minimize the impression one has of the actual scope of parent education.

There are several particularly noteworthy programs and services for parents in the countries studied. In Canada the Ontario Educational Communications Authority has produced a series of television programs, "Everybody's Children," "Foot-steps," and "First Years," that is also available on videotape for group use. The Family Folk High Schools in Denmark offer resident courses for parents and children. The family associ-ations in France offer a variety of educational services. The Open University in the United Kingdom has produced two multimedia courses, "The First Years of Life" and "The Pre-School Child." There are several "Universities for Parents" in the Soviet Union, and programs for parents are part of the regular school system. In the United States, the major federally-funded programs for elementary schools include a mandate for parent involvement.

Australia

Parent education is not a prominent aspect of adult education currently in Australia. Some information regarding parent education was located in reports of local providers, regional surveys or in annual reports of some state agencies. Hooper (1978), in a survey of providers of adult education in the Wollongong area of New South Wales, found that there were community health services and health support centers that offered preparation-for-parenthood programs. He did not indicate how many participants or how many such courses were offered. In 1973 the Sydney YMCA conducted courses on parent-child relationships (Newling, 1974). In 1978, the Workers' Educational Association listed in its annual report that it had arranged for courses on the One Parent Family (12 enrollments), How to Cope As A Working Housewife (6 enrollments), and Enriching Early Childhood (16 enrollments) (Workers' Educational Association of South Australia, 1979, p. 6).

While no enrollment figures were reported, the Victoria Council for Adult Education indicated its Discussion Service would include assistance to groups that wished to focus on particular issues such as Changing Family Patterns, Child Abuse, Child Care and Alternative Life Styles. It is of interest to note that only two instances of specific reference to parent education were found. In the University of Adelaide Department of Continuing Education annual report of 1978, attention was directed to the fact that classes in parent education and child development had drawn only four enrollments each. The second instance is found in the programming of the Victoria Council of Adult Education. Parent education annual enrollments during the years 1976, 1977 and 1978 fluctuated substantially: the figures were 362, 477, and 285. In 1978-79 parent education enrollments constituted less than 2 percent of all enrollments (Victoria Council of Adult Education, 1979).

Given these scanty references, it would appear that parent education is a very insignificant focus in adult education in Australia, accounting for less than one percent of all adult education participation.

Canada

The absence of any substantial comment on parent education in Coming of Age: Canadian Adult Education in the 1960s (Kidd and Selman, 1978) could be taken as a hint of the lack

of systematic and comprehensive information regarding programs and adult participation in parent education programs.
Apparently this is indeed the case and it is substantiated by
the remarks of Clark and Brundage in their paper in Part III
of this report.

On the other hand, there is indirect evidence of substantial interest in the subject. The Ontario Educational
Communications Authority (undated announcement) has produced
four extensive series of television programs on parenting and
child development. Everybody's Children is a series of eight
thirty-minute programs dealing with the family and social
influences that affect a child's emotional-psychological
development. Footsteps, twenty half-hour programs presenting
five families representing different cultural and economic
backgrounds, conveys the emotions, thoughts and self-doubts
universal to parents. The series offers alternative solutions
for parents within their own family environment. First Years
of Life, four half-hour programs, examines the developing
relationship of young children and their parents and how a
child adapts to the world. These four series are available on
videotape as a basis for study for parent groups and other
organizations.

One of the reasons for the absence of data on parent
education is that this subject cuts across a number of
governmental agencies and is not confined to ministries,
boards or statutory bodies concerned specifically with
education. This is illustrated in a publication of the
Provincial Secretary for Social Development for Ontario
(1979) which explains how several different ministries
impinge on the family as the focus of social policy. For
example, the Ministry of Agriculture and Food has a home
economics program for rural adults, the Ministry of Consumer
and Commercial Relations maintains telephone information
services for families regarding shopping, credit, home and
car repairs, and the Ministry of Health holds classes on
parent education per se (in which more than 19,000 parents
were enrolled in 1978). The Ministry of Health also offers
programs in pre-natal education (8,500 classes attended by
142,000 people in 1978) and family planning, for which
it organizes educational and promotional activities plus
individual counseling and clinical activities. And, of
course, the Ministry of Education itself includes parent
education within the scope of on-going continuing education
programming.

Denmark

There are programs in the Family Folk High Schools which involve participation of one or both parents and children. Originally a short summer course, there is now an extended form in certain of the schools. No other information could be uncovered on parent education in Denmark.

The Federal Republic of Germany

Available information gives no indication of programs specifically aimed at parents. The listing of categories and subcategories for Volkshochschule courses does not include any such grouping. Because courses or programs in the Volkshochschule are made available on evidence of demand, however, there is the possibility of providing such programs, and they undoubtedly are available in a variety of forms.

France

Family life and its preservation is highly valued, and many organizations exist to work in behalf of family interests. Documentation is lacking about adult education programs related to effective parenting, and participation in such activities seems to be excluded from French national adult education statistics. A well-developed network of services to families, however, has been established, and data are now being collected to learn who uses those services and how.

Services to Parents

Family associations, established in many French communities, focus on concerns of the family and how to improve services for them, but not necessarily on parent education. The National Union of Family Associations (L'Union Nationale des Associations Familiales) operates on a regional as well as national basis and serves as a lobbying and advocacy organization for families. It provides information to families on legal rights, available social services; it also creates and manages activities such as clothing exchanges and secondhand school book purchasing systems. The Union helps people reflect on family problems and intervenes in behalf of families, as a collectivity, in the administration and organization of programs which affect them. Its stated purpose is to ensure the "material and moral defense of families" (Comite du Travail Feminin, 1977).

The National Federation of Rural Families Associations acts in a similar capacity as a coordinating and advocacy body for rural families. Its goal is to help each family handle its problems better and to act collectively for the defense of family interests. This group does offer training courses, usually of one to several days duration. While there seem to be no enrollment restrictions, activities are especially oriented to the needs of professionals who provide family services. One group of courses is designed to impart general knowledge of interest to families. These classes focus on family legal rights, purposes of the federation, and on the nature of families in other countries (supplemented by trips or conferences). A second category is more targeted and includes information related to specific population sectors. For example, courses are offered on consumerism, family life, problems of women or older people, and also on leadership development for staff of such organizations as rural social centers or childrens' vacation colonies. A third tier of courses are those of "technical animation" (see the essay by Bernard and Leitard in Part III). These are organized particularly for family service professionals and contain information on how to conduct a meeting, oral and written expression, and relations with the media. Job training seminars for home aides, for example, or classes on psychological and affective development over the life span, are also typical.

Parent education occurs in self-help groups formed around common concerns to share information and provide mutual support. Parents of retarded children, for example, may establish their own self-help group. Supporting data are virtually nil, but interviews with French citizens and educators indicate that informal learning about parenting does occur in such groups, as well as in churches and other types of organizations.

There are l'Associations des Parents d'Eleves (Associations of Parents of Students) comparable to the PTA in the U.S., which function in school settings. These groups sponsor meetings which could be considered to be parent education, but rates of participation vary greatly.

In recent years there has been an increase, seemingly, in the amount of space and time given by the media to presentation of information on parenting. The creation of the magazine Parents, is a good example. Perhaps this distance learning approach is more palatable to French adults--less threatening and intrusive on private parental roles and responsibilities--than regular classes.

There are some general services available to mothers and children through federal or local government subsidies which appear to have an education component. The services of Protection Maternelle Infantile began in 1967 as pre- and post-natal health care. These services were extended in 1972 to include providing information, marriage counseling, family planning, and family education. Informal education on health, nutrition, and presumably on parenting, occurs.

To implement the French national family allowance policy, local offices of Les Caisse Nationale des d'Allocations Familiales are distributed widely. Under their sponsorship classes are held during the day on topics related to home economics; it seems logical that child care would be included. Representatives of the "Caisse" travel to small towns and villages to provide such classes in available space, when there is no local office. Once children are in school, health care services are available for them, and health personnel informally help parents to understand the particular needs of their child. It seems likely that other health programs and social services for children or women include an educational element, but that seems to be presented, if at all, as a secondary objective.

The Soviet Union

A model two-year lecture series for "improving parents' pedagogical sophistication" has been developed for presentation in schools of general education (Grebennikov, 1978; some details are given by Rosen in Part III). Among the People's Universities are (1) a number which are designated "Pedagogical Universities," which offer programs for parents and parents-to-be, and (2) several which are specifically "Universities for Parents" (Rosen, 1965). A great many shorter-term educational activities are also available for parents (see the Part II country report). A major emphasis of these programs is on showing parents how they can encourage and assist children in their schoolwork. Thus, as evidence of the effectiveness of programs for parents, one author (Grebennikov, 1978) cites the fact that, in one large city, the rate at which pupils dropped out of school before completing the eighth grade was reduced from 85 per 10,000 [sic] to 20 per 10,000 over an unspecified number of years.

Sweden

Sweden has no explicit national policy or programs for educating parents in childrearing roles. During recent years, however, more and more study circles have begun to focus on effective parenting. National statistics only list courses according to broad categories, so it is currently impossible to determine how many actual participants there are. However, the popularity of this topic seems to be growing rapidly.

In addition, the Ministry of Health and Social Welfare sponsors a number of activities related to parent education, including family planning advice, counseling for parents and children and courses in childbirth for prospective mothers and fathers.

Finally, a Royal Commission on preschool education is currently (1980) engaged in discussions concerning future directions for parent education.

The United Kingdom

There are no government policies and programs in the U.K. regarding parent education, and also no systematic information on the extent to which such educational opportunities may exist. Most certainly they do exist, most likely conducted quite informally in a variety of settings. Stock, in Part III, notes that there are, among others, child development, pre- and post-natal, and problem-centered (e.g., "teenage rebellion") courses--variously offered by university extra-mural departments, voluntary associations, LEA units, health clinics, parent-teacher associations, and the mass media. With the exception of the Open University courses described below, no descriptions of specific parent education programs were uncovered in our review.

The Open University. Possibly the best effort thus far to provide instruction in effective parenting in the U.K.--and an excellent effort by any standard--has come from the Open University. In cooperation with the BBC and the Health Education Council, the OU has produced two multimedia courses; their titles, respectively, are "The First Years of Life" and "The Pre-School Child."

To illustrate the OU format, "The First Years of Life" is described as "a complete course covering the progress of a baby from conception to his second birthday." The course is written for parents and covers the kinds of practical questions and problems that most parents have to deal with. Besides the eight books (in magazine format, with color drawings and photographs), there are four television programmes and four radio programmes specially made for the course. There is also a resource pack which includes leaflets, posters, records and assignments. The books have titles like "A New Life," "Progress in Pregnancy," "Birth and the Newborn Baby," "Getting to Grips With It All," "Who's in Control?" and "Happy Families?" The television and radio installments have names like "On the Way," "Mums and Dads, Husbands and Wives," "Down in the Dumps," and "Clash!" (The Open University, 1977).

The United States

The U.S. National Commission on the International Year of the Child recently reported provocative data on American children in difficulty: of 9 million under age 18 in the U.S. (in 1979), over 15 million, before they reach adulthood, will be recipients of federal assistance under the Aid to Families with Dependent Children program; one million are victims of child abuse and neglect each year; one million run away from home each year; 5.3 million youths between 14 and 17 have drinking problems; and nearly three-quarters of a million under age 18 are in prisons and correctional facilities. To this add the fact that more than half a million teenagers become mothers each year, with many presumably unready to accept full parental responsibilities.

What family issues are of greatest concern to Americans? Seven hearings have been held around the nation during 1979 and 1980 under the auspices of the White House Conference on Families. The concerns of participants in those hearings have been ranked. At the top of the list was sensitivity (or insensitivity) of government to family needs in social policy; fourth-ranked was childcare; eighth and ninth, respectively, were family life education (including preparation for marriage and parenting), and children and parents, including responsible parenting and supports for parents and children. Complicating the problem, many parents in the U.S. find it difficult to ask for advice or to seek help in parenting (Yankelovich, et al., 1977).

Since parenting is a heavily value-laden matter, goals for parent education differ widely. Given this variety of objectives, it is not surprising to find in the U.S. a range of models, programs and providers of parent education.

Government, religious institutions, social service organizations, schools and colleges, health agencies and self-help
groups all provide education for parents. Some approaches
stress the universality of specified behaviors and mis-
behaviors. Others stress the highly personalized and
individualized nature of parenting and human beings. Some
argue that there are no implicit standards against which all
parents or children may be measured, and no attempt ought be
made to impose one standard over another. Others make the
case that it is impossible to define a socially competent
parent in a pluralistic, changing society (Yankelovich, et
al., 1977). Even those programs promising to help adults
become "responsible" parents do not escape unscathed from the
definition and values dilemma. "Responsible" parenting may
mean close supervision of children by those who accept
the traditional values of one segment or another of American
society; to others it may mean emphasizing their children's
self-actualization and realization of individual potential,
by adopting a more laissez-faire attitude toward children.
Such contradictions underlie parent education in the United
States.

School-Based Programs

Federal programs and mandates such as Title I of the
Elementary and Secondary Education Act, Titles II and V--
Basic Skills Improvement and Training for Parents, Head Start,
the Education for All the Handicapped Act, and Project Follow
Through all call for parent involvement in their childrens'
education on the part of the primarily low income families
served. Head Start programs, for example, serve 387,000
preschool children and their families nationwide. Parents
may participate by volunteering in classrooms or on field
trips, by becoming involved in the decision-making process on
policy councils and committees, by choosing and organizing
activities which fit their interests (such as working on a
fund-raising event or as a speaker on job-interview skills),
or by working directly with children in cooperation with
staff at home or at school. Staff may visit a parent at home
to share information about his or her child and to discuss
ways in which each may help. Head Start developed a parent
education curriculum entitled "Exploring Parenting" which was
used during 1978 in an estimated 300 programs averaging about
30 parents each. The curriculum included films depicting
diverse families "at home." These were supplemented in
20 weekly three-hour sessions by audiotapes, a record on
coping with stress, posters, and booklets. Trained group
leaders facilitated and guided the discussions with these
9,000 low-income parents.

Parental involvement is required in the Head Start <u>Follow Through</u> program designed for children at the kindergarten through third grade levels. In 1980 there are 150 projects nationwide, 21 exemplary resource centers, and 19 educational or research organizations serving as sponsors. Parents of Follow Through children participate in governance on Policy Advisory Committees; in the instructional process as paid aides, volunteers, classroom observers; or as tutors of their own children. Parents are taught how to perform in these roles. There is also a career development component to provide education for nonprofessional and paraprofessional staff, often parents. Each Follow Through program employs a parent involvement coordinator. The specific nature of programs differs by site, but could include workshops on parent-child relations or nutrition, for instance; or staff could make home visits to work with parents on specific child-help tasks, returning later to assess progress.

Under Title I of the Elementary and Secondary Education Act, parental involvement on school site and school district level Policy Advisory Councils is mandated. These programs operate in 14,000 school districts, and monies may be spent to train parents about Title I and how it operates, but not to teach effective parenting skills. Teachers and staff, however, discuss with parents how they can help their child. A private membership organization, the National Coalition for Title I ESEA Parents, provides information, training, and technical assistance to some of the 5 million Title I parents in this country. With a membership of 5,000 to 7,000, the Coalition serves as an information clearinghouse, runs workshops at its annual conference, and provides training at the request of school districts. While most of the training focuses on Title I regulations and on roles of parents, some newsletter articles and convention sessions are devoted to "how parents can help their children to learn" or "effective parenting skills."

Parent-Teacher Associations provide services to parents, families, schools and children. Nationally, parent membership is roughly 6 million. Since 1972, in addition to local school programs which often focus on some aspect of parent education, there have been parenting education conferences in almost every state. Understanding what parenting is, and how to upgrade parenting skills have been topics. With 6,000 monitors across the nation, the PTA also has reviewed television programs, provided descriptions of them to parents and children, and given citations for excellence to networks and producers.

The Cooperative Extension Service of the U.S. Department of Agriculture sponsors parent education programs in every state. Participation data have not been aggregated nationally. One model, known as Parent-Child Interaction

(PCI), developed in Missouri, is focused on toy lending. Parents view a videotape, receive written materials, and participate in role-playing and group discussion about the use of a different toy which they take home to use with their child. With an average of 15 parents per class, this program is now in use in 50 to 75 percent of all states. Another Extension program, called Practical Education for Parents (PEP), developed in Ohio, focuses on improving parent's skills in communication, decision-making, and handling of discipline and punishment. Parents have homework assignments to practice the skills learned in class. At least 2000 parents in Ohio have taken this course, which other states are also using. USDA Extension provides a network to disseminate successful parent education programs.

Parenting education for adolescents is currently of particular concern in the U.S. The federal Administration on Children, Youth and Families as well as private sector groups such as the Child Welfare League, Planned Parenthood, the National March of Dimes Foundation and the American Home Economics Association have developed curricula for use in high schools. Some interested groups work directly with junior and teen-age youths; their parenting or pre-parenting education programs variously focus on nutrition, prenatal care, health and prevention of birth-defected babies, child care, and child growth and development, sometimes including a practicum. Adolescent pregnancy in the U.S. is a growing problem, with the National Alliance Concerned with School-Age Parents serving as a clearinghouse on programs and services.

Of the estimated one-half to one million self-help groups in this country (Evans, 1978), many provide information intended to help adults become better parents. These include, for example, groups of single parents, abusive parents, adoptive parents, and "fathers for equal justice."

Other Providers

Religious organizations long have been concerned about education for marital and parental responsibilities. With a constituency of 40 million people, the National Council of Churches, as well as most major denominations, has national staff to facilitate family ministries. Its Commission on Family Ministries and Human Sexuality reports a current movement to involve <u>families</u> in family enrichment, not only <u>couples</u> in marriage enrichment activities. Effective parenting is a concern. Current Commission foci, in addition to helping parents to become more effective sex educators in an attitudinal and informational sense, include remarriage of divorced persons and their reconstituted or aggregated families, family violence, and homosexuality and families.

The Family Service Association of America, a private nonprofit association of 260 sectarian and nonsectarian social service agencies, estimates that during 1978, 300,000 persons participated in family life education or family development programs through member agencies. Only about 10 percent of their agencies do not sponsor family education courses. While these community-based agencies, often partially supported by funds from the United Way (a nationally organized charity), offer individual or group counseling and problem-solving, such activities are separate from the education component. Individual agencies determine the nature and scope of offerings which may include topics such as parent-child interaction, parent effectiveness, or family money management. Family service staff also provide speakers to local organizations, participate in radio talk shows, or write articles of an educational nature. The impact of these diffuse parent education activities is difficult to know.

Programs of Parents Without Partners

The numbers of single parents are growing dramatically in the U.S., and one organization established to support them is Parents Without Partners. During 1977, membership totaled 150,000 in Canada and the U.S., with more than 900 chapters and an estimated past and present membership of 500,000. PWP uses four models of parent education (which also are used by other institutions throughout the country). One model is based on the Single Parent's Survival Guide: How to Raise Children, by Leroy G. Baruth. Using Adler-Dreikurs techniques, (described below), this program consists of five to eight discussion sessions, a guide for group leaders, a parent's guide for each participant and a copy of Baruth's book.

The other three models are also quite well known and widely used. Systematic Training for Effective Parenting (STEP), developed by Dinkmeyer and McKay, is designed for study group use. It assumes the equality, mutual respect and dignity of parents and children, and seeks to foster democratic rather than autocratic child-rearing practices. Motivating children to exercise responsibility for their own actions is a major task; using the natural and logical consequences of their decisions is the method. Hence, discussion topics include developing responsibility, communication/listening, and decision-making for parents.

Another model is Parent Effectiveness Training, based on the book by Thomas Gordon (1970). This program is designed to be taught in eight sessions of three hours each, and also assumes the egalitarian nature of family relationships. It focuses on mutual respect of parents and children and emphasizes conflict resolution rather than parental use of power. Major skill areas taught include: how to listen so your children will talk to you, how to talk so children will listen, how to resolve conflicts so nobody loses, and how to share values so everyone grows. About 35,000 people annually take the P.E.T. course in the U.S. through churches or synagogues, mental health agencies, community adult education, or under private auspices. Parents enrolled tend to have either children aged three or under, or children from 11 to 16 years old. A materials fee is charged and goes to the national offices of P.E.T.; teachers vary in the instructional fee they charge. This method is being used in a number of foreign countries (including most of those covered by this project).

The fourth approach is based on the work of Alfred Adler, as brought to the U.S. by Rudolf Dreikurs. Adler believed that all behavior was goal-directed, and this model seeks to teach parents how to recognize the goals of a child's mis-behavior (for example, attention getting, power, revenge, and displayed discouragement). Parents learn Adlerian principles and how to use this model in several ways. Through open "counseling" sessions--termed education, not therapy--a trained group leader talks with volunteer families before an audience. The leader seeks to understand the mistaken goal, suggests that to the child, and--with confirmation--then instructs parents in how not to encourage the misbehavior. Audience participation is encouraged. An estimated 20,000 persons are in such study groups at any one time.

UNDEREDUCATED ADULTS

All of the countries studied have learning opportunities for undereducated adults. They range from rather minimal provision in Denmark--where the need may be minimal--to fairly extensive opportunities in Australia, Sweden, the United Kingdom and the United States. All nine countries make schooling compulsory, usually for nine years, and failure to complete the designated period of compulsory education is the most usual definition given for "undereducated" (although concepts of minimal "basic skills" and "functional competencies" are gaining currency in the U.S. and U.K.).

In many industrialized nations, a large population group requiring literacy services are the thousands of immigrants, "guest workers" and refugees, who need to learn the language of their new country. In the nine countries studied, all but Denmark and the U.S.S.R. have experienced substantial inflows of non-native language speakers in recent years. France, in particular, has developed a broad range of educational services for foreigners. The German "folk high schools" (Volkshochschulen) conducted over a thousand classes in German as a foreign language in 1978, chiefly for the many immigrant guest workers.

With regard to basic skills and adult literacy programs more generally, perhaps most notable was the multi-organization, multi-media adult literacy campaign in Britain that ran between 1975 and 1978. In Sweden, reflecting a general government goal of targeting resources on the under-educated (see Rubenson's report in Part III), various "bridging education" strategies, including particularly the work of the municipal adult schools, have been initiated in the past decade. In the U.S.S.R. there is a noteworthy 1973 government regulation that requires employing organizations to send, at company expense, all employees under age 30 who have not completed secondary school to evening school.

Australia

Education is compulsory to age 16 in Tasmania and in all other Australian states to age 15. Secondary education

programs last five or six years after the seventh or eighth
year of schooling. Students complete secondary education at
the end of year 12; however, many leave after year 10. Most
students attend government schools: about 20 to 25 percent
attend private schools sponsored by religious orders. The
secondary school retention rate has been increasing. In 1967,
for example, 71 percent stayed through year 10 and 23 percent
stayed to year 12. By 1977, 88 percent stayed through year
10 and 35 percent stayed through year 12. Also, by 1977,
the retention of females was 36.6 percent vs. 34.0 percent
for males. While students can meet the requirements for
compulsory attendance at age 15 or 16 (year 10), the entry
standard to university is the higher school or senior
certificate award at grade 12.

If one accepts completion of year 10 as the line of
separation of educated vs. undereducated adults, the retention
rates of secondary schools for earlier periods, cited in
the preceding paragraph, hint at a fairly substantial portion
of the adult population being regarded as undereducated.
It has been estimated that 3 percent of the army was illiterate in World War II (Nelson, 1976). More recently Keeves
and Matthews have indicated that in basic skills areas
"...approximately 25 percent of school leavers, especially
those leaving at around the minimum legal age, do not have the
literacy or numeracy skills necessary for employment in many
occupations..." (D'Cruz and Sheehan, 1978, p. 249).

Programs for Immigrants. Literacy and numeracy have
been seen as special problems among Australia's substantial
immigrant population. In the early 1970's Goyen, through
actual testing of adults in the Sydney area, determined that
3.7 percent of Australian-born English speaking adults were
illiterate as compared to 43.3 percent of those whose mother
tongue was not English. She estimated that there were 220,000
illiterates in the Sydney area alone (Houston and Wesson,
1978). However, Goyen also noted that illiteracy increased
with age among those born in English speaking countries:
below age 30, 1.6 percent; age 50 to 59, 4.5 percent; and over
60, 11.9 percent (Goyen, 1976).

The literature about illiteracy among immigrants
repeatedly calls attention to the fact that migrants cannot be
treated as a group. Of those born overseas, for example, only
half came from countries with languages and cultures very
different from those in Australia (Williams, 1979, p. 497).
Moreover, among the aged migrants, 50,000 have come later
in life to be reunited with their families, whereas 300,000
came when young and have now grown old (Galbally, 1978).
Therefore, immigration and illiteracy are not invariably
paired and with substantial numbers of immigrants the educational concerns are not those of illiteracy, but rather in

developing an understanding of laws, systems of government, community services, and so forth.

A Department of Immigration and Ethnic Affairs report for fiscal year 1977-78 indicates that there were 75,732 new settlers that year including 18,800 who were 15 years or older from non-English speaking backgrounds, of whom 4,600 were Indo-China refugees (Mackellar, 1978). This report is the source of the following information about the Adult Migrant Education Program, which is funded and coordinated by the Commonwealth Minister for Immigration and Ethnic Affairs. At the state level, the costs of activities and services and their administration by state adult migrant education service units are reimbursed by the Commonwealth. State services arrange for courses, classes and teachers, and have immediate control over instruction. Some postsecondary and tertiary educational institutions and community groups contribute to adult programs and the Commonwealth reimburses costs. The ten-part program consisted of the following activities in 1977-78:

(1) Full-Time Courses. These are eight-week intensive courses consisting of 320 hours of instruction provided for professionally qualified immigrants. There are also 300 hour, 10-week accelerated courses for subprofessional and technical trades persons. There were 4,555 enrollments in 272 courses.

(2) Vacation Full-Time Courses. These are courses that are conducted full time over 6 or 7 weeks in January and February (to use school accommodations not being used). There were 330 enrollments in 18 courses offered in New South Wales, Victoria and West Australia.

(3) Refugee-on-Arrival Courses. These are full-time, part-time, or mixed courses conducted in hostels. There were 3,071 enrollments.

(4) Part-Time Courses. These are courses that last 10 to 20 weeks, with 6 to 20 hours of instruction per week. There were 11,886 enrollments in 546 courses.

(5) Courses-in-Industry. Courses for unskilled or semiskilled persons at their places of employment, consisting of 36 hours of instruction over 6 weeks. Seventy-five employers were involved in the offering of 317 courses to 3,187 persons.

(6) Continuation Classes. Part-time courses, 2 hours per week, offered at the learner's convenience. The average student receives 45-50 hours of instruction per year. There were 1,091 classes offered to 13,964 students.

(7) Correspondence Courses.   Two types of instruction are offered for those unable or unwilling to attend classes. Preliminary bilingual instruction, consisting of six lessons in Italian-English and Greek-English designed to help migrants prepare for the all-English course.   The latter course has 120 lessons in English and it is based on programs broadcast by the ABC Monday through Saturday.   The courses are also available on records.   Enrollment totalled 16,168, for which 79,807 lesson books were corrected.

(8) Home Tutor Scheme.   A program directed mainly at women.   A volunteer tutor meets students on a one-to-one basis, 1 to 2 hours per week at student's or tutor's home or during the course of some community activities.   Some 4,065 tutors worked with 5,030 students.

(9) Migrant Education Television.   You Say The Word!, a series shown on 12 stations.   It has been estimated that 800,000 migrant adults live within the stations' broadcast areas.   A preliminary study in 1978 indicated that 30 percent of the target audience are regular viewers.

(10) Living Allowances are paid in full-time and vacation programs.

Programs for Aboriginals.   Australia's Aboriginals constitute a special category of undereducated adults. When interpreted from the viewpoint of the main culture's educational system, Aboriginals are grossly undereducated. According to the 1971 Census, 25 percent of Aboriginals had never been to school, 43 percent had not gone beyond primary education, and only 2 percent had reached Year 10.   However, with the current social policy of Aboriginal self-management, questions arise afresh as to what may be the proper standards for assessing the status of educational development among the Aboriginal peoples.   For example, in a discussion of management training programs under development at the Aboriginal Training and Cultural Institute, the following position was noted: "Contrary to generally held opinion within the formal system, Aboriginal people do not need to have a high degree of literacy in order to perform significant management functions" (Aboriginal Training and Cultural Institute, 1979, p. 2).

When one seeks systematic statistical data on the provision of education for undereducated adults, one finds the same situation as regards adult education in general.   "There is no collection of nationally comparable statistics to reflect accurately the extent of educational services in adult literacy and numeracy throughout Australia or the enrollment in programs and courses" (Report of the Interdepartmental

Working Party, 1977, p. 26). This source goes on to indicate there is no Commonwealth adult literacy and numeracy grant program as such (Ibid., p. 19).

Canada

Canadian adult education authorities discuss the need and provision of programs of the undereducated adult with considerable concern and urgency. The Adams Commission (1979) summarized its discussion as follows: "In short, adult literacy in Canada is a serious social and economic problem which is largely being ignored" (p. 122). Adult Basic Education in Canada is described by Thomas (1979) as "...fragmented because of funding mechanisms and lack of clear understanding of, or commitment to, the holistic concept of Adult Basic Education on the part of provincial governments and others working in the field" (p. 5). Thomas goes on to report that "Proportionately we have greater numbers of people with less than grade 5 education than both the U.K. and U.S.A. and greater numbers of those with less than grade 9." (p. 18). Cairns (1977) said "...the majority of the present day inade-quately educated Canadian adults were too old to benefit from the post-war educational expansion. One might expect, there-fore, that their educational needs would be met by large scale adult basic education and literacy programs...this is not the case" (p. 43).

Perhaps part of the problem is how illiteracy is defined and measured. "There are...an estimated one million adults unable to read or write, with another four million who may be functionally illiterate. Census data for 1976 indicate that 856,000 Canadians have achieved less than a grade 5 level schooling and 3,520,595 between grades 5 and 8. This repre-sents 5.6 percent and 22.9 percent, respectively, of Canada's population aged 15 or over. While such figures are not entirely indicative of literacy levels, they attest to the under-education of a considerable segment of Canada's adult population" (Clark and Brundage in Part III of this report). As one might imagine, there are subsets within the illiterate category. Fifty percent of Native Indians and Innuits have not completed grade 8; Canadians who speak only French include 54.9 percent who have not completed grade 8; and 88.9 percent of those who speak neither French nor English have less than grade 8. Most of those regarded as illiterate, on the basis of their formal school records, are adults over age 44. The illiterates are disproportionately represented among the poor: 60.2 percent of adults with less than grade five earned no income and 30.6 percent earned less than $6,000. It has been indicated that grade 8 or less effectively bars an adult from many occupations, from employment in many companies and from participation in most forms of vocational education (Adams, 1979, p. 117).

Three programs of the Canada Manpower Training Program have been particularly directed at problems of illiteracy. Enrollments in these programs show a decided decline over a six-year period, as shown in the following table.

Number of Trainees: BTSD, BJRT, WAT

1972-73	55,671
1973-74	52,684
1974-75	47,791
1975-76	45,889
1976-77	44,910
1977-78	43,960

BTSD: Basic Training for Skills
             Development
BJRT: Basic Job Readiness Skills
WAT: Work Adjustment Training

Denmark

The length of compulsory education in Denmark was extended from seven to nine years in 1972-73. At that time, approximately 40 percent of the 20-25 year age group had less than nine years of education and over 85 percent of those over 55 had less than nine years. The projection for 1980 is that all of the 20-25 year group will have at least nine years. However, about one quarter of the 25-30 year olds, one half of those 30-35, two-thirds of the 35-40 group, and three-fourths of the 40-45 group will have less than nine years of education (Hansen, 1976). The recognition of this generation gap has led to efforts to provide opportunities for those individuals with less than the current level of compulsory education to bring themselves to at least this level.

The Labor Market Training Schemes, discussed in the section on Workers, provides assistance to the undereducated in developing vocational skills, but does little to improve their general educational background or provide educational certification. Continuation and Youth Schools provide alternative routes outside the regular educational system to examinations and certificates for those 18 and under but past the compulsory level. Leisure time programs offer vocational programs only where they are not otherwise available. As in most countries, there is a direct relationship between the amount of previous education and the degree of participation in leisure time programs in general, so these do not effectively close the gap for the undereducated (Himmelstrup, in Part IV).

Evening classes in the regular school system make it possible for adults to obtain matriculation and to take courses leading to the Higher Preparatory Examination. Experiments have been conducted in combining adult education institutions with other groups and the media to extend services to those with limited education (Nordic Council, 1976).

Federal Republic of Germany

Many of the philosophical statements of goals and purposes for adult education in the Federal Republic of Germany stress the importance of providing educational opportunities for those who have missed out for one reason or another. Many of the general statements of how adult education actually operates point out that those with more previous education are overrepresented in the various programs. There is recognition of this discrepancy between goals and achievement and much discussion of the reasons for it and of how it might be overcome.

The Federal Labor Office is authorized to provide funds for education courses for the unemployed. While this is not targeted specifically at the undereducated, they are represented in the unemployed group in a larger proportion than in the total population. In a survey during the first four months of 1979, two-thirds of the unemployed in Cologne had no recognized work skills. For more than 4,300 of the unemployed, German was a foreign language. Research-demonstration projects have been carried out to study the effect of counseling in guiding the unemployed into appropriate educational courses and in locating the site of instruction more appropriately to attract the unemployed. These provide the basis for recommendations to increase the attractiveness of such programs to the undereducated (Clyne, 1979).

There are expressions of the desirability to employers of raising the educational level, not only in the skills required for job performance, but also in the general awareness of social, economic and political issues. Perhaps many well above the compulsory level in school attendance could be included among the "undereducated" in such matters.

One of the problems mentioned with some frequency is that programs, under both the Labor Promotion Act and many of the trade union agreements, have the financial remuneration of the participant tied to his or her salary level. While this may provide for relative equality, in absolute terms it offers less incentive to the lower paid and often undereducated employee.

The courses of the Volkshochschulen are, of course, open to the undereducated, but the picture of participation is no different from the more direct vocational and labor oriented programs. More of the participants come from the higher educational levels. There are certain programs, however, that do serve more directly the undereducated. In 1978 there were 64,000 enrollments in courses in German as a foreign language. This represents 1.5 percent of all enrollments. There were also 50,000 in German for Germans, but how many of these would be considered undereducated is hard to say. The Volkshochschulen also offer courses for various of the regular school diplomas. Enrollments in these were 57,000, 1.4 percent of all VHS enrollments. These were taken primarily by younger people, two-thirds of them under age 25 (DVV, 1978).

France

Basic Education. Theoretically, adult basic education may be undertaken within the educational leave provisions of the 1971 law on continuing education. Participation data, however, are sparse on use of this option. While schooling is compulsory between ages six and 16, a rigid examination structure forecloses steady progress through the educational system for many. Over 16 percent of virtually all age groups have not completed primary schooling (von Moltke and Schneevoigt, 1977). Hence, there would seem to be an adult market for basic education.

Information about the character of this population and the programs in which these adults participate is fragmentary at best. Out of 400,000 men called for military duty annually, .6 percent are found to be illiterate, unable even to form letters in answer to selection tests administered by the Armed Forces (Pasquier, 1977). Over half,

17,500, of the conscripts enrolled in classes during 1976 were participating in primary education courses. This represents a total greater than the sum of those involved in secondary education, higher education, and technical courses.

The French League of Education (Ligue Francaise de l'Enseignement) and other voluntary organizations provide adult basic education, as do regular teachers during out-of-class hours. Members of the Retired Teachers' Association-- Mutuelle Generale de l'Education Nationale (MGEN)--in areas of Paris voluntarily organize and teach literacy classes. The numbers served are unknown.

Foreigners. Historically, a variety of educational services has been provided for another undereducated segment in France--immigrants and foreign workers. Recently migration has caused an annual population jump of 100,000 to 200,000 persons; but since July 1975, migration from non-European Economic Community countries has been permitted only for purposes of reuniting a family (Council of Europe, 1979). Hence the net flow has been stemmed, although accurate estimates cannot be made due to less than ideal migration registration procedures.

Because foreign workers, which comprise 12 percent of the labor force, may not have achieved ten years of compulsory schooling in a social and cultural environment comparable to that of an industrialized Western nation, they are accorded priority for entrance into adult training courses. This preferred position is maintained whether training is organized by public authorities, firms or nonprofit associations. Along with Labor and Education Ministries, the National Immigration Office (ONI) and the Social Action Fund (FAS), a special fund for migrants, intervene at the federal level to provide information, training and monies for migrant workers and their families.

Firms generally leave literacy training to voluntary groups because such courses for migrants are long and costly and hence would reduce available resources for French nationals and better qualified workers (Pasquier, 1977). Some social service, religious or political associations operate as bridges to regular certificate-rendering vocational programs of study. Young adult immigrants looking for work, as well as those already employed, are invited to participate at this level.

Finally, vocational training itself is available to foreign workers, as it is to French citizens, on the same state/employer shared-financing basis defined by the 1971 law on Continuing Vocational Training. Under the 1975 special legislation for migrants, occupational training occurs in centers having negotiated agreements with the state, or in AFPA national centers. Immigrants are integrated with French workers taking the same training.

Overall training enrollment figures for those foreign workers and their families who are undereducated is incomplete and imprecise.   It is reported, however, that during 1975 100,000 immigrants attended state-aided courses for foreign workers organized under state agreements, AFPA, or Social Action Fund monies for literacy courses (Pasquier, 1977).   It is further noted in the same source that probably no more than 20,000 immigrants attended training provided by firms, but 60,000-70,000 were enrolled in evening classes.

The Soviet Union

A term like "undereducated adult" is not apt to appear in the Soviet lexicon.   However, a "complete" (polnoe) secondary education of ten grades has been nominally compulsory since 1975--"nominally" because students are still permitted to leave full-time regular school at the end of the eighth grade and complete their secondary schooling through evening or extramural study, and because it is not clear that the latter procedure is rigorously enforced.   Nevertheless, this suggests that a person with less than a tenth-grade education would implicitly be regarded as "undereducated."   Further evidence of this supposition--and also a good illustration of the kind of inter-institutional "cooperation" that a highly centralized system is capable of--is a regulation issued in 1973 by the national Ministry of Education and "15 ministries associated with the national economy" (Darinsky, 1976b).   Under this rule, employing organizations were required to submit an annual report on their employees and were further obliged to send these employees to evening school "at company expense or with grants from social organizations," and to adjust the working conditions of these employees to facilitate their studies.   No information has been forthcoming on the effectiveness of this rule; one may speculate that employing organizations would not be overly diligent about reporting their undereducated employees, since they would then have to shoulder the burden of supporting their education.
Following the 1959 census, lists of the names and addresses of illiterates were drawn up and "transmitted to city and district departments of public education as a basis for the organization of further work" (Maksimov, 1974). However, no question about illiteracy has been included in subsequent censuses "because the 1959 census showed that illiteracy had been almost totally eliminated from the country" (Maksimov, 1974).

The major, if not the only, programs for adults with less than a secondary education are the evening and extramural schools, which are discussed in both the Part I overview and the country report in Part III.

Sweden

In the early 1960s Sweden adopted a system of compulsory comprehensive education which covered a total period of nine years and which combined the primary and the lower secondary schools. In contemporary terms, the concept of "under-education" is defined in reference to that system. Thus, one is "undereducated" if he or she has received less than nine years of formal schooling. The term also applies if a person has: (1) received nine years of elementary education under the unreformed system and is in need of supplemental instruction, (2) has received vocational training up to or beyond the nine year minimum but lacks background in "basic courses," or (3) is an immigrant who needs to augment the basic education acquired in another country (Stockholms Skolforvaltnings Utvarderingsbvra Pedagogiskt Centrum, 1979).

During the 1970s the overriding policy concern for undereducated individuals was to provide "bridging education" which would equip them with knowledge and skills equivalent to those obtainable by graduates of the contemporary comprehensive school. Various programs and incentives have been adopted by the Swedish government to assist adults in attaining the level of education to which they are entitled by law. All of the major national adult educational programs (study circles, folk high schools, labor market training, employer-sponsored education) contain special provisions for the undereducated. In addition, there are special municipal and state schools which are specifically organized as bridging institutions. Finally there are special subsidies and outreach activities available to facilitate participation of the undereducated.

Municipal Adult Schools. By far the largest program catering to undereducated adults is that of the municipal adult schools. These schools, created according to a plan enacted by the Swedish parliament in 1967, are operated by the school boards of each municipality. They offer instruction at the lower secondary school level (grades 7 to 9) and courses, both general and vocationally-oriented, at the upper secondary level. In many cases these schools are linked with regular comprehensive or upper secondary schools, and are generally staffed by regular school teachers working on a part-time basis.

Municipal adult schools are open to anyone who is interested in furthering his or her education and are free of charge. In 1973 roughly one-third of the participants in such schools were from among the undereducated. Since then new provisions for recruitments, leaves of absence and study grants have facilitated the return to education by this group, increasing their relative participation rate. In 1978-79, participants numbered in excess of 300,000, roughly 30 percent of whom were enrolled in lower secondary school courses (The Swedish Institute, 1979a).

Courses follow syllabi established for the regular schools. Among the courses offered at the comprehensive school level, English, mathematics, Swedish and German are the most popular. In addition to classroom instruction in such courses, the schools offer counseling and extra tutoring services when needed.

Central government subsidies to municipal adult schools cover the entire cost of employing a principal, a director of studies, a guidance counselor and the teachers. In addition, the state covers a portion of the costs of informational and outreach programs.

Study Circles. The well-known Swedish institution of the study circle also caters to the needs of the undereducated. As was explained in Part I, the Swedish study circles are organized by local branches of the country's ten voluntary educational associations, which are in turn sponsored by various popular movements (including labor unions, political parties, consumer and religious organizations). Originally the ten study associations were completely independent from central government policy and financing. In recent years, however, the associations and the activities have become more and more a part of the government's efforts to create an egalitarian society. Study circle activities are thus subsidized by national and local government funds.

Currently, state subsidies cover 75 to 90 percent of the costs of organizing courses and providing materials. For courses in priority areas catering to the undereducated, extra subsidies (up to 100 percent) are available. Priority courses include Swedish, English, mathematics and social sciences at a level corresponding to grades 7 to 9 of the compulsory comprehensive school. Immigrants are granted up to 240 hours of free Swedish language instruction during paid working hours, and providers of such courses receive grants covering 100 percent of the costs of teaching and materials. In 1974 the number of undereducated people attending study circles of all kinds was roughly 400,000.

Folk High Schools. Traditionally the organization which most catered to the needs of the educationally disadvantaged was the Swedish Folk High School (Jakobbson, 1977; Folkbildningsarbeter, 1977). Originating in the mid-19th century, the folk high schools were chartered to provide young rural adults with better opportunities for general (civic) education.

Today the folk high schools are owned either by county and local councils or by trade unions, churches, temperance societies, or other nonprofit organizations and are open to anyone over the age of 18. Although traditionally a 30-week "winter course" was the standard offering, today short courses of one week or less prevail. For example, in 1976-77 125,000 persons participated in folk high school courses; of these only 13,000 were enrolled in the 30-week winter course (The Swedish Institute, 1979a).

The folk high school winter courses still play an important role in the compensatory education of adults, however. According to national policy, anyone who adds two years of folk high school winter course participation to six or seven years of regular school attendance, or one year of participation to eight years of regular school attendance, can qualify for a comprehensive school certificate. Frequently the first year of a three-year folk high school winter course cycle will be based upon the elementary school curriculum, a measure to help the educationally disadvantaged catch up. In addition, those with the fewest years of formal training are frequently given top priority in admission to the winter courses.

Labor Market Training. Geared primarily to those who are threatened by unemployment or who are difficult to employ, labor market training--sponsored by the National Labor Market Board--also plays a role in providing bridging education for the undereducated. At special labor market training centers where occupationally-oriented courses of various lengths are conducted, those with only an elementary educational background are given an eight-week introductory course in general subjects. During vocational training the educationally disadvantaged continue to receive supplementary instruction of a more general or theoretical nature. In 1974, a year in which there was relatively little labor market training (less than one-half of that conducted in 1977), there were still over 40,000 labor market trainees in the undereducated category.

Other Programs. In addition to the programs described above, there are a number of smaller-scale programs which are geared to the undereducated. There are, for example, company organized on-the-job training courses in elementary occupational skills which are offered in conjunction with a local upper secondary school. Called "intramural company schools," these institutional arrangements are state sub- sidized. In addition, there are two central government operated adult schools which offer correspondence courses to people who do not have access to a municipal adult school. Finally, there are various kinds of educational radio programs which are generally integrated into some kind of basic education course sponsored by study circles, the Labor Market Training Board or labor unions.

Incentives. Although the reforms in adult education initiated in the mid-1960s were aimed at equalizing educa- tional resources, by the early 1970s it was clear that the gap between the educated and the undereducated was widening. It was noted, for example, that in 1973-74 only one-sixth of those with less than nine years of primary schooling took part in adult studies, whereas nearly one-half of those with higher education did so. Alarmed by this finding, the Swedish Government initiated in the mid-1970s a new series of reforms aimed at breaking down the barriers, both practical and psychological, to participation by the undereducated. In 1974 the Swedish Board of Education launched a series of out- reaching activities at both the work place and in housing areas using personal contact to encourage and recruit the educationally disadvantaged. In 1975 the Swedish Parliament passed an educational leave of absence bill which gave workers an unconditional right to take leaves of absence for studies that had to be pursued during working hours. Although the leave to which they are entitled by law is unpaid, assistance is available through hourly and daily study grants (CERI, 1976). In addition, provisions are made for locally sub- sidized child care for those who are working inside the home. These measures appear to have provided strong incentives for participation by the educationally disadvantaged.

Program Success. Two indicators of program success are overall enrollment and retention rates. Although the statistics which are available are not the most complete or up-to-date possible, they do give us some indication of program success. With respect to total enrollment, data for 1974 (the most recent year for which the appropriate breakdowns were made) indicate that 17 percent of those who had received no more than seven years of formal education participated in some form of adult education. Among those with eight or nine years of formal schooling, 19 percent were adult education participants. Since most of the incentive programs mentioned above began after 1974, these figures underestimate the level of current participation.

Retention rate, as noted, is one good indicator of the success of the incentive programs. Data for retention in Stockholm area municipal adult education courses (enrolling 37 percent of all municipal adult education participants) showed that in 1973 just over 30 percent completed the various two or three term courses (Stockholms Skolforvalthings..., 1979). These statistics refer to evening classes. A more recent survey revealed that in courses held during the day, the retention rate was 65 percent, reflecting already the greater incentives which educational leaves of absence and study grants provide (Rubenson, 1979).

The United Kingdom

This discussion of programs for undereducated adults in the U.K. is divided into two sections. The first deals with the adult literacy campaign which, while "over" in the sense of commitment of major resources by the DES and the BBC, has left a legacy of concern for literacy provision in the LEAs and voluntary associations. It also stands as a significant adult education undertaking worthy of consideration by other developed countries.

The second section deals with three current activities addressed to the needs of the marginally literate or educated: (1) the DES-funded Adult Literacy Unit based at the National Institute of Adult Education, (2) the TOPS Preparation Courses offered by the Manpower Services Commission (an agency of the Department of Employment), and (3) the Industrial Language Training Units, also funded by the MSC, which provide instruction in English to immigrant workers.

The Adult Literacy Campaign*

As noted in Part I, the adult literacy campaign, running between 1975 and 1978, came indeed to resemble a campaign, involving, as it did, many diverse organizations and an "army" of volunteer tutors. While the campaign itself may now be considered over, an Adult Literacy and Basic Skills Unit continues to function at the NIAE, and much literacy work

---

*The main source of material for this section is a report by Jones and Charnley (1979).

is still underway in the LEAs, the WEA and other voluntary associations.

Several developments came together in the early 1970s which led to the sizeable grants from the DES that fueled the full-scale campaign. A 1972 report, The Trend of Reading Standards, from the National Foundation for Educational Research, a book by Clyne (1972) which concluded that "two million adults...in England and Wales are deficient in their basic education," and the concern for the educationally disadvantaged expressed in the prestigious 1973 Russell report (on adult education) all helped to set the stage.

The key catalyst, however, was the literacy work of the British Association of Settlements,* whose small number of centers were pioneering the use of volunteer tutors and one-to-one teaching. The BAS' pamphlet, A Right to Read (1974), was particularly influential in urging the public education system to become involved. At about the same time, the BBC announced its intention to undertake a three-year adult literacy project.

The campaign itself involved three major institutions-- the BBC, the DES, and the LEAs--together with numerous supporting organizations. Beginning in the fall of 1974, the BBC piloted its prime-time television series aimed at making contact with potential students and urging them to seek aid, and its two radio series (one to train tutors, the other to give students practice reading). The BBC published its Adult Literacy Handbook for use in training tutors. The upcoming campaign was widely publicized. TESCO, the supermarket chain, agreed to give away 1.2 million sample units from the BBC's book for students. Finally, telephone link-up services were established (funded in part by the Ford Foundation) in all four countries of the United Kingdom.

In mid-1974, the Government announced its plans to make three annual grants of one million pounds to the LEAs for literacy work, and that beginning early in 1975 the National Institute of Adult Education would administer the grants through a unit called the Adult Literacy Resource Agency (ALRA). (A similar arrangement, involving 200,000 pounds, was entered into in 1976 with the Scottish Institute of Education.) The grants, which for each of the 104 LEAs were quite small, were chiefly used for training tutors, acquiring teaching materials, handling phone self-referrals, and matching tutors with students. ALRA, for its part,

---

*Settlements were formed around the turn of the century in deprived urban areas as voluntary, participatory organizations for social betterment.

initially in cooperation with the BAS, produced a series of instructional resources for tutors; assembled an advisory panel of experts who would consult with individual LEAs; and, beginning in 1976, provided (and funded) experienced staff for work in the LEA's. The DES viewed its grants as stimuli to the LEAs to contribute funds for literacy work from their own allocations (which indeed happened over the three years, in an amount roughly equal to the DES grants) and to make literacy training an integral part of LEA provisions for adult education.

The campaign got fully underway in the fall of 1975. The telephone referral service was in place. There was wide publicity in all the media. The BBC television series-- 50 ten-minute programs called "On the Move"--was shown every Sunday following the 6PM national news, with repeats the following Thursday at lunch time, and again on Saturday morning. Broadcast on BBC radio was the series consisting of eight 30-minute installments entitled "Teaching Adults to Read." A second series for students ("Your Move"), pitched at a slightly higher level, began in the fall of 1976, and a still higher level series ("Next Move") was introduced in the fall of 1977 (at which time all three programs were being broadcast). Both the BBC and, notably, Independent Television ran literally hundreds of "spots," usually giving a specific LEA telephone reference.

The main activity, of course, was down in the LEAs, some functioning more smoothly at the outset than others; but, in the words of Jones and Charnley, "...despite the cold winds of economy, they were moving with a tide of public opinion created by the media and the Government's grant; and if this tide of opinion did not wash down large resources, at least the awareness of it encouraged optimism."

Consistent with the realities of decentralized provision, 63 of the LEAs required no fees for the literacy training, while 40 did make charges of varying amounts, including four who charged "according to the student's circumstances" (Small, 1979). Overall, close to 80 percent of the students were men, and roughly 80 percent of the tutors were women.

Summing up the early stages of the campaign, Jones and Charnley observed that:

> The intention of the BAS was to instigate a national campaign, but in the British system this means pro-vision by the local authorities. The BBC intention was to stimulate people to seek local help, which had to be through local authorities. And a pump-priming grant for one year (later for two more), towards a BBC three-year project, could have no other purpose than to start the LEAs on a road that they must then follow themselves (p. 23).

Some statistics on the campaign for England and Wales are provided by Small (1979): a total of 125,000 adults had engaged in literacy training by February 1978; 80,000 volunteer tutors had participated as of that date; and resources were in place in 1978 for continuing provision of literacy training to 70,000 people.

The DES recently issued a report entitled Adult Literacy in 1977-78: A Remarkable Educational Advance. Numerous other (less partial) observers have also judged the campaign to have been a notable success.

Current Activities

The Adult Literacy Unit. With the conclusion of the DES' third grant in March 1978, ALRA ceased operation, as planned, and was replaced (at the NIAE) by the Adult Literacy Unit, with DES funding of 300,000 pounds for each of two years. In 1980, this agency was refunded and renamed the Adult Literacy and Basic Skills Unit. Both "Units" were concerned with "post basic literacy" as well as basic literacy training. The Units' functions have included provision of advisory services to LEAs and voluntary bodies, publication of relevant instructional materials, coordination and provision of training, and sponsorship of innovative Special Developmental Projects (some 30 in 1979).

TOPS Preparatory Courses. Beginning in 1977, the Training Opportunities Scheme has offered a limited number of courses in literacy, numeracy, and "life skills" as preparation for the regular TOPS vocational courses, and to otherwise boost employment prospects. The courses are normally full-time and last between 12 and 48 weeks. Courses are offered at the MSC-operated Skillcentres and at LEA institutions, the latter with grant support from the MSC. In 1978-79, some 3,700 people, of whom 3,500 were adults, completed "pre-TOPS" courses (TOPS SP1, 1980a).

Industrial Language Training Units. Another recent initiative by the Manpower Services Commission was the creation of the National Centre for Industrial Language Training (NCILT), which functions to promote English language instruction (under paid release arrangements) for non-English-speaking workers who have settled in Britain. NCILT trains staff, develops materials and provides information. Currently there are 28 Industrial Language Training Units operated by LEAs (financed by the MSC) which have a total capacity for about 3,000 trainees annually (Small, 1979). In addition to instruction in English, the ILTUs give attention to work-related social skills as well as to other information needed for "living and working in Britain," as Stock points out in Part III.

The United States

The definition of "undereducated adults" that would be most widely accepted in government circles in the U.S. is a rather straightforward one: individuals age 16 and older who are not in school and who have not completed high school. This is the so-called "target population," which numbers between 50 and 60 million Americans, as identified by the National Advisory Council on Adult Education (a presidentially-appointed program review and advisory group). While the original Adult Education Act (1966) specified "programs (to)...enable all adults to continue their education to at least the level of completion of secondary school," the Act, as amended, now also includes as one of its purposes, to "enable all adults to acquire basic skills necessary to function in society." Implicit in the current Act, then, are two types of definitions: one based on grade completion, the other, on "functional competence." Interestingly, a well-conceived national study of adult functional competencies, commissioned in 1971 by the Bureau of Adult Education, concluded that 57 million American adults are unable to function proficiently in American society (Northcutt, 1975). Thus, using either definition, the gross numbers are roughly the same.

Adult Basic Education

Adult Basic Education, or ABE, is the term commonly used to describe the programs for which funding is available under the federal Adult Education Act. Students in ABE programs, as indicated earlier, must be age 16 or older, not be (or are not required to be) enrolled in a school or college, and either not have graduated from high school or "lack sufficient mastery of basic educational skills to enable them to function effectively in society." Needless to say, the program gives many adults--including the 800,000 who drop out of school each year--a second chance to complete high school. In addition to (1) acquisition of basic skills and (2) completion of high school, the Act's third purpose is to extend opportunities for "training that will enable (people) to become more employable, productive, and responsible citizens."

The Secretary of Education makes grants to the 50 states and six territories for programs meeting the purposes of the Act. A base amount ($150,000) is allotted plus an amount based on a formula related to the number of persons in the state 16 and over and not in school. The federal share may not exceed 90 percent of total expenditures. From these funds, states make grants to local school districts and to public or private nonprofit organizations for program design and implementation. In FY 1979, federal funding amounted to $105.4 million. State funding for ABE varies greatly; in some states, it all comes from local sources. In 1979, state and local funding nationally totaled $540 million (NAPCAE, 1980). Nationally there are roughly four dollars from state sources for every federal and local dollar.

While state education agencies must prepare a State Plan for carrying out the purposes of the Act, and are ultimately responsible for all ABE programs in the state, decentralization and local autonomy are the rule; the primary initiative for conducting ABE programs rests in the local districts' adult schools.

ABE programs frequently cooperate in any of a variety of cosponsorship arrangements: with CETA and other job-training programs, welfare agencies, private employers, unions, prisons, housing developments, churches and other community organizations (see Mezirow, et al., 1975).

Hunter and Harmon (1979) cite government statistics indicating (in 1976) that 32 percent of ABE students were enrolled at the beginning level (grades 1 through 4), 33 percent at the intermediate level (grades 5 through 8), and 35 percent at the advanced level (grades 9 through 12). Eleven percent of the total of 1.7 million ABE students passed the high school diploma-equivalent General Education Development (GED) tests.

Most classes are conducted in traditional elementary school fashion, in local schools and in a variety of locations throughout the community. Drop-out rates tend to be high (Mezirow, et al., 1975). One-to-one tutoring and use of volunteers are not common practices, nor is inservice training for teachers of adults.

Various amendments to the original Adult Education Act (1966) now make available special grants to state and local agencies for educational programs for adult Indians, Indochina refugees, and adult immigrants.

Voluntary Literacy Organizations

Next to the federal ABE program, the voluntary literacy programs that operate in most populated areas in the U.S. probably represent the second most important learning opportunity for "undereducated adults" in the country. Compared to most students in ABE programs, the students served by the voluntary literacy organizations (VLOs) are starting at the very bottom. Most are essentially unable to read (or write or compute).

One may speak of two general categories of VLO students: native born illiterates, and foreign born immigrants who know no English. For the VLOs, the non-English speaking immigrants present fewer problems; typically they are motivated and quite able to learn a new language. The native illiterates, on the other hand, are usually not motivated--many go to great lengths to hide the fact that they cannot read.

The two major VLOs in the U.S. are the National Affiliation for Literacy Advance (NALA) and the Literacy Volunteers of America (LVA). Both are headquartered in Syracuse, N.Y. Both have roots in Christian service traditions.

Local VLO programs recruit and train (and certify) voluntary tutors (using materials from Syracuse); recruit students through advertising, word of mouth, and referrals from educational and social service agencies; match individual tutors and students; and, in the case of the NALA-affiliated units, provide instructional materials (from Syracuse). Tutor and student then decide on a mutually satisfactory place and time and frequency of meetings, for the one-to-one tutoring sessions.

The National Affiliation for Literacy Advance is the American (volunteer) arm of Laubach Literacy International, which for almost five decades has been active in literacy work outside of the U.S. Presently (1980) it has 458 affiliated councils or projects in the U.S. which served a total of 26,000 students during FY 1979. NALA publishes a wide array of materials both for training trainers (reading specialists) and for teaching reading and writing to illiterates (following the "Laubach Method"). Most of its extensive sales, a major source of income, are to ABE and other public and private organizations teaching reading, rather than to local affiliates.

Local units of the Literacy Volunteers of America (the "Lit Vols") are staffed entirely by volunteers and are totally self-supporting. Currently there are 150 local programs, which served a total of 12,000 students during FY 1979. Generally LVA units, particularly those that are termed "associates" (as opposed to the 91 "affiliates"), are more closely integrated with other community services, such as ABE and Right to Read, than are the NALA groups (Hunter and Harman, 1979). While LVA requires that all tutors complete a highly structured training course, it does not require that they use specific teaching materials.

Right to Read and Other Activities

Launched with some fanfare in 1971, the federal Right to
Read Effort's goal was to overcome illiteracy among people of
all ages "within ten years." It has attempted, in particular,
to stimulate state agencies and private organizations to
engage in literacy training. In 1976, Right to Read funded
numerous community-based, essentially demonstration projects,
including 80 Reading Academies intended for adults. The Right
to Read program was expanded in 1978 and renamed the Basic
Skills Program. The new program extends Right to Read
activities, helps local and state agencies coordinate and
improve diverse basic skills projects, and operates a grant
program to support states with minimum competency and achievement testing programs.

There are other sponsors of basic skills training
in the U.S. For example, some labor unions cosponsor ABE
programs with management; some run courses on English as a
second language for certain of their members (Hunter and
Harman, 1979); many require work on basic skills as part
of apprenticeship programs. ACTION, the principle federal
volunteer program, uses thousands of older adults throughout
the country as reading tutors for adults. Most of the
correctional institutions in the country provide literacy
and basic skills training, usually in cooperation with
local school district ABE programs and frequently with aid
from the voluntary literacy organizations. Finally, all
the military services provide basic skills training, including
GED preparation, for their many educationally impoverished
recruits.

PART III:

REPORTS BY COUNTRY CONSULTANTS

ADULT EDUCATION IN AUSTRALIA: POLICIES,

PROGRAMS AND STRUCTURES

Chris Duke

Director, Centre for Continuing Education
The Australian National University

Context

Australia is a large, and largely empty, country. Its fourteen million people are concentrated around the fringes of the southern half of the country, with some 85 percent living in metropolitan areas. Partly for reasons of history and national self-concept, partly because of the importance of farming and especially mining in remote areas, there is, however, a concern which finds some political expression with the isolated communities living in the outback. The population is mainly of European extraction, with a strong British emphasis but also very large immigrant communities from many parts of continental Europe especially since World War II, and smaller communities from many other parts of the world, including the Asian region, mostly of quite recent origin. The Federation was created at the beginning of the century comprising six States which had been established as separate colonies; in addition there is the Northern Territory, now approaching full statehood with government out of Darwin instead of Canberra, and the Australian Capital Territory, seat of the federal parliament and of much of the Australian (formerly called Commonwealth) Public Service.

Australia has until quite recently adhered closely to British traditions and approaches in many sectors of public affairs and administration, including adult education. The nineteenth century saw first mechanics' institutes and then in the nineties university extension closely modelled on British lines; the early 20th century saw the export of the workers' educational association also very much on British lines, through the person of Albert Mansbridge. Adult education till the Second World War remained very fragmented and impoverished; the Australian Army Education Service at that

time (1941-46) suggested to some adult educationists the
possibility of a peace-time national commitment to a national
system of provision including federal, State and local government involvement and support for the voluntary sector. This
found expression in a national conference in Sydney in 1944
and a report by W.G.K. Duncan to the Universities' Commission
the same year. This was the nearest Australia approached to a
national policy and commitment in adult education, and the
nearest to a charter analogous to the 1919 Report following
World War I in Britain. In the event the Duncan report was
shelved, the Commonwealth Government preferring not to take
up an issue which might cause conflict with the centrifugal
States, and a diversified pattern of provision continued
to develop at the State level which makes generalization
difficult. A national association, the Australian Association
of Adult Education (A.A.A.E.) was formed in 1960, but at the
end of the seventies there was still no Australian Government
commitment to, or policy on, adult education as such, and
no federal department or section of government with clear
responsibility for this area. Informal channels indicate that
an approach to the Australian Minister for Education by the
national Association in 1979 might possibly lead, perhaps late
in 1980, to the appointment of a Committee of Inquiry into
Adult Education, but this remains speculative.

Scope and Meanings

     Consistent with its British origins, adult education in
Australia tended formerly to connote the liberal and non-
vocational education of adults rather than all educational
opportunities for adults to learn. The membership of the
national Association has greatly widened this past decade,
reflecting a greater diversity of educational arrangements
for adults. However, partly because of different funding
arrangements for the provision of credit and noncredit
education in all three sectors of the Australian postsecondary
system (universities, colleges of advanced education, and
technical and further education or TAFE) adult/continuing
education normally refers only to noncredit provision of
education for adults. (Continuing education has become an
increasingly fashionable term largely interchangeable with
adult education.) This means that usage though wider than
the specific "great tradition" of (higher) liberal adult
education, and wider than the recreational and hobby-oriented
forms of provision which as a stereotype have tended to
overlay this tradition, still excludes learning opportunities
for adults leading to a degree, diploma or certificate.
Active membership of the A.A.A.E. reflects and confirms
this.

Open University type provision does not therefore warrant inclusion at this stage in an overview of Australian adult education. Because of geographical circumstances as well as social values and ethos, Australia has developed relatively open access to higher education during the present century. External studies with distance modes of teaching/learning have been a major part of the provision of five universities: Queensland, New England (in rural northern New South Wales), Macquarie (in northern Sydney), and very recently Deakin (in Geelong, Victoria) and Murdoch (Perth). Colleges of advanced education and TAFE colleges (as well as school systems) have also in some instances developed distance education and external and part-time study opportunities on a substantial scale. The scale and range of such provision, as well as the small and dispersed character of the population, led a Committee of Inquiry into Open Education of the Universities' Commission to recommend in 1974 against an Australian Open University and in favour of NIOTE--a National Institute for Open Tertiary Education--to stimulate further access and distance learning provision. (NIOTE has not been created because of reductions in public expenditure on tertiary education from 1975 soon after the appearance of the final report).

Although not all postsecondary educational institutions offer external studies, most allow part-time study. This means that there are opportunities for most adults to study part-time as well as full-time at a local postsecondary institution, as well as to enroll for external study through a more distant institution. By western standards access for postexperience adults is quite open except in the apprentice-ship area, and the proportion of older students entering military education has significantly, sometimes dramatically, increased in very recent years. Some institutions have introduced special adult entry schemes, with or without a quota, of various kinds. Data of this kind are not always easily identified, and may have to be drawn, possibly on a case study basis, from the records of postsecondary educational institutions. They are excluded from policy and statistical studies of adult education in Australia, and also therefore from this overview which follows Australian practice in limiting itself to noncredit or nonaward provision and which is also more circumscribed than adult education as now defined by UNESCO and OECD.

We are therefore referring only to adult/continuing education as defined administratively within Australia. Extension is another term which covers part of this work (the term extramural not being in common usage), although extension also embraces advisory services, where there is no deliberate educational arrangement within the precise scope of this project. The term community education has acquired currency

of late, but its meaning is vague and often confused: at the
one extreme it shades into community development, social
action and what is sometimes called informal education rather
than regular and systematised provision; at the other extreme,
and more commonly, it may be equated with enhancing community
involvement in and use of schools, perhaps simply the opening
of school premises for adult education purposes outside normal
school hours. Adult education also phases into counseling,
therapy, marriage guidance and similar kinds of service as
well as into social change programs. There is no consensus
about where the line should be drawn. While usage vis-a-
vis credit courses is narrower than in the current UNESCO
definition, some Australian adult educators feel that this and
similar definitions are too restrictive in terms of community-
based adult education and adult education to foster community
and organisational learning and change. The term further
education (usually in TAFE) is of quite recent Australian use,
and normally refers to the recreational and other noncredit
and fee-paying part of the TAFE provision; it is known
administratively as Stream 6. Onsite and offsite inservice
training is normally included within the scope of adult
education nowadays, although there are also still attempts to
distinguish education from training, more often a priori or
heuristically rather than descriptively. The informal learning
facilitated by broadcasting, libraries, museums, the press
etc. is normally excluded even though adult educators at times
join forces with such providers or engage in dialogue with
them at conferences. In summary, adult education in Australia
is quite broad and eclectic except in its exclusion of adults
studying courses for credit. It spans the whole range of
nonformal, noncredit provision and tends to flow further into
community and informal areas than definitions in some other
countries allow. The main negative consequence of this usage,
which flows from administrative practice and convenience, is
that it tends to separate adult educators from those working
for more open adult access within the formal system. Trends
towards recurrent education, for instance, may be overlooked
or ignored by those working as adult educators, and service
facilities for adults entering the formal institutions tend
to be provided separately from units dedicated to facilitating
adult/ continuing education.

Status of Data

There is a serious lack of statistical information about
adult education in Australia. The A.A.A.E. has not so far
succeeded in having such data collected through the periodic
census, and sample or other participation studies of the
general population are lacking. Providers have variable kinds

and quality of statistical data about their students, but much is incomplete and rudimentary. There is very little research into adult education although the TAFE Council has begun to sponsor some studies, and the Department of Further Education (DFE) in South Australia has conducted a number of enquiries. TAFE statistics are notoriously unsatisfactory (even to the point of having common criteria adopted by the different states); it is matter for speculation how far enrollment statistics correspond with numbers of students and how many multiple enrollments there might be. The position is made more difficult by the division of interest between federal and state governmental agencies and by the impoverished or voluntary basis of many nongovernmental providers; but even within, for instance, a single federal department, statistical data on participation have not been taken out in ways required for policy making in another section of the same department. Both for policies and especially for statistical information it is, therefore, necessary to rely on occasional illustrative studies of doubtful generalisability, annual and similar reports of variable quality and detail, and the impressions and opinions of senior policy makers and administrators about their own particular sectors.

Policies in Australian Adult Education

Australia is a centrifugal and largely laissez-faire society and polity. The diversity of adult education following the temporary centralised Army Education effort during the Second World War is a source of agonising and of both pride and divisiveness among the small and scattered community who define themselves as adult educators. (The great majority of those who teach adults see themselves as industrial or public service trainers, union educators, further education teachers and officers, or part-time tutors earning some overtime income through one agency or another, rather than, normally, as 'adult educators'.) A.A.A.E. is the main (quasi-)professional association, spanning all states and territories and most sectors of provision; as a nongovernmental agency it does not make policy, although it does make representations to federal government and occasionally to state administrations and to other bodies. It is somewhat distinctive in being unitary rather than a federation of state branches, although it is now encouraging the development of state or other local groupings and activities. Although its membership is wide, other associations express more specialised interests within the field of the education of adults: the Australian Institute of Training and Development (AITD); the Australian Institute of Human Relations (AIHR); the Australian Association of Community Education (AACE), which is essentially a Victorian

body; the recently formed Australian Literacy Education
Council; and, outside the noncredit fold but with some over-
lapping membership, the Australian and South Pacific External
Studies Association (ASPESA). Other groups such as university
adult educators, and agricultural extension officers, convene
on a more ad hoc basis from time to time.

This situation in the nongovernmental sector matches
governmental circumstances, except that there is no one
Australian government department or agency which makes policy
for adult education and to which the A.A.A.E. can regularly
and formally relate. The Association attracts a small grant
from the Australian Department of Education and occasionally
sends a delegation to meet with the Minister for Education or
with senior departmental officials. No officer has regular
and specialised carriage of a general adult education brief.
Within the Education portfolio there are several other, mostly
statutory, agencies and sources of advice, but the Secretary
(permanent head) of Education is the most senior person
within this group. Most significant for adult education is
the Tertiary Education Commission (TEC) with responsibility to
advise federally on all postsecondary education. Its three
Councils (UC, AEC and TAFEC) have superseded and largely
subsumed three earlier distinct Commissions--for Universities,
Advanced Education and Technical and Further Education. There
is no recognisable adult education interest or mechanism,
though a tri-Council adult education standing committee is
periodically mooted. Normally the 'further' sector of TAFE is
assumed to embrace all of adult education, even though adult
education (in the noncredit sense and apart from mature age
regular study) is funded through each of the three sectors.
The now superseded A.U.C. recommended in 1975 that all
universities should from 1978 be spending an additional one
percent of recurrent funds, over and above whatever was now
being spent, on (apparently mainly refresher) continuing
education, but this report was never accepted by Government
and did not become policy. Meanwhile the Colleges Council has
moved to an optional half percent formula (whereby up to half
percent of recurrent funds may at each college's discretion be
spent on continuing education); between a third and a half of
the seventy CAEs have acted on this clause.

Federal government acquired responsibility for funding
higher education in the early seventies, meaning the work of
the 19 universities (as there now are) and the colleges of
advanced education. In TAFE (as in school education, for
which there is a federal Schools Commission only marginally
relevant to this paper) the federal government has an indirect
role and makes available some supplementary funds for certain
purposes such as innovations and special programs. The TAFE
sector has been gradually expanded from an impoverished base
in recent years. The TEC provides a mechanism for containing

or reducing expenditure on higher education while increasing that in vocationally-oriented aspects of TAFE--the other component of tertiary, or postsecondary, education. There is no policy for adult education as such, although there are some incidental effects for the different kinds of adult education in the three sectors. In this tertiary (or postsecondary) arena the policies of the Department of Education and the TEC do not appear to conflict.

Within the Education portfolio there also exists a Curriculum Development Centre which, like the Schools Commission, has only incidental relevance for adult education, although interest in nonformal provision and social change has some implications in both cases. The Educational Research and Development Committee (ERDC) sponsors educational research and has included among its four priority areas recurrent education. This has meant that some research projects in adult education are funded from this source, and it is defined as a significant policy and R & D area. Another national body is the Australian Education Council (AEC), the meeting of all Ministers for Education; this has acquired enhanced significance and influence of late and has appointed a permanent secretariat, but its interests thus far are largely confined to schooling. It represents a possible alternative source of effective input into federal and national educational policy making.

Turning to the states, but restricting ourselves still to the Education portfolio, we find diversity of arrangement but some common trends. Again there is no explicit adult education policy as such, though policies may be deduced from administrative activities. In most states there is a single Education Department with different branches or divisions, an increasingly significant one of which is TAFE. In South Australia this sector broke away early in the seventies to become a distinct Department of Further Education under the Minister, making provision for both vocational and general education. Its higher profile and longer history have strengthened adult education provision and such ancillary services as R & D in that state, mainly through the network of TAFE colleges. Other major providers in that state, outside DFE control and policy, include the Workers' Educational Association of S.A. and the University of Adelaide's Department of Adult Education as well as various other nongovernmental providers for the community and recreational areas, and employers and other state government departments within their respective areas of responsibility.

In all states there is a tendency to rationalise and coordinate postsecondary education and in the process to define general or residual adult education as the fuzzy 'tail' of further education within TAFE. During the later seventies separate Adult Education Boards in Queensland and Tasmania were subsumed into the TAFE Divisions. Victoria sustained a distinct statutory Council of Adult Education which is both a providing and an advisory and facilitating agency for all forms of (noncredit) adult education. In New South Wales, where the TAFE and school systems (as well as universities and voluntary agencies) are significant providers, a new, largely advisory, Board of Adult Education was recently created; this suggests policy, disburses funds, and conducts inquiries. In the Northern Territory provision falls both to the Department of Education, which runs a large Aboriginal adult education service, and the Darwin Community College. The Capital Territory, after a brief phase of moving towards a statutory TAFE council or authority (in parallel with the Schools Authority which makes some adult education provision through secondary and evening colleges), reverted to federal control of TAFE through a section of the Education Department, with a Further Education Advisory Committee concerned mainly with TAFE provision and development.

In other words, at neither level of Australian government is there clear responsibility for policy making in adult education overall. Most States have some kind of advisory mechanism, but the trend has been towards subsuming what adult education is recognised as such into rationalised TAFE provision, possibly including modest grants to support the work of the more prominent nongovernmental agencies. Following committees of inquiry, in most states in recent years there has been a tendency also to create some form of post-secondary coordinating mechanism approximating the federal TEC arrangement; these new mechanisms are emerging as a significant factor for shaping postsecondary education in the states and for regulating the impact of federal policies and funds at this level. The clearest examples are the West Australian Postsecondary Education Commission (WAPSEC), the Victorian Postsecondary Education Commission (VIPSEC) and now the Tertiary Education Authority of South Australia (TEASA). The main responsibilities and outlets in terms of educational provision of these agencies are the three kinds of formal postsecondary educational institutions: the universities, CAEs, and TAFE colleges. There is no systematic adult education policy as yet from any of these bodies. In this sense, as in the thrust towards administrative rational-isation, the states closely resemble the central government, although the circumstances of noncredit adult education vary greatly, the situation being most healthy, from this perspective, with the continuation of the statutory Council in Victoria. That state has a rich and complex web of providing agencies, including many nongovernmental agencies such as learning exchanges and neighbourhood centres and country continuing education centres associated through VACEC--the

Victorian Association of Continuing Education Centres--as well as a strong community education thrust within the formal school system and other state provision in the TAFE, CAE and university sectors. The complexity, and the possibility of costly competition and duplication in postsecondary education, may have consequences in terms of a centralising and rational- ising policy for general adult education also, but at present this is a matter for conjecture only.

It is unlikely that any Australian government (state or federal) will quickly move to adopt anything like a policy for adult education, mainly because adult education has not come into focus as an area of significant need for the society. It carries the incubus of a marginal and recreational reputation, hence, in part, the tendency to abandon this for some other more prestigious or less encumbering term like continuing, further or community education. (The A.A.A.E. however recently determined that it had more to lose than to gain by tinkering with its title.) A major national Inquiry into Education and Training reporting in 1979 (the Williams Inquiry), despite the inclusion in its terms of reference of recurrent education, had nothing systematic to say for long- term policy development about this or adult education, although many specific points tucked away in the Report can be picked up by lobbyists keen to advance their cause. A subsequent, not yet completed, National Inquiry into Teacher Education (NITE, the Auchmuty Inquiry) was occasioned by readjustment needs of colleges of education in the CAE sector caused by the present serious oversupply of teachers. It is likely to have something to say relevant to adult education, whether it be about teacher updating only or including also possibly the use of the smaller colleges for other community education purposes.

However, the Education portfolios together account for only a part, perhaps the smaller part, of adult education activity and expenditure. While there is no adult education policy per se, there are important commitments under other names and ministries. Leaving aside the inservice training found in all government departments and agencies (and amount- ing to perhaps $400,000,000 a year in the armed forces at current prices) on the ground that this is internal provision of a management kind rather than a matter of public policy, we may identify two prominent areas where there is a clear political interest and commitment. One is provision of adult education for immigrants under the Department of Immigration and Ethnic Affairs. The budget for English language and similar classes supported by this department, which funds programs through different institutions but makes no direct provision itself, has trebled to over $24,000,000 over the past four years; the recent Galbaly Report on this subject was positively embraced by Government and the area identified for enhanced expenditure at a time when public expenditure generally was being reduced, especially in the social services. The second politically sensitive area where Cabinet has shown direct and close interest is in bridging, orientation, and retraining courses calculated to reduce unemployment. The main commitment, expressed jointly through Employment and Industrial Affairs (DEYA) and Education, is to transition programs for the 15-19 age group. The slightly earlier Educational Program for Unemployed Youth (EPUY) is now being evaluated; going back earlier through the seventies is the National Employment and Training (NEAT) Scheme with assistance for adults to retrain for new kinds of employment. This is also a responsibility of DEYA (formerly the Department of Employment and Industrial Relations). Although interdepartmental cooperation has increased of late, especially with the move of sections of DEYA from Melbourne to Canberra, where Education is located, there is a tendency for training schemes related to employment concerns to be the province of DEYA, and formal education to rest with Education. DEYA itself does not administer courses; all provision is through the states and their educational institutions, which, as so often in Australian political life, means that much energy goes into the sensitive federal-state interface. High youth unemployment--the exact level of which is a source of continuing disagreement but clearly in excess of 20 percent with much higher pockets and approaching 100 percent for instance for Aboriginal youth--has attracted most Cabinet and DEYA attention to this area. However, perceptive individual officers, for instance in Education, are asking what will be the consequences for, and the needs of, other age groups. There has been a significant drop in participation of older workers and of women in the workforce, which incidentally means that unemployment levels are higher than figures indicate; if women and older workers sought reentry those identifiable as unemployed would increase further.

If there emerges any significant policy for adult education it is likely to be in relation to employment. Yet another national inquiry, on the impact of technological change, is due to appear in 1980; it could clearly have implications for adult education related to work and the loss or lack of work; at present the debate about the likely employment and wider societal impact of microprocessing, in particular, is energetic but inconclusive. A National Training Council created at the beginning of the seventies remains weak and of surprisingly little significance, although it has done useful work through specialist committees in relation to training needs for different industry sectors. Despite some proposals to strengthen its role, it remains purely advisory. There is no other body concerned officially with workers' education as such, although clearly this resides with DEYA, which also has responsibility for the Trade Union Training Authority set up by Labor in the early seventies; this operates largely without political interference to provide union education both nationally and within each state. Again, it would be hard to deduce a policy toward union education in the present government, except in the sense that it has allowed the continuation of TUTA with some restrictions of a statutory kind and some contraction of resources. It could be that a manpower type policy for "workers' education" in the broadest sense is emerging, as a subsystem of manpower/employment policy, although scepticism about the possible contribution of adult education to solving structural and systemic economic and employment problems may militate against this.

Other branches of government have provision, and implicit policies, for adult education within their areas of authority. To take one example, the Department of Aboriginal Affairs has a responsibility for overseeing matters relating to the well-being and treatment of Aboriginal peoples, although administration is from the federal Education Department, which has an Aboriginal Scholarship Section. D.A.A. emphasises the importance of Aboriginal adult education of a traditional or spiritual kind, which takes place outside schooling or formal education, and objects to equating adult education with schooling. Its interests embrace community development and the training of Aboriginal primary health care personnel, paralegal officers and community leaders of other kinds. A little money goes directly to national training programs but most of it is disbursed through the states, and both control and statistical data are unsatisfactory from a national policy making and administrative perspective.

Structures and Programs

It is evident that in the particular circumstances of the Australian constitution and tradition, one cannot speak of a policy for adult education, and one cannot with confidence measure the allocation of resources to and participation in adult education in this country. The A.A.A.E. survey of needs and provision conducted in 1978 did no more than gather indicative data, and point out the need for governmental data collecting in this field if sound information was to exist as a basis for policy. In practice this means that while there is no one Australian adult education policy, there are many sectoral policies, a few of them explicit, the majority to be deduced from administrative behaviour rather than found on the statute book. Large numbers of institutions in the post-secondary formal education sector as well as nongovernmental agencies have their own different policies within the broad

framework of what law and finances permit. This laissez-faire
situation is actually enshrined in the advice to government of
bodies like the Universities' Commission from time to time;
the AUC for instance in 1972 recommended that individual
universities should be allowed to provide adult education if
they wished, and to expand it also on a self-financing basis
over whatever was the chosen core, to the extent that entrepreneurial ingenuity might permit.

Given this circumstance, and given the heterogeneity that
is found among states, no simple account of structures and
programs would be accurate; we are again restricted to broad
generalisations and some illustrative examples. It is better
to refer first to structures (insofar as they are not already
clear from the preceding section) rather than to programs,
given that for most adult educators--and their clients--
this latter word connotes the annual provision of a particular
providing agency. A number of information services seek to
provide information about different structures and programs:
the CAE in Victoria and the Board in New South Wales, LINK in
the A.C.T., as well as several more local and nongovernmental
agencies, most prominent of which over the years has been
the Malvern Learning Exchange in Greater Melbourne. Most
promotion and provision, however, is on an agency by agency
basis, sometimes, though certainly not always, in part
competitively.

An attempted overview of structure of provision would
need first to distinguish governmental from nongovernmental or
voluntary provision. Nongovernmental provision includes some
commercial or profit making adult education and training
enterprises. Some of these provide instruction leading to
formal qualifications of a general (e.g., matriculation) or
specific vocational kind (e.g., public service examinations,
examinations for entry to certain bodies). Strictly speaking,
in Australia these would be excluded from adult education
defined as noncredit oriented. In practice most profit making
provisions, for whatever purpose, tend to be looked down upon,
even though fee paying private education at the school level
is a very substantial, albeit somewhat socially divisive,
enterprise. Other profit making adult provision includes
management education of various kinds by bodies like the
Australian Institute of Management as well as management
consultant organisations, and a few exclusively management
training concerns. A distinct category would be the very
large and diverse category of incompany training schemes of
various forms, ranging from on-the-job and in-plant training
to placements in educational institutions, secondments and
sabbaticals. All these are conceived as in some way enhancing
the capacity of the employee for the organisation and at the
organisation's partial or complete expense; of course some
such arrangements may bring business to the profit making

enterprises just mentioned. In Australia long service leave (three months after ten years) is a normal right; some argue that this provision may act as a deterrent to the introduction of paid educational leave schemes for specifically educational purposes. Public sector employees, as well as educational institutions, also have various educational leave arrangements: five hours a week for approved courses for Australian Public Service employees, with some opportunities for full-time study leave on full pay to complete a course of study. The high proportion of very small--and currently economically straitened--businesses in Australia means that for many any kind of adult educational opportunity on the firm's time is a luxury which can no longer be afforded, if indeed it ever could.

Employees, then, may look to various kinds of provision, and--depending on the economic viability, market situation and outlook of the employing organisation--they may obtain some assistance in the form of time off to undertake general, vocational or union education; or they might in their private capacity pursue one or another kind of updating, upgrading or personal development education at a local institution. In this latter capacity, as citizens and individuals rather than as employees, they might look to different forms of governmental provision but also, to return to our first distinction, to various forms of nongovernmental, voluntary, provision. Some of this attracts small subsidies from one or another department of government as clearly educational provision; other agencies may funds for a noneducational purpose and provide courses on the side; still others may be entirely self-supporting, and charge fees to participating adults in courses to meet at least the visible costs. Categorisation becomes difficult in some situations. People practising in the human relations and related therapy and growth areas--including many forms of meditation, Eastern mysticism, acupuncture and so forth--might be defined strictly as nonprofit-making yet may derive an income, or supplementary income, from such work. The amount of such provision is unknown, but is probably very considerable. No account of organisational structures which excluded it would be other than grossly incomplete; yet no attempt to include it could with present data give even an informed guess as to the scale.

More recognisable, and no doubt more acceptable to those nearer the traditional core of adult education, is the provision that borders on the recreational and on entertainment as provided inter alia by the YMCA and the YWCA, the Country Women's Association, sport associations, language societies, ethnic clubs and even general entertainment clubs--large leisure enterprises which in New South Wales generate large revenues from the 'pokies' or 'one-armed bandits' game-of-chance gambling machines. Whereas these last named clubs are only marginally involved in formal adult education in recognisable ways, at the other end of the spectrum are the two surviving W.E.A.s, in New South Wales and South Australia (the former adhering rather more closely to the Mansbridge tradition than the latter); more recently, community or neighbourhood learning centres have sprung up, especially, but not only, in Greater Melbourne. The mission of these centres, as of the W.E.A., is exclusively educational; this takes the form of a significant measure of consciousness-raising among isolated suburban housewives as well as, for example, formally preparing them for matriculation courses to enter university. Some such community and interest-based groups and centres come to attract ad hoc and even regular government funding (state or federal), as do, for example, the W.E.A.s; others remain entirely self-supporting, relying much on voluntary endeavour and on modest fees charged to their students. Whether one employs financial and administrative considerations (profit, nonprofit, subsidised, unsubsidised), sense of mission (social change, educational, recreational), or some other criterion (representatively managed, advancing the interests or expressing the expertise of their management) there is no easy categorisation for the diverse plethora of nongovernmental providers of adult education which has yet been tested, and found acceptance, in Australia.

While there is no common system of government adult education in the different states, the picture is easier to see here than outside the governmental sector. We have noted the distinction between job-oriented and general courses (as well as the distinction between credit and noncredit, which tends to hide from those preoccupied with adult education the increasing access of adults to formal education, and the trend towards "recurrence" in adult learning opportunities). Adults interested in some kind of study may look to a technical and further education college not only for a trade or certificate course at one level or another but also for a (Stream 5) bridging course to transfer from one level to another or, particularly, to acquire the basic qualifications to move into general higher education where these are missing from their school days; or they can take for payment of a fee a (Stream 6) noncredit and intendedly nonvocational course for payment of a fee, which might be in car maintenance, gemstone polishing or, for that matter, in typing. They may also get a short updating course in a field of trade practice if this is taught at the TAFE level, or if it is at the 'higher education' level, seek it instead at a CAE. Both CAEs and most universities offer a sometimes bewildering and usually quite ad hoc range of refresher, diversification and updating short courses, and they may act as agencies for federal or

state government funded programs for special groups, such as
English for immigrants qualified in their own country in
nursing or computing. Continuing education may be subsidised
in part by the institution out of its recurrent funds, or
offered entirely on a fee-for-service self-supporting basis.
It may be centralised within the institution as a single
program, with or without a special purpose central for
continuing education, or handled by those individuals and
departments with an interest in such work. Where there is a
special unit it is likely that the annual program offered will
include at least some kind of general liberal education for
the local community (as distinct from financially viable or
profitable professional refresher courses) and possibly some
special conferences and workshops which reflect a sense of
mission or social purpose and which are at least indirectly
subsidised by the parent institution rather than being
completely self-financing. It might nonetheless be inaccurate
to talk about this as the policy of that university; more
frequently it is a somewhat laissez-faire situation in which a
purposeful unit develops a direction and style of provision
which, so long as no crisis ensues, the institution allows
to continue.

If this seems unsatisfactory as a description of structures and provisions, it accurately reflects the hotch-potch
state of adult education in Australia. We can speak about a
gradually rationalised (as it presently looks) system of
postsecondary education, and recognise various forms and
manifestations of adult education which are tolerated or
encouraged within this, often in the interstices and on the
margins rather than as a result of conscious policy and
direction. We cannot talk about adult education structures as
such, other than in the different segmented areas mentioned in
the previous section.

Similarly we may speak about major programs in certain
sectors, especially English for immigrants (sometimes called
new Australians) and, nowadays, transition and other training
programs especially for unemployed youth. We cannot yet point
to any concerted retraining strategy, nor to any general
refresher or renewal program analogous to the mandatory
CEU-type provision emerging for various professions in
various of the United States, although there are small
signs in this direction in the deliberations of some professional associations. Concern about the level of functional
illiteracy in the adult population may lead to some more
concerted thrust to tackle this problem, largely, if so, as a
subset of policies intended to reduce unemployment through
educational means. It may be that other special groups such
as the elderly, the preretirement, Aborigines, prisoners,
the physically and mentally handicapped, most of whom are
acknowledged as adult education indigents in at least a token

way, will win more support for special purpose adult education programs; but it seems likely that the more effective of these will secure opportunistic resource reallocation through special funding at the level of the individual educational institution rather than any clear new policy or organisational structure. To this extent, provision of adult education in Australia, especially away from areas thought to relate directly to unemployment, is likely to evolve as a product of the skill and opportunism of groups in need and agencies able to respond with acceptable provision, rather than through any clear overarching policy or concept of a system.

ADULT EDUCATION OPPORTUNITIES IN CANADA

Ralph J. Clark and Donald H. Brundage

Department of Adult Education
The Ontario Institute for Studies in Education

General Overview

There exists in Canada a rich and varied tradition of adult education that may be traced to the establishment of the ordre de bon temps at Port Royal (Montreal) in 1604. Early efforts took the form of literary societies, book clubs, and music, art and handicraft associations. Adult education became more predominantly associated in this century with remedial night school programs and the extension activities of universities and government agricultural departments. The promotion of adult education and the inception, in 1935, and subsequent development of the Canadian Association for Adult Education were primarily a product of educators engaged in university and agricultural extension and those in voluntary associations. Many organizations committed to adult education in Canada, among these being the Y.M.-Y.W.C.A., mechanics' and farmers' institutes, and the Workers' Education Association, were influenced by external developments. Others have been distinctly Canadian and have achieved national and international prominence. Included among these are: Frontier College, the Canadian Army's WWI Khaki College, Farm Radio Forum, Citizen's Forum, the National Film Board, and the Banff School of Fine Arts.

When placed in the broad sphere of education, however, Canadian adult education can best be described as having been, by and large, a relatively small undertaking. Despite its contributory and often unique nature, adult education has been poorly funded and seen as peripheral to the formal school system. It remains unrecognized and little understood by many Canadians. Recent publications by Faris, Kidd and Selman, and others signal the beginnings of a more substantial examination of our adult education heritage (Faris, 1975; Kidd and Selman, 1978).

Within the last three decades, a marked growth has occurred in the number and range of courses and programs available to the adult. A shift in emphasis from private to public institutions has been particularly evident. The introduction and establishment of community colleges in the mid-1960's in Ontario, Quebec, Alberta and Saskatchewan accounts for much of the growth in opportunities for adult learning. In the same period, the federal government became involved in a large way with technical and vocational training. Enrollments by adults in the public schools and universities also noticeably increased.

Expenditures on education in Canada during the period 1968 to 1977 underwent an almost fourfold increase (in constant dollars) (Statistics Canada, 1979d). Overall expenditures in the year ending 1977 exceeded $15.2 billion. This accounts for 7 percent of Canada's GNP and represents approximately 17 percent of federal, provincial and municipal government expenditures, second only to the outlay of funds in the field of social welfare. Expenditures vary considerably by province and reflect relative size and economic strength and prosperity.

Information provided in the reports of educational institutions, school boards, ministers' reports, public accounts and the reports of federal government departments and agencies indicates that during the fiscal year 1976-1977, roughly 1.7 million Canadians were involved in continuing education. This compares with the 5.9 million engaged in full time learning at all levels. The participation rate for adults was 118.1 per 1,000 population that same year.

Enrollments in Continuing Education and Participation
Rates per 1,000 Adults in Canada, 1976-1977
(Ibid. pp. 106-107. Table Adapted)

		Enroll-ments	Partic. Per 1,000 Pop.
School Boards	credit	100,005	6.7
Departments of Education	noncredit	539,079	36.2
Correspondence Courses	credit	84,344	5.7
Departments of Education	noncredit	7,162	0.5
Colleges	credit	131,922	8.9
	noncredit	318,231	21.4
Universities	credit	347,369	23.4
	noncredit	226,966	15.3
TOTAL	credit	663,640	44.7
	noncredit	1,097,437	73.4
GRAND TOTAL		1,755,078	118.1

Clearly, a significant segment of the adult population is actively involved in continuing education. At the same time, there is a need for the provision of technical and industrial training, professional and para-professional upgrading, language training and citizenship skills development, and for a greater response to the under-educated, unemployed, older adults, and women (Thomas, 1972). The distinction between participation and potential for participation is evident in the examination of part-time adult learning statistics in Ontario conducted by Waniewicz (1976, pp. 13-14 and 114 ff). The study indicates that nearly 30 percent of the province's adults, aged 18 to 69, were or had recently been involved in some form of systematic learning. Another 18 percent expressed the wish to undertake some type of study in the near future. Cited obstacles to learning included competing work and family responsibilities, cost factors, accessibility problems, and lack of suitable information and counselling services. Such factors were seen as debilitating to the aspirations and interests of adults, particularly those who are disadvantaged.

Programs and policies of adult education in Canada are tempered by demographic and cultural factors and are substantially influenced by political ones. Canada is the second largest country in the world and covers an area of 3.8 million square miles. Its topographical and climatic differences are immense. Its population is small, at 23,742,000. Language of use for approximately 60 percent of Canadians is English; and 27 percent, French. Nine of Canada's ten provinces are predominantly anglophone, with Quebec being largely francophone. Concentrations of French-speaking Canadians reside in Ontario, New Brunswick, Alberta, and Manitoba. Roughly 20 percent of Quebec residents are English-speaking Canadians. A third of all Canadians are neither of British nor French descent, but rather European and, increasingly, Asian, West Indian and South American.

Canada is a federal parliamentary state comprising ten provinces and two territories. While subsidiary to the federal government, the provinces possess a relatively high level of autonomy and are conscious of their constitutional prerogatives. One of these prerogatives of particular relevance is education. Only in the Yukon and Northwest Territories is education a federal preserve. Even here it is administered at the territorial level.

The situation is compounded by the fact that there exists a strong federal presence in education. Directly or indirectly, Ottawa spends approximately $2 billion annually for education in the form of transfer payments for post-secondary and bilingual education, student loans, adult occupational training, programs for native citizens, and a host of other arrangements. This presence is generally tolerated by the provinces, according to an OECD report, "as long as nobody calls it educational policy and as long as there are no overt strings attached to the money coming from Ottawa" (OECD, 1976, p. 90).

As a consequence, there is no one educational system, but rather twelve distinct systems, variably articulated, serving the provinces and the territories as well as federal government activity. A second major consequence is that of the integration of adult education with specific development needs relating to regional disparities, industrial development, poverty, unemployment and bilingual and cultural diversity. A third result is that adult education documentation and research tends to be uncoordinated and piecemeal. Documentation in one of the country's official languages is not always to be found in the other. With the exception of a survey conducted under the direction of Sandiford (1935), a detailed and systematic national examination of adult education in Canada has never been undertaken.

Mechanisms for the exchange of information among the provincial authorities responsible for adult education are not well developed. Linking mechanisms such as the Canadian Education Association and the Council of Ministers of Education provide for liaison among educational authorities and for the consideration of policy coordination, yet have only been peripherally concerned with adult education. The Canadian Association for Adult Education (CAAE), its franco-phone counterpart, the Institut Canadien d'Education des Adultes (ICEA), and provincial continuing education associations have been active in the promotion of issues in the field of adult education as well as serving as vehicles for the exchange of information, yet lack the necessary resources.

The overriding feature of Canadian adult education is its diffuseness. There does not exist, in Canada as a whole, a coherent articulated system of adult education. It can best be described as complex, highly decentralized, variably funded, and largely invisible. The system is characterized within each province by a further stage of decentralization to municipal, regional school board, college, university, and volunteer organization jurisdictions. A White Paper by the CAAE (1964) provided the following comments:

> In spite of improvements, it remains a patchwork of courses, schools, programs and systems: a confusing jumble of opportunities, upon which too many adults have to stumble if they discover it at all; an oppor-tunistic, short-term, sporadic enterprise exploited by the nation in time of crisis and left to private and desperate chance when the emergency is past.

A less harsh yet similar view has been expressed in two more recent studies. In a document prepared in 1972 by the Canadian Commission for Unesco, Canadian adult education was described as being a diffusion of geographic and operational responsibilities with little universal agreement on social and political objectives (Canadian Commission for UNESCO, 1977, p. 3 ff). The review of national education policies in Canada conducted by the OECD (1976, pp. 19-21) gave recognition to the vast array of adult education programs and their success in attracting adults, yet commented with respect to education policy:

> There is no clearly-formulated concept of education policy set in the context of a comprehensive frame-work of general social policies. Reforms in education are almost totally pragmatic...(and are) derived from no explicitly-stated overall conceptions of the country's interest.

The delineation of adult education policies is made difficult by the fact that they are rarely rooted in legislation, but rather are in the form of ministerial directives and pragmatic and often shifting, policy statements. Jurisdiction for adult education may be delegated, as is generally the case with school boards and postsecondary institutions. Adult education is not viewed solely as the prerogative of education ministries. Programs having implications for adults are found in numerous ministries concerned with health, community and social services, labor, recreation and culture, and the like.

The sub-populations of workers, older adults, women entering the labor force, parents, and the undereducated are not always designated as specific targets of national or provincial level policies. Programs and information on programs affecting women, older adults, and parents, are woefully inadequate. Nevertheless, federal involvement and recent developments at the provincial level have implications directly or indirectly for these populations.

Major Developments in the Provinces

Administrative structures for adult education vary considerably and are less well-defined in the Maritime provinces of Newfoundland, Nova Scotia, New Brunswick, and Prince Edward Island. In Ontario, a Senior and Continuing Education Branch of the Ministry of Education was created in 1979 and currently is developing a policy statement. The most prominent development has occurred in Quebec and in the western provinces of British Columbia, Alberta, and Saskatchewan.

In Alberta, a process of policy development was spurred by the Report of the Alberta Commission on Educational Planning, entitled A Choice of Futures (1972). Among other matters, the report advocated the development of a system of lifelong learning in the province. A distinct approach to adult education was introduced in April 1975, with the implementation of a further education policy on the basis of the document Further Education: Policy, Guideline and Procedures by the Department of Advanced Education and Manpower. The policy views further education as "planned educational experience designed to be integrated on a part-time basis into the ongoing life-style of adults as part of a system of recurrent education" (Province of Alberta, 1975). It gives recognition to the variety of agencies, institutions and government departments which play a role in adult education.

The policy introduced guidelines for the formation of Local Further Education Councils (LFEC) and a granting system in support of non-credit courses. LFEC members are generally, but not exclusively, representatives of various agencies and organizations within a region. Regions are defined in terms of city, county or school division boundaries. The purpose of the LFEC is to mobilize resources in a comprehensive and coordinated way and to localize initiative for adult learning. The LFEC coordinates non-credit further education on an interagency basis.

Grants are made available to members of an LFEC sponsoring courses. The locus of programs (local Hosting Authorities) is generally public and private agencies, educational institutions, and organizations such as the Y.M.-Y.W.C.A., Agricultural Societies, Arts Councils and Women's Institutes. To be eligible for grants, LFEC proposals must meet a number of criteria. Courses must be planned teacher-learner situations, be in excess of 100 hours, involve eight or more adults, and be nonprofit. Grants are made available on the basis of instructional hours and are scaled such that funding is greater in courses involving community problems, citizenship courses, adult basic and literacy education, and English and French as a Second Language.

The need still exists in Alberta's Further Education Policy for more highly trained field staff, increased grant expenditures, a greater manpower training dimension and a student finance system (Falkenberg, 1976). Grant support for elderly adults is presently provided, and a system of bursaries covering tuition fees, supplies, travel and baby-sitting services to a maximum of $300 for part-time noncredit learners is now being considered.

Participation in further education courses offered by hosting authorities has increased steadily since 1971-72.

Further Education Participation Statistics
1971-72 to Dec. 31, 1978
(Alberta Department of Advanced Education)

Year	School Authorities	Courses	Participants
1971-72	24	1,300	14,000
1972-73	40	2,200	28,200
1973-74	74	5,400	76,000

	Hosting Authorities/ Public and Private Agencies	Courses	Participants
1975-76	120	9,700	148,000
1976-77	107	12,000	165,600

	Hosting Authorities	Courses	Participants
1977-78	106	12,500	180,400
	111	13,427	200,396

The most noteworthy development in Saskatchewan adult education has been the establishment by the Department of Continuing Education of a regional college system which now numbers fifteen institutions. Enabling legislation passed in 1973 preceded the introduction of the system by one year. The distinct feature of Saskatchewan's college system is the absence of permanent campuses and faculty. The colleges are essentially administrative and coordinating organizations utilizing existing facilities and relying heavily on volunteer advisory committees (600 of them) in the province. College boards, which are the regional policy makers, receive a global grant and, within broad policy guidelines on tuition recovery and program/administration ratios, allocate approximately $500,000 per region annually.

The formally stated purpose of the colleges is "the maximization of opportunities for continuing education through a decentralization of formal adult learning opportunities and the organization of programs at a community and regional level to meet informal learning needs," and that "colleges be developed on a regional basis with priority in development

given to rural areas" (Kutarna, 1972).   Specific mandate
areas include adult upgrading, general educational development
(GED), Canada Manpower and Non-Registered Indian and Metis
(NRIM) programs, general interest courses, and university
and technical institute courses.   The colleges serve in a
brokerage capacity for the latter.   In 1978, 96,538 adults
registered in 6,756 college programs with a participation
rate of 14.2 percent.

College Enrollments in Saskatchewan by Percentage,
1977-78 (Kutarna, 1972)

	Percent
Adult basic education	3.3
Adult secondary education	5.1
Employment training	6.1
Agriculture - farm related	4.0
Institute-related certificate	0.5
University credit	2.1
Fine arts and crafts	19.0
Physical development	12.2
Home skills related	31.1
Personal development	11.8
Family-community related	4.9

100.0   (96,538)

Educational leadership in needs identification, the
rationalization of overall objectives, and project evaluation
have been singled out as areas yet to be substantially
addressed (Sissons, 1977).   New initiatives may be expected
in the areas of technical and vocational training and the
possible introduction of campus models as a counterpart
to the present system.

Since 1976, the Ministry of Education in British Columbia
has undertaken an extensive review of educational policies and
practices in adult education.   The most influential of these
has been the 1976 Report of the Committee on Continuing and
Community Education (Faris Report) (Province of British
Columbia, 1976).   The Report advocated that the concept of
lifelong learning be adopted as basic to the planning of the
total educational system in the province.   The Committee
recommended that adult education legislation emphasize:
a more systematic and localized provision of services,
a greater emphasis on the process of adult learning and
the development of skills to enhance it, increased public
participation in decision making, the maximization of existing

resources through the increased cooperation of institutions and agencies providing adult education, and sufficient decentralization of resources to ensure greater equality of access. Populations designated as high priority groups were the handicapped, older adults, women, and immigrants. Areas in need of development included adult basic education, career information and educational counselling, and English as a Second Language.

As a consequence of the Report's recommendations, there has ensued a series of programs, investigations, discussion papers and policy proposals. The Report of the Committee on Adult Basic Education (January 1979) cited adult basic education as an area of neglect and low priority at all levels (Province of British Columbia, 1979a). It provided 46 recommendations, principal among these being the need for a provincial directorate responsible for communications, material development and distribution, data collection, in-service training, program evaluation and funding procedures. The Advisory Committee on English as a Second Language for Adults (February 1979) recommended a five year plan for the systematic improvement by institutions of ESL services, improved funding, development of outreach programs, and formulation of a central resource center for curriculum development and staff training (Province of British Columbia, 1979b). The Report on Non-Traditional Learning Programs for Women at B.C. Post-Secondary Institutions (February 1979) advocated the development of provincial coordination with adequate funding, support for Women's Access Programs, comprehensive needs assessment, and systematic review of institutional policies and practices (Province of British Columbia, 1979c).

Continuing education at the community level has received considerable attention. A Continuing Education Pilot System introduced in 1977 provides grants for each school district and college. Since its inception, 143 projects have been funded, involving as participants and recipients over 150,000 people. Projects have entailed seniors' continuing education projects, life skills, volunteer trainings, curriculum development, and family education. A review of the system indicated access was a problem for those unable to pay, that procedures for consultation and follow-up were in need of clarification, and that funding ($500,000 in 1978-79) was insufficient to adequately seed projects. At the same time, the system was viewed as an excellent means of promoting innovative and valuable projects, successful in allocating funds for developmental projects at a low cost and by a rational system, and supported by college and school board administrators (Province of British Columbia, 1978).

Public educational institutions play a major role in the provision of adult education in the province. Continuing education enrollments in schools, universities, colleges and technical institutes totalled 319,940 in 17,121 courses in 1976-77 (Province of British Columbia, 1976-77). The recently introduced Draft Policy on the Provision of Community Education and General Interest Education (January 1980) and the Draft Policy on the Provision of Continuing Education together indicate the extensive role and potential of public educational institutions in continuing education (Province of British Columbia, Nov. 1979d). Specific areas of responsibility for adult basic education, community education, general interest education, academic and technical education have been accorded to colleges, school boards, universities and technical institutes in a comprehensive and coordinated fashion. Support in the form of policy development, advocacy, coordination and liaison, provincial needs assessment, program planning and development, financial allocation and system-wide monitoring will be provided by the Division of Continuing Education, supported by a Ministry Advisory Committee on Adult and Continuing Education.

A delivery system for the provision of distance education has been introduced. Prominent distance learning programs in Canada are provided by Newfoundland's Memorial University, Quebec's Tele-universite, Alberta's Athabasca University, and through television and radio broadcasting under the auspices of educational authorities such as ACCESS (Alberta) and OECA (TV Ontario). The distinguishing characteristic in British Columbia is its comprehensiveness and potential. The province's fourteen community colleges serve as a primary vehicle for the delivery of distance education courses. The most active of these has been North Island College which operates out of limited traditional facilities and has a network of college centers with mobile classrooms and tutors, and a system of drop-off centers providing reference material. Television, telephone, video-tape, audio-tape, print material, simulation, and satellite have been used for program delivery by Okanagan, Northern Lights and East Kootenay, as well as other colleges (Province of British Columbia, March 1978). The Open Learning Institute officially began in September of 1979 (Shore, 1980). Its admission procedures are modelled after those of the British Open University. Seven pilot courses have been introduced, incorporating three university-level courses and a full grade ten completion program. Ultimately, course offerings will include vocational and pre-vocational programs, university degrees, secondary school completion and basic literacy studies.

Quebec's system of adult education is the most comprehensive in the country. Influenced by two commissions of inquiry--one into adult education (Ryan Commission) in 1964 and another into education (Parent Commission) in 1966--the government created la Direction generale de l'education des adultes (DGEA) within the Ministry of Education in 1966, and introduced a new organizational structure. An inquiry into the province's adult education needs and resources (Operation depart) and research on a theoretical model of education permanente (Operation depart Montreal) led to the establishment of a new system of adult education jurisdiction (Ministere de l'Education, 1970). The system is based on regional school boards (CS) and delimits nine regions within which are fifty-six territorial divisions.

In 1972, a new service program, SEAPAC (services educatifs d'aide personnelle et d'animation communautaire), was introduced to facilitate adult learning in the regions. The technical resources of the school boards and the use of animators (animateur-formateur et animateur-consultant) are the principal support forms. The form of SEAPAC in each region is determined through the collaboration of local groups with the Direction's services de l'education des adults (SEA).

Underlying SEAPAC's educational approach is a heavy reliance on adult participation in decision-making and the use of media resources. Prior to its introduction, a series of experimental projects were initiated by the Direction. SESAME (Sessions d'enseignement specialise aux adults par le ministre de l'Education) was an experiment in adult learning methodology and the training of adult educators (Lachine, 1974). TEVEC, a multi-media regional development project in the Saguenay-Lac Saint John region involved 32,000 participants in adult basic education projects and in selected sociocultural theme courses broadcast by television (Lallez, 1973). Another 60,000 viewers were attracted to various broadcasts. TEVEC served as the basis of Multi-Media, a third major program (Gouvernement du Quebec, 1978). In operation between 1972 and 1978, Multi-Media was a strategy for the development of human resources using a wide range of instructional methods and modes of intervention, based on mass media and social and educational animators. Various projects involved 25,000 adults in specific courses, a viewership of 134,000 for weekly broadcasts, and up to 35,000 subscribers to an educational publication series.

A multi-media approach remains a dominant theme of adult education in Quebec. Recent legislation is likely to increase the use of radio and television broadcasting in the province. An act passed in June 1979 specified the establishment by Radio Quebec of a provincial educational broadcasting firm, responsive in content to regional committees (Assemblee Nationale du Quebec, Juin 22, 1979). A second act followed in November authorizing financial and technical support for firms broadcasting educational programs. Educational broadcasting is defined in the act as "programming that must favor the exercise by citizens of their right to education, promote their access to their cultural heritage, promote their access to economic and social well-being, or favor the exercise of their right to information" (Assemblee National du Quebec, Novembre 27, 1979).

The Direction generale de l'education des adultes (DGEA) is reponsible for two major educational areas. The first is in workers' education and training (formation du travailleur). Most programming, which takes the form of retraining, up-grading, certification, reentry to the labor force, and general education, is found within the framework of federal schemes. The second rests on the principle of self-directed learning (autoformation) and relies heavily on media based guidelines formulated from the experiences found through TEVEC, SESAME, and Multi-Media. Referred to as citizenship development (formation du citoyen) its purpose is to:

> Vise a rendre les membres de la societe concients des problemes qui se posent dans leurs relations entre eux et dans leur milieu, presents et participant aux prises de decisions qui les concernent, ouverts et responsables face a la prise en charge de leur devenir collectif (Gouvernement du Quebec, 1978b).

Under the umbrella of citizenship development are programs within the school boards, unions, voluntary associations, and colleges. Additional support is provided to the boards in the form of financial and technical assistance (l'animation communautaire et le support a l'action communautaire) for community development projects. In 1979, 48 such projects were funded involving 417 groups and 7,142 adults. The DGEA also provides direct subsidies to voluntary associations (l'aide populaire dans les organismes volontaires d'education populaire OVEP). Six hundred projects with 350 organizations were funded that same year (Ministere de l'Education, 1979). Close to 90 percent of OVEP projects in 1976-77 entailed programs on the family and animation and human relations (Gouvernement du Quebec, 1978a).

Despite developments in Quebec, a number of concerns need to be addressed. The Conseil superieur de l'education reported in 1979 the need to better integrate general and professional education, to resolve the conflict in jurisdiction between education and training, to clarify socio-cultural education and community animation in the school boards, and to attend to the tension between autonomous organizations and adult education services (Gouvernement du Quebec, 1979c). Despite past programs such as SESAME, Multi-Media, and programs in Point-St-Charles, Youville a Beaubarnois, and other locations, adult basic and literacy education has not been adequately addressed, according to Hautecoeur (1978).

In 1978 the government stated its intention to elaborate
a more comprehensive policy on adult education. This has been
underway and is still evolving. Its immediate effect will
be to increase, by 6 percent, funding (now at $124 million)
for general and sociocultural education in 1980-81. Women
(particularly in areas of non-traditional occupations training), cultural development, language training, energy use, and
disadvantaged adults (undereducated, handicapped, native
people) will receive increased attention (Ministere de
l'Education, 1979).

Despite developments at the provincial level, policies
and programs respecting the undereducated, older adults,
workers, women entering the labor force, and parents, are less
than extensive or comprehensive. Except for federal policies
and programs dealing with technical and vocational education,
women entering the labor force, and the undereducated,
together with some provincial input, programs in these areas
remain outside government jurisdiction, are generally not
subject to coordinated effort, and have not been systematically evaluated.

Part-time enrollment in 1978-79 totalled 460,204 with
another 39,375 full time. A specific breakdown is given
below:

Education des adultes, Clienteles, 1978-79 et 1979-80
(Ministere de l'Education, 1979b, p. 94)

Formation a temps plein	1978-79	1979-80*
Formation general	12,988	12,933
Formation professionnelle	26,387	28,372
TOTAL	39,375	41,305
Inscriptions a temps partiel		
Formation general	100,885	113,945
Formation socio-culturelle et animation communautaire	276,770	313,613
Formation professionnelle	70,196	85,802
Formation en industrie et petites et moyennes enterprises	12,353	13,410
TOTAL	460,204	526,770

*Forecast

Programs for Workers

There are serious inadequacies in Canada's system of education and training. The report to the federal Department of Labour by the Commission of Inquiry on Educational Leave and Productivity (Adams Commission) in June 1979, indicates that most training in industry is shortterm, job specific, available to a minority of employees only, and that few reasonable alternatives to postsecondary education exist for those in search of vocational training (Report of the Commission of Inquiry on Paid Educational Leave and Productivity, 1979). Apprenticeship training, the principal form of general vocational training provided by employers, is underdeveloped and the availability of systematic industry-based training for vocational competence in skilled jobs other than apprenticeships tends to be the exception. According to the report, the acquisition of technical qualifications for working people by means of a combination of practical experience and inclass instruction is, in fact, becoming increasingly more difficult. For instance, only 5 percent of the 16 to 24 year-olds in the labor force were registered apprentices in the fiscal year, yet application/position ratios are often 20 to 30 to 1.

A number of factors account for the lack of long-term training by employers. Included among them are: the fear on the part of employers, particularly those with limited funds, of providing mobile skills; the encouragement of youth to remain in school because of high unemployment rates; and educational policies that foster dependence. In addition, there is no single agency to advise prospective industrial trainers, with the exception of the Ontario Training in Business and Industry (TIBI) program and the federal government's Canada Manpower Training programs (CMTP). In a report submitted to the Canada Employment and Immigration Comission in 1978, 92.5 percent of companies surveyed knew about available government grants yet did not utilize these because of a preference for selecting their own trainers, the desire for designing their own training programs, the high administrative costs in dealing with Manpower and/or the inability of Manpower officials to fully comprehend the company's problems (Robertson, Nickerson, Group Associates, 1972).

An Adams Commission survey indicates that only between 27 percent and 32 percent of the enterprises responding to a questionnaire had a plan or policy on training and development during working hours (Report of the Commission of Inquiry on Paid Leave, p. 144). Since large organizations were much more likely to undertake training, 68 percent of all employees in the sample worked for an organization with a training plan. With respect to employment distribution, 99 percent of covered employees worked in an establishment allowing time off for job-related training, 25 percent for labor studies, and 40 percent for general and social education. Although the vast majority of employees work for organizations with a training plan, only 15.1 percent were reported as having received training in 1978.

All provinces have manpower training policies which generally rely on institutional training. Major programs of continuing education in the workplace have been provided by the federal government and by the Ontario government.

Federal programs in the field of technical and vocational training are sponsored by the Canada Employment and Immigration Commission (CEIC). Federally-funded training programs have been directed towards the continuing education of workers and the undereducated. Significant federal involvement in this area dates from the passage of the Technical and Vocational Training Assistance Act (TA) in 1960. Giving impetus to the establishment of the act was an economic recession in Canada in the late 1950's and early 1960's, and an increased public awareness of poverty, undereducation and unemployment. The act was superseded in 1967 by the Adult Occupational Training Act (AOTA) which is the current enabling legislation. The AOT Act authorizes training to increase earning capacity or opportunities for employment through the provision of skills needed for the labor force. Programs sponsored by the act have also been expected to serve other purposes as well--maximizing employment, reducing inter-regional and interpersonal income disparities, reducing unemployment by withdrawing workers from the labor force, and meeting the demands for income supplementation and social development for various groups (Employment and Immigration Canada, 1977).

Training under the AOT Act is provided either in industrial settings (Canada Manpower Industrial Training Program) or in institutions (Canada Manpower Training Program). Under the institutional training provisions, arrangements are made with the provinces for the purchase of training provided by the community colleges, technical institutes, trade schools and vocational centers. The plan provides funding for provincially registered apprentices who are required to attend educational institution training classes for up to twelve weeks annually. An Occupational Skill Training component is also incorporated within institutional training. This generally entails classroom learning and encompasses some 800 different courses involving skill acquisition at the subprofessional level. Three additional components: Basic Training for Skill Development, Basic Job Readiness Training, and Work Adjustment Training, are more directly concerned with the undereducated.

Under the Vocational Rehabilitation for Disabled Persons Act (VRDP), the federal government also provides 50 percent of the costs incurred by the provinces in undertaking training programs for the disabled (Statistics Canada, 1979e). Federal responsibility has been borne by the Department of National Health and Welfare under the Canada Assistance Plan scheme since 1973. Participants in the program in 1976-77 totalled 7,054.

In the industrial training programs (CMITP), funds are provided in support of employer-centered training. Courses may be part-time, of short duration, or up to one year in length. The industrial training program is intended as a cost-sharing arrangement with employers. Costs of such items as administration, production materials used in training, and fringe benefits are the responsibility of the employer. The federal government assumes the full cost of instructors' salaries, travelling and living expenses (where applicable), training aids, and the rental of premises and equipment. When all or a portion of the training is provided by an outside institution, the program also provides for a reimbursement of course fees to a maximum of 75 percent and of trainee travelling and living of up to 50 percent. The industrial training program was introduced in 1974 and replaced a number of previous programs. It provides consultative and financial assistance for employers initiating training or expanding training capacity. The objectives of the program are:

(1)   To fill positions for which skilled qualified workers are not available;

(2)   To retain employees who might otherwise be laid off because of technological or economic changes;

(3)   To participate in the support of industrial development strategies in various regions of the country;

(4)   To fill new job vacancies that have resulted from the expansion of company operations; and

(5)   To provide jobs and training for people who find it especially difficult to obtain and hold permanent employment (i.e., "special needs" workers) (Employment and Immigration Canada, Appendix A, pp. 3-4).

Between 1967 and 1977, annual expenditures in purchasing and subsidizing training and in paying training allowances averaged $500 million. Total participant numbers averaged roughly 250,000 yearly. Expenditures have increased slightly and totalled over $600 million in the 1978-79 fiscal year. Full-time and part-time trainees totalled 286,494. Information on enrollments and expenditures are given in the tables on the next page.

Canada Manpower Training Program, Trainee Starts, 1978-79
(Employment and Training Canada, 1979)

	Number of Trainees
Full Time Public and Private Institutions	
Skill Training	65,024
Language Training	5,720
BTSD	31,364
Job Readiness Training	7,094
Work Adjustment Training	1,537
Apprenticeship Training	51,417
Total Full Time Training	162,156
Part-Time Institutional Training	45,402
Total Institutional Training	207,558
Industrial Training	78,936
TOTAL	286,494

Canada Manpower Training Program, Institutional and
Industrial Expenditures, 1978-79
(Employment and Training Canada, 1979, table adapted)

	Expenditures
Institutional Training	
Purchases	$331,697,455
Allowances	116,993,377
Unemployment Insurance	102,668,073
Total	551,358,905
Industrial Training	83,697,475
Training Improvement Costs	2,294,198
TOTAL	$637,350,578

The evaluation of training outcomes is made extremely difficult due to the complexity of the program (Duquet and Field, 1976). Follow-up of 1973/74 graduates, for example, indicates that the overall employment rate for the skill component of institutional training was 76 percent, with two-thirds of the employed working in a training related occupation. Employment rates were 36 percent for language training. In the industrial training component, 79 percent of the trainees were employed after training, with increases of 35 percent—twice the increase of averages in the country. At a national conference on adult occupational training held in 1976, Gunderson, in describing the program, concluded:

> Many individuals have been raised out of poverty by Canada Manpower Training; however, the effectiveness of training remains an open question. It appears that the disadvantaged receive substantial wage gains from training and yet higher costs of perhaps less lengthy benefit periods imply low benefit-cost ratios. This appears to be especially the case for preparatory training (Gunders, 1976).

In examining manpower training in Canada, conference delegates pointed to: the need to integrate the process of manpower training more thoroughly into the overall education system in Canada; the need for more congruity between adult occupational training and the rest of adult education; the need for an overall perspective, not just planning in the context of purely economic criteria; and the need for more comprehensive (polyvalent) curriculum in the content of training in order to respond to both immediate training needs and the social context of the worker and the work place (Canadian Association For Adult Education, 1977).

A program entitled Training in Business and Industry (TIBI), comparable yet distinct from the CMITP, has been introduced by the Ontario government under the aegis of the Ministry of Colleges and Universities. The focus of the program is skills upgrading for employed adults below the supervisory level. TIBI courses tend to be of shorter duration than CMITP courses. Most are less than fifty hours. The range of courses is a broad one and includes training in the use of technical equipment, sales, human relations management, problem solving, family workshops, supervision fundamentals, and personal fitness programs. Over one-half of the participants in 1977-78 undertook training in four occupational categories—merchandising and sales (22.2 percent), medical and dental services (15.6 percent), management (8.1 percent), and transportation and communications (7.7 percent). Almost 85 percent of the training conducted is on company premises. A network of 22 community colleges serves as the program delivery vehicle. The province funds one-third of the training costs, the largest expenditure being the salaries of teachers. Generally these are college instructors, although company officials also serve in this capacity. The remainder of the costs is borne by the individual companies. In the 1977-78 fiscal year, 85,283 adults were involved in various TIBI courses. This program has been cited by college staff for the wide range of courses offered and an excellent cost-benefit ratio.

There are a number of creative schemes in the public and private sectors designed to improve the acccessibility to educational opportunities for working people (Statistics Canada, 1973c). Space limitations allow only a few to be highlighted.

The Saskatchewan Government Administrative Development Program

The plan qualifies clerical personnel (largely women) to move into managerial and administrative positions through the provision of courses in economics, sociology, administration, accounting, writing and government at the University of Regina, the University of Saskatchewan, and La Ronge Community College. Courses are offered one or two afternoons each week and time off with pay is provided. The program generally takes two and one-half years but may be completed in a shorter period by taking evening classes. Total enrollment is about 50, and 40 percent of the first two years' enrollees have received promotions.

Technical Training at Moffat

A system of certification in different technical areas has been introduced. The number of specializations and certifications varies according to employer skill levels. Ten specializations exist for technicians and six for supervisory personnel. Courses average five weeks in length, but may take from four weeks to six months depending on individual skill level. Bonuses of $5 or $6 per specialization per month are provided. Many employees train on their own time, and the union has agreed to waive the collective agreement on overtime to hasten the process leading to obtaining bonuses. The program has been cited as of potential value to industries and companies that incur slack periods during the year.

The Union Education Program of the United Auto Workers

This is a block release program for local union leaders involving five periods of four days' instruction combined with two weeks of home study. Employer payments of one cent per hour per employee into a union-controlled fund provides for the program. Subject areas taught include introduction to learning, economics for trade unionists, communications, collective bargaining, and human, social, and economic problems such as health and safety, and human rights legislation. The locus of the program is the U.A.W. education center at Port Elgin, Ontario. In the first year, 93 union members participated in the program.

The Petroleum Industry Training Service (P.I.T.S.)

P.I.T.S. is an independent multi-employer training program offering courses in technical skills. Advice is provided by committees representing various sectors of the petroleum industry. Courses may be contracted to consulting firms or educational institutions or given on site, using educators, consultants and industry experts. Employers designate trainees and in most cases provide for expenses including salaries. Total enrollment is between 6,000 and 7,000 annually.

With respect to labor education, much of the initiative is provided by the approximately 130 labor councils in Canada and the country's largest central labor body, the 2.3 million member Canadian Labour Congress (CLC). Historically, the labor movement has initiated, planned and financed its own programs (Adams Commission, 1979). Most union education is concerned with steward's or grievance training, local union administration, labor and social legislation, and collective bargaining. Major forms of labor education provision are weekend institutes, evening courses, and one-week schools. Since 1963, the Labour College of Canada has provided both residential and correspondence courses in trade unionism, economics, political science, sociology and other disciplines. Labor studies programs are now available at Ontario's Niagara and Humber Colleges of Applied Arts and Technology, and at McMaster University, the University of British Columbia, Simon Fraser University, the University of Quebec at Montreal, and St. Francis Xavier University's Atlantic Region Labour Education Centre.

Accessibility to union education varies considerably. Verner and Dickenson reported in 1974 that education and

information services provided to members tended to increase as
the size of the union increased (Hepworth, 1979). Resources
to mount systematic educational programs were generally
available only in the larger (industrial) unions. In
69 percent of the local unions there proved to be no person
assigned a specific responsibility for education. This was
the case in three-fourths of the unions not affiliated with
the CLC or Quebec's Confederation of National Trade Unions
(CNTU). Of 118 national and international unions affiliated
with the CLC, only 18 had a recognized education department.
In addition, the Adams Commission found that relatively few
employees covered by collective bargaining agreements worked
in enterprises allowing either short-term or extended leave
for union studies.

Availability of Leave for Union Studies
(Verner and Dickenson, 1974)

	A	B	C	
	No. of Estabs. with Plan	Labour Force in Estabs. with Plan	Number of Employees Covered by Collective Agreements	Percent Covered by leave Arrangements (B as % of C)
Extended Leave				
Exec., prof., managerial	171	64,837	108,107	60.0
Office	164	124,576	312,886	39.8
Non-office	167	174,170	1,032,960	16.9
All		363,583	1,453,953	25.0
Short Term Leave				
Exec., prof., managerial	227	69,482	108,107	64.3
Office	206	139,768	312,886	44.7
Non-office	358	235,979	1,032,960	22.8
All		444,229	1,453,953	30.6

Since the adoption of the ILO convention 140 by the CLC in 1976, paid educational leave has assumed a higher priority by unions in Canada. The United Auto Workers has arranged 116 collective agreements providing leave for union training. Particularly active also, have been the United Steelworkers of America, the Canadian Paperworkers' Union and the Canadian Union of Public Employees. Labor education possibilities have also been enhanced by an agreement beween the federal Department of Labour and the CLC in 1977. Since then, the Labour Department has provided a grant for the promotion of labor studies. The grant covers a five-year period with $2 million allotted annually to the CLC and another $600,000 yearly to labor groups not affiliated with the Congress. Both of these actions should have beneficial results for labor education in Canada, although the extent of these gains remains to be seen.

Programs for Older Adults

While educational opportunities and policies for working Canadians have been the subject of recent studies, this is not the case for older adults. Most research in gerontology is directed towards areas other than education. Sufficient research to guide policy is lacking. Communications among educators and others who work with older people have been described as little·more than chance and haphazard (Adams Commission, 1979, p. 128). With the exception of studies by Waniewicz (1976), Falee and Nusyna (1975), Vigoda and Ellis (1979), and the Third Career Research Society (1976), little research has been directed toward the education of older adults (Riddell, 1978).

The general finding of these studies is that interest is highest in instrumental areas such as financial management, legal issues, health care, and consumer-related studies, and that much of the learning that occurs takes place in public buildings whose principal function is not educational. A study for the Alberta government by the Third Career Research Society found that 66 percent of the respondents wished to participate in continuing education programs. Interest declines considerably among urban retirees (20 percent) and is less among rural retirees (Waniewicz, 1976; Fales and Nusyna, 1975). A recent survey of 1078 Ontario men, aged 63, by Vigoda and Ellis (1979), found that 23 percent were engaged in some form of learning during the previous twelve months. Subject areas were reported as shown in the following table.

Distribution of Subject Areas Reported by
Educational Participants According to Sponsoring
Institutions, 1979

(Third Career Research Society 1979)

Subject Areas	Total Reported		Nonformal Institutions		Formal Institutions	
	No.	%	No.	%	No.	%
Job-Oriented	141	47.5	115	48.5	26	41.9
Hobby-Recreational	63	21.0	50	21.1	13	21.0
Personal Development	34	11.4	21	8.9	13	21.0
Religious Studies	25	8.4	25	10.5	0	0
Public Affairs	17	5.7	16	6.8	1	1.6
Academic Subjects	14	4.7	6	2.5	8	12.9
Home and Family	5	1.7	4	1.7	1	1.6
TOTAL	229	100.0%	237	100.0%	62	100.0%

Leadership in Learning Opportunities for Older People
(LLOOP), a volunteer organization of adult education faculty
and graduate students at the Ontario Institute for Studies in
Education, as well as others in the field, represents the sole
organization in Canada that has, as its primary concern, the
continuing education of older adults and the provision of
support to practitioners in the field. Within the last two
years LLOOP has begun a process of network development,
research, information exchange, and leadership training.
Recent actions include a workshop on "Counselling the Older
Adult," the development of a training kit on Interpersonal
Skills for Involvement with Seniors (ISIS) and a preliminary
survey of preretirement courses available in Ontario.

Even an adequate portrayal of programs for older adults
is next to impossible due to the paucity of data. In an
Issue Paper forwarded to the Canadian Association for Adult
Education in September 1979, LLOOP described the response
to the learning of older adults in Canada as "inequitable,"
with no effort towards a Canada-wide or even regional inter-
institutional cooperative attempt to redress the situation
(Vigoda and Ellis, 1979). In an October 1979 meeting to
discuss "the state of the art" sponsored by the CAAE, a common
conclusion reached was that:

There appears to be no data base to determine who
the potential learners are; adult education seems to
still reach those who appear to need it least. There

is no clearinghouse for information about what courses are offered, and how they are developed. It was perceived that there is a need for consciousness-raising among the educational leadership, to learn about normal aging and how to be better facilitators (for learners of all ages). There is a lack of a range of opportunities for learners of all ages across Canada, and especially there is almost no opportunity for inter-generational experiences. It was observed that physical accessibility is a problem as a result of poor transportation and the isolation of many educational facilities. It was generally accepted that there was a lack of recognition of the needs of the older adult (Newsletter, IQRT, 1980).

Notable activities or developments might include the actions of two Toronto-based organizations, the AGORA Foundation and the Third Age Learning Associates (TALA). Both organizations are operated by seniors and provide educational counselling and seminars and workshops for older adults. A weekly CBC Toronto television program From Now On has received critical acclaim. It offers programs for older adults on such matters as fitness, money management, meal planning and nutrition, medical information, legal advice, gardening techniques, and coping with widowhood and divorce. More than twenty stations in the country now rebroadcast it. In November 1979, an Office on Aging opened at McMaster University. The purpose of the Office is to coordinate on a multidisciplinary and multifaculty basis research on the elderly and on the education of adults.

Many government agencies are directly and indirectly involved with older citizens, yet coherent policies in gerontology and educational gerontology do not exist. Papers presented at a National Symposium on Aging in 1978 evidenced the need for the systematic planning and coordination of programs and services at all levels (Ibid., p. 29). The reformation of provincial adult education policies should result in increased attention to the older adult. Establishment of senior citizens' advisory committees in a number of provinces should also aid the formation of government policies. Statistics Canada projections of 2.3 million Canadians aged 65 and over by 1981 and between 3.3 and 4 million by the year 2001 point to the urgency for policy development in this area.

Programs for Women Entering the Labor Force

Women constitute 51 percent of Canada's population. The number of women participating in the labor force has increased from 33.6 in 1966 to 45.9 in 1977 (Ontario Ministry of Community and Social Services, 1978). Participation rates vary in the provinces from a high of 50.3 percent in Alberta to 32.0 percent in Newfoundland. Increased participation has been fueled by the influence of the women's movement, a reduction in family size, the increased necessity for women to supplement family income, and an increase in the number of single women.

Women still tend to be disproportionately represented in traditional occupations and suffer startling disparities in income when contrasted with men in the labor force. Incomes for full-time working women have been calculated at slightly over half those of men, with the gap widening. Lifetime earnings of women in Canada from those with no education to those with university degrees, as a percentage of men's earnings, range from 34 percent to 48 percent (Labor Canada, 1977). Of Canada's female labor force of 3,900,340 in 1976, 326,000 were in medical and health occupations, representing 75.5 percent of all people so employed. Another 1,265,000 women in clerical occupations represent 75.3 percent of all people employed in such occupations (Cook, 1976). Women in publicly supported vocational training are concentrated in four traditional areas: stenographic and clerical trades (22.1 percent); fabricating, assembly and repairing textiles (14.3 percent); service occupations (12.2 percent); and food and beverage processing (8.9 percent (Labor Canada, 1977). Women in federal training programs are decidedly under-represented in institutional, apprenticeship, and skill training programs:

Characteristics of Full Time Institutional Trainees
(1975/76) and CMITP Trainees (1974/75)
(Statistics Canada, 1979)

Component	Male	Female
Skill Training	61.6	38.4
BTSD	45.8	54.2
Language Training	47.7	52.3
Apprenticeships	96.9	3.1
CMITP	76.5	23.5
Labor Force	65.0	35.0
Unemployed	68.3	31.7

Human rights codes in Canada prohibit discrimination because of sex or marital status in recruitment and hiring, training and apprenticeship, promotion and transfer, dismissal, and terms and conditions of employment. Affirmative action by the provincial governments in the form of community outreach information, referral and consultative services have been introduced. A major shift in employment policy at the federal level was announced in March 1979. Termed the National Plan of Action on the Status of Women, its purpose is to enhance access to the labor force by women through the provision of special assistance programs. This is to be facilitated by a Women's Employment Section located in the various CEIC regions in Canada. Specific action in the regions will vary according to regional needs. Common to all will be affirmative action with unions, employers, and professional associations, mini-workshops on <u>Creative Job Search Techniques</u>, the use of a computer-based vocational assessment and occupational information system entitled CHOICES (located in 50 CEC centers), increased referral of women to apprenticeship training, and job creation schemes such as Canada Works and the Local Employment Assistance Program (LEAP). While some action preceded the formal adoption of the plan, many programs are in an incipient stage and system-wide assessment has yet to be conducted. Data collection, when undertaken, is done at the local CEC level.

The Ontario Region has taken the lead in operationalizing the Women's Employment Policy and has issued an Employment Operating Plan for the 1979-80 fiscal year. The goals of the Plan include:

(1) Using advertising to inform women of accessibility of training for non-traditional occupations, particularly indicating those where women have priority;

(2) Purchasing and utilizing the Introduction to Non-Traditional Occupations (INTO) program to orient women to alternative occupations;

(3) Promoting the participation of women in nontraditional CMITP contracts;

(4) Participating in seminars/meetings with employers and employer associations, the agenda of which will include the dispelling of myths concerning women in employment;

(5) Encouraging female participants in JET (Job Experience Training) to enter nontraditional areas;

(6) Ensuring that referral of women to Canada Works projects is proportional to their unemployment levels in the community; and

(7) Undertaking special initiatives such as the use of Career II and to provide women with the necessary assistance to participate equally in the labor market (Employment and Immigration Canada, 1977).

Special programs for women include:

(1) Career II. A 16-hour program that operates over a period of from two days to eight weeks in the local CEC's. It is a group information-sharing program providing labor market information, job search techniques and confidence-building in preparation for women reentering the labor force.

(2) Creative Job Search Techniques. A two-and-a-half-hour mini-workshop provided at the local CEC offices. CJST focuses on interviewing techniques and resume writing. A special module exists for women.

(3) Encouragement for women to enter employment development programs such as:

Canada Works. Special projects are to be funded with women as the target group employing women as managers and workers. Activities range from projects to assist women reentering the labor force and centers assisting sole-support mothers.

Local Employment Assistance Program. Approximately one-quarter of the projects funded will have women as the target group. Day care subsidy is provided for women in most LEAP projects.

(4) Support for programs such as Search of Self (Womanpower Inc.) and Introduction to Non-Traditional Occupations (described below) (Canada Employment and Immigration Commission, 1979-80).

Introduction to Non-Traditional Occupations (INTO) is a full-time eight-week course funded by the CMTP and designed as an orientation program for women to nontraditional occupations. Course content includes assertiveness training, labor market information, labor legislation, job search techniques, budgeting and financial management, coping with the dual role of worker and homemaker, plant tours, and "hands on" exposure to jobs. INTO courses are available in 17 Ontario community colleges and have an annual enrollment of approximately 900 women.

Search of Self (S.O.S.) is a program for women operated by Manpower, a vocational counselling agency in operation in London since 1978 and sponsored by the CEIC. Sole-support mothers are the designated target group. The purpose of S.O.S. is to assist women in exploring the implications and opportunities of entering or reentering the work force. Womanpower has a full-time staff of five and employs 23 women as home care providers in the neighborhoods where women attending S.O.S. reside. A daily program covering five weeks and encompassing groups of up to 20 women focuses heavily on self-assessment financial planning, resume writing and assertiveness training. Womanpower has designed and produced an employment resource kit for immigrant women wishing to enter or reenter the labor force. The kit is available to other centers through the Women's Employment Section.

The number of community-based organizations of a similar nature has increased in recent years. Funding arrangements vary and include grants from all three levels of government, school boards, and the private sector. Their primary functions are information and training, counselling, self-assessment and referral. Notable examples include: Prime Time, Victoria; Women's Career Counselling Service, Ottawa; Opportunity for Advancement, Weston, Ontario; Women Alone in Saskatoon, Saskatchewan; Women's Trade Association, Winnipeg; and the Y.W.C.A. Focus on Change in Toronto.

Only in British Columbia has there been some coherence in the development of centers for women. The Ministry of Education provides funds for seven resource centers modelled after the University of British Columbia's Women's Resource Center. A comparable program to INTO, entitled Employment Orientation for Women (EOW) has been in operation since 1968-69 and now entails 27 courses at nine colleges and the Pacific Vocational Institute.

Learning and training opportunities for women, according to the Canadian Committee on Learning Opportunities for Women (CCLOW), a group affiliated with the CAAE, have suffered from an insufficient power base by women to influence policy and have been characterized by the difficulty of securing the survival of worthwhile programs, let alone ensuring their necessary expansion. Major concerns still include problems associated with reaching the disadvantaged woman, linking education to realistic employment goals, changing attitudes to work, institutional and funding barriers, and alternate delivery systems for programs. In addition, MacKeracher cites as inhibiting factors lack of subsidized day care, lack of time by many women for the completion of academic upgrading and occupational training programs, and poor future employment prospects (Willis, 1978).

Parent Education

The most prominent feature of parental education in Canada is the tremendous increase in interest and concern about parenting and a corresponding growth in the number of courses, programs, therapy sessions, lectures, workshops, and discussion groups on the subject. Equally noteworthy is the virtual absence of documentation on the nature of these activities, their content, distribution, frequency, or numbers participating.

In a study conducted in 1970 by Vanier Institute of the Family on family life education in the media, 34 percent of media personnel judged parent-child relationships to be of the highest interest to adults (MacKeracher, 1978). In a more systematic study by the same institute in 1973, a survey of family life education in voluntary associations identified parent-child relationships as the most active concern, except for personal growth and development (Vanier Institute of the Family, 1970). Over 3,500 organizations were contacted. These included neighborhood associations, Y.M.-Y.W.C.A.s, Women's Institutes and Homemakers' Clubs, Associations for the Mentally Retarded, clubs for Parents Without Partners, community centers, family planning centers and groups, and religious organizations, among others. Recipient numbers were identified at about one and one-half million. However, this contact ranged from the receipt of a brochure to listening to public speakers. Actual participation was cited at 235,000 and estimated, when including nonrespondents, at 350,000. The most common family target group, cited by over 50 percent of the respondents, was both parents, followed by 44 percent for parents and children. This varied according to type of organization. Classification of associations and survey data on the extent of concern with parent-child relationships are shown below.

Classification of Voluntary Associations (percentages)
(Vanier Institute of The Family, 1973)

Level	Religious	Educational	Health/ Medical	Welfare	Women's Organizations	Recreational or Social	Other
National	28	8	28	20	2	6	8
Provincial	18	24	24	21	2	6	5
Local	67	6	4	9	11	2	5

Number of associations: national, 5; provincial, 160; local, 3,332

Concern for Parent-Child Relationships by Type of
Association (percentages)
(Ibid. p. 37)

	Reli-gious	Educa-tional	Health/Medical	Wel-fare	Women's Organi-zations	Other	All Associ-ations
No Concern	-	-	4	4	11	1	1
Major Conc.	65	80	59	67	25	72	64
Minor Conc.	25	11	21	19	32	19	23
Incidental	10	9	16	11	33	8	11
Number	1,957	166	123	220	159	105	2,730
(Percent)	(72)	(6)	(5)	(8)	(6)	(4)	(100)

The concept of family life education is a broad one.
Documentation describing it does not allow for the abstraction
of formal courses or programs in parent education. The formal
offering of parent effectiveness training or parent education
courses occurs in such settings as the continuing education
noncredit sectors of the colleges, night schools, libraries
and community centers and organizations. Provision of such
courses does not generally follow a set pattern but occurs
in response to demand or according to the availability
of instructors. Many of these are social service agency
personnel who teach courses in their spare time. Others have
essentially no credentials. Investigations into the number of
instructors, courses, and participants has not been undertaken. They may be subject only to very rough estimates.

Government ministries are involved in parent education
essentially by providing life planning and parent education
classes. As an example, the Ministry of Health in Ontario
holds a series of classes on health supervision, nutrition
growth and development, infant stimulation, immunization and
behavior problems. In 1978, forty health units gave 1,900
classes with an enrollment of close to 20,000 (Ontario
Provincial Secretariat for Social Development, 1979). In
addition, the Ontario Education Communications Authority
recently presented a series of 20 half-hour programs on
parenting and child development. Despite these efforts,
parent education has not been the subject of government policy
in any comprehensive fashion. The family as a unit is
not a major focus for development in Canadian social policy
(Armitage, 1977). Social policy development tends to be
problem- or issue-oriented and concerned with such matters as
poverty, crime or illness. Other issues such as childcare,
housing, juvenile justice, and community services as these
relate to the family, take precedence.

Programs for Under-Educated Adults

There are in Canada an estimated one million adults
unable to read or write, with another four million who may
be termed functionally illiterate. Census data for 1976
indicates that 856,000 Canadians have achieved less than a
grade 5 level schooling and 3,520,595 between grades 5 and 8.
This represents 5.6 percent and 22.9 percent respectively of
Canada's population aged 55 or over. While such figures are
not entirely indicative of literacy levels, they attest to the
under-education of a considerable segment of Canada's adult
population. Labor force participation rates and unemployment
rates for those having had schooling below grade 8 are 44.3
percent and 11.5 percent respectively. This compares to an
average of 62.1 percent and 8.6 percent across all levels
(Statistics Canada, 1979d).

A number of organizations are involved in adult basic
and literacy education. Over 100 have been catalogued
by Anderson, et al., with a similar number uncatalogued
(Anderson, et al., 1978). Many of these are of a voluntary
nature or, alternately, rely heavily on volunteer support.
Both the National Affiliation for Literacy Advance and
Literacy Volunteers of America are active in Canada in providing training and material support. Frontier College has
been involved with the undereducated, generally in remote
areas in Canada, for eighty years. The College received
recognition from UNESCO in 1977 for "meritorious work in
literacy." Most active in conducting research, promoting the
need for concerted action, publishing materials and serving as
a clearinghouse for those in the field of literacy work, has
been a nonprofit group, the Movement for Canadian Literacy.
Common to all of these groups is a lack of resources.

Attempts to deal with Canada's undereducated can best be
described as tentative. The participation of school boards in
adult basic literacy education is not extensive. A survey of
school boards by Thomas in 1975-76 found that in the Atlantic
region, night classes are under other jurisdictions--the
provincial Department of Continuing Education in Newfoundland,
the federal Department of Regional Economic Expansion in
Prince Edward Island, and the New Brunswick Community College
system in New Brunswick. Only in Nova Scotia were school
boards active in adult basic education. In Manitoba and
Saskatchewan, the college is the ultimate authority rather
than the boards. In Alberta, British Columbia and Ontario,
school boards have handed responsibility for continuing
education classes to the colleges, except for a few that still
operate independently. In Quebec, the regional school boards
serve as the vehicle for both provincial initiative and the
federal training program (Thomas, 1976).

The largest ABE program in the country is provided by the federal Canada Manpower Training Program by means of three specific programs. Basic Training for Skill Development (BTST) is designed to upgrade the academic qualifications of adults for labor force entry or specific skill training. Two additional components are subsumed under the BTSD program. Basic Job Readiness Training (BJRT) provides academic upgrading, supplementary work experience, job search techniques, and basic life skills training. Work Adjustment Training (WAT) is designed for clients having difficulties in obtaining and maintaining employment and in need of developing attitudes and skills consistent with the demands of the work place. Trainees are selected by CEIC counsellors. To be eligible, clients must be one year past the school leaving age in the province of residence, have been out of school for at least one year and be viewed as able to benefit from training. Courses average 17 weeks in length and cannot exceed 52. Training allowances are provided full-time trainees either directly or in the form of Unemployment Insurance Benefits. The community colleges and, to a lesser extent, training centers or modules serve as the vehicle of the program.

The Canada Employment and Immigration Commission has increasingly viewed its role in academic upgrading as inappropriate for federal government involvement; such programming should belong in the jurisdiction of provincial education ministries. BTSD enrollment has declined since 1972-73 when 55,671 trainees were enrolled in the program, to 43,960 in 1977-78 (Canada Manpower Training Program, 1977-78). In 1980, BTSD below grade 7 will be phased out entirely.

A number of innovative instructional methodologies have been developed in Canada. Funds made available by the Department of Manpower and Immigration in 1965 and, later, the Department of Regional Economic Expansion, led to the establishment of the Canada New Start Program. The purpose of this program was "to develop through action-research and experimentation, new methods for motivating and training adults, particularly those who are disadvantaged as to their education (Thomas, 1979a). From New Start came DACUM (Designing a Curriculum), BLADE (Basic Literacy for Adult Development, LINC (Learning Individualized for Canadians), and life skills. These methodologies are in common use in Canada.

Approaches to instructing adults with low educational attainment vary considerably. Thomas states, "Some approaches work better in some settings than others; some have been derived to meet gaps in convential delivery systems; others to respond to particular geographic needs and social conditions" (Ibid., p. 48). The BTSD exemplifies this. The most commonly used instructional material, as reported in a recent survey, was self-developed material (Clark and Draper, 1979-80).

Roughly a fourth of the BTSD and BJRT programs reported activity in developing instruments for assessing literacy attainment, extending adult basic education programs, improving administration of programs, and examining literacy retention. The dropout range of from 5 percent to 80 percent in the BTSD and BJRT programs is indicative of the variation in program effectiveness.

A complete enumeration of effective adult basic education programs is not possible. Some of note are: The London Adult Basic Education Program, the volunteer literacy movement in Nova Scotia, Project R.E.A.D. in Ottawa, Winnipeg's International Centre, and the Adult Learning Centre in Calgary's Forest Lawn Public Library (Thomas, 1976). Particularly noteworthy is Frontier College. A private non-profit agency chartered by an Act of Parliament, the College is funded by foundations, corporations, unions, service organizations, and federal and provincial governments. Each year it sends approximately 100 field workers called laborer-teachers to mining towns, lumber camps, fishing villages, construction sites, and railway crews, in remote parts of Canada. In addition to working full time, laborer-teachers initiate adult education activities. In 1977-78 activities in 82 locations included: recreation (18); life skills (6); community development with native peoples (23); English or French as a second language and adult upgrading (58); youth activities and childhood education (10); women's programs (5); and cooperatives and small business management (13) (Frontier College, 1979).

Undereducated adults constitute one of the country's most pressing social and economic problems and have been subject to neglect. Provincial policy vacuums have been filled by the CMTP program and volunteer groups. An increase in support has occurred through the introduction of adult day schools in the larger urban centers, programs delivered by staff in a number of library systems, and the growth of literacy councils. Nevertheless, substantial provincial involvement will be required to address this problem.

Conclusion

It is difficult to provide a concise, yet comprehensive, account of programs and policies dealing with the populations considered in this report. Reference has been made to programs and policies of note but these do not constitute, in any sense, a complete picture. At the provincial level, only the most prominent activities have been cited. A number of developments having varying implications for these subpopulations have not been included. Among these, as examples, are the use of public educational broadcasting in Canada, initiatives to improve access to educational opportunities by individual postsecondary institutions, the establishment of community learning centers in Newfoundland in conjunction with the extension services of Memorial University, and the recent review of education and training in the federal penitentiary system conducted by the Department of Adult Education at the Ontario Institute for Studies in Education (Thomas, 1979b). The report reflects variations in the availability of information and the general state of change that adult education in Canada is presently undergoing.

Because of its largely indigenous nature, adult education in Canada manifests itself and is evolving in different ways in the provinces. Jurisdictional distinctions at the federal and provincial levels have, as a consequence, a lack of articulation between education and training and labor force planning. Hence, large gaps exist in the provision of adult education opportunities. This is particularly evident in the case of the undereducated, workers, parents, women, and older adults. Policy neglect, limited funding, and insufficient documentation reflect the relative powerlessness of these populations in Canadian society, and the lack of attention given to them.

The kinds of activities subsumed within each of these populations are not all amenable to national or provincial level policy. Programs, particularly for the older adult, the undereducated, and parents are characterized in large part by local level initiative and voluntary action. As a result, they take a variety of forms and constitute an exciting feature of the field of adult education. However, the sharing of experiences for those involved, the engagement of adult education practitioners in a useful and more far-reaching manner, and the conducting of research have been hampered by the diffuse nature of the programs in these fields.

Evident in Canada is an increased awareness of, and responsiveness to, these populations. The introduction of new programs and policies to facilitate entry and reentry of women into the labor force, the examination of industrial training policies and paid educational leave, and the funding agreement with the Canadian Labour Congress in support of union education by the federal government, signal a beginning. The nongovernmental level has been characterized by an expansion effectiveness and increased activity of community-based women's organizations and a wide range of programs in parental education and in adult basic and literacy education. Most significant has been the development of structures and policies of adult education in many of the provinces, and the present examination and appraisal of future directions.

Provincial adult education authorities have yet to deal substantially with these populations. Nevertheless, noteworthy changes have occurred in the responsiveness to adult education needs in the last decade. The overriding feature of new adult education structures in the provinces has been a decentralization of control and initiative to the local and regional level. To what extent this will lead to increased accessibility for those traditionally excluded is of critical importance and remains to be resolved. Concomitant with this will be the question of how to facilitate access and respond to needs without exercising undue control. Detailed investigation, increased funding, more systematic policy formation, and coordination of effort among the provinces and with the federal government will be required.

ADULT EDUCATION OPPORTUNITIES IN DENMARK

Per Himmelstrup

Vice Chancellor, Sydjysk Universitetscenter

Introduction

In 1978 an OECD expert group of four examined the Danish National Policy for Education. It was a routine examination, but it was closely linked with the ambitious long-term planning effort called U-90 (Danish Educational Planning and Policy in a Social Context at the End of the 20th Century).

In the V-90 report, published in 1979, Denmark was described in the following way:

Denmark is a small country with a population of 5 million people occupying 43,000 square kilometres of Northern Europe between the North Sea and the Baltic. It comprises the Jutland peninsula and no fewer than 406 islands, excluding Greenland and the Faroe Islands. Communications are nevertheless very good.

Denmark has very few natural resources and virtually no energy base. Nevertheless, while its gross economic output is small in relation to that of several other European countries (for example, 11 percent of France and 9 percent of Germany), it ranks fifth among the countries in the OECD world on a per capita basis (7,600 U.S. dollars in 1976), placing it just behind the U.S.A. and Norway. The standard of living has reached a very high level, and in the other three Scandinavian countries the Danes have the reputation of being carefree spenders. This may well be an exaggeration but there is at least no doubt that most Danes today experience a sense of material comfort.

This was not always so.   The Danish economy, and
with it the way of life, has been gradually trans-
formed since the middle of the 19th Century.   The
pace of economic change quickened in the aftermath
of the worldwide breakdown of international trade
during the Depression.   Though still vitally important for its export trade, agriculture is no longer
dominant.   Expansion has been spectacular in the
manufacturing and tertiary sectors.   Denmark has
been particularly adept at developing export industries, especially of the consumer durables and high
investment goods type, in the domain of high level
technology.   In 1976 the export of goods and
services accounted for 33 percent of G.D.P.   This
remarkable leap forward in national wealth has had a
profound impact on individual aspirations and
community expectations, indeed on the very essence
of the Danish character.

In the 19th Century, following severe military
defeat, the Danish accepted the reality of no longer
being a European middle power, but a relatively
small nation able to survive only by concentrating
on the homeland.   This led to a conscious effort to
develop a Danish mind, soul and spirit revolving
around ideas of personal enlightenment and savoir
vivre.   The result is that Denmark has become an
unusually close-knit society with few minority
group problems.   The people prefer informality to
formality in their social and political institutions
and in everyday life.   This liking for informality
does not denote any lack of order or efficiency.   On
the contrary, life in all its aspects is unob-
trusively well organized, the outcome of ripe
experience in seeking social harmony and pragmatic
solutions to problems.

Social class differences exist but are not noticeably divisive.   Much of the nation's wealth has been
used to build a welfare state of which the Danes are
intensely proud.   They tend to think in terms of
collective social responsibility and to believe that
everyone must be properly cared for, so that public
expenditure on the social services is high by
international standards.   Taxation is accordingly
severe, forcing income levels to fall within a
relatively narrow band.   Of late there has been a
certain reaction against the burdens placed on the
taxpayers. However, this expresses itself not so
much in questioning the need for an enlightened and

generous welfare system but rather in condemning the increasing power of experts and technocrats at the expense of the people and the shift of influence from the localities to the centre.

For one of the most striking features of Danish society is that while nurturing a collectivist approach towards satisfying human needs it cares deeply about local rights and is extraordinarily tolerant of non-conformist behaviour, whether by groups or invididuals. To some outside observers it seems odd for such a small country to have twelve political parties represented in the Parliament (the Folketing). In fact, this apparent political fragmentation is really a mark of the determination of various interest groups to be seen and heard. Another manifestation of this tendency is due to the fact that a very high proportion of farms and commercial and manufacturing business are still relatively small by Western European standards.

The open-mindedness of the Danes is today illustrated in a multitude of ways. The springing up of communes, the latitude given to the young to experiment with a variety of life styles, the emancipated status of women, the lack of censorship and the acceptance of sexual freedom, are examples. Underlying this is a tradition of moderation and common sense, a confident belief that human beings behave most reasonably when encouraged to make their own decisions.

While conscious of the distinctive qualities of their way of life, the Danes are far from being chauvinists. They feel a strong affinity to the other peoples of Scandinavia. Indeed, over and above their uniqueness they recognise a Scandinavian entity. Beyond that they see themselves as having and indeed being obliged to have, a strong European and internationalist outlook. Virtually devoid of natural resources, Denmark can survive and prosper only through energetic and successful trading. Being thus acutely aware of the need to cultivate close relations with other countries in Europe than the Scandinavian group, it has elected, as the only Scandinavian country, to join the European Economic Community with all the political and social implications that such an attachment entails.

In general, it recognizes the necessity of bringing
up the young with a strong international awareness
and of ensuring that its citizens can command
foreign languages and adapt to living in and working
with countries in all parts of the world.

Denmark has, however, now experienced the beginning
of a period of some uncertainty. We noted how
during the period of full employment in the 1960s
and early 70s the welfare state expanded with
particular vigor. This is seen by some people to
have had marked and undesirable effects on living
and working patterns: a rapid drift of population
from the farms; diminution of family functions;
lessening of popular participation in owner co-
operatives and local government as smallness has
yielded to the consolidation of farm and factory;
increasing competition not only for market shares
but also for status and power in the hierarchies of
expertise created by the new means of production.

Along with other OECD countries, Denmark today is
also contending with dual problems of inflation and
unemployment. The slackening of economic growth--
about 1 1/2 percent of G.D.P. in 1977--has led to a
widespread re-thinking of values, principles and
practices in the public sector. Denmark faces
an additional difficulty--a balance of payments
deficit, amounting to 2 1/2 percent of G.D.P.
(1977), linked with a heavy dependence on imports
(38 percent of G.D.P.) and a traditional resistance
to governmental intervention in trade matters.
There is a dawning recognition that Denmark may have
been living beyond its means and that, despite the
good will of its commercial partners and external
investors, a harsh reckoning awaits it unless some
creative compromises can be reached and unless its
entrepreneurial and research and development prowess
can be applied to find new outlets for its productive capacity and reserves of human capital.

This introduction is concluded by reproducing from U-90
three illustrative figures. The first one shows the development of public expenditure on education as a percentage of
G.D.P. since the mid-1930s.

The second figure (on the next page) shows the distribution of students between ages 13 and 24 in various types of
study. Up to the age of 15, the primary and lower secondary
school is dominant; then upper secondary education, higher

preparatory education* and vocational training become predominant with continuation schools** as a special supplement.
At the age of 18, only 50 percent of the young are following a
course of formal education.

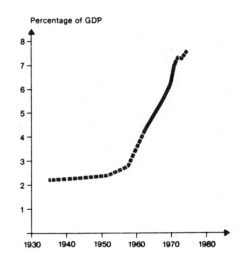

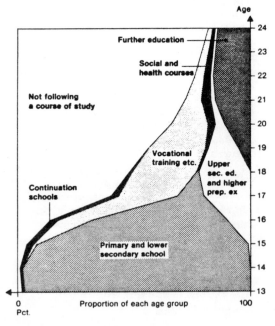

---

*An alternative to upper secondary school.
**An alternative to lower secondary school/long-term
  residential colleges.

The third figure gives estimates of the extent of formal schooling by age, in the population in 1977. About 65 percent had less than 9 years of schooling, which today constitutes the period of compulsory education. It is estimated that in 1990 there will still be 40 percent of the population in the age bracket 20-65 years with less than 9 years of schooling.

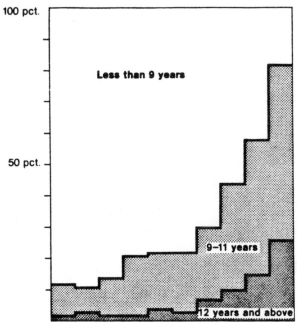

Year of birth: 1908-12 13-17 18-22 23-27 28-32 33-37 38-42 43-47 48-52 53-57
Age: 65-69 60-64 55-59 50-54 45-49 40-44 35-39 30-34 25-29 20-24

Participation in Adult Education

In the mid-70s the Danish Institute of Social Research carried out a study of participation in various adult education activities.

The study indicated that the "education gap"--differences in school education and training levels between the younger and the older sections of the population--has become wider in recent decades. It also showed, however, that the proportion of the population with no vocational training has been drastically reduced--from over 50 percent of those aged 50-59 years to about 30 percent of those 20 to 29 years old (20 percent for men but 40 percent for women).

The study also showed that in 1975 33 percent of the adult population (over 20 years of age) took part in some kind of educational activity. Or in other words, 67 percent did not take part.

Fourteen percent attended courses related to their work, while 16 percent attended general, liberal adult education courses.

When asked if they had ever attended adult education classes, the "yes" answer ranged from 64 percent for unskilled workers to 89 percent for superior civil servants.

These attendance figures may be broken down as shown in the following three tables:

School background	Adult Education Participants	
	Men	Women
7 years or less formal education	18%	23%
8-10 years	38	44
11 years or more	58	63
All categories	30%	36%

Vocational training or professional education

	Men	Women
University education or equivalent (3 years or more)	46%	70%
Shorter academic education (1-3 years)	65	60
Apprenticeship or basic voc. training	32	47
Short courses (max. 1 year)	31	43
No training/education	13	23
All categories	30%	36%

Social group*

	Men	Women
I and II	45%	76%
III	29	64
IV	40	48
V	17	30

*The social groups range from I at the top to V at the bottom (unskilled workers).

Review of Major National Policies and Programs

Background. During the Enlightenment (late 18th century), when Denmark was still an absolute monarchy, an extensive reform policy furthering rural development was formulated and carried out from above.

This work was concluded by the Elementary School Act of 1814. According to this act, it was the obligation of the school master to offer evening classes twice a week to young people who had left school. The aim was not only to offer "refresher courses" in Danish, mathematics and writing but also to familiarize youth with "obligations which ensued from maturity and changed living conditions."

Thirty years later the first Folk High School was founded in Rødding (1844). It is a long-term residential college for young adults (minimum age 18) inspired by the thinking of the scholar and clergyman, N.F.S. Grundtvig (1783 - 1872). Within a few years these colleges developed into the kind of institutions we still know. This was mainly due to the work of Kristen Kold, a schoolteacher, who founded Ryslinge Folk High School in 1851. The Folk High School concept is by no means rigid; methods of learning vary from one school to another. But they have certain features in common. They are residential, and the collective experiences of the students form the basis for discussions and debates. Another common feature is the absence of final examinations, reports or competence-based testing.

While the evening classes prescribed in the 1814 Act did not really flourish (mainly because the teachers were not paid to teach them), the Folk High Schools spread throughout the country and became an important element in national and socio-political development. This was especially so after the free constitution (1849) turned Denmark into a democracy.

The Grundtvig-inspired educational thinking has marked adult education in its diversity. Not only have other types of residential colleges (Continuation Schools, Domestic Science Colleges, and others) been established, but also "evening schools" run mainly by associations whose main--or only--task is education for adults.

Vocational training has also been influenced by the "enlightenment tradition" underlying the Folk High Schools. Learning is primarily for one's personal development, expression and emancipation.

Present Trends. As indicated above, the majority of those pursuing adult education attend "enlightenment" schools and courses: that is, they seek general, liberal, non-vocational adult education without any particular connection to the educational core (or the formal system). However, two other kinds of adult education parallel the educational core:

competence-based or second-chance (qualifying) education for adults and courses that may supplement or complement the educational core (retraining, further, and reconversion training schemes).

Definition of Adult Education. Even though adult education in Denmark dates back as far as the middle of the 18th Century and received its first legislative provision as early as 1814, it has no clearly formulated or officially stated aim; no definition or demarcation of this area has ever been made.

Adult education has developed as the need has arisen, without any overall plan. The result is that this "alternative system" is today spread amongst various ministries, giving adult education a broad and varied, but little-coordinated, mandate and domain.

During the 1970s a more or less general understanding developed that understands adult education as any educational activity outside the formal system and organized for adults--irrespective of content, level and methods.

U-90 went a step further by stating that "in principle the teaching which may be termed 'useful' that which participants consider to be valuable for their own situation." But this statement is more a sign of resignation than of approval --let alone enthusiasm.

National Policy. Adult education is rarely debated in Parliament. A general debate took place in December 1972 (following the UNESCO conference in Tokyo), but during the past two or three years attempts to generate political debate in Parliament have been futile. The aim of such a debate should be (contrary to the 1972 debate) to formulate a programme for future action in the field.

As mentioned, education for adults today takes place according to many different administrative, legislative and financial regulations. The closest one can get to a general policy for adult education may have have been the declaration of intention in the white paper on long-term planning (1971) called "Perspective Plan for 1970-85." This report notes a lack of continuity, coherence and long-term objectives in practically all sectors of the Danish educational system.

The Perspective Plan (PPI) expected adult education to develop considerably in the coming years, for a number of reasons, and that this development would result in:

(1) A great part of the population in the productive age group pursuing further education and "up-dating" courses, and

(2) A significant part of the active population demand-
     ing continuation training via specially prepared
     courses or via already existing forms of education.

The PPI established three main objectives for adult
education:

(1) To give adults with insufficient basic education
     further education (qualifying or second-chance
     education),

(2) To provide retraining and possibly reconversion
     training for adults with respect to current develop-
     ments in science and technology (vocationally-
     oriented adult education), and

(3) To provide the opportunity of leisure-time instruc-
     tion of a supplementary and orienting nature
     (general liberal nonvocational adult education,
     i.e., enlightenment).

Another long-term plan (PP II--1972-87, published in
1973) stated briefly that "there is thus every reason to give
adult education a high priority" and pointed out that for
reasons of scarce resources it would be necessary to consider
the possibility of a redistribution of means within the
education system as a whole, e.g., to allocate more funds for
retraining programmes.

Supporting this supposition were the following factors:

(1) About 75 percent of employed persons have had only
     seven years of basic education;

(2) A considerable percentage of employed persons are
     skilled in trades which they have left or that,
     through changes in social structure and industry, no
     longer exist;

(3) The increase of leisure time leads to an increasing
     demand for leisure-time instruction;

(4) The efforts regarding initial schooling in the 50s
     and 60s have created a generation gap and will
     encourage inequality;

(5) The increase in effectiveness and specialisation
     and their consequent psychological pressures will
     necessitate "breathing spaces" which will afford
     development of self-expression and creativity; and

(6)   It is increasingly vital to create a general framework for communicating across the limitations of
specialization.

In consequence of the Leisure-time Instruction Act (1967)
and the legislation on residential adult education (Folk High
Schools, etc. in 1970), the 1970s were envisaged as the decade
of adult education.

Few concrete programs come into being, however, and a new
long-term plan, this time exclusively for education (U-90),
again in very general terms stated a declaration of worthy
intentions:

...finds that adult education plays a very important
part in the total future educational strategy, and
that this applies to the entire range of different
activities within the field. Adult education must
be accorded a higher priority in the future educational policy, i.e., more attention should be
devoted to it, and more resources allocated to the
field of adult education.

Also the OECD examiners stated in their report on Danish
education that "a positive national policy (in the field of
adult education) is lacking. The principles of recurrent
education underlie much of the argument in U-90, but we see
few signs of pragmatic proposals to apply them."

Responsibility

From previous parts of this report it may be deduced that
the responsibility for adult education is everybody's--and
nobody's.

As has been indicated, important features of Danish adult
education are rooted in the popular movements of the 19th
century and are influenced by the Enlightenment. That means
that subjective emotional experience (of the participant) and
influencing attitudes (from the tutor)--aiming at personal
development and the development of a personal competence--
has been more important than learning aimed at achieving
recognized formal competence (qualification).

This is, unfortunately, presently changing in favour of
education for recognized qualification (credentialism).

But the special Danish tradition of "enlightenment"
(general liberal adult education) is closely related to free,
private initiative.

The most independent providers of adult education are no
doubt the Folk High Schools. There are now about 85, most of
them rather small (from about 50 to about 250 students) and

all of them founded by individuals or organizations, and all now run as independent self-governing private bodies. They attract about 10 percent of adult students each year. The state has no influence on the programmes offered and the methods used, although it pays 85 percent of the running expenses related to education. In 1977-78 there were 9,000 students in the long term courses (12 weeks or more) and 25,000 in the short courses (1-2 weeks). The state support amounted to Dkr. 128,000,000 excluding subsidies to the students. Subsidies for students at the "free-schools" (Folk High Schools), continuation schools and agricultural schools amounted to Dkr. 87,000,000). The minimum age for students is 18 and no qualifications are required and no formal credentials are obtained. Although each school has an advisory board, the major educational responsibilities lie with the principal, who is solely responsible for employing and dismissing tutors.

The activities of the Folk High Schools are regulated by the 1970 Act on Folk High Schools, Continuation Schools, Domestic Science Colleges and Agricultural Colleges.

In all, these "Free Schools"--as they are called--attract about 25,000 young people every year, half of whom are over 18.

Next on the scale of independent responsibility is the system for general, liberal, nonvocational adult education. It was previously called "evening school" though now it is also termed "leisure-time instruction" --in consequence of the Act on Leisure-time Instruction which was passed in Parliament in 1967.

The most important sponsors of activities in this field (which attract 16 percent of all adult Danes) are the independent educational associations, i.e., organizations whose main (and as a rule, only) task is to undertake education for adults. There are about a dozen nationwide educational associations with different bases both politically and philosophically.

As a rule the politically-based educational associations have been established in order to use enlightenment/adult education as a tool in the efforts to form future society.

But thanks to free initiative, anyone can start an adult education class, so besides the national education associations, educational opportunities for adults are organized by individuals, by local groups/organizations and by municipalities.

According to the Act on Leisure-time Instruction of 1967 (with many later amendments), conditions are in principle exactly the same for national educational associations, local organizations, individuals and local authorities. Public authorities pay 75 percent of teacher salaries (evenly shared by state and municipality), and facilities (classrooms with necessary equipment, heating, light, cleaning, etc.) are available free of charge. Any facility constructed with public funding is available for use, including nonvocational adult education. It should be noted that the actual number of individuals taking part is smaller; there are no individual statistics, and one person may take two or more courses.

Program for the Handicapped. For physically or mentally handicapped people two types of education are offered.

One aims at compensating the handicap. Tuition is free and classes must be held if two students register. Free transport is arranged if needed. Teachers must be qualified for this special kind of education. It may be sponsored both by private bodies (educational associations and others) and by local authorities, and is paid for by the county.

The other type takes the handicap into consideration. The aim in this instance is to give handicapped persons equal opportunities for adult education. Tuition is free; expenses are evenly divided between state and municipality.

The general trend is that public authorities in one way or another assume a more active, responsible role to the extent the program has credentialing or occupational objectives.

Thus, in 1978 qualifying education for adults was separated from the Act on Leisure-time Instruction and was given its own legislation. This legislation applies to qualifying education corresponding in the 3 top classes in lower secondary schools (8th, 9th and 10th grades) and to upper secondary schools (11th and 12th grade). This development of second-chance education started in the late 50s and was largely organized by traditional sponsors of adult education. But in the early 1970s a process was begun to coordinate these opportunities (called preparatory courses) by county, on the basis of collective planning which considered such factors as density of population, public transportation, training centres, and an action radius of not more than 20 to 25 kilometres.

The Act on Preparatory Courses of 1978 transferred the total responsibility to the County Councils. By 1977-78, the last year of free-initiative preparatory courses, 42,000 students were enrolled. Experiments are presently going on in qualifying (credential-oriented) education at the post-secondary (or university) level, and also in introducing part-time students to the Danish university world. There are numerous alternatives.

In some cases the established higher education institutions will accept some part-time students. In that case the responsibility lies completely with the institution, and courses are not changed in any way to meet the special needs of the new clients. This system has been in operation for several years now.

Another approach is to take the courses to the potential students. For example, tailor-made short job-oriented courses (one to three years) called KVU will attempt to draw upon existing resources and thereby reduce existing institutional barriers.

Yet another plan is to take regular university courses out to potential students and to make it easier to attend at a slower pace.

In the last two cases, a special regional board (comprising several counties) will probably be established and will be responsible. This board will be appointed and approved by the government and expenses will be paid by the state.

Adult Education and the Labour Market

Trade unions are responsible for a wide variety of courses related to workers' rights, the national economy, wage policies, industrial economy and cooperation. They often cooperate with the Workers' Education Association (AOF) and with the three Folk High Schools operated by the labour movement.

Employer associations are responsible for courses dealing with leadership problems, management and production techniques, administrative rationalisation, systematisation, marketing, etc. They run three residential training centers.

In addition there are many Labour Market Training Schemes, many of which are run by the state, either under the auspices of the Ministry of Education or the Ministry of Labour. This is training organized for adults who have not been in a learning situation for some time. Courses may be full- or part-time, but they all aim at introducing the participants to a trade or to a specific occupation. Since the 1960 Act on Vocational Training for Semiskilled and Other Workers, special training schemes have been carried through for semiskilled workers, for retraining of skilled workers and for reconversion training.

Semi-skilled worker training schemes are arranged by special Branch Committees consisting of both employer and employee representatives. Most of the courses are held at training establishments for semiskilled workers (special-arbejderskoler), of which there are about 25. Twenty are independent self-governing private institutions; the rest are owned by the state. Some courses are held on the job. The courses are short (up to six weeks) and conform to pre-established standards. The training schemes are based on a correlated course-level system, each level constituting an

independent module.   In 1977-78 more than 29,000 adults
attended these courses.

Retraining schemes are arranged and run jointly by both
sides of the labour market and by the Technological Institutes
(of which there are four under the Ministry of Commerce) and
the Commercial and Technical Schools (under the Ministry of
Education).
They are designed on the same model as the training
schemes for semi-skilled workers and run mainly as day courses
(1 to 3 weeks). Over and above bringing students' basic
training up to date, they have the additional aim of teaching
students new skills and competencies applicable to new production methods and techniques. In 1977-78 almost 25,000 adults
attended these courses.
Finally there are the reconversion training schemes
designed to help people in the adjustment process accompanying
a change of trade, and to assist the unemployed and those
returning to the labour market. Reconversion training
programmes as a rule have concrete objectives and can be
sponsored either by a particular industrial concern, by labour
exchanges or by labour market organizations. Only 325 adults
took part in these courses in 1977-78.
It may be added that there are limited provisions for
vocational training under the Act on Leisure-time Instruction.
They include various basic and retraining schemes, for
instance in social welfare, health, secretarial work, and
agriculture, of which the last has by far the largest number
of courses.
Since its beginning in the 1920s, there has been a desire
to use radio --and later television--for educational purposes.
Radio/TV in Denmark is a state monopoly; there is only one
station, Radio Denmark. From the beginning, language courses
have been the most important part of the programme. But
during the past 25 years the spectrum has been widened
considerably, and Radio Denmark often cooperates with outside
sponsors of adult education.
In 1976 the education department of Radio Denmark became
tax-financed--until then it had been financed by normal
license fees. Simultaneously, the Ministry of Education,
through the newly established National Centre for Teaching
Equipment and Audio-Visual Aids, assumed responsibility for
the station. Three advisory councils, one of which deals with
adult education, advise the ministry on the broadcasts.

Adult Education for Whom?

In principle, general liberal nonvocational adult education is, of course, offered to all adults living in Denmark.

And there are in practice no limitations on the subjects offered.

One of the ideas behind the Act on Leisure-time Instruction is that adult education must be offered throughout the country. For this reason municipalities are obliged to offer adult education if there are no (or not enough) private sponsors. That is also why there are certain regulations regarding number of participants and other details in sparsely populated regions.

Though all adults (above 18 years of age) are eligible, only some 16 percent take advantage of the opportunities available.

Qualifying (or second chance) courses are, of course, offered to those who did not make use of the opportunity when they were the "right" age for it. As has been indicated above, this applies to about two-thirds of the adult population. The Danish education system has traditionally been very selective, but the general democratization has changed this pattern and at the same time pressed for alternative (second chance) opportunities for adults.

It goes without saying that radio and TV serve the total population; however, only a very small proportion register for organized courses when they are offered. Labor maket programmes have well-defined target groups.

Financing

In general it can be said that the more general and liberal or hobby-oriented a course is, the less it is financed by public means. The costs are, as much as possible, borne by the participants themselves. At the present time, between a quarter and a third of teachers' salaries are paid by the participants. They also pay for materials used, while facilities are at their disposal free of charge.

This has not always been the case. Until 1971 most education--including adult education--was free of charge. And it is still so to the extent that there are no precalculated limits to public support. If classes are established according to regulations and participants pay their share, the public authorities are obliged to pay their part, and to provide physical facilities.

The more courses serve credentialing or vocational purposes, the more it is financed by the state. Most courses are free of charge for the participants, and often they will also receive books and other materials free.

In the field of labour market training, participating organizations have, by general agreement, established a fund. The state pays the largest part of the costs related to courses according to the 1960 Act. A minor part (about 10 percent) is paid by the municipality from which the participant comes.

Goals and Purposes

As stated in the introductory paragraphs of this report, there is no national policy. There is a general desire for more equal opportunities, a belief that education is a good thing in itself, an effort to make leisure time more meaningful, and objectives related to democratic participation.

But in order to identify formulated goals or purposes for the activities, it is necessary to study the individual sponsors. And there are hundreds of them. Some have stated goals and purposes in their statutes, but many of them would probably be in difficulty if asked to do so.

Major Problems in Achieving the Goals of Adult Education

If adult education's goal is to reach almost all adults and to engage them in an active process of personal development or in some kind of education, then Denmark still has a long way to go. Even though about 30 percent participate yearly--and about two thirds do take part sooner or later-- there is still 25 to 35 percent of the adult population who will never avail themselves of the education planned for them.

We must remember, however, that many adults wish to and are capable of developing themselves and learning on their own. They do not need to register, and they do not need a tutor. But they may need access to modern aids of different kinds. So a task for the 80s may be to render all educational resources accessible to the individual and independent learner.

A serious, and growing, problem is an attitude of rejection of education in favor of entertainment.

This problem is also related to the mass media, especially television; it also has to do with politics and the central administration. But it is also a school problem. Work at school should not only make it seem a natural and logical thing to go on with the process of personal development and learning, but it should stress that learning does not only take place in childhood and youth, but throughout life.

Lifelong learning is verbally accepted by most Danes, but it has yet to reduce barriers between educational institutions at the same level, not to mention vertical barriers between institutions at different levels.

School experiences are still often negative, very often because academic work is stressed, and practical, manual work is depreciated.

During the past ten years there has been great interest in "the residual group." Efforts have concentrated on out-reach activity. Results are not impressive, and it may be stated that the main problem is motivation. Learning opportunities exist in Denmark, or they can easily be organized.

In recent years it has been acknowledged that radio and TV are more effective in motivating people than in educating them; perhaps the mass media should be used differently in the future.

Guidance, counselling and information are keywords if the goals of adult education are to be achieved, especially in relation to second chance education but also for more serious academic subjects. A longstanding problem is curricula and materials designed for adult students. As it is now, materials from upper and lower secondary schools are used, and there are often complaints about the lack of material especially prepared for adults.

Among more trivial obstacles to participation are:

(1) baby-sitting;

(2) distance: since the new municipal structure (1970), there has been a trend toward concentrating activities in the main urban centres thereby neglecting the rural areas and villages;

(3) an increasing formalization and bureaucratization of liberal general adult education; and

(4) dislike or disapproval on the part of the spouse. This is especially felt by wives, particularly since course fees have been introduced.

Finally, a problem and an obstacle stem from the fact that Denmark has no national center or institute for adult education. Adult education is still in a marginal position and is in many respects an appendage to the educational core, especially to the elementary school system.

Very little research is being done in the field. Political debate is minimal. Training of adult educators has improved considerably during the 70s but could still be improved. A center for research, documentation, and exchange of ideas would strengthen the entire field of education for adults, especially if it could help reduce barriers between the different providers of education described in this paper.

ADULT EDUCATION IN THE FEDERAL REPUBLIC OF GERMANY

(With Special Reference to the German "Volkshochschulen")

Helmuth Dolff

Director, German Volkshochschul-Verbandes

Statutory Arrangements for Adult Education

The realization that adult education is a necessary element in the educational system of the Federal Republic emerged after the 2nd UNESCO World Conference in 1960 in Montreal, and since then it has been given increasing emphasis.

The German Committee for the Educational System (a committee of experts appointed by the President of the Federal Republic) had already in 1960 described and substantiated the importance of adult education in a comprehensive report. In 1970 the German Education Council (also appointed by the President) made the following statement about adult education in its "Structural Plan for the Educational System":

> Continuing education can neither be regarded and treated as subject to private discretion nor as a measure only serving sectional interests. We rather have to assume a strong interest of the entire society in a universal and permanent continuing education of a desirably great number of people-- similarly strong to the interest of society in school education for all. The first educational phase remains incomplete without a complementary continuing education. The whole field of continuing education therefore is part of the educational system; advanced training, reorientation and adult education are to be implemented within the framework of this field. These tasks sketch perspectives for the shaping and extension of continuing education. The general principles relating to the first educa- tional phase apply also to the whole range of continuing education.

A so-called Bund-Lander-Kommission (mixed federal-state commission) formed by representatives of the federal and the Lander authorities made the attempt in its "Bildungs-gesamtplan" (Comprehensive Plan for Education) ratified in 1973 to be more concrete by saying:

> Continuing education is the pursuit or resumption of organized learning after the termination of a first educational phase and after the entry into professional activity.

> To meet the growing social and professional demands that are changing more and more quickly, in the future more people have to be able to acquire new knowledge and skills. Furthermore adults have to be granted the opportunity in their professional activities and their spare time to develop creative talents and to acquire access to new spheres of interest.

> All the measures adopted in this field aim at the establishment and consolidation of a continuing educational system as a main component of the educational system, which is a public task even though the initiative for continuing one's personal education remains with the individual. According to their respective areas of responsibility, the federal, Lander and local authorities will make sufficient provision for educational measures that meet modern standards. To ensure adequate services, the non-public (voluntary) providers are given an equal share in all the measures and utilities as well as in public promotion.

> In the field of continuing education a detailed educational provision shall be offered. This demand is being anticipated by the numerous initiatives and activities of the different provider agencies. Nevertheless a minimum of systematization and distinctness has to be guaranteed by institution-alized cooperation. The areas of professional, general and political education are to be considered as correlated.

> In order to accomplish these aims, the actual efforts in the field of continuing education have to be coordinated at a local, regional and supra-regional levels.

Article No. 30 of the Constitution charges the respective Lander with the "Execution of State Powers" and the "Accomplishment of State Duties" in all those cases where the Constitution does not explicitly charge a federal organ with the responsibility. On the matter of education and cultural policy, the federal structure of the West German Republic is particularly distinct. There the responsibility of the federal authorities is limited to only a few areas. Legislation and administration of the inner cultural activities are exclusively executed by the respective Lander. Within the scope of the Lander constitutions, certain tasks can be assigned to the municipalities, or administrative arrangements with federal authorities can bring about their cooperation in the state's pursuance of cultural tasks.

According to the Constitution, therefore, only the Lander are in a position to issue sovereign regulations (laws and administrative orders) for the field of adult education. Because of the diversity of the individual Lander there has been a wide range of developments, laws and structures.

This state of affairs has been one of the compelling reasons that brought about in 1969 a modification of Article 9 of the Constitution, according to which cooperation between federal and Lander authorities shall also extend to the area of educational planning as a common task. Consequently the federal and the Lander governments instituted in 1970 the mixed federal-Lander commission for educational planning as a standing discussion forum for all questions of the educational system relating to both federal and Lander authorities. Composed of the ministers of education and the ministers of finance as representatives of their respective governments, the commission was ordered to prepare a comprehensive plan and a budget for education.

Seven out of eleven of the presently valid Lander constitutions contain provisions on the regulation of public responsibility for adult education (Baden-Wurttemberg, Bavaria, Bremen, North-Rhine-Westphalia, Rhineland-Palatinate, the Saar, Schleswig-Holstein). In the respective articles of the constitutions, the municipalities are generally designated as the main providers of adult education. Only the constitutions of Berlin, Hamburg, Hesse and Lower-Saxony do not contain any regulations on adult education. Hesse and Lower-Saxony, however, have issued separate laws on adult education, and in the town-states of Berlin and Hamburg, Volkshochschulen are run as state institutions.

The regulations of the Lander constitutions concerning public financing of adult education are supplemented by rules of the Land laws in the municipal and county codes. According to nearly all of these codes the municipalities and counties are assigned to provide, within their sphere of action and within the scope of their capacity, those public services that are necessary for the economic, social and cultural well-being of their inhabitants. It is generally accepted that adult education by helping its participants to learn, to orient themselves, to form their own opinions, as well as to develop individual activities, serves the social and cultural well-being of the community's and county's inhabitants. Therefore adult education has to be counted among those communal or county tasks for which the communal and county codes decree the provision of public services.

In nearly all the Lander the supplementary laws on academic, vocational high school and school education contain directions and decrees on the different sections of adult education. There are also existing miscellaneous programmes promoting continuing education, for example in the fields of agriculture, handicraft, trade, politics and public health.

This extraordinary abundance of laws undoubtedly led during recent years to an enormous development in adult education. It must not be overlooked, however, that the heterogeneity of legislation resulting from the federal system often leads to a scattering of efforts and obstructs a desirably homogeneous conceptional development of adult education. It has to be stated, nevertheless, that all these laws and decrees start from the principle of autonomy of teaching and curriculum planning for the institutions of adult education and also guarantee freedom of instruction to those working in these institutions.

Actual Status of Adult Education

The attempt to obtain a survey of the existing situation in adult education on the basis of the available material will reveal variations that have their origins in history as well as in differences of content and socio-political background. To all appearances, adult education in the Federal Republic of Germany follows a fixed plan, is badly structured and is still in a rudimentary stage, even though the progress of recent years cannot be disregarded. It is true that in public consciousness the Volkshochschule has asserted itself success- fully as a central institution of adult education, and it is also true that its courses and short programmes alone are attended by about 8 million citizens. Nevertheless a large proportion of the population is not attracted by the pro- grammes that are offered within the scope of adult education, and government grants for them do not exceed 2 percent of the entire government spending on education. Development of adult education still lags far behind development of the other spheres of education, such as the universities, schools and vocational training.

In addition to the Volkshochschule as the prototype of an institution of adult education which is independent ideologically and socio-politically, there exists a wide range of institutions, public as well as private, which are mostly specialized in their orientation.

Some of these institutions for adult education are:

(1)   The bodies of self-management in industry under public law, whose educational programmes are directly cut out for the requirements of industry. The first elements of an integration into a coherent system can be perceived in certain fields where it has been possible to institutionalize cooperation with the Volkschochschule.

(2)   The academies which increasingly address problems of adult education. In this area close relations among institutions of adult education arise, particularly in vocational training and continuing education of staff.

(3)   The broadcasting stations with their educational and informational programmes and their growing tendency to genuinely cooperate in a media alliance where partners are trying to harmonize their contributions (radio and TV, written material, accompanying study circles at, for example, the Volkshochschulen).

(4)   The trade unions with their special educational programmes for employees at local, regional and central levels. Through the working combination, "Arbeit und Leben," special means for cooperation with the Volkshochschulen have been provided.

(5)   The great number of competitive voluntary sponsoring bodies among which especially the churches and the trade associations (for instance the farmers' association) have to be counted, as well as other communal institutions or associations.

(6)   The institutions of adult education in the form of boarding schools, among them boarding Volkshochschulen with different sponsors, trade-union schools, Protestant and Catholic academies, Europe Houses, political academies, Youth Courts, etc.

(7)   The system of correspondence education whose non-commercial part is still relatively small, indeed,

whose importance will grow through federal regulation as well as by the foundation of the first
distance (television) university in Hagen.

In addition there are the various institutions of special
vocational training, the political parties, the educational
work in the armed forces, the public libraries, etc., which
are important to consider in order to round out this general
survey.

All the sponsoring bodies and institutions mentioned here
agree in their efforts to establish an all-covering system of
adult education in the Federal Republic of Germany. Every
adult citizen shall be granted the right and the facilities to
participate in it. There are different opinions existing
among the groups responsible, but only with regard to the
proper steps to be undertaken in order to reach this aim.

The opinion supported by the Volkshochschulen starts from
the conviction that the state is obligated to provide its
citizens with an all-covering system of adult education which
is publicly supported, publicly guaranteed and publicly
controlled. The state has to accomplish its obligations
through the provision of public utilities such as, for
instance, the Volkshochschulen.

The German Volkshochschule as the Central Public Institution for Adult Education

The Volkshochschulen as public centres are not only open
to all who are already motivated to take part in their programmes of activities, they are also concerned to stimulate
and encourage participation among people whose previous
experience is not such that it would prompt them to come
to the Volkshochschulen of their own accord.

Education and culture are an indispensable element of
local community development. Within the framework of the
many cultural and educational activities supported by local
authorities, Volkshochschulen contribute to the social,
intellectual and cultural development of the general public.
They provide essential knowledge and skills; they encourage
insights and attitudes by means of which the community gains
more active and more responsible members.

The institutional connection accords with the close
relationship between the local community and its Volkshochschule; Volkshochschulen are provided by local authorities in
various statutory forms. This support requires the disclosure
of their finances, the content and aims of their educational
programmes, the organisation of their work and the statistics
of participation. It documents the Volkshochschulen's claim
to be regarded as public institutions for the provision of
adult and continuing education.

Financing the Volkshochschule

In the Federal Republic the VHS have for many years been building up a position in the educational system commensurate with their tasks. The improvement of public financial support and the increasing number of full-time staff are matched by a steadily growing volume of teaching, expansion of the range of programmes offered, improvement of the types of activity and teaching methods, as well as a steadily growing number of participants.

The present qualitative provision of VHS remains inadequate and needs further investment to provide the support and development required to meet the demands of educational policy being made upon them. The present state of development indicates above all the following shortcomings:

(1) Development of educational policy in the Lander is so uneven that comparability of standards with respect to the position and aims of the VHS can only be gained with difficulty and the achievements of the VHS receive very varied recognition.

(2) There is a regional sliding scale of educational provision within the Federal Republic, as a rule with a similar distinction between town and country. The quantity and quality of programmes of continuing education differ between industrial and rural regions, sometimes appreciably so. Within cities there are serious imbalances in the provision of programmes enjoyed by different districts.

(3) Those social strata where there is less familiarity with education and less cultural activity have, both in rural and urban areas, fewer opportunities to find stimulating programmes of continuing education which are tailored to their needs.

(4) The programmes offered by VHS, both in individual subjects and in multi-disciplinary fields of activity, reveal educational shortcomings resulting from lack of time to prepare curricula and instructional materials.

(5) The facilities of the VHS are insufficient with respect to full-time qualified staff and appropriate purpose-designed premises.

Expansion of the work of the VHS will cost money. A programme of investment in the area of public continuing education is a foremost priority for Lander and local

authorities and should be guaranteed on a long term basis
through legislation. The sources of finance are of equal
significance:

(1) Finance through the body providing the VHS, which
either within the framework of the statutory
responsibility placed upon it or through the Land
promotes and guarantees the expansion of investment (including basic provision) in the public
central sector of continuing education through
special grants towards capital investment and
staffing costs.

(2) Finance by students who through course fees and
supplementary individual expenditure (travel costs,
literature, equipment) make a contribution which
greatly varies among the different Lander and
local authorities.

Mixed financing from various sources will also be the
appropriate method in the future. In addition, federal and
Land government grants should support central development and
service activities and guarantee long-term work in the central
service institutes of the VHS and their Land Associations.

Public financing of the VHS is at present inadequate.
With the VHS share of the financing of public education
standing at less than one percent, it is clear that equal
status for adult and continuing education is still far from
being achieved.

Programme Provision of the Volkshochschulen

The extensive responsibilities of the Volkshochschulen
(VHS) as public institutions for the provision of adult and
continuing education require a broadly conceived and methodologically varied programme directed towards the needs of the
participants.

To plan in accordance with the needs of participants
means attempting to take account of the different circumstances which arise as a result of age, sex, social origin,
school education, linguistic milieu, vocational experience and
individual abilities. It does not contradict the principle
of openness for the VHS to prepare parts of their programmes
for specifically defined groups.

The starting point must be that groups which are
alienated from certain programmes by reason of their background and social situation can more easily be persuaded to
cooperate if a direct approach is made to them within the

framework of their own lives, making it possible for them to meet the kind of people with whom they are familiar and with whom they can converse easily.

In statements about the role of the VHS, three different functions have long been identified as being of equal importance and value: to help people study, to help people gain a perspective and a critical sense, and to help people acquire habits of independent activity.

Taking account of these general objectives, special points of emphasis can be developed depending on local and regional conditions. These might include:

(1)   study skills
(2)   society, politics, law
(3)   educational issues, psychology, philosophy, religion
(4)   literature, art, music, the media
(5)   mathematics, natural sciences, technology
(6)   economics, commercial practice
(7)   languages
(8)   housekeeping
(9)   health, gymnastics, hygiene
(10) games and modelling
(11) late acquisition of school qualifications

This listing of subject areas serves to give a general idea of the programme. The VHS, however, also offer interdisciplinary work in order to relate their programmes to the individual situations of participants. The differing expectations of those to whom the VHS address themselves are also matched by a broad spectrum of learning objectives. To meet the varying prerequisites and expectations of their public the VHS offer courses which vary in the degree of student commitment required, in standards and in objectives.

The following general types of study activity can be identified:

(1)   Those leading to examinations uniformly organised at the federal level on the basis of systematically constructed courses with standardised objectives (Volkshochschule certificates);

(2)   Those organised in accordance with supra-regional didactic models which contain recommendations as to content, methods and objectives and can be varied according to local conditions;

(3)   Those based on local agreements which can be developed depending on the local situation, if appropriate, through contact with interest groups; and

(4) Those in which the participants themselves decide on the teaching methods to be used, in which case procedures are worked out by the course itself, or in the context of a self-study programme.

Alongside content, objectives and degree of commitment, the structure of VHS programmes is characterised by efforts to do justice to the varying levels of ability represented by the students. There is a continuum which stretches from elementary instruction to academic disciplines. It is equally possible to obtain an elementary school certificate and to take part in academic post-graduate study.

The views of participants as regards their readiness to be involved and the form that this involvement should take may vary. The VHS therefore offer various forms of educational activity. Each requires a different kind of involvement.

Distinctions can be made among:

(1) Courses of instruction which prepare for specific learning objectives and require regular practice;

(2) Study groups in which issues are analysed and which require independent-minded and critical participation;

(3) Conversation circles which provide for exchange and consideration of experiences and points of view;

(4) Autonomous working groups to promote personal activity in which, under leadership, different creative patterns are developed and applied; and

(5) Series of lectures and special meetings (platform discussions, braintrusts, individual lectures with discussion) in which information is made available and it is left to the participants to make whatever use of it they wish.

There is a long tradition of such activities on an evening basis. In addition there is an increasing number of daytime meetings. Possibilities include:

(1) daytime courses
(2) weekend seminars
(3) longer-term full-time courses
(4) seminars of a week's duration within the framework of paid educational leave
(5) short and extended study trips

(6) exhibitions
(7) individual opportunities for study on an ad hoc
     basis

A type of VHS activity developed in the last decade is
the media-linked course. These courses, e.g. in collaboration
with television and radio programmes and supported by accompanying printed material, offer the opportunity to explore
more fully what has been heard and seen.

Demands on and Problems for the Volkshochschulen
───

The interdependence of all people and the accelerated
pace of change in all areas of life have created a situation
in which it is more than ever necessary to provide adult and
continuing education to help people cope with their daily
lives.

Formerly learning was considered a matter for young
people. For a long time this traditional attitude determined
the conception of the adult's role. Scarcely any attention
was paid to the continuing education of adults and no support
was provided for it. Only in very recent times has a gradual
change in this attitude become apparent.

The need for adult study is penetrating the public
consciousness more and more, based on the effects that
scientific and technological development have brought about
and the efforts to shape our communal life in a way that makes
a high degree of autonomy and cooperation possible.

Scientific and technological development has led not only
to changes in the organisation of work which bring about
changing demands in people's working lives, but, with its
innovations, it also has had a profound effect on the shaping
of everyday life and leisure. The changes in consumer
society are causing more and more people to ask what is the
point of the demands and distractions of modern life. Fewer
and fewer people declare themselves to be satisfied with a
pre-arranged life. More and more attempts are being made
to avoid the hurly-burly, and instead to develop forms of
activity in which people can discover their own potentialities
and which at the same time stimulate communication. Corresponding initiatives develop to some extent informally. But
at the same time demands on institutionalised adult education
thereby develop. The VHS can meet these demands through
programmes of a kind which allow scope for the participants'
needs for personal experience and personal development.

The demands made on the VHS are also based on the fact
that adults are today at a disadvantage compared with the
younger generation. Today's adult will have had comparatively
fewer educational opportunities in his youth. And today's

adult has to adjust to living conditions for which he was not given preparation in his youth.

The lost ground that adults have to make up is particularly obvious in the case of school-leaving certificates. This makes it necessary for adult education to be linked into the primary, secondary and tertiary sectors of the school system. Opportunities for cooperation are available through activities of the VHS. The proper way of developing them further entails, even for courses which lead to recognised school-leaving certificates, choosing content material and developing types of programmes that are appropriate for the situation and experience of the participants. Educational organisation of this kind is appropriate for adults when it can be carried out within the framework of a modular system. An example of this is the recognition being accorded to the VHS Certificates. Students must be enabled to repeat final examinations, in full or in part.

The principle of the modular system is also applicable to vocational adult education. In the context of the labour market it concerns the foundations of material existence. Education for adjustment to the market is therefore of foremost importance. The VHS offer courses which are appropriately related to vocational qualifications. But they can also see obligations that go beyond this, for a narrow and purely functional conception of vocational adult education will not meet the actual need for variously applicable qualifications nor do justice to the fact that the way in which qualifications are acquired plays a part in determining attitudes to other people and to social pressures. The demands on adult education are therefore met when the VHS, even in the context of vocational learning processes where a high standard is required, develops a style of work which supports and fosters individual self-confidence.

It is therefore to satisfy part of the demands on adult education that the VHS should create opportunities to learn how to learn, and this is achieved through the use of examples and problems which, being rooted in life situations, motivate and stimulate adults to find their own ways to solve problems.

Parents. Education of parents of the kind that has long been practised by VHS in courses and working groups was for a long time concerned mainly with upbringing in early childhood. For all the significance that should still be attached to this today there are nevertheless demands which go beyond this sphere. Differentiation in the school system causes parents to be intensely concerned with problems of schooling.

The relationship of the generations to one another, influenced by the rapid changes in living conditions, has taken on forms which present adult education with a very particular challenge. The problem is to develop forms of communication which strengthen the self-confidence of the age groups and at the same time increase knowledge about and encourage mutual respect for different backgrounds.

Older People. The relationship between the generations appears to have suffered particularly with respect to the situation of older people. The proportion of this age group will increase considerably in the near future. It is in their interests and the interest of everyone that they should not withdraw from life. Bound up with this is the need to prepare oneself for advancing years and for encouragement and help to be given in the preparation. Adult education for older people through the VHS is therefore not a matter of "care of the aged." Rather it should comprise efforts to stimulate them to take part in cultural and social life.

Problems of public life cannot be solved at the present time within national boundaries alone. The extent and speed with which influences and disturbances are spread has woven for us a web of worldwide dependencies. The extraordinary intensification of trading relations has brought possibilities of communicaton and exchange among people that were not previously known. The world has become smaller. European cooperation is a challenge to multilingualism.

Here adults have a particularly large amount of ground to make up. This is met by a programme of language courses through the VHS which makes possible realistic, applicable language learning. This can contribute to the understanding of the social and cultural situations of other peoples and countries. The ability to communicate which is acquired thereby enables better use to be made of the enlarged scope that now exists in work and leisure.

Discovering and trying out ways of self-expression and formative creativity both as an individual and in a group, for which the VHS provides opportunities, can extend the scope for creative development. Experiences gained thereby encourage people to become more self-assured. They foster conviviality and release forces which enable one to enhance the humane side of social life.

Developing the humane side of social life assumes some relationship to cultural tradition, which once lay right at the centre of the work of the VHS, and remains topical today. Sensitivity to artistic endeavour in various periods can lead to a consciousness of history which, when applied to the present day, provides insight into complex interrelationship of life and helps prepare for the future.

Educational Leave

It is still too early to report on substantial experiences with educational leave as the laws in five of the Lander of the Federal Republic of Germany are still relatively new and also quite different. Some remarks on the general situation can be made, however.

Since the sixties educational leave has been publicly discussed in the Federal Republic of Germany. The term has generally been accepted. Misunderstandings connected with this designation very rarely arise now. Strictly speaking, it should be understood as follows, however: "Paid leave of absence from other work for the purpose of continuing education." This formulation was also used by the Educational Council in its so called "structure plan" of 1970. According to the future conception of the Educational Council and in its overall concept, educational leave is an integral part of the system of continuing education.

Educational leave is therefore not only supported by the trade unions, it is considered to be necessary from an educational research and policy point of view as well. One can, from the emancipating as well as from the economic aspect, advocate educational leave. Accordingly, there are recommendations for educational leave from UNESCO, the "General Conference on International Labour Organization" and from the "Council of Experts for the Overall Economic Development in the Federal Republic of Germany."

The problem of financing is unresolved in public discussions and in the implementation of existing laws. The originally envisaged solution--namely that costs for the period in which no services are rendered by the absentee were to be borne by a compensatory fund from employers, that programme costs were to be taken over by public funds, and that participants' fees were not to exceed normal costs of living--could not be realized due to the economic situation of both private industry and public authorities.

Taking all these various aspects into consideration one can say, in a highly simplified way, the following: The laws concerning educational leave which were enacted recently in the Lander of Bremen, Hamburg, Hesse, West Berlin and Lower Saxony have not received immediate approval of potential consumers, as had been expected at the beginning of the discussion on educational leave.

Due to the labour market situation there is the risk that only those employees who are already qualified and who do not care if they eventually lose their jobs as a result of participation will take advantage of their right to educational leave.

The question of how to distribute the financing of educational leaves could not be solved due to the economic situation.   Therefore decisive elements of stimulus and orientation are missing that would fully integrate educational leave into the overall system of continuing education.

Since at the moment much more emphasis has to be placed on short-term job security and job provision, it is particularly difficult to convince employees of the long-term chances and advantages of educational leave and to motivate them for participation.

The laws on educational leave in the Lander mentioned above were enacted without sufficient experience with a methodologically and didactically new form of continuing education.   It is only now, with programme models being initiated in a larger context, that experiences with them can be used to create better conditions for future regulations.

Due to the lack of appropriate elements in the various laws, it is extraordinarily difficult to gain an insight into how many employees really make use of the legal possibilities. It seems certain, however, that only a relatively small percentage of employees are able to and do make use of opportunities for paid leave.

Local institutions of continuing education are by no means in a position, not even in those Lander in which laws on educational leave exist, to provide the necessary facilities, personnel and course content to fulfill the legal claims of the vast numbers of employees.   It would take some time before the need could be fully satisfied.

There is continuing discussion of whether educational leave as a whole should best be implemented within the framework of an overall reform of the educational system and thus also of continuing education.

ADULT EDUCATION IN FRANCE: THE SOCIO-CULTURAL

OR VOLUNTARY SUB-SYSTEM*

Pierre Besnard and Bernard Lietard

Universite Rene Descartes

Introduction

This report provides us with a systemic and socio-pedagogic view of adult education in France. From the systemic viewpoint, the French system of adult education is divided, as is true for most other foreign systems, into three sub-systems:

(1) The School Sub-System. This includes those forms of adult education which are linked to or integrated into the body of initial education, or which, with respect to different institutions, are under the direction of administrations responsible also for initial education.

(2) The Occupational Sub-System. Included here are the various forms of training which are connected with enterprises or with vocational organizations, with the exception of apprenticeship training which is considered a part of initial education.

(3) The Socio-Cultural or Voluntary Sub-System. This sub-system consists of those forms of adult education, formal or informal, which are not linked with the two above-mentioned sub-systems. It includes more particularly what we call

---

*This report is adapted from a much longer paper furnished to the project by Besnard and Lietard. Included here is material dealing in particular with socio-cultural "animation" and the work of the "animateurs." These are topics that are not discussed in detail in Parts I and II.

"the out-of-school" system, the voluntary sector, social and cultural activities, "animation," and personal education. The prevailing characteristic of this sub-system is its informality. Because of this informality, and given the fact that participants are not registered, statistical data are very difficult to obtain.

From the socio-pedagogic viewpoint (Besnard, et al., 1978), we are considering the education process in its totality, as a social product and as a product of trans-formation. The socio-pedagogic approach attempts to analyze not only the act of education, but also institutional, sociological, economic, and political determinants. It also studies interrelationships among elements of a structure with several levels (such as educational background, the institution, the educational system, and the social system).

The Socio-Cultural or Voluntary Sub-System

As we have said, adult education in France can be analyzed into three sectors: school, vocational, and socio-cultural. The last sector is relatively more autonomous than the others and, when compared to the total adult education system, it is in that sector that the most innovative initia-tives concerning education and culture have developed.

Coming from the French "Education Populaire" (Popular Education), it is similar to the American recreation system in some ways, to Yugoslav self-management activities, to the cooperative currents of the Scandinavian countries, and to the British "community development."

This sector is very complex: multiple establishments at all levels intermingled with diverse social practices, activities led by very different types of instructors (occupa-tional specialists, technicians, volunteers, militants, etc.), equally varied publics. No study can as yet fully describe it. We will sketch it with the help of recent publi-cations (Besnard, Poujol, and Labourie, 1978; Besnard, 1980; Besnard, in press).

This form of adult education, called "animation socio-culturelle," is a type of educational and cultural movement that aims, through local facilities (communities, districts), to develop cultural or personal educational activities usually during participants' free time. Many voluntary associations, local communities, the State and Ministries, the large educational and cultural federations that are legion in France, and various cultural, educational, sports movements are taking many initiatives in this field. "Animation socio-culturelle" can be associated with the definition of adult education given by Johnstone and Rivera in their important book <u>Volunteers for Learning</u> (1965) regarding all the forms of education and culture chosen by participants. In this sense, socio-cultural animation is sometimes introduced as a "parallel school," even as a "counter-school," able to contribute to the renewal of the whole education system through its initiatives and innovations.

Organization and Structure of Socio-Cultural "Animation"

The history of popular education and the sociological and cultural aspects of socio-cultural "animation" reveal a great diversity because of the diverse origins of the many public and private institutions, organizations, and associations--all different in nature and size--that form its structure.

There exists a complex network of federations with thousands of members, of clubs, and of sections of various departments that oversee "animation" activities and control them through subsidies. Moreover, due to the law of 1901 concerning voluntary associations, new organizations are created every day to promote such interests as ecology, group motorbike riding, stamp-collecting, nudism, conservation of monuments or sites, disco music, "football" (i.e. soccer), walking tours, silk painting, cable TV, photography, majorettes, street theater, cultural tourism, "third age" clubs, playgrounds, volunteers at work sites, scientific clubs, etc.

Animation was organized in institutionalized forms within the last 30 years, particularly under the dual efforts of private initiative and State financing, by setting up socio-cultural facilities and creating positions of professional "animateurs."

There is no need here to give an exhaustive list of all establishments. We will only present the actual organization of current socio-cultural animation in France, by citing examples of some typical institutions in the socio-cultural field representing different levels, from voluntary associations to national federations, to ministerial departments, passing by intermediary regional or local structures (a field in which we include cultural, sports and educational activities).

Overall Structure: Toward a System of "Animation"?

Socio-cultural animation could be considered perhaps as a part or sub-system of the cultural and educational system of society and analyzed as such. But this hypothesis should be questioned. Indeed, it is a coherent whole composed of such elements as institutions, organizations, associations, facilities, animateurs and publics--that are all related. These relationships form the structures that characterize the type of organization of this system.

Operating Levels of "Animation"

(1) Informal, Spontaneous, Natural Groups. This would include groups of children, adults, pairs, and "pals" with various interests such as sports, culture, etc. (for example, children who play together without "animateurs" and without registered associations, or adults who meet to spend an evening together, etc.). It is impossible to inventory them all. Even if it is not an institutionalized type of animation, it is a very important part of cultural animation, worth mentioning.

(2) Voluntary Associations. This is the natural framework of animation. Just as Tocqueville called the phenomenon of association the "nerve of the democracy," so it is the subject of renewed political and theoretical interest, becoming more and more important in the "animation" of local community life. Indeed, association structures permit the exercise of participation and power, and the development of expressiveness and an identity that religious and socio-political organizations (parties, churches, schools) could not implement because of their size, tendency to adopt bureaucratic and technocratic guidelines, and neglect of individual aspirations that are inconsistant with large abstract orientations.

In 1976, the D.A.P. (Developpement des Associations de Progres/The Association for the Development of Associations of Progress) observed that in 100 days 8,000 associations were "born." One out of four French people is a member of an association and many belong to several. There are an estimated 250,000 associations at the present time (and roughly one million since the law of 1901).

Of the 2,500 associations founded each year since 1973, 15 percent are of the socio-cultural type, 8 percent leisure, and 20 percent sports. Thus about 43 percent are part of the larger socio-cultural sub-system (that includes the sports sector) (Labourie, 1978).

We must point out that a good number of associations are not specifically social and cultural, but still perform the functions of social and cultural "animation." This leads us to believe, thanks to the voluntary sociological framework, that socio-cultural animation covers a field widened to include the voluntary and is not limited to only registered socio-cultural institutions.

This explains the considerable statistical difference between the number of professional "animateurs,"--estimated at 10,000 in 1976--and the number of volunteer "animateurs,"--estimated at 275,000 (Ruet, 1976).

From their numbers, one realizes the importance of the voluntary associations and of their volunteer "animateurs" for socio-cultural animation, compared to the reduced battalion of professional animateurs who may be regarded as the "career army" for future animation.

Other reasons for the growth of this phenomenon of associations are the greater and greater diversification of cultural interests which give rise to the associations (such as ecology, women, jazz, video), problems related to daily life (quality of life, third age or older persons, etc.), and the defense of the rights and interests of different categories of people (consumers, tenants, users, etc.) that resemble types of animation in British and Danish communities. Those associations constitute a means of social expression and a true apprenticeship of power; they play an undeniable role in the advancement and selection of the social elite (Poujol, 1978).

(3) Local Communities: Animation on a Human Scale. If we have insisted upon the significance of these voluntary asociations as basic elements of socio-cultural animation, it is because they are the sources of initiatives and the catalysts of the socio-cultural dynamic. This dynamic will expand more at the local level, with the necessary institutional means and material. Local communities* play the role of "Maecenas" ("Mecene," patron of the arts) more and more, by encouraging socio-cultural initiatives through subsidies, equipment and facilities, and paid personnel--especially since the 1960's. Following official incentives, towns increasingly are providing social-cultural facilities in new areas (youth homes, cultural centers and clubs). Local communities not only grant subsidies for operating them, but also support their total realization.

A good example of socio-cultural action is that of the C.A.F. (Caisses d'Allocations Familiales/Family Allowance Funds). The C.A.F. not only pays allowances to families, but also contributes to the realization and operation of facilities such as social centers, young workers homes, leisure centers, holiday centers, etc. (through loans,

---

*In 1975, France had 36,394 communities, of which only 20 had more than 150,000 inhabitants (figures cited by Labourie, 1978).

subsidies, and payments for services). Depending on the region, the C.A.F. devotes 50, 60, even 70 percent of its social appropriations to the realization effort under direct management. They participate in ",concerted actions" at the department level, with the "Conseils Generaux" (General Councils), in ministerial management and direction (Conseil Social et Culturel de la Moselle/Social and Cultural Council of Moselle, for example) and at the town level (Office Social et Culturel de Rennes/ Social and Cultural Office of Rennes, for example).

In 1974, the C.A.F. employed 1,900 social assistants (social welfare workers who are usually women) and 113 socio-cultural "animateurs," while also subsidizing associations, social centers, and young workers' homes. Their instigating and innovative actions have been "capital" in the development of social and cultural animation of new areas of urban buillding. Besides those, there also are other organizations and multiple socio-cultural facilities, which have more specialized and local activities.

These would be the following:

(1) Leisure centers for children: open air centers (2,290 in 1970), leisure centers (6,141 in 1975), childhood homes, children's libraries, clubs and technical workshops;

(2) Homes of Youth and Culture: polyvalent (study circles, workshops, sport and leisure clubs, summer camps, etc.) which went from 180 in 1956 to 1,235 in 1965;

(3) Vacation centers (colonies): which attracted 1,400,000 children (1975) from 6 to 14 years old, and which included 7,135 centers in 1965;

(4) Social and socio-cultural centers: some 700, which mostly provide cultural services such as book rentals, educational workshops, and art or handi-craft workshops; and

(5) "Les maisons de la culture" (culture homes): numbering 12 in 1975, they are more devoted to cultural than social improvement, and tend to identify themselves more by cultural activities than "animation." They orient their efforts toward creation and diffusion from a decentralized perspec-tive. They are "heavy" facilities, the prototypes of which are in Bourges, Amiens, and Grenoble. The "maisons" have been influenced by Andre Malraux's conception of the culture that presides at birth:

the culture of the creators--an elitist conception
of a culture elaborated in a particular aristocracy
(the "avant garde", "intelligentsia", cultural
producers). Their staff are on ambiguous terms with
animation and with animateurs, who are considered
too often as assistants, diffusers or disseminators,
"relais," slaves, creators as well as revealers of
an unstable popular culture.

In their expenditures for culture, local communities
devote an average of 25 percent of their budget for socio-
cultural animation, while the ministries devote 14 percent to
it. Thus, there is an important and increasing contribution
of local communities (whose financial resources are less than
one-fourth that of the State budget).

(4) Intermediate level: Socio-Cultural Institutions--
Movements and National and Regional Structures. Socio-
cultural animation also owes its development and its national
and regional dimension to institutions, movements and structures strongly intermingled in the social and cultural
life of the country. They are relatively more important than
the local voluntary associations (with whom they frequently
cooperate or federate).

Labourie's Typology of Socio-Cultural Institutions

As already pointed out, these institutions, movements,
and organizations are ambiguous, and their socio-cultural
realities are complex. R. Labourie's book (1978) presents
37 types of socio-cultural institutions. They are mainly:

"Movements" and Institutions. Their dimension is often
regional or national; they combine or federate local and
departmental groups or sections. Among the "movements"
(called "popular education" for some time), the following
two general kinds can be identified:

Youth movements such as Scouts, Catholic action, Protestant action, lay or secular action, etc.

Movements and federations such as "People and Culture,"
Leo Lagrange, youth hostels, women's unions, civic
unions, social unions, sincere friends, rural centers,
etc.

Socio-Cultural Structures and Facilities. Even if they
have a certain number of traits in common with the movements

and institutions, particularly regarding their historic origins and birth, their dominant characteristic is to act as service agencies in more "neutral" ways than the above-mentioned movements, and often to play a complementary role, or to replace the Public Service. Some of them intervene as investors and promoters of socio-cultural facilities, and their influence is important in social and cultural life; some examples are real estate promoters, HLM officers (Habitation a Loyer Modere/Moderate Rental Housing), and family allowance funds staff.

Centers of cultural animation, numbering 23 in 1977, operate from the same perspective as "les maisons de la culture" in implementing the policy of the Secretary of State for Culture. The facilities are "lighter;" they try to integrate animation directly into the schools, firms, and districts, in order to disseminate or diffuse the culture.

Local community cultural centers, 280 of them in 1974, are linked to municipal governments, which act in liaison with les maisons de la culture" and cultural animation centers, homes of youth and culture, and associations following diverse objectives which vary according to town.

Finally, beyond the above two general categories, numerous other types of socio-cultural organizations may be identified:

Educational and cultural centers (such as the new towns of Yerves, Istres, Evry, etc.) created from a perspective of integrating social, educational, cultural, sport and other functions;

Socio-cultural, school, new town centers, which are polyvalent (information, welcome, animation, advice, sports, audio-visual etc.);

Leisure and open air centers and playgrounds;

Libraries (created either by public bodies, firms, or associations) and museums;

Information centers for youth;

National parks and environment initiation centers;

Work sites (15 associations and 1,500 volunteers);

Cine-clubs for special or old movies (10,000 presently in nine federations);

"Les clubs aux armees" (330 agricultural, 2,000 leisure in 1971);

Youth clubs (speleology, bridge, photo, scientific etc.);

Third age clubs for older persons (8,000 in 1977);

Various hostels for "young workers" (rural, socio-educational);

Family vacation houses and vacation villages;

Works councils in firms and their role in animation: libraries, vacation centers, social tourism, etc.;

Festival committees and visitor information centers that participate in local animation;

Social and cultural offices which are responsible for coordination between municipal governments and local associations, and which play a part in the socio-cultural environment and act as organisms of "concerted action" at the municipal, county, departmental and regional level, depending upon the case; and

National organizations, such as the Franco-German Office and the Franco-Quebec Office, whose objective is to develop relations and exchanges between two national cultures.

The "Animateurs"--Essential Agents of the Socio-Cultural Sector

Once the complex universe of socio-cultural animation is penetrated, persons called "animateurs," who are essential as well as ambiguous, appear. Who are they? Volunteers or professionals? Militants or civil servants? Revolutionary idealists? Skilled technicians of recreation or merchants of leisure?

Sometimes they are called socio-cultural "animateurs," sometimes socio-educational "animateurs," and sometimes cultural or social "animateurs." Their different names reveal the multiplicity of their tasks, as well as of the publics they reach and the institutions in which they work. The only constant is the term "animateur" itself. The various definitions below will indicate their main characteristics and duties, and also give some notion of the level of professionalization and training of these agents (Besnard, in press).

Definitions of Socio-Cultural "Animateurs"

Definitions of "animateur" preceded definitions of "animation." Ten years ago, definitions were few; then they began to proliferate, often by expressing the duties and tasks of the animateurs (functional definitions), or the ideal personality type of an animateur, or by stating appropriate value systems (ideologies). Sometimes the definitions referred to a specific sector of social and cultural activity to which they pertained, amd sometimes they simply referred to the type of payment or employment (professional animateurs, paid or volunteer, full-time or part-time, permanent or temporary).

Below are several definitions that illustrate this diversity:

(1) The "animateur," a professional agent of socio-educational animation, is a social worker. His duties are to give rise to and develop activites with educational, cultural and sport objectives. These activities apply to everyone: they lead to continuing and global education.

(2) The "animateurs" are specialized agents, whose role is to promote and assure socio-educational animation. Thus, their duties are to give rise and develop educational and cultural activities (civic, economic, artistic, sports) that facilitate total cultural development.

(3) The socio-cultural "animateur" is a man at the "crossroads" where all the needs, wishes and dreams of men and society converge and telescope.

(4) The animateur is the one who calls himself animateur because of the main activity he performs.

(5) The animateur can help people to understand social mechanisms, to reproduce them, to make them more responsible for themselves, to get them acquainted, to help them attain their projects, to advise them, to relax them, to facilitate the integration of "marginals" (outsiders).

From the viewpoint of Jean Hurstel, animateur in Montbeliard, the definition of the functions of the animateur derives from confrontation with daily practice and a commitment in the name of certain values:

> The first duty of the animateur is to play the traditional role attributed to him in another way. It is a matter of total refusal of the system in which the profession is established--which breaks with the idea of a career, with established powers, and with the cultural producer-sellers (creators) and consumers (public) system. The privileged field of animation is the working class, peasant, or the middle classes. The animateur is a creator of forms (like the educator) and a creator of contradictions, and animation in that sense is neither a technology nor a methodology, but a mode of social transformation which aims to establish a cultural democracy. The animateur is the carrier of a question and of a desire; he cannot be content to reproduce an institutional operation--he is a creator.

Animateur: Function or Career?

To avoid confusion, it is necessary to recall a key phenomenon of social and cultural life: that is that the great majority of the social actors are volunteers (250,000 of them) who participate in socio-cultural animation in all its forms but especially within the association framework. If one considers that animation is not only the field of professional animateurs (a maximum of about 10,000), but of volunteers, one finds volunteer animateurs are an immense number compared to the small "career army" of animateurs. The latter are very often "militants" responsible for the objectives and means of their animation, that is to say, for the same policy concerning their movement, institution or organization.

A tree must not be taken for the forest, and animation must not be represented as identifiable with (identical to) professional activities. There are two types of cultural agents who intervene in an associative or complementary manner: the volunteers and the professionals.

Another comment concerns the training of animateurs: to be an animateur is not the monopoly of the professional animateurs who have had certified training (CAPASE) and present a certificate, adhere to professional rules, and have other recognized qualifications. Many volunteers have trained themselves in animation by different ways and often "sur le tas" (by experience). Many excel in a function of an animateur, which they have not made a career (even if some of them end up by moving from the function to the career).

Thus if one considers, beyond the occupation, the function of animateur--that everyone can perform in his social, cultural, or political life--one finds there are not only 10,000 or 250,000 animateurs, but millions of natural ones, who act or operate with groups of young people, friends, old people, people of any category, on various topics and who depend on the "needs expressed by the populations with whom they live."

Functions of Socio-Cultural Animateurs

It is only since 1966-68 that one finds detailed descriptions of the functions of animateurs, while the professional training of the animateurs was becoming more specific, presaging the advent of a genuine profession or career of socio-cultural animateur.

In 1966, a work group formed under the authority of the Ministry of Youth supplied the first elaboration of the functions of the animateur. Following that work group, a national commission including representatives of the State and of the associations produced a document which served as a basis for "general principles" regarding the status of professional socio-educational and socio-cultural animation personnel. It specified the various functions performed by animateurs, including global and technical animation, coordination of activities, administration/ management, research and creation, training, and general responsibility (orientation/inspiration).

The F.O.N.J.E.P. in 1974 launched the first important inquiry about socio-cultural animateurs, which led to interesting outcomes at the national level. Below are the main results concerning the functions and characteristics of the animateur:

Work Location. Fifty-six percent of the animateurs work at one unique location (mainly youth centers and young workers' homes). Forty-four percent work at multiple locations and social centers. Specifically: popular education, 18.5 percent; music centers, 7.4 percent; youth movements, 7.2 percent; C.E.M.E.A., 2.5 percent; municipal animateurs, 2.0 percent, and U.F.C.V., 1.5 percent.

Framework of the Function. For more than 92 percent of the animateurs, their employer is an association under the law of 1901. This verifies the essential role of the associations

in the social dynamic of the animateur, playing the role
of a veritable out-of-school cultural "service" (with the
help of local communities and the State). Townships employ
6.5 percent of animateurs; family allowance funds (C.A.F.),
5.1 percent; private firms, works councils, missions, etc.,
a minimal percentage.

Special Features of the Function. All animateurs perform
different categories of functions regularly: work with
individuals, 72 percent; relations with a group, 56 percent;
with publics, 42 percent; coordination, 43 percent; training
(of animateurs and staff) 31 percent; management, 37 percent;
documentation/research, 31 percent; and specialized activities, 35 percent.
    Thus, the socio-cultural animateur appears to be
essentially a middleman engaged in specialized activities
and research. He is also a coordinator and manager, and
occasionally a trainer.

Some Sociological Characteristics of Animateurs. Masculine dominance is very strong (78 percent of animateurs are
men). However, one notes a progressive "feminization" of the
occupation. Socio-cultural animateurs are rather young on the
whole: 72 percent are between 26 and 46 years old; 93 percent
are less than 47 years old. New generations are replacing
the founding and veteran animateurs of 1936-1945. Most
animateurs come from the middle classes.

Publics Served. The publics served by animateurs include
a variety of social categories: 80 percent are scholars
and young workers; 74 percent, employees; 41 percent, blue-
collar workers; 38 percent, staff/ executives; 36 percent,
housewives; and 29 percent, retired people. And for some
animateurs who are more "specialized": 23 percent work with
migrants; 22 percent work with delinquents; 19 percent work
with "social associations."
    The overall survey reveals, in short, great diversity
in the functions of animateurs, as is the case also with
activities, socio-cultural institutions, and publics reached.
Furthermore, the authors of this report are of the opinion
that animation penetrates the whole of daily life more and
more and tends to extend beyond the bounds of specialized
cultural facilities, culture "houses" (centers), etc. It
touches the full range of life spaces and lifetimes of
individuals and groups.

The Profession of Socio-Cultural Animateur

Most studies and statements about animation conclude
with doubts: Does animation exist? Is an occupation of

animateur possible? This type of doubt can be compared to
Raymond Aron's definition of sociology as "permanent self-
interrogation."

It can be observed, however, that this sector of social
life is following ineluctable institutionalization. It has
seen establishment of genuine occupational training recognized
by diplomas, such as CAPASE--DEFA, and also progressive
elaboration since 1969 of occupational statutes regarding
animateurs. The occupation of animateur, however, is a
reality: a "career army" estimated at 10,000 permanently
employed will increase its ranks, according to most recent
analyses. The literature on the topic obviously shows
evidence of increasing professionalization.

Statutes Related to Animateurs

In spite of the resistance, doubts, and "critiques" that
come from institutions, animateurs, the unions themselves,
and although a single unique national statute could not be
successfully established, a certain number of rules have been
codified progressively. Types of statutes have been established corresponding to different categories of animateurs.
The distribution of responsibilities in this field, the
plurality of conceptions of animation, the complexity of the
structure, and the multiplicity of types of animateurs make
the problem particularly difficult to deal with.

Since 1966, when the question of a statuatory basis for
animateurs arose, matters have progressed considerably. For
example, one recalls the action of the FONJEP in that field
as early as 1967. There was also the work of the parity
reflection group (State and associations) organized around
that question in 1968 that led to the 1970 publication of the
Act giving birth to the profession of Animateur, entitled
"Agreed-Upon General Principles" (circular of September 22,
1970).

In that Act, the animateur and his functions were
defined, motives were explained, and an occupational rating
"grid" was presented which related levels of competencies,
occupations, diplomas or qualifications, and wages. Additionally, a 1970 circular specified the conditions of recruitment
and hiring of animation personnel by local communities. It
indicated several binding ethical principles of this occupation, about which there has been much ink spilled, since its
provisions concerning the ideological freedom of animateurs
was highly ambiguous. A ministerial draft decree from the
(Home) Interior Ministry is expected; it sets forth the
conditions and career perspectives for municipal animateurs.
Other statutes (animateurs county, departmental, civil
servants, without status, contractual, "ditaches", etc...)

have seen the light of day since then, as have numerous collective agreements, especially for the personnel of large federations (FFMJC; Leo Lagrange League, township cultural centers, young worker's homes).

There are many opportunities as well as guarantees of security for animateurs that accompany this "irreversible historic process of professionalization" within a particular context of employer-employee relationships. These statutes and texts drew their inspiration largely from the Agreed-Upon General Principles, which fixed the overall framework of the occupation, while guaranteeing the autonomy of providing institutions against State monopoly.

The delicate question of the moral obligations of animateurs remains. Involved are problems of reference values, secrecy, and ideology, which reside in the always ambigious or equivocal domain of reflection, and in the absence of formal codification.

The Occupation of Animateur--Summing Up

Briefly stated below are a number of characteristics of this new occupation:

A largely masculine population, but in the process of feminization--especially in certain sectors;

Dominance of relatively young people (25 to 35 years old);

Personal experience in animation as well as professional diplomas and qualifications as criteria for entry into the occupation;

Emphasis on qualifications acquired on the job associated with long training periods (increasingly certified by the CAPASE);

Previous occupational qualification earned outside the animation field as an entry criteria;

The brevity of the "career";

A population that is often "overeducated" at the university level;

A shift from the volunteer to the professional;

A "militant" occupation which joins competence and an ideal--an "open, multiform occupation" and an occupation of "giving" (vocation and charisma);

The key role of training and of the CAPASE as a professional and pedagogic reference model;

Ambivalance of this occupation at all levels: ideological, institutional, pedagogic, research, creation, relations, etc.;

Pay variation by position and function, but within a narrow range--from 2,000 FF to 4,000 FF monthly (in 1978);

Workweeks often lasting 50 hours or more, with major work performed during the leisure time of the "animated";

Rather great freedom to organize one's time and a rather large power for initiative;

A profession said to be rather tiring, but where the energy flow is entwined with a militant and vocational gratification (which sometimes has neurotic aspects);

Recognition of the animateur as a "middle" level executive; for many, this means "social promotion" (compared to their original social class backgrounds);

For animateurs of higher class origins, the opportunity to exercise interesting responsibilities within a culturally valued sector, not directly linked to production;

Large number of candidates for this "function-profession-vocation" (36 percent believe it plays a political role of social transformation and 40 percent, an educational role);

For professional defense or protection, no overall organization for animateurs (such as, for example, the Association Nationale des Assure's Sociauz, for social welfare workers), although there are unions claiming to serve the interests of animateurs; and

Existence of animation professionals in the absence of a unique "profession" defined by codes and statutes.

It has been said that "it is truly because they exist as 'professionals' that animateurs can take the liberty of doubting their profession." Maybe it is time for animateurs to end this doubt and feeling of incapability once and for all, and to affirm without reserve a social practice and an identity that nobody contests.

The Role of Government in the Socio-Cultural Sub-System

A Limited Liberal Policy with Incentives. In the absence of an overall cultural policy (despite initiatives under Malraux), the action of the State in the field of animation is midway between liberalism of good form (whose dominant cultural models receive their inspiration from the coupling of elitist culture and mass culture), and a democratic conception respectful of cultural pluralism.

If there is a cultural policy, it is a policy of selectively backing up and encouraging here and there--according to criteria needing to be clarified--the multiple initiatives of the associations and local communities (which increasingly bear the financial burden).

The problem is ambiguous: at a time of increasing demand for self-action in many ways of life (self-training, self-achievement, self-animation, self-management), who would complain about this respectful and non-interventionist policy but those who wish an intensification of the influence of the "State-Ogre" (Besnard, 1977)--or those who realized that this liberal attitude could have a reverse effect through increased sterility in the matter of appropriations?

Incentives of the State toward out-of-school activities during the 19th and 20th centuries first were moral, and material aid was secured first through private initiatives and local communities. In 1936, the creation of a State Undersecretariat on Sports and Leisure marked the beginning of limited but genuine State aid in the socio-cultural field. After 1945, a certain number of cultural innovations developed (paradoxically, under Vichy) thanks to public aid: these included training centers for youth, a High Commission for Youth, youth homes, rural homes, etc.

The Planned Culture? Although there is no overall policy of culture and of animation, there are a number of important trends, and directions of the State in this field:

(1) Liberalism of incentive and working in concert (public and private);

(2) Neutral goodwill and limited financing;

(3) Setting-up of progressive planning of facilities and equipment, and of socio-cultural development in the Sixth Plan (Houses of Culture, other facilities);

(4) Aid to private training centers;

(5) Establishment of training centers;

(6) Creation of diplomas or degrees for animateurs; this is the first step toward statutes, professionalization, and occupational training;

(7) Overall encouragement of social and cultural participation;

(8) Decentralization, deconcentration and joint management;

(9) Emphasis on "concerted cultural development" (the Conseil du Developpment Culturel was created in 1970, and reaffirmed in the 1979 reorganization of the Ministry of Culture); and

(10) Encouragement of experimental activities, of "multipliers," and of polyvalent facilities.

A survey cited by Labourie (1978) gave the distribution of cultural expenditures among the different ministries: Culture, 42.5 percent; Education, 29.1 percent; Foreign Affairs, 9.7 percent; Youth and Sports, 6.9 percent; Agriculture, 3.3 percent; Others, 8.2 percent.

Fourteen percent of these expenditures concerned animation (cultural and socio-cultural) with the largest allocation for Youth and Sports (70 percent). With those structures--partly private, partly State--and with its very diversified organizations and purposes, socio-cultural animation does not appear as a formed system but as a system being formed, and operating throughout the cultural, school, and occupational training systems.

Although there have been various interpretations of it, animation does not appear to be an ideological device of the State. This is because of its pluralistic structure (State, associations, organizations, local communities) and also because of the multiple ideologies existing in it, which are much more subtly diversified than the political parties. Animation does not appear as a simple method of sociocultural development or even as a recreational technique, since it originated in popular education and in philosophical and militant ideals. It is more like a composite whole of practices and multiple organizations which act in the socio-cultural field with diverse objectives, and for various publics. Particular thanks should go to those cultural agents--volunteers and professionals--called "animateurs," whose characteristics and work within the "system of animation" in France have been analyzed in this report.

ADULT EDUCATION IN THE U.S.S.R.

Seymour M. Rosen*

United States Department of Education

The U.S.S.R. (Union of Soviet Socialist Republics)
stretches across the Eurasian landmass and is the largest
country in the world in area. It is the third largest in
population, the first being the People's Republic of China and
the second, India. The U.S.S.R.'s population totalled some
262 million in 1979.

The country is divided administratively and territorially
into 15 union-republics, each populated by and named after a
dominant nationality group but containing many other ethnic
groups as well. The Slavic group of republics consists of
the Russian S.F.S.R. (Soviet Federated Socialist Republic),
the Ukrainian S.S.R. (Soviet Socialist Republic), and the
Belorussian S.S.R. The Baltic group, not recognized as
constituent parts of the U.S.S.R. by the United States, is
composed of the Lithuanian, Latvian, and Estonian S.S.R.'s.
The Central Asian union-republics consist of Kazakh, Uzbek,
Kirgiz, Tadzhik, and Turkmen S.S.R.'s. The Caucasus group
contains the Armenian, Georgian, and Azerbaidzhan S.S.R.'s.
The fifteenth republic is the Moldavian S.S.R.

Slightly more than half of the U.S.S.R. population is
ethnically Russian, but it is likely that Russians will be a
minority in the near future, since other nationality groups,
particularly the Central Asians, have higher birth rates.

---

*This report was prepared in the author's capacity as a
doctoral candidate at Catholic University of America.
Mr. Rosen is author of, among other works, Education and
Modernization in the USSR (Reading, Mass.: Addison Wesley,
1971).

Along with ethnic and cultural differences, there are religious differences between the Slavic and other groups. Seventy percent of the population is reported to be atheist-- the favored "religion" supported by the Communist Party and the government (which includes the school system). Eighteen percent of the population is reported to be Russian Orthodox, and nine percent (mostly in Central Asia and the Caucasus) are reported to be Moslem. The numbers of religious sympathizers are probably higher than the reported figures.

The U.S.S.R.'s political, social, cultural, and economic system is dominated by the Communist Party and Marxist-Leninist doctrine. In doctrine and in law, the Party is the guiding institution of the country, and the "party line" rules ideology and practice. The Communist Party leadership provides the guidelines for the major national economic annual and five-year plans, which include directives for funding education as well as industry and for the determination of manpower priorities in every field. Party offices in every major social, cultural, and economic institution, including education, monitor daily performance for conformity with guidelines.

The U.S.S.R. is the world's second-ranking industrial power, out-produced overall only by the United States. The Soviet Union is largely self-sufficient, with significant oil and other fossil-fuel deposits, large supplies of waterpower and timber, and other natural resources. The country has highly developed mining, metallurgical, chemical, and machine-building industries.

The U.S.S.R., even granting reporting discrepancies, is one of the most literate countries in the world. Literacy has reportedly been achieved by 98.5 percent of the population between the ages of nine and forty-nine. The median level of educational attainment of the population is estimated to be between the eighth and ninth grade. For the needs of its current economy, however, Soviet officials have argued that at least a tenth-grade general education is needed, with components of "polytechnical training."

Adult education is a major means of achieving national manpower, economic, social, and cultural goals in the U.S.S.R. Its history goes back to Tsarist times. Literacy committees were established by enlightened gentry and others in the mid-19th century to begin the process of combatting massive illiteracy. So-called zemstvo schools for adult elementary education in rural areas, and Sunday schools for general adult education, were initiated at this time. Correspondence and evening education began late in the 19th century. Groups or societies for self-education by correspondence, using published journals and other aids to self-education, were formed. Evening classes were usually divided into illiterate, semi-literate, and more advanced groups. Adult pupils who passed the elementary level examination were granted an elementary school certificate. Some courses in evening schools provided education at the secondary level, and technical as well as general subjects were introduced.

After the Soviets came to power in 1917, they developed adult education programs on a large scale. Most notable were the literacy campaigns of the 1920's, which were massive attempts to teach the illiterate, predominantly in rural areas, by virtually anyone who was literate. (There was no post-testing to measure literacy retention.) In addition, "workers' faculties" (rabfaks) provided accelerated day, evening, and correspondence courses for workers and peasants who had not attended or completed secondary school, following which they were admitted to higher education institutions. A variety of other adult education programs were developed in the 1920's and 1930's, forerunners of today's informal as well as formal adult education programs.

Adult Education Policy

Broad policy in education in the U.S.S.R. is determined by the Communist Party leadership, which issues its own education directives as well as joint decrees with the national government. Policies are elaborated in implementing legislation and in regulations of the education ministries. A summary of U.S.S.R. policy on adult education is provided by Soviet officials in the field (Onushkin and Tonkonogaja, 1978):

> Education not only includes the period of direct general education but also embraces the whole system for providing further training for various categories of workers and raising their ideological, political and cultural level, and is conceived of as a process that continues throughout the active life of an individual....

> Adult education in the U.S.S.R. is one of the most important social factors for solving the strategic problems outlined in the programme of the Communist Party of the Soviet Union, namely the establishment of the material and technological foundation of communism, the improvement of socialist social attitudes, and their transformation into communist attitudes, and the moulding of men in the spirit of communist society.

In March, 1976, the 25th Congress of the Communist Party of the Soviet Union issued a directive on "Main

Directions for the Development of the U.S.S.R. National Economy in 1976-80." Like previous Party Congresses, it expressed concern for education in general ("USSR Economic Development Plan," 1976):

> The public education system is to be further developed in accordance with the demands of scientific and technical progress and the tasks of steadily raising the working people's cultural, technical, and educational level and improving the training of skilled cadres of workers and specialists.

The directive also provided a mandate to improve adult education:

> The training of qualified working people and other workers of the mass trades is to be improved and their qualifications are to be raised. The work of evening (shift) schools is to be improved... The further rise of the level of training and ideological-political education of specialists and workers is to be considered a major task...The network of mass libraries and clubs is to be expanded. The people's universities are to be developed and their activity improved.

Currently effective national legislation in all areas of education, including adult education, was issued in July, 1973, under the title "Fundamentals of Legislation of the U.S.S.R. and Union Republics on Public Education." Article Three of the "Fundamentals" law, entitled "The Right of Citizens of the U.S.S.R. to Education," cites free tuition for all types of education, state education stipends, and the availability of various forms of industrial training. The article calls for raising the qualifications of workers and broadening the network of out-of-school institutions.

Articles 26 and 33 of the "Fundamentals" law are specifically concerned with aspects of adult education. Article 26, "Secondary General Education Schools for Working Youth," states (Rosen, 1975):

> For persons working in various branches of the national economy and not having a secondary education, secondary general education evening (shift) schools and correspondence schools are organized. Enterprises, institutions and organizations participate in bringing working youth into the evening schools and create the conditions necessary for combining work with instruction and for normal work of these schools and studies of pupils.

Article 33, "Training and Raising Qualifications of Workers in Industry," states:

> For youth entering production after completion of general education school, and for persons working in the national economy and wishing to receive a new vocation or to increase their qualifications, evening (shift) vocational-technical schools.and other forms of training and increasing qualifications directly in industry, are organized...

Responsibility for implementing adult education policy resides in government ministries and committees, under whose administrative control school programs are carried out. The U.S.S.R. Ministry of Education and its counterpart ministries in the 15 constituent republics of the U.S.S.R. supervise and fund (out of the national and republic education budgets) elementary and secondary schools of general education for adults as well as for children. Directly administered by local departments of education, these were previously called "schools for working youth" and "schools for rural youth," but now are generally called evening or (work-)shift schools. These designations, when used loosely (as they often are in Soviet legislation and statistics), also include correspondence or extramural schools.

The U.S.S.R. State Committee for Vocational-Technical Education and its republic counterparts control evening (shift) vocational schools, for upgrading the qualifications of workers. More advanced technical training and higher education for adults falls under the supervision of the U.S.S.R. and republic Ministries of Higher and Secondary Specialized Education. Virtually all higher educational institutions have correspondence departments and most have evening departments.

In addition, the U.S.S.R. has at least 16 higher education institutes (two evening and 14 correspondence institutes) completely devoted to higher education programs for working adults. As with adult education at the elementary-secondary level, funding emanates from a national government budget earmarked for education, and the national allocation from that budget to the 15 republic governments.

Major Programs

Elementary-Secondary Evening Programs. Evening schools of general education are administered and financed through the Ministry of Education by local departments of education in each of the 15 republics of the U.S.S.R. The schools follow an evening schedule, or a shift schedule to accommodate groups of adults who may be working during the regular evening school hours. About a third of the evening schools are reported to have their own buildings and premises, while two-thirds use the premises and facilities of regular day schools of general education.

The schools offer grades three to eleven, combining grades three and four into one school year. Grade eleven allows an additional year beyond the 10-year regular day school program to cover secondary subject matter. Generally there are 20 class hours a week through grade eight and 19 hours in the upper grades. Each school year is 36 weeks. A variant schedule for a school year of 28 weeks entails 25 hours a week through grade eight and 24 hours a week thereafter. The school week in the U.S.S.R. is a six-day week, which extends the hours of school each evening somewhat. The schedule is heavy for working adults, averaging three or even four classroom hours per night. Most of the time is devoted to classroom instruction, with three to four hours per week allowed for practical activities, testing, and examinations.

The schools use model or standard curricula, syllabi, and textbooks prepared by the U.S.S.R. and republic Ministries of Education. The subjects covered in the evening courses for adults are similar to those in regular day school programs, primarily language and literature, mathematics, history, geography, biology, physics, and chemistry. A foreign language is optional rather than required as it is in regular day programs, and four subjects of day schools are not included at all: music, drawing, physical education, and manual training.

As in regular schools of general education, students completing the eighth grade take a school-leaving examination and receive "incomplete secondary" certificates. Students completing the eleventh grade take another school-leaving examination and receive a certificate of (complete) secondary education. These certificates provide evening school graduates with rights similar to regular school graduates in competing for further education or meeting higher job qualification requirements.

Some of the problems of evening schools and attempts at their solutions are cited by a leading Soviet research administrator on adult education (Darinsky, 1976b):

> However, the evening schools are different from regular schools both in terms of student body and of teaching techniques. Students in these schools often lack basic knowledge due to long absences from school over the years. There are less hours of instruction in every subject, and there is also less time available for homework, as evening school

students are generally working or have a family
to take care of in contrast to the normal school-age
child.

Taking into consideration the differences in the
characteristics of the students of the two types of
schools, it became obvious that a special curriculum
is needed for students at evening schools, who have
to progress further in a shorter time...

Special textbooks geared for adults are available in
about half the subjects taught in evening schools, though the
extent of their distribution is not clear. The rest are
standard texts prepared for use by children and youth in
regular schools. Another problem is obtaining teachers
adequately trained or experienced to teach adults of varying
ages, backgrounds, attitudes, and study habits. Teachers have
difficulty in selecting the essentials of each subject and in
covering the program material without being superficial. The
majority of evening school teachers are not full-time adult
educators, but part-time evening teachers working during the
day at regular schools for children and teenagers.

As the education level of the population has risen,
enrollments in evening schools of general education have
declined in the lower grades. Only about 300,000 were
reported enrolled in grades one to eight in the 1977-78 school
year. The upper grades (9-11), however, have maintained
strong enrollments, reportedly numbering about 4.5 million in
1977-78. These figures are only rough indicators, however, as
they include correspondence as well as evening enrollments.

A large proportion of the enrollments in evening schools
are working youth, both urban and rural. These are teenagers
and youth in their twenties who for various reasons discontinued regular day school and joined the labor force. At the
same time there are also enrollees in fair numbers in their
thirties and older.

Elementary-Secondary Correspondence Programs. Correspondence programs of general education are administered and
financed similarly to evening programs, through the Ministry
of Education. They also offer courses of study in grades
three to eleven. In contrast to evening schools, however, the
number of contact hours between faculty and students is small
(eight hours per week or less), less subject matter is introduced although the same subjects are covered, the courses are
structured differently, and the program is more compact.
Textbooks frequently are in the form of self-instruction
manuals, and most study is done away from a school setting.
Correspondence programs generally have older students than
evening schools and many fewer teenagers. Attendance at

classes by correspondence students is optional, in contrast to compulsory attendance in evening schools.

The essential correspondence component of the program involves students at home preparing their lessons from booklets of "control tasks." These tasks involve self-instruction, solving problems at the end of each lesson, and mailing them to the instructors for corrections, notes, and remarks. Textbooks are often similar to those of regular day and evening students, but the aim is to develop special textbooks for correspondence courses.

A special feature of the program is the system of individual and group consultations, the latter appearing to be the principal form of student-faculty contact. These are generally held on the premises of evening schools and may even be part of an evening-school program. Individual consultations are provided to one or a few students who cannot come to scheduled group consultations because of work schedules or distance from the schools. Individual discussions relate to specific problems students are having in their studies rather than being a general review of the subject matter or lecturing. Because of this personal contact, it would be more appropriate to translate the Russian word (zaochnyi) used to describe these programs as "correspondence-extension" rather than as merely "correspondence." However, the simpler usage will be followed here.

The ages of students in secondary correspondence programs range from the teens to the fifties; students appear mostly to be office clerks or factory or farm workers, although other groups are also served by the programs. No separate statistics on national elementary-secondary correspondence enrollments are available as distinct from evening school enrollments.

At the secondary level, in addition to correspondence programs in general education, there are technical correspondence programs, combining vocational and general education. These are administered by the Secondary Specialized Administrations of the Ministries of Higher and Secondary Specialized Education in the Soviet republics. The schools are called "tekhnikums," and hundreds of technical specialties are taught, providing for entry into industries ranging from communications to food preservation. Students in these schools are generally working in factories and seeking advancement on their jobs. The tekhnikums send the factories periodic notice on standard forms concerning the progress of the students in their studies. This procedure applies to evening as well as to correspondence students.

Higher Education Evening Programs. Evening programs of higher education for working adults are offered in evening divisions or faculties of regular higher education institutions. They are given in a majority of the specialized fields of study in most of the higher educational institutions in the U.S.S.R. Administrative control, as in the regular day programs of universities and institutes, is generally in the Ministry of Higher and Secondary Specialized Education of the constituent Soviet republic in which the institution is located. However, the leading Soviet university, Moscow State University (and its evening programs), is directly under the national Ministry of Higher and Secondary Specialized Education.

Many specialized institutes and their evening programs are administered by the ministries in the fields of study they offer, i.e., agricultural institutes by the Ministry of Agriculture, communications institutes by the Ministry of Communications, pedagogical institutes (teachers colleges) by the Ministry of Education, and medical institutes by the Ministry of Health. The U.S.S.R. Ministry of Higher and Secondary Specialized Education, however, maintains an over-view of their evening and other academic programs and provides general guidelines. Financial support, as with other academic programs, is filtered down from the national and republic government budgets, according to the annual national economic plans.

Graduates of secondary schools of any age who are gain-fully employed are eligible to apply for admission to evening programs of higher education. Those admitted attend classes some 16 hours a week on a compulsory basis. As compared with regular day programs, the class hours and the amount of subject matter covered in the evening schools are curtailed, but the total period of study is six months to a year longer. Evening school students are entitled to paid leave from their places of work for laboratory classes and examinations, such leave increasing from 20 to 30 days a year as the student progresses to the senior years. Extra leave time is allowed for final state examinations and diploma projects.

The Soviets have experimented with evening programs in separate higher educational institutions but have not adopted this as a general practice. Two such institutions are known to exist, the Moscow Evening Metallurgical Institute and the Norilsk Evening Industrial Institute, both under the Russian S.F.S.R. Ministry of Higher and Secondary Specialized Education. In addition, for the convenience of workers in selected industrial complexes, there are four higher technical education institutions directly attached to plants, in the metallurgical, automotive, agricultural machine-building, and polytechnical fields. All have large evening divisions.

Evening programs of higher education served some 650,000 students out of a total higher education enrollment of about five million in the 1978-79 school year. Enrollments in evening programs have remained relatively stable in the past decade.

Higher Education Correspondence Programs. The pattern of
Soviet government sponsorship, administrative control, and
financial support for correspondence programs* is the same as
that for the evening programs of higher education, described
in the previous section.   While most higher educational
institutions have evening programs, virtually all of them have
correspondence programs.   These programs serve a much larger
adult working population than evening programs.   In the
1978-79 school year, enrollments in higher correspondence
programs totalled 1.6 million, about two and a half times the
evening program enrollments.

As with day and evening programs, correspondence programs
of higher education are aimed at producing specialists to meet
the state's requirements for scientific, technical, economic,
social, and cultural manpower. Unlike the case with evening
programs, a very large proportion of correspondence students
are enrolled in institutions that offer only that type
of program.   These special correspondence institutes are
officially accredited as higher educational institutions.
Most of them are headquartered in Moscow, with affiliates or
branches throughout the U.S.S.R.

The correspondence system has been described in an
earlier publication by this writer (Rosen, 1965):

> Once a year (in some cases twice) each correspon-
> dence student comes to the university or specialized
> institute for 5 weeks (7 for upperclass students)
> for a series of consultations, examinations, and
> orientation.   In addition, students who live
> near the correspondence institute or department may
> attend regular evening consultations during the
> school year.
>
> The consultation may include laboratory practice,
> small informal lecture-discussion groups or large
> lecture sessions.   Materials upon which the student
> is to be tested comprise the subject of the consul-
> tations, which are followed by examinations.   For
> those who pass, a 2-week orientation is held, during
> which professors lecture on the highlights of
> the students' subjects, aspects meriting special
> attention, books to be used, and techniques for
> students engaged in correspondence study.

---

*As with the analogous programs at the secondary levels,
it would be more accurate to call these "correspondence-
extension" programs.

The student then goes back to his job, working on his studies at night or on weekends, preparing "control tasks" according to the set timetable he was given at the institute or university. If conveniently located, he may come in person to a "consultation point" near his place of work to attend special review lectures... Otherwise, the student depends upon his correspondence with the institute for the answers he cannot find in his study materials.

Contributing to [a degree of] success of this correspondence program are two factors: (1) The student receives paid leave from his job, in addition to his normal vacation, for the time he spends "on campus" each summer, (2) he is given a rebate for all mailing costs and for 50 percent of the cost of transportation to the university for the 5-week summer session.

The correspondence system of higher education includes supplementary lectures on radio and television, but the extent to which these are incorporated into the formal program of studies is not clear. Despite the appeal of lower per-pupil cost of the correspondence programs, the adequacies of the program in producing fully qualified specialists have been questioned, particularly in the theoretical as contrasted to the practical aspects of the specialties. As a result of quality problems and the problem of dropouts, in the past decade enrollments in correspondence programs have declined somewhat. During this same period, regular full-time enrollments have almost doubled.

  Adult Education Research. A national government organization is responsible for research on adult education in the U.S.S.R., the Scientific Research Institute (SRI) for the General Education of Adults. The Institute is one of twelve educational research institutes within the U.S.S.R. Academy of Pedagogical Sciences, the research arm of the U.S.S.R. Ministry of Education. The SRI for Adult Education is located in Leningrad; all the other institutes of the Academy of Pedagogical Sciences are located in Moscow.
  The Institute carries out research on adult education in three major areas: general elementary and secondary education, inservice training, and informal education. Research on general elementary and secondary education is concerned with organization of admissions, methods of teaching, the psychology of adult education (attitudes and motivation, and development of mental functions, of adult

learners), development of curricula and syllabi, and prevention of dropouts from adult education programs.

Research of the Institute on inservice training is
generally concerned with the further training of teachers and
"raising their ideological, political, and general educational
and cultural standard." A model has been developed of the
ideal contemporary teacher to meet the requirements of
present-day Soviet society. This model has been compared
with an empirical model of the professional activity and
personality of the teacher performing in the school today,
and the comparison forms the basis for revising the further
training of educational personnel.

Adult informal education, sometimes called "self-
education" in Soviet sources, is also an area of Institute
research. Such "self-education" takes place in public lecture
halls, libraries, clubs, cultural and political education
centers, and associations of various professional groups.
The focus of recent research has been on the organization,
content, and methods of operation of the People's Universities
as they differ from formal educational institutions, frequently being developed through local initiative, not being
subject to uniform standards or limitations on admission, and
reflecting the interests of students rather than the state-
defined needs of the national economy.

Research of the Institute is published in monographs on
an ad hoc basis, and in occasional collections of papers of
all the institutes of the U.S.S.R. Academy of Pedagogical
Sciences.

At the higher education level, there is a Scientific
Research Institute for Problems of the Higher School. It
functions as the research arm of the U.S.S.R. Ministry of
Higher and Secondary Specialized Education. None of the
Institute's ten research departments is primarily concerned
with adult education. However, among the six "sectors" of the
Department for Theory and Methods of Instruction is one sector
concerned with evening, correspondence, and post-diploma
study.

Programs for Selected Sub-populations

Workers. Programs for workers, specifically designed
to encourage their further general and vocational education
while working, are developed by the national and republic
governments. Guidelines for programs providing general
secondary education are issued by the U.S.S.R. Ministry
of Education and various national ministries such as those
responsible for the metallurgy, chemical, coal, and machine-
building industries. Similar guidelines for vocational and
technical training are issued by the appropriate government
ministries and committees.

The guidelines for furthering the general secondary education of workers are described as follows (Darinsky, 1976b):

In 1973-74, the Soviet Ministry of Education and 15 ministries associated with the national economy issued common guidelines for the further development of general education for young people working within public enterprises. These measures called for an increased enrollment of young people in evening schools. Companies must submit a yearly report on employees under thirty who have not received secondary education, and they are obliged to send them to evening school at company expense or with grants from social organizations. Companies must also create suitable conditions for these evening school students, so that they can combine work with study. Such students must not work overtime, and certain privileges are granted to them under law; leaves are permitted only in the summer, at times when classes are not being held. The ministries also require that material and moral incentives be given to those studying. Such students are granted priority in hiring and promotion over people without a secondary education...

Additional benefits to workers attending secondary evening or shift schools of general education include a day off from work each week at 50 percent of their normal wages.

Full-time workers attending higher educational institutions are also given benefits which vary somewhat by their year of studies and whether they are in evening or correspondence programs. Evening students in the first two years of higher studies receive 20 days paid leave annually for laboratory work and end-of-year examinations. From the third year on they receive 30 days paid leave annually. In the final year, evening students may take four months leave (presumably on a fixed stipend rather than their work salary) for diploma projects and preparation for final examinations. Correspondence students in their first and second years are given 30 or more days leave per year with pay to attend lectures and consultations and to take course examinations. Third- and fourth-year students are given 40 days or more paid leave from work, and fifth- and final-year students 70 days. As with evening students, final-year correspondence students may take up to four months leave for their diploma project and final examinations.

Workers may receive vocational training in programs of vocational schools and tekhnikums. In addition, many industrial plants and collective farms provide short-term apprenticeship and training courses in particular skills or to upgrade skills and qualify workers for a higher wage category. This training is specifically job-related, may last a month or several months, and has no broad theoretical or cultural content.

A special factory program which introduces a few subjects in general education along with primarily technical subjects is the "School for Masters" or "School for Foremen" program. It provides what is considered the equivalent of an eighth-grade education to generally older workers (30- to 50-year-olds), with the object of raising their qualifications to skilled worker, assistant foreman, or foreman.

Women.   The great majority of women of working age are employed in the U.S.S.R. Special services are focused on provisions for their children during working hours rather than on special educational provisions for housewives entering the labor force.

The problem for working mothers may be seen in a typical schedule. Children come home from school in the early afternoon, while parents do not get home from work until 5:00 or 6:00 p.m. For several hours, six days a week, a grandmother must take care of the working mother's children, or alternative care must be available. The state's solution is nurseries, kindergartens, and "schools of a prolonged day."

Nurseries and kindergartens frequently have schedules that extend for the full period of the working hours of the mothers they serve. Often they are located within the plants where the mothers work. Thus, mothers may drop their children off at the plant's nursery in the morning and pick them up at the end of the work day or even after a training program if the mother is attending one at the plant. Nursing mothers are permitted to leave their work periodically during the day to nurse their children. There are also nurseries where infants can be left during the week and taken home on weekends. These are primarily to accommodate single parents and mothers with large families.

Except for single parents, there is a fee for the use of these facilities, the amount of the fee depending on the size of the family and its income. There are occasional criticisms in the Soviet press of the inadequacies of these services, both in quantity and quality, although certain model programs in large cities (generally those shown to observers from western nations) are of high quality.

At the elementary-secondary level (grades one to ten), there are schools which remain open at the end of the regular school day, providing a range of activities and meals for students waiting to be picked up by working parents. These are called "schools of the prolonged day." The parents pay for their children's meals, but otherwise the costs of these schools are borne by the state, or by the taxes that citizens pay either directly or indirectly. These schools have been a successful alternative to the more expensive boarding schools, reserved primarily for single-parent families, orphans, or children with special problems.

Soviet statistics lump prolonged-day and boarding-school enrollments; together they totaled 9.9 million in the 1978-79 school year. It is likely that most of these are in the prolonged-day schools.

Young women preparing for motherhood have gynecological consultation sessions in "maternity homes" or medical infirmaries or clinics. Women's consultation centers have special classes for pregnant women on what to expect during delivery and how to care for the newborn baby. The centers also provide special booklets on baby care. Lectures for women in health care are presented in various institutions, such as the Palaces of Culture and People's Universities, described in the section on "Informal Adult Education Programs." Other assistance and advice to mothers on upbringing of children of all age groups is described in the following section on programs for parents.

Parents. There is a broad range of special programs for parents to aid them in the process of child-rearing, or "upbringing" (vospitanie), as it is commonly called in the U.S.S.R. However, it is not clear how widespread the programs are or what the caliber is of their staffs. A number of the programs are models or experimental programs, or they are fully developed only in the large cities. The aspiration of the U.S.S.R. Ministry of Education and the Research Institute on General Problems of Social Upbringing is to have these programs multiply. They are outlined here to indicate their variety.

Nurseries (for infants of a few months to two years of age) and kindergartens (for children of three to six years of age) conduct sessions for parents once a month. A uniform series of lectures is provided at these meetings on the upbringing of small children according to their specific age group. Parents of six-year-old children, who will be first-graders in the following year, are given a series of exercises on "How to Prepare Your Child for School." A Soviet monthly popular journal called Pre-School Training provides nursery and kindergarten staff and parents with articles and discussions on the problems of upbringing in the pre-school and the home.

Schools of general education provide a lecture series for parents. An example of the topics of such lectures is available for one city (Grebennikov, 1978):

The general school lecture series, which is designed
essentially for two school years, begins with the
topic, "The Twenty-Fifth Congress of the CPSU on the
Task of Educating the Younger Generation."   The
following problems are then studied: the tasks and
principles of the communist education of the younger
generation and the role of the family; Soviet
legislation on the family; psychological, physio-
logical, and pedagogical principles in the education
of school pupils; the age-related features of pupil
development and their consideration in education in
the family setting; the content, basic forms, ways,
and means of educating school pupils in the family;
difficulties and errors in familial education and
ways of overcoming them; avenues for interaction
between the family and the school, the Young Pioneer
and Komsomol [Communist Youth] organizations...

For parents of students in the senior grades, the
lectures become increasingly concerned with instilling
Communist ideology, with such topics as "inculcation of
political awareness and communist morality" and "development
of a communist attitude toward labor and public property."

The schools also have parent committees, open houses for
parents, and meetings of the parents of pupils in particular
classes to discuss their children's problems.   Parents are
counseled by teachers or by other members of the parent
committee if their children are behavior problems in the
school.   Work sites also have parent-school councils, the
members of which include employees and probably Communist
Party, Komsomol, and trade-union representatives as well.
These councils are used to assist the schools, presumably in
supplying some equipment and training, and they are also
forums for admonishing parents to improve the school behavior
of their children.

At the informal education level, Palaces of Culture have
"young family clubs" in which both spouses receive advice
from teachers, doctors, dieticians, and others, view films on
upbringing, and hold discussions.   Radio, television, and
the press also have frequent discussions on problems of
child-rearing.

Informal Adult Education Programs.   Aside from adult-
education programs for academic credit, there is a range of
informal programs for strengthening ideological convictions,
raising the cultural level, and imparting a variety of skills.
Some of these may be aimed especially at older persons.

Adult-education facilities called "Palaces of Culture"
and smaller "Houses of Culture" offer the working and retired
population many social, artistic, technical, recreational,

and hobby activities--creative writing, handicrafts, radio assembly, automobile repair, photography, etc. They frequently have a chorus, orchestra, or drama group. Palaces of Culture in large cities are sometimes housed in former royal residences, or they (and Houses of Culture) may be in buildings adjoining or affiliated with large industrial plants or with collective or state farms. Often Houses of Culture are sponsored by trade unions, which may contribute to their financial support while the expenses of buildings, utilities, and equipment are covered by the plant for whose workers the House of Culture is maintained.

"People's Universities" provide systematic, noncredit adult-education courses and programs. In 1974, there were 29,000 People's Universities, with an enrollment of about 7,000,000. These "universities" are sometimes located in Palaces or Houses of Culture. They may specialize in one field or another--e.g., there are People's Universities of culture, of scientific knowledge, of musical education, of health, and others. Adults who enroll in the People's Universities attend lectures two or three times a month for several months, or for as long as three years.

A major national organization for dissemination among adults of Communist ideology and the Communist Party's position on various domestic and world issues is Znanie, the All-Union Knowledge Society (a title shortened in recent years from the original "All-Union Society for the Dissemination of Political and Scientific Knowledge"). Every year, thousands of Znanie lecturers provide propaganda and popular-science lectures to millions of Soviet adults at their places of work or in Palaces and Houses of Culture.

Znanie has its own publishing house and a "House of Knowledge," a "House of Scientific-Technical Propaganda," and a "House of Scientific Atheism," which presumably provide display and lecture facilities and distribute literature. The publishing house produces books and lecture materials for adults, as well as several journals, including International Life, Science and Life, and Science and Religion.

How Znanie is funded is not clear. People's Universities are supported by their founding organizations, which are described as follows (Darinsky, 1974):

> People's Universities can be founded by public organizations, scientific and technical societies, creative unions (composers, writers, artists, architects, etc.), museums, research institutes, higher and secondary specialized educational establishments, local ministry and board bodies, industrial enterprises, collective and state farms, transport organizations and servicing establishments.

Undereducated Adults. The U.S.S.R. provides no definition of "undereducated adults." It points with pride to the
virtual elimination of illiteracy in its population, but
reports no national data on semi-literates or adults who have
dropped out of school in the early grades. However, a rough
count of undereducated adults can be inferred from official
Soviet statistics which give the number per thousand of the
population of 10 years of age or older with a higher education, a complete (10-year or 11-year) secondary education, or
an incomplete (7-year or 8-year) secondary education. In 1979
these categories totaled 863 per thousand in urban areas and
693 per thousand in rural areas (Naselenie SSSR, 1980).
Residually, then, about 13.7 percent of the urban working
population and 30.7 percent of the rural working population have less than a seventh- or eighth-grade education.
According to the results of the 1970 Soviet national census
("Statistical Profile," 1974), about 19 million persons of
age 16 and over (18 million persons of age 20 and over), had
completed no more than an elementary education. An additional
28 million persons of age 16 and over (22 million persons
of age 20 and over) had achieved an incomplete secondary
education.

Programs which serve the needs of undereducated adults
have been described in the sections above on elementary-
secondary evening and correspondence programs.

Summary and Conclusions

Adult education in the U.S.S.R. is well-developed
and varied, including the major types of formal education
at every level and a large range of informal programs.
It affects a large proportion of the adult population,
providing general education, training and retraining, and
development of economic, social, and cultural skills. At
the same time, it is a means for imparting to the adult
population the Communist ideology, Communist Party directives, and the current Communist leadership's program for
the population.

Adult education in the Soviet Union has strengths
and weaknesses, both of which may be of interest to those
concerned with adult education in the United States. An
obvious caveat is that the adult-education programs developed in one country are intrinsically interwoven with its
particular political, social, economic, and cultural system.
What appears to work or malfunction in adult education in the
U.S.S.R. is only indicative or suggestive for a country with a
markedly different political, social, economic, and cultural
system.

Strengths of Soviet Adult Education

(1) The variety of programs provides something for nearly everybody, whether the adult interest is merely a hobby or socializing or is the completion of a program of studies leading to a secondary school or higher education diploma.

(2) The elementary-secondary programs involve co-operation between places of work, the adults working and in adult-education programs, and places of study. Most notable are the worker-leave and subsidy elements provided by the places of work and the reports to them by places of study on the progress of adults in their programs.

(3) At the higher education level, correspondence-extension programs provide a large percentage of adults seeking a higher education while working with an opportunity to obtain it, when they might not otherwise be involved in further education.

(4) Research on adult education is supported and co-ordinated by the national government, in an institute devoted solely to adult education within the national research academy. Adult education research findings can be translated into programs by virtue of the academy's affiliation with the national Ministry of Education.

(5) Various subgroups in the adult population have programs or services geared to their needs. These include young adults, workers, working mothers, parents, and profes-sionals.

Weaknesses of Soviet Adult Education

(1) The staffing, content, and quality of adult educa-tion programs of all types is uneven. Statistical reporting of the numbers of adults served by various programs probably includes large numbers involved in nominal or substantially inadequate programs.

(2) Elementary-secondary programs are particularly inadequate in rural areas, where a substantial portion of the population resides, with shortages of trained teachers, equipment, and supplies.

(3) Higher education correspondence-extension programs are weak on the theoretical aspects of fields of study, laboratory training in relevant fields, and instructor-student contact. Problems of dropouts and other problems have led to government decisions not to expand the programs further.

(4)   Adult subgroups whose special needs are not particularly addressed are women entering the labor force (as distinct from mothers, who have services provided) and senior citizens.   Their needs are partially met by general programs for all adults.   Nursery and kindergarten services for children of working mothers range from very good in selected institutions in large cities to grossly inadequate in some urban and rural areas.

(5)   What might appear to be a strength to the Soviet Government but a weakness to a western observer is the utilization of adult education for massive propaganda and indoctrination.   Programs of citizen education do not present adults with a range of views and ideas or with opportunities for developing individual judgment and decision making on political and social issues.

ADULT EDUCATION IN SWEDEN

Kjell Rubenson

Stockholm Institute of Education

Sweden's way of life has often been called the "middle way," because it combines private enterprise with a government that greatly influences the development of the economy. The Swedish government operates one of the most far-reaching social security systems in the world. The government provides free education and largely free medical service. It pays pensions to old people, widows and orphans. After most Swedes retire, they receive annual pensions of about 60 percent of their average earnings during their 15 highest paid years. The government also provides health insurance and financial aid for housing.

Sweden is a little larger than California but it is thinly populated (52 inhabitants per square mile) and has about two-fifths as many people as that state. Forests cover more than half of Sweden and only about a tenth of the country is farmland.

Sweden's economy is based mainly on its three most important natural resources--timber, iron ore, and water power. The large Swedish merchant shipping fleet transports cargoes to and from all parts of the world, and provides an important source of income for the nation. About 90 percent of Swedish industry is privately owned. The Gross National Product is divided as follows: services, 53 percent; industry, 42 percent; and agriculture, 5 percent.

Sweden has a parliamentary government built on a party system. The Social Democratic Labor party was in power from 1932 to 1976, practically without a break. The 1976 elections resulted in a majority for the nonsocialist parties, and for the first time in 44 years Sweden has a nonsocialist government. The monarchy is constitutional and the King's authority is of a purely formal nature.

Historical Background

In Sweden, society's continuously growing interest in adult education is a relatively new phenomenon. During the fifties and sixties, when radical reforms were taking place in primary, secondary and higher education, very little or no attention was paid to recruitment for adult education. Only later--in fact, at a point in time when much of the great educational optimism of the sixties had been gnawed away--did adult education gain prominence.

This late interest can be contrasted with the fact that, during the whole of this century, adult education has played a significant role in Sweden.

In the late nineteenth and early twentieth centuries, adult popular education (adult education associated with the popular movements, e.g., folk high schools and study associations) began to acquire an increasingly established form. A characteristic feature of Swedish adult education is that, from a very early stage, there has been a broad, integrated and well-organized adult education sector that influences the power structure in society. For leaders in the workers' movement, adult education has come to function as a parallel system to the formal educational system, which in most European countries acted as a means of preparing political leaders. The absence in Sweden of society's involvement, despite its established position, most probably has to do with the independent standing of the voluntary educational associations in relation to official authority.

Having adopted a parsimonious attitude toward these associations for many years, society has, to a great extent, taken over financial responsibility for this sector during the post-war years. During the last decade, free and voluntary popular adult education has increasingly begun to be seen as an integrated part of the adult education sector and has come to be used directly as an instrument for achieving the overall goals of educational policy.

As a modern labor market policy took shape, it provided for public labor market training (AMU) which is specifically intended for the unemployed and for people in danger of losing their jobs.

In 1968 the state-run system of adult education was augmented by a municipally-sponsored system, which gives adults greater opportunities to study at levels corresponding to the senior level of primary school (i.e., the last three grades of basic compulsory education) and to the secondary school (i.e., upper secondary education, which is voluntary).

Correspondence schools and courses arranged by the broadcasting media and the labor organizations are other important forms that have developed.

Adult Education Policy

The goals of adult education as prescribed in official documents can be divided into four broad categories:
equality, democracy, the economy, and the satisfaction of
individual preferences. The overriding goals of educational
policy as defined by the Government and Riksdag represent a
declaration of political intent. These broad goals are often
vague and even contradictory. They need to be interpreted and
analyzed with reference to their value origins, consequences
and conflicts (see Cohen and Garet, 1975).

The Government Bill (1967:85) on adult education marked
the start of an extensive reform period. In order to understand the policy and goals as stated in the bill, we need to
consider the environment of education policy at that time. As
a result of a very selective and hierarchically-constructed
education system, the proportion of graduates among the
economically active in Sweden was only 2 percent in 1960, a
relatively low figure compared with other industrialized
countries.

Early in the sixties, economists began to point to the
significance of education for economic development. Denison's
analysis of development in the USA had shown that investment
in education and research would be three times as profitable
as investment in real capital (Denison, 1962). These research results gave added fuel to the growing optimism about
education.

The idea of giving adults without upper secondary school
education the opportunity of gaining a higher education was
given further nourishment by the studies of the "reserve
talent" carried out in Sweden in the 1950's. The primary aim
of these studies was to provide a foundation for changing
and broadening the narrow intake to upper secondary school
education. However, the studies were also decisive for the
reforms carried out in the 1960s aimed at giving adults
broader opportunities for study at the upper secondary and
postsecondary levels.

Coming back to the four categories of goals, we would
conclude that the economic and service (i.e., the satisfaction
of individual preferences) goals were predominant in the 1967
reforms. This is not to say that equality was out of the
picture. The reform gave talented adults a second chance to
acquire the education they had been denied because of a selective and hierarchical educational system. These broadened
opportunities represented a legitimate demand for fairness
for adults after the nine years of basic schooling was made
mandatory.

Bill 1970:35 signified a change in values in adult education and precipitated new discussion concerning reallocation.

No longer was the "intellectual-reserve" the focus; the new focus was on the undereducated and the underprivileged. How is this change to be explained? If the 1967 bill was to be understood as a response to perceived changes in the economy, then the answer to the change in values lies in the policy.

During the 1960s the Swedish economy showed rapid growth giving companies a higher than ever net profit. Despite the steady growth in the economy, there was an emerging awareness that resources in Swedish society had not become more equally distributed. The Swedish survey of living standards revealed that vast differences still existed between different socio-economic groups (Johansson, 1970). As a result we can see a radicalization taking place in the trade unions. This expressed itself in far-reaching demands for industrial democracy involving a share of the capital stock and a general reallocation of resources in society. Briefly, it should be mentioned that the trade union demands resulted in major reforms in the Swedish labour market in the middle of the 70's.

The unions' philosophy on allocation policy was not limited to reforms in the labour market but also included adult education. In 1969 the Swedish Confederation of Trade Unions (SCTU) published its first report on adult education, which demanded allocation reforms in adult education. In addition, SCTU, together with the Workers' Educational Association (ABF), wrote to the government asking for immediate action in carrying out experiments aimed at reaching the educationally disadvantaged. SCTU's and ABF's demands are reflected in the 1970 bill which was an important turning point in policy on adult education.

In the period following 1970, the allocation policy (equity and democracy) was increasingly articulated, reaching its climax with the 1975:23 Bill on adult education in which equity is the dominant goal. The goal of individual preferences has steadily diminished in importance compared to the goal of equality. The more subordinate role allotted to the economic objective in policy documents for adult education can, according to Brostrom and Ekeroth (1977), be ascribed to its more direct relation to labour market policy, particularly as it affects labour market training. It is also worth pointing out that the opening up of secondary and higher education in Sweden had created a vast increase in skilled labour. This, in combination with an increasing distrust in the human capital theory, is also a part of the explanation of why the economic goal has come to be more subordinate in official documents.

Financing

Except for study circles, the types of adult education described here are in principle entirely free of charge, although in practice there may be some expenses for study materials. The tuition fees paid by participants in study circles, however, are quite low.

Adult education accounts for a rapidly growing share of the government budget. More than one-tenth of the national outlay for education goes to the various kinds of adult education that are described here. On top of that, an equal amount is spent on allowances to students enrolled in labor market training, which is entirely government-financed.

Local authority expenditures on adult education have also increased rapidly. Municipal governments pay about one-third of the costs of municipal adult schools and about the same proportion of the costs of study circles.

National, municipal and county governments together employ more than one-fourth of Sweden's working population. Their staff training programs are extensive and are aimed at all categories of employees. Thus, through direct payments, subsidy systems and financial assistance to students, the national, county and local governments pay the lion's share of adult education costs in Sweden. Other contributors to these costs include the popular movements, political and non-profit organizations, trade unions, and private companies.

As of 1976, employers began paying a special payroll contribution for adult education. This money is used, among other things, to implement the allocation policy.

Hourly and daily study grants provide compensation for loss of income. Studies which must be pursued for longer uninterrupted periods qualify for a special adult study allowance which is mainly intended for persons of low previous educational attainments.

The payroll fee also finances study circles in "high-priority subjects," for example, Swedish, English, mathematics and social science, as well as outreach programs at workplaces and in residential areas. These funds are distributed by special regional adult education councils.

Outreach programs are aimed primarily at establishing contact with people having less than nine years of primary schooling. The outreach programs at workplaces are administered by local branches of trade unions, and outreach programs in residential areas are handled by the voluntary educational associations. In the latter case, priority is given to establishing contact with immigrants, the handicapped, housewives and others working in the home.

Further, all employees enjoy an unconditional right to take leaves of absence for studies that must be pursued during working hours. Although the leave to which they are entitled under law is unpaid, certain grants are available through hourly and daily study grants and special study allowances. At present the government provides means for 25,000 full-time study allowances.

Forms of Adult Education in Sweden

Folk High Schools

A specifically Scandinavian form of adult education is the folk high school, a type of boarding school. The folk high school is not the form of adult education with the greatest number of participants, but it is the oldest one. The first folk high schools were founded in the mid-19th century to give young rural adults better opportunities for general education.

Today there exist 110 folk high schools, which are owned either by county and local councils or by trade unions, churches, temperance societies or other nonprofit organizations. Each school determines its own curriculum within the framework of the Folk High School Code. There is no official syllabus or compulsory subject matter for Folk High Schools. Studies focus on topic areas rather than on single subjects. A significant feature of these schools is the high degree of student participation in educational planning and implementation.

The folk high schools have made an effort to improve facilities for handicapped persons. More and more schools have been adapted to accommodate physically handicapped persons; assistance to the blind and deaf is increasing; and about 20 schools work with mentally retarded persons who are integrated into ordinary school activities as much as possible.

In the course of the school year 1978-79, 150,000 persons participated in folk high school courses in Sweden. More than three-fourths of these people participated in courses of one week or less. About 15,000 persons participated in the so-called long-term folk high school courses with a length of 30 weeks or longer. It is the students participating in these long courses that form the backbone of the folk high schools and their work. Usually it is this group of people one thinks of when talking about folk high schools in general.

The short courses are, as a rule, arranged in collaboration with organizations, institutions and authorities. Experts from the cooperating organization often take over the teaching during such short courses and are paid by the school with money set aside for this purpose. But it is always the school that is responsible to the government for the planning and accomplishment of such short courses.

Voluntary Educational Associations and the Study Circles

By far the largest number of today's adult learners attend the study circles organized by the local branches of Sweden's educational associations. In fiscal year 1978-79, study circles attracted about 3 million participants, of whom slightly over half were women. That figure should be put in relation to Sweden's total population of about eight million and its adult population (aged 20-67) of about five million. But since any one participant may take part in more than one study circle, no net figure can be given. These study circles are sponsored by ten voluntary educational associations, of which the largest, ABF (the Workers' Educational Association) accounts for just over one-third of the total study circle hours qualifying for national government subsidies.

In the regulations for awarding government subsidies to voluntary educational associations, a study circle is defined as "an informal group which meets for the common pursuit of well-planned studies of a subject or problem area which has previously been decided upon." The group itself determines how its work is to be planned and carried out. A circle leader has certain coordinating and administrative tasks but does not act as a teacher in the ordinary sense. There are no formal requirements for circle leaders.

To be eligible for subsidy, a study circle must have between five and twenty members. It must meet for at least twenty class-hours spread over at least four weeks. Each meeting may last no more than three class-hours. The subsidy, fixed at a certain amount per class-hour, covers slightly more than 45 percent of the costs, with the remainder coming from fees and municipal grants. Study-circle activity is supplemented by programs of public lectures, which also receive government subsidies.

Two subject areas account for two-thirds of the study circle hours: aesthetic subjects and civics. Study circles in Swedish, English, mathematics and social science at a level corresponding to grades 7-9 of compulsory comprehensive school (sometimes lower) have been given higher priority through a system of extra State subsidies.* Priority is also

---

*The Commission on Popular Adult Education (SOU 1979:85) has suggested that the financing system should be changed so that priority is given to selected groups, not selected programs. The Riksdag will deal with the report in the autumn of 1980.

given to union and immigrant circles as well as to study circles for the handicapped. More than a third of all study circles fall into these high-priority categories. For many of those attending high-priority circles, their studies are the first phase of a recurrent educational process of varying length.

There are also study circles at university level. So far the number of participants in such circles has been about one percent of the total. A person who has completed an approved-curriculum study circle at university level may take a special examination at a university and earn credit points there.

Immigrant education has grown rapidly in volume and has come to loom ever larger in the total course offerings at the educational associations.

Study circles are politically valuable, as a conduit between the population and the government. For example, recent circle discussions were held on whether or not Sweden should use nuclear energy as a future power source--prompted, incidentally, by the government. Swedish leaders have in this way received highly accurate readings of current popular thinking on this volatile question.

During recent years the study circle has also come to be used as an instrument by groups to find solutions to serious problems confronting the group. Circles in villages threatened by loss of job opportunities have, for example, investigated the possibilities for alternative production.

The study associations have likewise made a great effort to provide study possibilities for the mentally retarded and those with serious physical handicaps. The government has provided special money for research and development in order to facilitate participation for these groups.

Municipal Adult Schools

The municipal adult schools are operated by the school boards of each local authority. They offer instruction in accordance with the uniform national curricula for the lower secondary school level (grades 7-9) and for the various study lines and courses in upper secondary (2-4 years beginning with grade 10). However, compared with the education of youth, the normal time schedules for adults imply a reduction of between 30 and 70 percent.

A system of special vocational training operates along-side the education that follows the curricula for the compulsory comprehensive and upper secondary schools.

Most courses are offered in the evening, although eligibility for leave of absence since 1975 and for special adult study allowance since 1976 has increased the proportion of daytime students. Most students study part-time, but many daytime students attend full time.

The increased possibilities for financial aid for study during daytime have led to a decrease in dropout rates from the municipal adult schools. A 1973 study of evening courses in Stockholm (constituting 37 percent of all participants in Sweden) reported that just over 30 percent completed the whole program (Borgstrom, et al., 1979). A follow-up study of day courses showed that as many as 65 percent completed the courses (Rubenson, 1980b).

The purpose of full-time or part-time studies is often to acquire the actual skills and satisfy the formal pre-requisites that will qualify a person for further studies at higher levels or to meet the requirements of a certain profession.

In recent years the municipal adult schools have increased their enrollments to about 310,000 students per year. Over 40 percent study general courses at upper secondary level, while just under 30 percent each take lower secondary school courses and vocational courses under the upper secondary school's curricula. The trend has been toward larger numbers in general courses and some decline in the numbers studying vocational subjects. This trend, though, is slowly changing. The thrust and design of the vocational courses are the subject of development projects launched both by the National Board of Education and through local initiatives.

A parliamentary decision in 1977 has given municipal adult education new tasks to perform on behalf of adults with no previous or deficient earlier schooling. The so-called basic education of adults is meant to give all grown-ups, whether they be Swedish-speaking or immigrants, a minimum standard of knowledge and skills so that they can practice a trade and take part in the society's other activities.

English, mathematics, Swedish and German are the most popular subjects at compulsory comprehensive school levels and in the general upper secondary school courses. Among vocational training programs, the dominant subjects are industry and handicrafts, home technology, and commercial and office subjects.

The teachers in municipal adult schools have the same training as those who teach the same subjects in upper secondary schools. Since 1975, it has been possible to create special teaching positions within the municipal adult schools. But most teachers are connected to secondary school or upper-level compulsory comprehensive and teach only part-time in the adult school. The Stockholm Institute of Education offers a special program for those wishing to teach in municipal adult schools. Admission requirements are the same as for applicants to the secondary-teaching credential programs, i.e., the equivalent of a fil.kand. (roughly, Bachelor of Arts) degree.

All students at municipal adult schools have access to educational counseling if needed. Extra tutoring and financial aid are also provided. Study assistance grants were improved considerably by an Act of Parliament in 1975. Part-time grants in particular (hourly and daily study assistance) have increased. Certain local authorities also arrange child-care services for their adult students.

For organizational purposes and depending on scope, municipal adult education is linked either to a compulsory comprehensive or upper secondary school, or it is conducted in a separate unit.

State subsidies to the municipal school systems for adult education cover the entire cost of employing a principal, a director of studies, a "SYO functionary" (i.e., a person who is in charge of educational and vocational guidance) and the teachers, plus part of the cost of information and outreach programs. Instruction is free of charge but students may often be required to pay for their own study materials.

State Schools for Adults

Study programs equivalent to the municipal adult schools are available at two adult schools (at Norrkoping and Harnosand) directly administered by the central government. These schools are intended for students who do not have access to adult education in their home towns and for people who cannot attend regular day or evening courses. The courses take place either entirely on a correspondence basis or by correspondence combined each term with relatively short and intensive in-school courses.

Labour Market Training

The system of labour market training originated in the need to act swiftly against imbalances in the labour market, both by helping under- and unemployed workers to improve their employability in occupations with better opportunities, and by increasing the supply of skills in industries where a shortage of suitably trained personnel tends to exacerbate inflationary pressures. The labour market training system now has a running capacity of more than one percent of the total labour force. With courses lasting for an average length of four to five months, more than three percent of the labour force can be reached in the space of one year.

The main provisions of this scheme are as follows: Persons unemployed or with precarious employment conditions (threatened by unemployment due to working in declining sectors or troubled by personal difficulties) as well as those who are willing to leave their employment (or take educational leave of absence) in order to take training for skills in short supply, can attend training courses arranged by the labour market authorities in cooperation with the school authorities or with employers. Courses are free of charge and trainees receive subsistence allowances. The pay to trainees exceeds the unemployment benefits per day, amounting to some 80 percent of ordinary wage income after taxes.

The courses vary in length and level of qualification from a few weeks for introductory courses, designed to accustom participants to working situations outside their experience, up to two-year courses for skilled workers and technicians, partly at academic levels. In recent years, half of the participants have been women. One of the important functions of this activity is to pave the way for female entry into the labour market.

Most of the training is carried out at permanent or temporary and often rapidly improvised training centers, administered (jointly but with a great amount of delegation to their county subsidiaries) by the Labour Market Board and the National Board of Education or by arrangement with vocational schools, which are now integrated with the system of upper secondary education. In the year 1978-79, 78,000 people participated in this kind of training.

The Labour Market Board can, when the employment situation so warrants, pay temporary training grants to private firms and municipalities so as to compensate for introductory training costs. Similar subsidies can also be given to employers hiring handicapped or older workers, and to municipalities organizing sheltered employment. Employers who let women try male occupations (or vice versa) can obtain special grants. In regions with a limited demand for labour, employers can receive training grants for new employees. A subsidy is also available to employers who arrange training of old or new employees in connection with a net increase in their work forces. For cyclical and other reasons, it can sometimes be advisable to support the in-plant training activities of business enterprises. Firms abstaining from laying off workers during a slack period and giving them training instead can receive a special subsidy per hour and trainee up to a maximum of 960 hours. This part of in-plant training expanded rapidly during the past recession, when the number of participants in 1976-77 rose to more than 100,000 compared with roughly 10,000 in the previous year. In 1978-79, when the economy had started to pick up, it was down to 50,000.

Training is used not only to improve the level and amount of industrial skills among workers but also to spur "investment in human capital," the aim being to offset cyclical and seasonal variations in employment by counter-cyclical variations in its volume.

Solution of the administrative problems connected with this policy for "rapid action" against employment variations demands a considerable freedom of decision-making by local employment offices in cooperation with municipal and school authorities, trade unions and employers. It also entails a centrally organized provision of educational material (equipment, books, teacher training) and holding a reserve capacity in permanent or temporary training centers during high-employment periods, so that courses can rapidly increase their intake as soon as the employment situation in an area begins to deteriorate.

The primary objective of the labour market training is to ensure steady jobs for the unemployed. Regular follow-up studies show that of those who have taken vocational courses and who then enter the labour market, some 85 percent have obtained jobs within three months of course completion. Approximately 85 percent of these people have, in turn, obtained work within the occupation branch for which they were trained.

A substantial proportion of those enrolled in labour market training have no educational attainments beyond six to eight years of elementary schooling. To give these groups a wider range of choice on the labour market is a major redistributive goal of manpower training.

Higher Education

"Regular" higher education has usually not been con- sidered a part of adult education. However, the Swedish reform in higher education (1977) obscures this distinction. The reform could be seen as an attempt to evolve a coherent approach to opening post-secondary education to adults. A cornerstone here has been to accord increased value to work experience as a ground for admission to higher education.

The Swedish admission system makes a fundamental distinc- tion between general qualifications (eligibility) and special requirements. The new admissions scheme defines four main ways of obtaining general eligibility for higher education. They are:

(1) To have completed a three-year stream of upper secondary school;

(2) To have completed a two-year stream of upper secon- dary school;

(3) To have equivalent education from a "folk high school;" or

(4) To have more than four years of work experience and
to be over age 25 (the 25:4 qualification).

In these admission rules, work experience is given wide
interpretation; any kind of work experience including child
care and military service can be included in the four years
required for the 25:4 qualification. However, the <u>special
requirements</u> often mean that the equivalent of upper secondary
school knowledge in certain subjects is required in addition
to the general requirements (which also include knowledge of
Swedish and English).

Work experience also has a second function as an additional selection criterion to restricted programs. Previous
to the 1977 reform, selection had been entirely based on
school grades. In selection to full degree programs, the
applicants are placed in so-called quota groups corresponding to the four grounds for general eligibility. Each
group is alloted places in proportion to the number of
applicants in the group.

Applicants in all categories can add credit points for
work experience to their school marks. The broad definition
of work experience which is used for general eligibility is
also used for selection to restricted programmes. Applicants
must have at least 15 months of work experience (in addition
to the four years included in the general entrance requirements for 25:4 students).

Staff Training in the Public and Private Sectors

Some government authorities train their own employees.
In certain agencies, for example, the Customs Service, the
Post Office and the Labour Market Board, a complete vocational
training course is provided. More advanced training in the
form of short and long courses is available within most
government agencies.

The county councils and larger municipal governments have
extensive staff training programs. Nursing staff in county
hospitals and other county-operated health care institutions
receive vocational training. Advanced courses are also
available. The Swedish Association of Local Authorities
and the Federation of County Councils each have training
departments which sponsor courses for various staff categories
and for elected municipal and county officials.

Most large private companies have training departments
which carry out educational planning and sponsor courses.
Employees of small and medium-sized firms are eligible for
training courses sponsored by the various employer federations
and their affiliated trade associations. A number of joint
employer-employee bodies also sponsor training to meet

the needs of working life; among these are courses for shop stewards.

As a rule, the employer pays the cost of staff training and the participants pay no fee. Staff training programs within local governments and private companies are not generally eligible for national government subsidies. An exception is on-the-job training of an elementary vocational nature sponsored by an employer in collaboration with the local upper secondary school, referred to as "intramural company schools."

Training Programs Sponsored by Employee Organizations

Sweden's two largest employee organizations, the Confederation of Trade Unions (LO) and the Central Organization of Salaried Employees (TCO), have extensive study programs of their own. They are designed to give union members a solid background in union affairs and other social matters. They also supply trained union officials at local, regional and national levels. Most courses are residential and last one or two weeks, but some last up to six months. The national government provides subsidies for these programs.

A vital task for the trade unions as well as for the organized employers is to give all employees information and training on the various labour-law statutes that have been enacted in recent years. The most important of these from the educational aspect is the Law on Employee Participation in Decision-making, which came into force on January 1, 1977. So far all public employees have been assured of at least two days of information about this law on the strength of special contracts. But knowledge must also be spread about the Law on Security of Employment and the Act Concerning the Status of Shop Stewards.

Radio, Television and Correspondence Schools

Educational programs on radio and television are produced by a special corporation which operates with government funds. The programs are aimed at the regular schools as well as at adult students and undergraduates in higher education. Broadcast programs are usually supplemented with printed study material. The broadcasting media collaborate with various sponsors of adult education.

Two correspondence schools, Hermods and Brevskolan, dominate this educational medium. Hermods designs courses chiefly aimed at helping people fulfill the formal requirements for completion of courses at primary, secondary and university levels. Brevskolan mainly caters to the needs of various special-interest organizations.

In recent years the traditional type of correspondence course has been increasingly combined with other forms of instruction, especially study circles and educational broadcasts. This type of combined course generally leads to more effective learning than pure correspondence courses.

Public Libraries and Teaching-Aid Centers

Public libraries and the audio-visual or teaching-aid centers operated by local authorities play a vital role in the work of both the educational associations and the municipal adult schools. The public libraries lend out books, magnetic tapes and film strips to study circles and individuals. Teaching-aid centers tape educational broadcasts and lend out copies of them. The libraries arrange exhibitions, lectures, concerts and so forth, which often serve as adjuncts to study circles and courses.

Special Programs for Subcategories of Adults

The five populations of interest here--workers, older persons, women entering the labour force, parents, and the undereducated--are highly affected by the general measures taken to implement the allocation policy. Thus, the following paragraphs are more a description of steps to recruit persons with low resources than to accomodate the specific subcategories.

Several important reforms have been launched to enable employees to take greater part in adult education. The Swedish act concerning a general right to educational leave imposes no restrictions on the nature or duration of the studies pursued. Outreaching (recruiting) activities at workplaces are possible in Sweden through the labour market legislation, which gives trade unions the opportunity to pursue this activity during working hours. The regional adult education committees are responsible for funds for outreach activities which would be put at the disposal of the trade unions.*

Labour market training is the major instrument to help women enter the labour market. Another route is through municipal adult schools. In order to reach housewives, the

---

*The Commission on Adult Popular Education (SOU 1979: 85) has suggested that these funds should not go to the trade unions but to the voluntary educational associations.

voluntary education associations are receiving a subsidy for outreaching activities in the housing areas. In some instances this contact forms the start of a process leading to entry into the labour force.

Recently the voluntary educational associations have started a variety of study circles directed towards the special needs of older adults and parents. This is often carried out in cooperation with organizations representing these groups. The care centers are also involved in parent education. These courses are directed towards preparing the parents-to-be for the birth and for parenthood.

Available statistics on participation do not allow a clear separation among programs directed to the five sub-categories and participation in general.

Experiences from the Swedish Adult Education Reforms

Information

Research on channels of information has shown that various forms of personal contact have great significance in stimulating an interest in studying. When the person has decided to pursue education, such channels of information as advertisements, brochures and other printed matter in the letter-box help the individual to choose a special course. However, they do not to a great extent affect the basic attitude towards adult education.

In order to recruit disadvantaged groups, the government financed a variety of experiments on outreaching activities (the Committee on Methods Testing in Adult Education, 1974). Trying to interest people in adult education through personal contacts is, of course, not new; on the contrary, it has a long history in Swedish popular adult education. The new feature is that the outreaching activity was given a more established form and organization on the basis of earmarked state funds to act as a recruitment model.

It is usual to distinguish between outreaching activity in housing areas and at workplaces. Judging from the number of persons recruited, it is obvious that the greatest successes have been achieved at workplaces (Rubenson, 1979). Several interacting factors contribute to this.

In housing areas the study organizers quite simply do not make contact with everyone. Another reason is that the groups who are outside the labour market are often the really disadvantaged and hard-to-recruit groups. Particularly exposed groups are people on early retirement pensions and the long-term unemployed. Other groups are immigrants, the handicapped and those working in the home.

A fundamental difference is that the contact within housing areas is directed at individuals, while contact at the workplace is collective. Thus, the success at the workplace depends partly on the fact that the outreaching activity has included the overwhelming majority of the work group, thus affecting not only the individual but also one of his most significant member-groups. For obvious reasons, it is more difficult to build on the target group's member and reference groups where outreaching activity in housing areas is concerned.

The ambition of outreaching work at the local level is dependent on how the goals of educational policy, as they are formulated by Parliament and Government, are interpreted. Characteristically, as noted earlier, these goals are often unclear. As a result, the tendency at lower levels is to give old procedures new names more in time with the new tunes. Thus, one of the lessons from the experiments is that, at the local level, the goals of educational policy and the consequences these ought to have for the activity have not been analyzed sufficiently (Brostrom & Ekeroth, 1976).

The design of the subsidy system is probably the strongest tool for directing the level of ambition. The general character of the subsidies makes it difficult for organizations who seek to obtain allocation effects. As they can not compensate for the increased costs involved in recruiting the underprivileged, they will be forced to concentrate on other groups.

Financing

Evaluations of the Swedish reforms in adult education show that, with the exception of labour market training, there has been too much faith in what a general strengthening of resources for adult education could lead to. If one tries, through one and the same measure, to fulfill both allocation and service-policy goals (meeting individual preferences), one must be aware that the allocation effects will be very limited and will be accomplished at the price of great service-policy costs (Brostrom & Ekeroth, 1977).

To bring about a change, it is necessary that future subsidies be earmarked to a much larger extent than has previously been the case. This, however, requires one to identify more exactly the group whose living condition should be equalized, and it presupposes a deeper knowledge of which study methods and which content can create the desired allocation effects. This is a fundamental aspect which hitherto has not been the object of close analysis (see Rubenson, 1980a).

Content

It is not enough to observe how total recruitment changes without bearing in mind also the groups that choose a particular education. What, for example, has happened in Sweden during the recent great expansion in the voluntary educational associations? The increase has primarily been in aesthetic and civic circles. In the latter case this has partly been due to a greater increase in internal recruitment of those active in trade unions--an already relatively strong resource group. The aesthetic circles are of particular interest, as this is the subject which dominates among the undereducated. The crucial question is, what resources do these kinds of circles create?

In this connection it may be worthwhile presenting one of the findings from a Swedish survey of study needs and study impediments among the undereducated (Rubenson, et al., 1976). The most revealing result, bearing in mind that the subjects of this study were undereducated persons, was the great interest which people took in education relating to their present occupations. The data indicated that this interest is not mainly a bid for advancement, but rather the manifestation of a need to master more thoroughly the tasks with which one is confronted, even though one can already cope with them satisfactorily. This may be due to a desire for greater job satisfaction, or else to apprehension about failure.

To meet these needs it was suggested that the existing programs should be supplemented by study circles connected to the work role which would help participants to view their work situation in a broader context.

Experiments carried out within the Workers Educational Association show that, through occupationally-related study circles, it is possible to recruit persons who had never previously considered participating.

Concerning the participation of employees, particular interest is attached to the line taken by the trade unions. The changes in adult education in Sweden that have been discussed have, to a large extent, come about through the involvement of trade union organizations in matters connected with adult education. The significance of the trade unions is that they have become capable of acting decisively to bring into being a scheme of adult education that both enables systematic change and provides the collective with a means for obtaining a better life.

Educational Process

With the reorientation in adult education policy in the 1970s from the service-policy goal towards the allocation goal, a shift of emphasis followed such that undereducated persons came to constitute the main target group, not only for adult education in general but particularly in municipal adult education.

The change in policy could be seen as a change in the normative pattern. New norms rarely, if ever, become effective unless accompanied by institutional innovation. In other words, normative innovations are only successful when accompanied by effective organization. The institutional changes that have taken place following the allocation goal have to do with the link between the target population and the educational institution. Instead of waiting for the student to come, the institutions have responded to the changed policy by being much more active in the recruitment process. Since the rest of the system (the actual teaching process) operates much in the same way as when the target group was the "educational reserve," the changes in the selection process have led to a state of normative inconsistency. The explanation for this inconsistency is that municipal adult schools are a part not only of the adult educational sector, where the allocation policy is formulated, but also of the formal school system, where the allocation aspect is less pronounced. Despite a change in policy, the institutional values are very much the same as before (see Borgstrom, et al., 1979; Hoghielm, 1980). This is one of the problems that the present Commission on Municipal Adult Schools has to tackle (see SOU 1979:92).

Coordination

Another experience from the Swedish reform period relates to the difficulties involved in establishing a comprehensive strategy for using the various components of the adult education system.

For example, the introduction of municipal adult schools has led to considerable friction between representatives from the voluntary associations regarding what kind of programs they should provide.

Coordination is made even more difficult by the fact that the voluntary education organizations, to a growing extent, are trying to develop distinctive images in relation to one another. There is an increasing awareness that the price for the enormous growth in the number of study circles has been the disappearance of the unique culture of each voluntary organization.

One of the distinctive features of popular adult education is that it should be free and voluntary. By freedom is meant the independent standing of voluntary educational associations in relation to official authority levels. How this freedom is to be maintained in view of the increasingly large economic dependence on society (government) has, therefore, become one of the most fundamental issues within the voluntary educational associations today.

The results of various research and development activities have been recently reviewed by the Commissions on Popular Adult Education (SOU 1979:85) and Municipal Adult Schools (SOU 1979:92). Based on the experience so far, the Commissions are suggesting complementary actions to strengthen the allocation policy. Thus, we can soon look forward to even further reforms in Swedish adult education.

ADULT EDUCATION IN THE UNITED KINGDOM

Arthur Stock

Director, National Institute of Adult Education

Introduction

It must be stated at the outset that much of the following text, under the various section headings which follow, is concerned with the adult education which is readily observable in England. Although, at the present time, the legal basis for provision in Wales is precisely the same as in England, the historical, cultural and language differences of Wales produce certain differences in the institutional and functional elements as compared to its larger neighbour. In Scotland and Northern Ireland there are different legal bases for the respective adult education services; and the administrative patterns and organisational style of these two countries are markedly different from those of England.

Nevertheless, there are more similarities in the service of adult education in all four countries of the United Kingdom than there are differences; and so in this brief account it will be sufficient in each section to refer to these differences in respective countries as they occur, rather than undertaking a four-nation study with each national section having its own range of chapter headings.

A further initial consideration must be in relation to the scope and range of what is meant by "adult education." The tradition in the UK, common to all four countries, was to regard the term "adult education" as being synonymous with "non-vocational" educational courses, classes and programmes for adults. Vocational, professional or work-oriented programmes were often designated as "further education" or "training." Indeed, such traditional usages die hard: even in the recent (1973) governmentally-sponsored Committee of Enquiry into Adult Education in England and Wales under the chairmanship of Sir Lionel Russell, their terms of reference were directed to examine "...the provision of non-vocational adult education." In fact, the Russell Committee found it very difficult to adhere to this limitation, as on numerous occasions the evidence presented to them was not able to be separated on the basis of the simple polarity "vocational" vs. "non-vocational." The Education Act 1944, which informs the administrative practice of England and Wales, uses the term Further Education as a generic one to subsume various elements of a continuum, from narrowly defined professional training and education at one end to personal, social and cultural education at the other. Clearly the many forms of academic, technical, community, family-related, political or religious education in between may be either "vocational" or "non-vocational" according to the circumstances and motivation of the individual student.

In the event, the Russell Committee made the following statement in their final report: "We therefore see no virtue in attempting a sharp line of division anywhere across this spectrum, but have taken our terms of reference as being simply a convenient way of indicating that we should exclude the major areas of higher, technical and art education."

Even this neat side-stepping of the major hazards in the Committee's terms of reference is hardly adequate. Consider the Open University, which is specifically designed to be open to all adults whatever their educational qualifications, and yet offers high level education in arts, sciences, mathematics, humanities and technology; clearly it cannot be categorised as "non-vocational," is obviously "higher," and yet equally clearly is <u>adult</u> education.

Conceptually then, the notion of adult education is coming to mean "the provision of non-formal and informal education for adult people: that is, courses excluding the normal range of provision in colleges and universities for young people immediately following the statutory school leaving age, but including the full range of recurrent educational opportunities designed for people of more mature years, and related to any or all aspects of adult life."

More recently again, the Advisory Council for Adult and Continuing Education* issued a discussion document entitled

---

*Constituted by the Secretary of State for Education and Science, the ACACE's purposes are to (1) promote cooperation between the various bodies in adult education and review current practice, organisation and priorities, with a view to the most effective deployment of available resources; and (2) promote the development of future policies and priorities, with full regard to the concept of education as a process continuing throughout life.

Towards Continuing Education (ACACE, 1979c). This report referred to "initial" and "post-initial" education: the former includes the formal school/college/university system in which there is a legal requirement to participate during the ages five through 16 years, and fairly substantial "end-on" voluntary involvement of about 40 percent of relevant age-cohorts up to the age of 19, and much less (many first degree and post-graduate students) into the early twenties; whereas post-initial education refers to all the provision undertaken after a period of employment, often at recurrent intervals throughout life, and typically of fairly short-cycle or part-time. Thus post-initial education would include occupational training and education, traditional "liberal" adult education, general academic education, cultural and physical education, basic education, role education and others as mentioned above. And this sector (i.e., post-initial) would require an infusion of extra resources in the future.

It is fair to say that the majority response from informed opinion in the field has not been favourable to this conceptual divide and the Advisory Council may yet return to the more common distinction as between "compulsory education" and "post-compulsory education," accepting that many of the operations within the post-compulsory education sector (e.g., vocation preparation for 16 to 19 year-olds, or traditional end-on-to-school first degree work) would be the priority concerns of others. The Council could still concentrate on those aspects of post-compulsory education of particular concern and interest to adults such as recurrent opportunities for mature-age, entry/re-entry into further or higher education programmes, locally available cultural/academic and physical education, political education, community education and specific role education.

However, administratively the old divisions (i.e., vocational vs. non-vocational) persist. This fact, amongst other inconsistencies, illustrates the present great paradox of adult education in Great Britain, where the concepts and practice of the service frequently strain the bounds of the legislative and administrative framework in which they are based.

Historical Development

The history of adult education in Great Britain is certainly the most highly developed and minutely studied forms of investigation into this sector of education. The bibliographies abound with historical theses, studies,

pamphlets, articles. Much for the general or professionally
interested reader is contained within the 420 pages of
Professor Thomas Kelly's definitive <u>A History of Adult
Education in Great Britain</u>.

To reduce the long historical tradition (and indeed the
massive scholarship upon it) to a few pages introducing this
paper is an impossible task. We shall try to fly over the
centuries picking out one or two crucial events in passing,
and bringing us to the immediate post-war period when other
chapters can take up the narrative more effectively.

The primitive roots of British adult education can
be traced back to the early mediaeval church, and to the
concern of several bishops of the church to ensure that
their priests and others in holy orders had the necessary
skills to present The Word to the people and to maintain The
Faith in the face of exceedingly troubled and difficult
times as one wave of continental invaders succeeded another.
There was the further need to maintain a cadre of literate
people who could read and write the Scriptures and other holy
books. Thus it can be fairly said that, notwithstanding
the founding of the ancient universities in the twelfth
and thirteenth centuries, the concentrated knowledge,
scholarship and its effective transmission for future
generations was in the hands of the Church.

The opening of the sixteenth century saw rapid change:
the printing of the first complete English Bible in 1535;
then the study of preaching from that Bible by the growing
band of Protestants; later the Reformation and the subsequent impositions of Counter Reformation and Anglican
orthodoxy. And not least the powerful waves of Renaissance
influence were widening the minds and perceptions of more
than merely an elite to alternative considerations of the
arts, sciences and the human condition.

The seventeenth century brought Protestantism and with
it the establishment of specific institutions to be devoted
to the education of the poor and unenlightened in the
message of the Scriptures, and also in good works. As a
continuation of the same organisational logic the very
first public libraries were established. Later again public
lectures in coffee houses, debating and scientific societies; and the first (though totally impractical) plan for
comprehensive adult education, by Gerrard Winstanley in
1652, contained in his "Law of Freedom in a Platform, or
True Magistracy Restored."

Towards the end of the seventeenth century a few of the
science, engineering and debating societies began to attract
middle-class and even artisan members. As the eighteenth
century came in there was a renewed upsurge of religious
commitment to the education of the public, resulting
in the formation of the Society for the Propagation of

Christian Knowledge --an organisation which flourishes to this day. The SPCK devised highly structured reading and study courses based on the Bible. As a breakaway from the rather arduous and costly SPCK courses, Griffith Jones, Rector of Llandowror, Carmarthenshire, set up the first Welsh Circulating School in 1731. The system was essentially one of three months' intensive course in literacy based on the Bible and other religious literature; whereupon the school, its teacher(s) and assistants would move on to another church, chapel or village hall in another part of the region. The schools catered to adults as well as children.

This early Welsh example of what would now be called "non-formal" educational provision was just a part of an immense movement of religious commitment allied to various forms of basic education, and particularly associated with the growth of Methodism. In extreme rural (e.g., the Highlands of Scotland) as well as intensely urban areas (central Birmingham) further examples of Methodist Schools and Societies can be found. It was, however, not until 1798 that a specifically Adult Sunday School was established in the city of Nottingham "... for Bible reading and instruction in the secular arts of writing and arithmetic...."

The nineteenth century was the great era of expansion in Great Britain, linked with the massive Industrial Revolution, the major acquisition of the Empire overseas, the need for new classes of occupations and the pressure to consider new ways of understanding and controlling the ravages of urban industrial society. The most typical innovation in adult education was the founding of the Mechanics' Institute movement. The first as judged by its curriculum rather than its name was the Edinburgh School of Arts, founded in 1821. Its primary concern was to provide for working men systematic courses of lectures "... in such branches of physical science as are of practical advantage in their several trades." In addition to the chemistry, mechanics and mathematics so provided, there were fifty additional classes at more elementary levels of functional literacy and numeracy, together with a library, and a collection of models and apparatus for experiments. By 1851 there were close on 700 Mechanics' Institutes throughout the country. In several instances the original foundations, particularly in larger cities, formed the basis for over a century of educational development to the present day. Thus the Manchester Mechanics' Institute has become today's University of Manchester Institute of Science and Technology (UMIST), the London Mechanics' Institute gave rise to the foundation of Birkbeck College of London University, a college entirely devoted to continuing higher education for adults--mostly on a part-time basis.

That same turbulent century saw many other adult education developments which have a modern counterpart in today's service: the early cooperative societies, the Working Men's Colleges, the Evening School movement, the Technical Education Act, the introduction of University Extension Lectures (by Cambridge) in 1873, the founding in 1899 of Ruskin College as a residential college for the continuing education of working people, and in 1903 the founding by Albert Mansbridge of An Association to Promote the Higher Education of Working Men, which later became the Workers' Educational Association.

These early years of the twentieth century also saw the beginning in primitive form of the fourfold partnership which persists to this day of central government, local education authorities, universities, and voluntary agencies.   This partnership experienced many vicissitudes but also benefits from the two world wars of this century: in both cases the absolute necessity for specific and general forms of education for adults was perceived during and immediately after both holocausts.   Unfortunately, again in both cases, the early post-war flush of enthusiasm drained away into apathy on the part of political masters of the day, so that although gains were made, the impetus has never been maintained nor the potential fully realised.

As a footnote we should perhaps mention that in 1921 the British Institute of Adult Education was founded by a band of enthusiasts and activists including Mansbridge, Haldane and Tawney.   It continued successfully as a "personal membership" organisation right through the Second World War, when it was the major instrument in forming the Army Bureau of Current Affairs and the Council for Education in Music and the Arts. The former was later incorporated into the work of the Royal Army Educational Corps, and the latter the Arts Council of Great Britain.

In 1946, following the new Education Act, a National Foundation for Adult Education was set up by a group of activists who were dissatisfied with the British Institute of Adult Education because it had neither institutional members nor formal recognition as a national body uniting the whole adult education movement; and it serviced the many authorities and organisations which now had new responsibilities for adult education thrust upon them.   For three years the two organisations--the National Foundation and the British Institute--existed side by side.   But in 1949, after some hard negotiating, they agreed to merge within one joint constitution, and thus formed the National Institute of Adult Education.   NIAE has continued to evolve throughout the years, now being committed to much research, development, documentation and publication work, as well as being the major coordinating and consultative body for the education of adults.

Perhaps unfortunately, the new duties upon Scottish local authorities suggested the need for a specifically Scottish Institute of Adult Education, based in Edinburgh, and such was formed, breaking away from the former whole Kingdom organisation. Nevertheless the two sister Institutes work closely and amicably at all times.

Legal Bases

It should be noted at the outset of this section that the legal basis for public (and some private) services of education for adults is regarded by many professional, administrative and academic practitioners as quite inadequate to meet the needs of the present, let alone to cope with the rapidly changing demographic, technological, economic and social scenarios of the future. This view is to some extent endorsed by central government, as exemplified in the second main term of reference of the 1978-formed Advisory Council for Adult and Continuing Education, which requires that the Council shall:

> promote the development of future policies and priorities with full regard to the concept of education as a process continuing throughout life.

The situation is futher complicated by legislation and regulations relating to education for adults promulgated by several other Ministries than the specific Department of Education and Science (e.g., Department of Employment provision relating to labour-market education and training, or the Home Office support for the education of immigrants, communities suffering inner-urban deprivation, or inmates of penal establishments). Hopefully, in the not-too-distant future, a major reappraisal will be undertaken, and new legal enactment will follow.

Postwar Education Acts

The base line for modern adult education services in all four countries of the UK is a series of Acts of Parliament passed in the immediate post-war period. Inherent in all of these was the principle of developing "... a national service, locally administered." For this purpose certain levels of local government, either the old counties or the more recent urban municipalities, were designed as local education authorities (LEAs). These LEAs were charged with considerable responsibilities to provide educational services to meet the needs of their respective areas. The notion was to devolve much detailed planning and management to this local level, but to insist on certain national standards being maintained. Thus in the very first Section of the Education Act (1944) for England and Wales, it states the following:

> It shall be lawful for His Majesty to appoint a Minister,* (hereinafter referred to as 'the Minister') whose duty it shall be to promote the education of the people of England and Wales and the progressive development of institutions devoted to that purpose, and to secure the effective execution by local authorities, under his control and direction, of the national policy for producing a varied and comprehensive service of education in every area.

Similarly this Act, and the sister Acts in Scotland and Northern Ireland, set out the three fundamental stages of the statutory system of education. It should be noted that the universities and certain other institutions and organisations including several in adult education were outside this devolved LEA responsibility. Thus certain prestigious secondary schools, a few independent colleges, all the universities, plus a number of adult education organisations received direct financial support from central government. But Section 7 (below) was at the time a very considerable step forward in requiring a great variety of educational services to be provided for all members of the community, rather than a selected minority.

> The statutory system of public education shall be organised in three progressive stages to be known as primary education, secondary education and further education; and it shall be the duty of the local education authority for every area, so far as their powers extend, to contribute towards the spiritual, moral, mental and physical development of the community by securing that efficient education throughout those stages shall be available to meet the needs of the population of their area.

---

*Currently the title of this Minister is the Secretary of State for Education and Science.

Acts Affecting Adult Education

Three sections of the Act crucial to the continuing education of adults are Sections 41, 42 and 53. Section 41 reads as follows:

> Subject as hereinafter provided, it shall be the duty of every local education authority to secure the provision for their area of adequate facilities for further education, that is to say:
>
> (a) full-time and part-time education for persons over compulsory school age; and
>
> (b) leisure-time occupation, in such organised cultural training and recreative activities as are suited to their requirements, for any persons over compulsory school age who are able and willing to profit by the facilities provided for that purpose.

Section 41, at the time of its introduction, was quite revolutionary: for the first time ever the provision of education beyond the statutory school leaving age, raised to 15 years of age in 1947 and to 16 in 1972, became a duty and responsibility of local authorities rather than merely a hoped-for possibility. In fact, several progressive local authorities had introduced adult education provision during the 1920s and 1930s and the London County Council founded some Literary Institutes even before 1914. However, most had not done so in any determined way, although the majority had introduced "evening institutes" for the vocational or remedial education of young workers whose educational needs had not been met before the (then) statutory school leaving age of 14. These latter institutes always attracted a proportion of adult students although their courses were not geared, either in content or method, to the needs of adults.

Thus, in the late 1940s and 1950s there was an expansion of evening institutes and a gradual change in the nature of their courses and clientele towards adult interests and adult involvement. Predominantly though, their ethos was still that of "catching up" on deficiencies in required educational qualifications, although there was a small but growing proportion of non-examination courses pursued for their intrinsic interest rather than for the acquisition of a certificate or diploma. This expansion obviously required increased expenditure by local government which was in part supported by pro-rata grants from central government. But even during those early years of the new dispensation, the inadequacies of the Education Act's wording, from the point of view of adult education development, became apparent. In other sections of the Act, it was stated clearly and unequivocally that it was the duty of each local education authority to provide a school place for every child resident in that particular LEA. Thus the extent of primary and secondary education provision was determined on the basis of demographic extrapolation, i.e., the forecasting of numbers of children who had to be provided for. But in the further education sector the law merely stated that "adequate facilities" had to be "secured," thus leaving the scope, range and extent of such facilities to the local interpretation of the word "adequate." In practice, over the thirty or so years since the first implementation of the Act, the interpretations have been so varied that the educational opportunity available to an adult in different parts of the country also varies greatly.

The extent of this variation, which was never envisaged or intended in the original drafting of the legislation, could have been checked by a more rigorous application of Section 42 of the Act, which spells out in some detail the requirement upon local education authorities to prepare, discuss, and gain ministerial approval of plans for the further education services of their respective areas. With hindsight it may be judged that some of these specific LEA plans which were accepted by the Minister in the period 1949-51 should have been tightened up considerably, as in subsequent periods of financial stringency the adult and further education services have frequently been the first target for cut-backs and limitations. In short, the perception of what is "adequate" in good times seems to deteriorate in bad times.

Section 53 of the Act stresses the importance of social, physical and cultural recreational facilities being readily available to all the people of a local authority area. It empowers local authorities to set up recreational centres, holiday camps and classes, swimming pools and other facilities. The implication of the wording is clearly that of integration, i.e. of educational, social and cultural facilities so that the buildings, equipment and other facilities whether "educational" or not, shall be available to all who wish to use them in a responsible fashion. Here again though, the Act is permissive rather than mandatory: it encourages and empowers the securing of facilities without sufficiently specifying basic requirements. The result has been an equal diversity of styles of provision--from large campus, multi-purpose community colleges to scattered, organisationally-fragmented facilities.

This immense diversity in the form, structure, extent and style of local education authority provision is often seen as a great strength of British adult education: there can be a quick and appropriate response to local needs, and the decision making is much closer to the "grassroots" of a society than is the case in highly centralised models. However, as previously mentioned, the contrary aspect of highly decentralised local decision making, especially within a somewhat loose framework of national legislation, is the inequality of opportunity which results in certain parts of the country as compared to others.

Responsible Bodies

It was previously briefly noted that certain organisations providing adult education had special legislative consideration, at least in England, Wales and Northern Ireland. The universities of these three countries with Extra-Mural Departments, the seventeen English and Welsh Districts of the Workers' Educational Association and the Welsh Council of Young Men's Christian Associations are designated as special Responsible Bodies for the providing of education for adults. The work of these Responsible Bodies is therefore additional to (or ideally complementary to) the programmes of the various local education authorities throughout the country. Special regulations have from time to time been drawn up to administer "district grants" from the central government towards the costs of these organisations. The major part of this finance takes the form of up to 75 percent grant towards the teaching costs. There is no requirement in law to assist either the university departments or the voluntary organisations with their organising and administrative costs. In practice the university extra-mural departments acquire this organising and administrative finance from university sources; whereas the voluntary organisations receive arbitrary, annually-determined grants from central and local government sources. For example, the overall breakdown of income for English and Welsh WEA Districts in 1973-74 was: 60 percent DES; 20 percent LEAs; 20 percent voluntary effort. Additionally, certain other voluntary organisations not included in the Responsible Body list (e.g., the National Federation of Women's Institutes, the Seafarers' Education Service, the Long-term Residential Colleges) also receive annually determined direct grants to assist them to carry out their educational work.

The present legal framework for this is the Further Education Regulations (1969), and the relevant sections read as follows:

Grants to Responsible Bodies:

25.(1) Subject to the provisions of this regulation, the Secretary of State may pay a grant to a responsible body towards the cost of providing tuition in any course of liberal adult education included in a programme approved by him for the purposes of these regulations.

(2)   The amount of any such grant shall be determined by reference to the general standard of the courses included in the programme (having regard to the syllabuses, the quality of teaching, the length of courses and the arrangements for written work, reading under guidance and other forms of private study to be carried out between meetings), the needs of the area, the activities of other bodies providing further education in the area and the fees paid by students.

(3)   It shall be a condition of grant under this regulation that the appointment of full-time lecturers and tutor organisers for any such programme shall be subject to the approval of the Secretary of State; and regulation 20 (refers only to the conduct of voluntary establishments under the Education Act 1944) shall apply in respect of any course included in the programme as it applies in respect of courses provided by voluntary establishments.

Grants to national associations:

26.   The Secretary of State may pay to any national association grants towards expenditure incurred by them in providing educational services otherwise than in or in connection with the provision of courses to which regulation 25 (1) applies.

Grants to other organisations:

29.   The Secretary of State may pay grants to any other voluntary organisation, and in particular to any youth organisation, in respect of expenditure incurred by them, whether as part of wider activities or not, in providing, or in connection with the provision of facilities for further education within the meaning of Section 41 (b) of the Education Act 1944.

It should be noted that in Scotland, the Responsible Body list of designated direct grant organisations does not exist. Scottish universities have adult, extra-mural or continuing education departments with their full-time adult education staff financed entirely by the universities; there are three WEA Districts and numerous small voluntary organisations; but all have to negotiate their necessary finances from local education authorities, annual grants from central government, special foundation grants and of course tuition fees. In this respect there is a major legal and operational difference between Scottish adult education and the rest of the United Kingdom.

Other Regulations

A variety of specific "regulations" is designed to implement this rather loose legal framework, some of which has been outlined above. Two further examples are worth specific emphasis, both relating to the support of adult students undertaking particular forms of continuing education. The first provides mandatory grant support on a means-tested sliding scale for those adult students undertaking the highly concentrated courses promoted by the so-called long-term residential colleges (Ruskin College, Plater College, Coleg Harlech, Fircroft College, Hillcroft College, Northern College, and Newbattle Abbey). The colleges themselves also receive direct grants from the Department of Education and Science towards annual recurrent expenditure, and a minor proportion of the costs of approved building programmes. The second is of similar nature for those adult students accepted by universities and polytechnics for fully designated first degree courses, whereby such adults are eligible for mandatory grants structurally similar to those provided for young first degree students who are normally in the 18 to 22 age range. It should be stated, however, that the acceptance of such mature adult students without the normal requirements of high grades in appropriate subjects in the Advanced level of the General Certificate of Education is dependent entirely on the views of individual universities or polytechnics, or even of individual relevant faculties or schools within them. In short, it is very arbitrary and is by no means widespread or adequate.

Finally, one should mention that the responsible Ministers in the respective countries can sponsor, if they so wish, change and development in the local authorities by the issue of Administrative Memoranda, Administrative Circulars or Circular Letters. None of these has the absolute force of governmental laws, decrees or regulations. However, Administrative Memoranda are regarded as strong injunctions for action. Most of these since the war have related to financial matters--building cost limits, fee increases, minor works programmes. One salutary Administrative Memorandum, issued in June of 1963, strongly encouraged the development of conversion, purchase or occasionally new construction of suitable buildings for the organisation and conduct of adult education; and also indicated a basis for the employment of full-time staff at local authority centre level. This memorandum had a marked effect on the general professionalisation of the service.

Organisational Structures

The structure of British adult education, like the culture on which it is founded, is essentially pluralistic. The long tradition of "voluntary" provision organised by societies and associations with social, moral or political aims, a century of university commitment plus the more recent legislative enactments encouraging substantial local authority intervention, all contribute to that essential pluralism.

This situation was further emphasised in the previously mentioned Russell Report which recommended the setting up of cooperative liaison bodies (Development Councils for Adult Education) at local, regional, and national levels. Similarly, the Alexander Report recommended a National Development Council for Community Education in Scotland. In all these more recent structural additions the recommended purpose was to involve all the interested parties: local education authorities, voluntary associations, universities, teachers and students; and to identify cooperatively the unmet needs and to agree to collaborative approaches, where appropriate, to tackle the problems so identified. However, it is true to say that in the past, this ideal state of cooperation between "partners" in a perceived joint enterprise has not always been achieved. It is not that one or the other type of provider of adult education was actually hostile or openly competitive. Rather, they have frequently just followed their own interests and concerns without consulting other partners.

Basically then, there are four major organising foci for continuing education for adults in all four countries of the United Kingdom: the Local Education Authorities (called Regional Authorities in Scotland, and Education and Library Boards in Northern Ireland), the Universities, the Voluntary Associations, and Central Government Departments.

The Local Education Authorities

The largest in every dimension of measurement is the local education authorities. LEA-provided courses and programmes account for just over 85 percent of all known adult education enrollments. The LEAs are responsible for the vast majority of buildings, equipment and human resources (i.e., teachers and ancillary staff) available: adult education colleges, centres and institutes are mostly LEA owned and financed--only a few independent centres remain; the Colleges of Further Education and the Polytechnics, many of which undertake substantial amounts of educational work for adults, are also part of the LEA structure; similarly, the day schools for children (many of which are used in the evenings for adult courses), together with the specially built multi-purpose school-centred campuses such as the village or community colleges, are all LEA operated. Of the part-time teacher force, approximately 80 percent (145,000 in England and Wales) are LEA employed, of whom about 40 percent are qualified day-school teachers and the other 60 percent are qualified in a particular subject or skill, but not teacher-trained. There are currently about 2,200 full-time adult education "organisers"--principals, wardens, managers, heads-of-department, tutor-organisers in the United Kingdom, of whom about 1,600 are employed by LEAs.

Within this large LEA sector there are three major styles of organisation, as follows:

(1) The "area" adult education centre/college/institute. In this instance an area principal has the responsibility for arranging, publicising and supervising a wide-ranging pro-gramme of courses for adults, conducted in a variety of buildings within a determined geographical area. The majority of courses are taught in the evening, using the classrooms, laboratories, art and practical rooms of day-schools primarily built for children. Increasingly these 'evening-only' facilities are supplemented by specially built or converted facilities available throughout the daytime as well as in the evening. Such a special adult centre or college will often be the organising centre and will house the office of the principal and his subordinate full-time staff.

In addition, especially in rural areas, village and church halls are hired to provide meeting places for classes and groups. Sometimes there are well-established satellite centres, with either full-time or part-time 'centre-heads' responsible to the overall area principal.

(2) The community college or village college. In all examples of this organisational form a secondary school, with all the usual range of specialist teaching facilities, has

additional accommodation and staff for the provision of adult education programmes, and often for informal youth service activities as well. Such conglomerate arrangements were pioneered in the county of Cambridgeshire during the 1920s and 1930s, under the inspiration and guidance of the then Director of Education, Mr. Henry Morris. The concept has been developed and extended particularly in semi-rural and small town situations in several other local education authorities such as Cumbria, Devon, Leicestershire and Nottinghamshire, where extensive facilities are brought together on a campus, and designated as a community college. The overall management of all the services--school, youth and adult--is usually in the hands of a single principal or warden, assisted by specialist adult, community or youth tutors. Sometimes these latter attain the status of vice-principal. Adult classes and activities are largely organised on the main campus, although related 'out-centres' are not unknown. The intention, in this pattern of provision, is to offer a totality of educational services conveniently grouped together and central to a given neighborhood allowing ready access to classes, library, clubs, societies and recreational facilities.

(3)   The Adult Studies Department of a College of Further Education. This style of organisation uses as the base for adult education services one of the many district technical or further education colleges originally set up to provide employment-related education for the immediate post-school years, i.e., for those of ages 16 through 19. Increasingly in their professional education programmes, these colleges have been catering for older people: retraining courses, "topping-up" courses, management programmes or new technology courses. Some local education authorities took the logical step of extending the range of provision to the whole area of adults' educational needs, setting up special departments with staff aware of the techniques of teaching adults and of the special factors associated with adults learning. The principal of the college has overall direction of this work, as of all other departments in the college; but much of the management of the adult studies department will be devolved upon a specialist adult educator designated as Head of Department of Adult Studies.

In all three models outlined above, much of the teaching of adult students is carried out by part-time staff, especially in Model (1). There is a larger incidence of the use of internal full-time day-school teachers or college lecturers in models (2) and (3); but even in these cases part-time teachers are still needed from outside the teaching profession to cater for diverse subject specialisms. Thus, induction and in-service training is particularly necessary to help these part-time teachers to work effectively.

The Universities

The British universities have a long and honourable
tradition in the field of adult education. In 1873, the
University of Cambridge began a service of Extension Lectures,
which encouraged liberal-minded teachers and scholars to give
courses of public lectures in industrial centres throughout
the country. The practice was followed five years later by
the University of Oxford. Lecturers from these two ancient
universities ranged over incredible distances and often
attracted vast audiences in public halls in all the major
cities of the country. Later still, some of the 'receiving'
cities organised their own municipal Extension Committees;
and in several instances these became the bases for the
development of civic universities. Indeed, one major part of
the present University of Manchester was so formed; and
another major part, its Institute of Science and Technology,
was developed from the Manchester Mechanics' Institute. Thus,
that university, which has in recent years trained hundreds of
adult educators scattered throughout the world, can truly
claim that its dual ancestors were of that same sturdy
tradition of adult education.

As previously noted in the section on legal matters, the
twenty-five English and Welsh universities which serve their
respective regions of the country with varied services of
extra-mural education at university standard are designated as
Responsible Bodies. Thus, subject to the agreement of Her
Majesty's Inspectors as to the programme of courses and
its congruence with the Further Education Regulations 1969,
their courses are able to attract a central government grant
of up to 75 percent towards teaching costs. The remaining
tutorial costs, together with the cost of administration, have
to be found either from the individual university's finances
or from local grants together with fees charged to students.
Similar financial arrangements apply to the two universities
in Northern Ireland providing extra-mural programmes. However, in Scotland, where seven universities have established
extra-mural departments, the financial resource, although
still highly diverse, cannot depend upon central government
direct grants towards tutorial costs. Instead a much larger
proportion of support costs has to be negotiated from local
education authority sources although, as previously noted, the
costs of the full-time adult education staff are a charge on
the respective universities. Indeed, the recent Committee of
Enquiry into Adult Education in Scotland under the Chairmanship of Professor K. A. Alexander, recommended a continuation
of this special Scottish system, in spite of strong representations from some quarters that university extra-mural work
should qualify for direct central government grants, as in
England.

The one common characteristic of all university adult education courses is that of "university standard," that is to say that the conceptual level of the courses, the requirement upon students and the presentation, should not fall below that of the first or second year of undergraduate courses or at the very least that the tutor's qualifications should be of a university teaching level. However, the style of discourse--including much more interaction than is common in university intramural classes--and the lack (for the most part, but not entirely) of externally applied assessments and examinations indicate major differences from internal university teaching and learning. It is true that there is a small core of certificate and diploma courses organised for extra-mural students and examined by written papers and dissertations (and occasionally by viva voce); but these are the exception.

A major difference of the university sector from other branches of adult education lies in the full-time staff to student ratio. The universities throughout the United Kingdom employ just over 500 full-time specialist adult educators, mainly as subject tutors (i.e., teachers of classes) but also as supervisors of part-time tutors in a given subject area. These appointments are administered and paid as equivalent to internal university lecturers and senior lecturers. The directors of the extra-mural departments have (mostly) professorial status and salaries. Additional to the expertise of the special extra-mural staff, the extra-mural department of a university should be able to involve staff and resources from any internal department of the university and channel them into the service of the communities in the surrounding region. In practice, most internal departments do so co-operate; but others do not, regarding extra-mural work as draining off energy and commitment from "internal" research and teaching purposes of the department.

The Open University

Finally, of course, there is the newest and most "adult," of all British universities, namely the Open University. This is an establishment providing distance education courses at four levels leading to ordinary first degrees (after three levels) or honours degrees (after the fourth level). Additionally there is a limited number of post-experience and advanced degree courses. Entry to the university requires no previous educational qualifications whatsoever (in marked contrast to entry into the other British universities which have rigorous entry qualification requirements, often much stiffer than the official minimum for entry into higher education).

Teaching is carried out via three main media: correspondence, television and radio, face-to-face tutorials, and
seminars at local study centres. Of these the correspondence
element is the major one, carrying the main teaching units,
the books and references, the written tutorials and assessments (including regular computer marked assignments).
All this central resource is written and published at the
University's main campus at Milton Keynes, some 40 miles north
of London. The television and radio programmes are produced
in association with the BBC, mostly in London studios but
increasingly (and totally, in the future) at Milton Keynes.
Each of the 13 regional divisions of the OU is responsible
for setting up and supervising a number of study centres in
its area and recruiting suitable part-time tutor-counsellors.
These local study centres are often located in local education
authority owned colleges or centres, by agreement with the LEA
concerned. Students are not compelled to attend local study
centres. They are, however, required to attend one week's
residential summer school in most subject areas. Thus, in
addition to nearly three hundred central academic and senior
administrative staff at Milton Keynes, there are about one
hundred and fifty regional full-time academic and senior
administrative staff based on the thirteen regional offices,
and readily available to counsel, advise, and tutor students
if required, and to assist or supervise the relatively more
numerous part-time staff recruited from local universities,
polytechnics and adult colleges who work in the local study
centres. Organisationally speaking, the Open University is a
much more centralised style of provision than is usual in the
United Kingdom; although even in this instance strongly
developed regional offices each with their own regional
director and professional staff help to mitigate the danger
of remoteness of a central institution operating through
technological media.

The Voluntary Associations

The third great sector of British adult education is that
of the voluntary associations. As might be expected in this
highly pluralistic society, the number of such associations is
considerable. There are fourteen long-standing associations
who are corporate members of the National Institute of Adult
Education (England and Wales) and many more not so affiliated.
There are also several associations in Scotland, Wales and
Ireland unique to those countries, and additional to those
which cross the boundaries of all four countries.

The Workers' Educational Association

The largest and internationally best known voluntary body is the Workers' Educational Association. Apart from the Welsh National Council of Young Men's Christian Associations, it is the only voluntary association to be given the status of a Responsible Body in England and Wales. Strictly speaking, each of the Association's seventeen Districts (or regional federations) in England and Wales is a Responsible Body, and each administers the direct grant finances from central government disbursed on the same formula as already described in the section about the universities' provision. Altogether in the whole of the UK there are twenty one Districts to which are affiliated, in regional groupings, the 950 branches of the Association. So far as the programme organisation is concerned, the local Branch Committee is autonomous and all-powerful in its own domain. It is a source of great pride to the WEA that its real democracy extends so much wider and deeper than in many other national bodies. Of course, the Branch Committee will usually welcome advice in its programme formulation from one of the full-time tutor-organisers employed by the District, or alternatively from the local university extra-mural staff tutor who will often take an interest in local WEA affairs. Another source of strength is the large number (more than 2,000) of local, regional and national trades union and workers' organisations affiliated to the Association.

Structurally, the Association should be considered from the Branch upwards. Each local Branch will have a group of voluntary officers and an executive committee which decides upon the educational programme which is within the budget. Certain funds are available to Branches for special events and for their small administrative costs. Each Branch elects a delegate to the District Council; and it is at this level that the disposition of the central and local government grants is decided and District budgets balanced through required class fees. Each District employs a full-time District Secretary, most a Development Officer and a small number of full-time tutor-organisers. These latter are more often appointed on the basis of academic knowledge and qualifications than on organising skills. All twenty-one Districts futher federate to form the third or national level. Thus there is a national Honorary President and Deputy President, full-time salaried General Secretary, Assistant General Secretaries and National Development Officer, together with supporting ancillary staff at a central headquarters building in London. This national headquarters represents the whole Association in negotiations with central government, in meetings with other providers and in general public relations. It also publishes a bi-annual newspaper and develops a range of teaching materials and resources.

Other Voluntary Associations

Besides the WEA a number of voluntary organisations such as the National Federation of Women's Institutes, the National Union of Townswomen's Guilds, the Marine Society, the National Council of YMCAs, all receive central government grants for their central organising and promotional work in education. And there is a much larger number which receives no regular direct government grants, although occasionally they are able to attract local or central government grants for particular programmes or activities. More recently a number of voluntary groups specialising in social and educational work with the most deprived and disadvantaged sections of the populations have received special grants in respect of literacy work, or English-for-immigrants courses or parent education programmes.

Organisationally, these are very diverse. The larger of the women's organisations have county and district secretaries on a salaried basis as well as substantial headquarters staffs. The rural women's organisation (the National Federation of Women's Institutes) also maintains a residential college of adult education promoting an extensive programme of courses for the Federation's membership of over half a million. Other important 'voluntaries' are the National Federation of Community Associations, the Educational Centres Association, the Trades Union Congress Education Department, and the Cooperative Union.

Officially (and legally), the National Institute of Adult Education (England and Wales) and the Scottish Institute of Adult Education are voluntary organisations officially registered as charities under the appropriate Acts. They nevertheless receive a substantial proportion of their overall finance from public sector sources either as "core" finance, research contracts or special development programmes such as adult literacy and basic education.

Linkages

A structural weakness which is currently being tackled in piece-meal experimental fashion is that of linkage between the various sectors and dimensions of post-school education. Two examples:

(1) The Open College in the North West of England is a consortium of Further Education Colleges linked to the University of Lancaster, and providing "new opportunity"/ "fresh horizons"/"return to study" programmes for adult students who, on successful completion of same, achieve credit for entry at various levels into certain first degree courses of Lancaster University.

(2)   The Open University and the Council for National
Academic Awards (which validates all the degree programmes of
the Polytechnics) have recently concluded an academic credit
exchange agreement.   This allows students successfully completing elements of degree programmes in the Open University
to transfer to second level stages of polytechnic degree
courses, and vice-versa.

     It should also be added that a recently concluded
Feasibility Study into wholesale academic credit accumulation
and transfer in the higher education sector has reported
favourably upon the notion and has recommended the inception
of a pilot project.   This could be of great importance
in furthering a broad-band system of continuing educational
opportunity for adults.

Programmes

Fields of Study

     In a rather approximate normative way, the different
organisational forms of adult education in Britain have an
influence upon the subject areas and fields of study undertaken.   By tradition and by regulation, the organisations
receiving direct grants from the central government under
the Responsible Body regulations concentrate on fields of
study which lend themselves to a more academic or cognitive
approach.   Occasionally this leads to some curious anomalies
as, for example, the regulations encourage "appreciation" of
music courses, but discourage the actual performance of music
by the students.   Similarly in other arts subjects the extra-
mural departments and the WEA frequently study drama, various
aspects of the visual arts, literature, opera and ballet
without directly engaging in the creative activities themselves.   However, the fields of study of these older, more
traditional forms of adult education also include the social
sciences, physical and natural sciences, history (with local
history and archaeology being particularly popular) and
international, intercultural combined studies.

     With this tradition of academic curricula having been
promoted for many years, there was a tendency during the rapid
growth of LEA adult education in the 1960's for the LEA adult
evening and day centres to cater for the alternative fields of
practical, cultural, physical and creative subjects in which
students could actually practise the particular activity as
they learned about it, rather than studying and analysing it
in a "once-removed" way.   In more recent years these rather
simplistic demarcation lines have been increasingly blurred,

as more LEA adult colleges and centres have successfully promoted rigorous intellectual courses in addition to (or occasionally complementary to) the pottery, drama, music-making, needlecraft, dance and language learning.

In some towns, particularly the larger cities, it is increasingly common to find one college specialising in more advanced work in several of the more demanding fields of study, collecting students at second, third and fourth year levels who have already received a grounding in the subject at an adult centre nearer to their home neighbourhood.

Overall, the most popular field of study includes those courses related to the home and family. Thus, there is a wide variety of needlecraft courses, furnishing courses, woodwork and craft metalwork, home improvements, including painting and decorating, motor vehicle maintenance, gardening, cookery and other aspects of home economics.

Second in the popularity lists are courses involving a large measure of physical activity such as keep fit, dancing (folk, modern and special movement systems), sports and outdoor pursuits (e.g., orienteering, pre-ski) and yoga. Sometimes such courses are linked to serious study in other fields: an angling course linked to marine biology, a sub-aqua diving course linked to marine archaeology.

Close in demand to the physical activity courses is the field of modern language learning. The most popular languages are French, German, Spanish, Italian, in that order, although some large-city colleges have a remarkable range including Russian and several "small" European languages, together with an increasing spread of Asian languages.

The next large field includes the arts and artistic crafts courses. Pottery, painting, sculpture, leatherwork, embroidery and lace are prominent; also choral singing, group instrumental music making and drama.

All other fields tend to be much smaller in the extent of participation but remarkably consistent in their occurrence. Thus "basic education" (including literacy, about which there has been a recent successful multi-media campaign), history and archaeology, natural sciences, social sciences, local/community studies and action groups, first aid and health education. In addition there is a continuing and fairly constant demand for courses which enable adults to pass the General Certificate of Education normally taken by children at ages 16 or 18 for Ordinary level or Advanced level respectively. Indeed, there has been a rather belated realisation of this fact by the GCE examination boards who are more frequently offering better syllabuses for courses which are relevant and interesting to adult people of more mature years.

Other certificate courses include a large range of office skills courses: typewriting, shorthand, accounts and bookkeeping, office machinery etc. Others again are more technological, relating to basic qualifications in the engineering, building and electrical industries. More often when older adults are involved in such technological studies, it is either for purposes of retraining following redundancy in another type of work, or for up-dating as new knowledge and new methods are introduced. Usually these latter courses are organised in technical colleges or polytechnics (sometimes in universities) as the facilities and resources for the specialised studies are more readily available.

Industrial Studies

Another interesting and developing field in the work-milieu is that of industrial studies provided by institutions of both local education authorities and Responsible Bodies. This field generally includes industrial relations, health and safety at work, introductory economics and statistics and industrial law. Although all these subjects have been studied by adults in traditional institutions for many years, more recently there has been considerable success--including a much greater involvement of industrial workers themselves--by arranging the classes and study groups (with the cooperation of management and unions) within or nearby the industrial plant; and whenever possible negotiating an agreement between management and trades unions to allow the workers (say) two hours paid leave each week to undertake these studies. This process of in-factory provision with paid release has, until recently, entirely been a matter for local or regional agreement between management and trade unions. But very recently two new Acts of Parliament reached the Statute Book: the Health and Safety at Work Act (1974) and the Protection of Employment Act (1975); and both of these include clauses allowing paid release for educational purposes for certain categories of workers' representatives. No doubt this will accelerate the progress towards a more universal law of paid educational leave. Furthermore, the Trades Union Congress is in receipt of an annual grant from the Department of Education and Science to support accredited courses of Trades Union Studies.

Of course, as in most industrialised countries, there is a great deal of management education, from foremen and supervisors, to line and middle management, and occasionally top management. Much of the first two categories is catered for by short specialised courses in polytechnics, colleges of further education or residential adult colleges. The latter category (and often middle management too) is provided for by universities, (including a substantial amount by university extra-mural departments), and notably by the specialist

Business Schools attached to the universities of London, Manchester and Strathclyde (Glasgow).

In short, the range of educational provision for adults is immense, from the most basic education in literacy, numeracy and domestic skills to advanced, highly specialised courses of university post-graduate standard, i.e., at the highest level of Higher Education. And these extremes of content may often attract the same person: quite recently the writer was talking to a business man who had just returned from an advanced computerisation course at a university business school, and who was worried about having missed some valuable sessions of his local evening centre pottery class.

Programmes for Women

A particular development area has been in the field of new opportunities for women, sometimes organised separately (occasionally with a strong feminist element), sometimes as part of more general "Return to Study" or "Fresh Horizons" programmes. The main informing notion is that of "experiential learning," i.e., that women wishing to return (or become involved for the first time) into the world of work or higher education should be able to "sample" various subjects and programmes in order to readjust to the style of procedure and discipline and also to make more informed choices as to the fields of study. Such programmes have been organised at universities, polytechnics, local further education colleges and at adult colleges and centres. Both day and evening programmes have been available, but the day programmes seem to be more successful.

Another approach to the same objective has been via the Training Opportunities Scheme (TOPS), sponsored by the Manpower Services Commission --the latter an agency of the Department of Employment. TOPS schemes are essentially devised for the training or retraining of unemployed adults for occupations where there are shortages of labour. Although women takers for these programmes are still in a minority overall, there are several specific courses where women have been recruited in large numbers (notably in new commercial, office and other service-industry sectors), and where the access of confidence and skill has induced further motivation to proceed to more advanced levels of general education. It should be noted that adults recruited on to TOPS courses receive support moneys ("wages") for their attendance which is significantly, though not largely, above the basic unemployment allowances given to registered unemployed persons.

Programmes for Workers

Part-time educational provision for working people is extensive, and mostly related to the specific occupational requirements. A better understanding of this area has recently been achieved by the recent (1979) Survey of Paid Educational Leave in England and Wales, undertaken by the National Institute of Adult Education. The PEL survey studied all provision made in 1976/77 for employees aged at least 19 years at the commencement of the respective courses. Careful estimates indicate that between three and four million workers received PEL of varying duration during that year. This relatively large figure, representing approximately 17 percent of the work force, was achieved mainly by either dispensations of the various employers or by collective agreements between unions and employers. There is no universal law of PEL as is the case in France. The only specific legislation relates to Health and Safety at Work Act of 1974 and the Protection of Employment Act of 1975, both of which provide for compulsory paid educational leave for elected worker representatives to attend appropriate courses.

The great majority (almost two thirds) of the 3 to 4 million were in receipt of provision made directly by the employers, i.e., mostly "in-house," the rest were in a variety of public educational establishments such as colleges of further education, polytechnics, and a sprinkling of universities and private sector establishments. Conventional public sector educational establishments provided only approximately one-sixth of all student-places for workers on PEL; but they also provided the longer courses, so that approximately 40 percent of student-attendances (i.e., student-hours) took place in such establishments. It should also be noted that the Trades Union Congress is grant-aided by the Department of Education and Science to sponsor courses in trades union studies, as well as other specific courses as required under the two acts previously referred to. Thus, "trades union" worker education in its various forms (with paid educational leave to undertake it) accounts for approximately 30,000 places per year.

In spite of this apparently fairly healthy scene in worker education, the following caveats need to be noted.

(1) Those under 30 years of age are eight times more likely to receive out-of-house PEL than those over 50.

(2) Whereas two in five workers are female, only one in six of those who receive out-of-house PEL are women (and probably less in "in-house" provision).

(3) The liability to receive PEL varies greatly with occupational category, with the rate per annum for managers, scientific and professional workers being 1 in 5; supervisors 1 in 3; clerical workers 1 in 8; and manual workers 1 in 8. More than half of all places go to the "top" 15 percent of the work-force.

(4) Very little of this large amount of PEL supported educational activity is of the general, academic, or "personal development" nature, except where it is complementary or intrinsic to the occupational concern, although some enlightened employers (notably central and local government and certain science-based industries) do allow limited PEL for the general academic advancement of their employees.

The Industrial Language Training Units in the United Kingdom are a fairly recent phenomenon, specifically designed to help non-English-speaking immigrants to gain a knowledge of functional English together with other information relevant to their living and working in Great Britain. The Units' staff negotiate with particular industrial, commercial or service enterprises which employ high proportions of immigrant people, so that the workers concerned are able to gain paid release from work for this type of study.

The provision is not only of language learning, but also social skills which are specific to that industry. On the basis of careful investigation, this highly skilled team from the Industrial Language Training Unit will design a training plan. Wherever possible this plan will include educational material and programmes which are for the immigrant workers on the one hand but also for the English work force, particularly the supervisors and managers and the leading trade unionists on the other. They will then, if this is accepted, conduct these courses.

Also part of the offer on the Industrial Training Unit is an assessment and evaluation of not only the courses, but also of the possibilities for continuation of the process within the work place; or to put it another way, the means for this process of education to continue without so much support from the ILTU but with the possibility of consultation and further help if required. All of the money for funding the ILTUs and their activities comes from the Department of Employment's Manpower Services Commission; in most cases there is a time allowance from the employers for the workers to undertake these courses during working time, and the workers are paid at their normal rate of pay whilst they attend the courses. So there is a financial contribution from the employers insofar as they continue to pay the workers' wages and in many cases provide a suitable place for the educational work to go on.

There are some 28 ILTUs, and there is a central servicing body, the National Centre for Industrial Language Training, based at one of the working centres in London, which designs materials which can be adapted to local circumstances and also informs and educates the trainers working in the field.

Although there has been tremendous success, both in language learning and the encouragement of employment for immigrants by this intervention, not everything goes easily. In several parts of the country there are difficulties in persuading certain types of industry to participate in this sort of activity. One example is the hotel and catering industry, which traditionally employs a large number of migrant workers. This is an area which requires a considerable knowledge of the English language, plus health and safety considerations, but it has been very difficult to persuade employers to release workers for education and training.

Much of the success of the ILTUs relates to the vocational motivation on both sides of industry. Further, the materials and the curricula are highly varied and seen by the participants to be very relevant to their immediate concerns; there is no predetermined package which has to be either taken or refused--each course is designed to be specific, highly functional and relevant to the needs of all participants.

Basic Education and Literacy Training

The decade of the 70's saw considerable developments in the provision of basic education for adults whose self-perception of their inadequacy in the face of society's requirements was such as to require specific tuition in reading, writing, elementary computation, acquisition of or improvement in the English language; and, more recently, "social and life skills."

The exact figures are not known; but the pure literacy provision caters for about 80,000 adults per annum, the ESL and numeracy rather less; and the social and life skills provision is still in its infancy.

Apart from these grossly disadvantaged people, the locally available provision for adults (particularly that occupationally related) does involve just over a million people who left formal schooling at the minimum school-leaving age (currently--since 1972--16). Thus a substantial proportion of the adult population can be identified as "under-educated" by the standard of national minima in schooling terms. It should also be noted that various studies have indicated that such people are less likely to perceive the advantage of continuing education and less likely to take it up, except when its immediate utility (i.e., work or a preferred recreation or interest) becomes obvious.

The latest contral government initiatives in this field are the funding of the Adult Literacy and Basic Skills Unit, operated by NIAE, and the pre-TOPS courses (i.e., pre-Training Opportunities in Basic Education for the unemployed), sponsored by the Manpower Services Commission.

Parent Education

Parent Education is a field without any mass provision in the UK, although contributory elements to a comprehensive programme do occur, as follows:

(1) Child psychology/child development courses: offered by university extra-mural departments, WEA and some LEA centres and colleges;

(2) Pre- and post-natal courses: sponsored by local authority health education departments and clinics;

(3) Problem-centred courses (e.g., teen-age rebellion, vandalism, etc.): organized by local community groups, some LEA centres, and parent-teacher associations;

(4) Media-based courses (mostly BBC, some commercial TV): child development, single-parenting, relationship to schools, etc. Some courses have links with correspondence courses, with voluntary "support" groups, and with the Open University.

There is no record of the numbers involved, and no reliable estimate is possible.

Pre-Retirement Courses

The growing proportion of retired and elderly people in the population has led to a substantial growth in the provision of pre-retirement courses. Most local education authorities now run courses designed to help those approaching retirement (and the recently-retired) to cope with the various problems of retirement from employment and increasing age.

Often the courses take the form of a series of talks (followed by discussion) by visiting experts on subjects such as finance, health, leisure and part-time work, social and family changes and personal attitudes to retirement. Under the "leisure" heading, the development of interests and hobbies through attendance at adult education classes is invariably mentioned, and in fact retired persons do make up a substantial proportion of students at adult centres, WEA and extra-mural classes, particularly those organised in the daytime, and at the colleges offering midweek or weekend residential courses. (It might be mentioned here that most LEAs allow a reduced rate of fees for pensioners attending classes.)

Many private firms also provide similar courses for those of their employees approaching retirement age, often in collaboration with the Pre-Retirement Association which, among other activities, publishes a monthly magazine for the over-fifties. These private courses vary considerably in length and comprehensiveness, ranging from a one-hour talk on pension arrangements to several months of weekly sesions on a wide range of topics.

Instructional Methodology

To compress all the methodology of adult teaching and learning into one half-section of a short paper is an impossibility. Instead, this writer prefers to identify certain trends, emphasise certain contrasts between British practice and elsewhere, and point to some innovations.

It is important to understand that, in a highly decentralised system of education as applies in the United Kingdom, centralised determination of curricula and methodology is hardly feasible even if it were desirable. It is true that Britain has a Schools Council, which is a central curriculum development body for those sectors of education catering for small children and young people, i.e., mostly within the statutory ages for attending school (5 through 16). However, even this prestigious body has recently been severely criticised, partly in relation to specific alleged deficiencies, but also as exemplifying the larger criticism about what is often referred to as the "Centre-Periphery Model" of curriculum development. In short, there is in the United Kingdom considerable doubt about centrally produced packages and systems and about their suitability or adaptability for local circumstances.

Probably the answer is somewhere between the polarities of total "classroom" determination of content and method on the one hand, and totally centralised curricula and systems on the other. Indeed the Open University in its multi-media system demonstrates most aptly how centrally produced "learning units," with television and radio back-up, still benefit greatly from face-to-face teaching and learning in local study centres. In many respects, and particularly with the most difficult learning content, the local tutor is "interpreting" the central teaching resources according to the problems and needs of individual students.

To return to the mainstream of British adult education, one could state unequivocally that although there is still perhaps an over-use of the "presentation mode" (e.g., lectures, lessons, demonstrations, highly structured seminars), there has been more of a move towards "interaction mode" (e.g., many varities of discussions, case studies, simulations, project groups etc.) than in most other sectors of education. Only early primary schooling has greater interaction and search modes of teaching and learning. This third, i.e., "search mode" (e.g., discovery learning, research projects for individuals and groups, field trips, model building, etc.), although employed by enterprising teachers, is not as frequently used as one might expect. There is still a reluctance in some teachers (and in many students) to abandon the old "dependency-role" relationship, and to encourage students to launch out from the calm, safe--but essentially limited--waters of the "known," where everything is told to them by an omniscient teacher, into what is often perceived as the dangerous "unknown" of self-managed learning. In this regard the very interesting "discovery learning" research and development conducted by Drs. Meredith and Eunice Belbin and their collaborators at the Industrial Training Research Unit at Cambridge has enabled adult educators to perceive ways of structuring and assisting students' progress by "search" mode towards a learning objective. Whilst achieving little gain in time and short-term retention, the method was obviously appreciated and readily adopted by older workers, and displayed marked advantages when longer term retention and performance were tested.

Another trend, as much organisational as methodological, is occurring in foreign language teaching (and the teaching of English as a Second Language), where courses are being organised on an "intensive commitment" basis, requiring students to attend centres two, three or even four times a week for demanding rigorous combination courses of face-to-face, audiovisual/language laboratory, individualised or small group programmes of language learning. These use a high proportion of pre-packaged material; but the key factors appear to be the high commitment and motivation of these self-selected groups plus the high frequency of reinforcement and practice of the language skills being learned.

Yet another innovative trend is the designing of multidisciplinary yet related courses which are taught by "team-teaching"--i.e., a group of specialist teachers working as a team dealing with a relatively large number of students in open-workshop situations. An example known to the writer was a home economics programme which included early stages in cookery, dressmaking, millinery, soft furnishing, electricity in the home, health and safety and consumer economics. Yet another team project was for poor readers and writers (semi-literate): as well as individualised and group skill exercises in reading and writing, the team taught the rudiments of producing a community newspaper which eventually published reports, stories and even poems by these same students.

The Literacy Campaign

A final example on a nationwide scale is the successful literacy and basic education campaign, begun in 1975, which included attractive popular programmes at a peak viewing hour on television, the broadcasting of telephone referral numbers in all four countries of Great Britain, the projection of a nationally recognised logo or motif, the recruiting of nearly 50,000 volunteer tutors for one-to-one or team teaching under professional supervision, and the matching of over 100,000 enquirers to tutors or groups. Obviously a crucial element in this relatively large-scale operation was the training of volunteer tutors; and for this purpose and certain other expenditures on teaching materials, equipment and support staff, a central government "pump-priming" grant of (L)1,000,000 per annum was given, and was disbursed by the National Institute of Adult Education through its Adult Literacy Resource Agency to local education authorities in England, Wales and Scotland, plus many voluntary agencies, to carry out the work as a partnership. This special central government direct grant was continued in 1976/77 and 1977/78. Much has been learned (and is still being learned) about the particularities of literacy provision for a largely concealed minority in a developed country. Although useful insights have been acquired from literacy work in the developing countries, the special nature of this problem in a western European country with a long tradition of formal education prevents the wholesale translation of models and methods from other countries. (Reports of research undertaken by the National Institute of Adult Education are currently available.)

Participation Statistics

It would be pleasant to be able to refer with confidence to the annual volumes of statistics produced by the Department of Education and Science, and thereby to be able to determine conclusively how many of this or that type of person attend adult education courses in Great Britain. Unfortunately, this desirable degree of accuracy is not possible, as most of the statistics gathered are based on a single date in November survey of enrolments in LEA institutions, together with annual retrospective returns made by the universities, WEA and residential colleges. The categories and the nomenclature are hopelessly out of date. Furthermore, the systems of collection and analysis, although the same in England and Wales, are different in Scotland and Northern Ireland.

Nevertheless, some further analysis of the available statistics in England and Wales, plus extrapolation from special studies undertaken by the National Institute of Adult Education and the Russell Committee, enable us to indicate certain proportions and trends as to the involvement in courses of study of the population at large.

Extrapolating from the figures of the academic year 1976/77, (the last when full statistics are currently available) we may judge that there were approximately 3.3 million adults in England and Wales (combined) engaged in systematic study in LEA establishments or Responsible Body institutions. Of these we may calculate that about 2 million were not pursuing courses leading to diplomas or certificates, whereas the remaining 1.3 million were engaged on courses of such a character, either relating to a recognised qualification or general education certificates or diplomas required as a preliminary to such courses of professional qualification.

Comparable figures for Scotland and Northern Ireland are not available at the time of writing.

The figures represent about 9 percent (in any one year) of the adult population (legally, all those who have attained the age of 18 years). We may fairly hypothesise that a further one percent of the adult population is regularly involved in educational activities sponsored by the several small voluntary agencies, the private correspondence colleges and the Open University. In addition, approximately 2.5 million are involved in in-house occupationally related training or education in industry and commerce. Thus we may estimate that roughly 15 percent of the adult population has some systematic educational experience in any one year. In the public sector the proportion of women to men is approximately 4:3; and in non-certificate courses 2:1. In industrial training the proportion of women to men is 1:6.

Of course, summing totals in this way does not greatly help us to determine informative detail about those who join adult education, and more particularly those who do not join.

The most detailed analysis of population categories connected with adult education was undertaken by the National

Institute in the late 1960s and published in 1970. This
showed that, as compared to the whole-population profile,
the profile of adult education participants was skewed away
from lower socio-economic groups, being particularly deficient
in its recruitment of semi-skilled and unskilled workers and
their wives. By contrast, professional, managerial and
supervisory categories were over-represented as compared to
their proportions in the total population. Nevertheless the
single largest group (in absolute numbers) of participants
were people (including wives) classified as skilled manual
workers; although here again their proportion in adult education was lower than their proportion in the population.

Only the Open University analyses its student body
annually and in great detail. A recent analysis of Open
University applicants according to their occupation background
reads as follows (in percents):

	1976	1978
At home	13.8	14.4
Armed forces	2.8	2.7
Administration and management	4.6	4.5
Education	23.1	21.2
Professions and arts	11.5	12.2
Science and engineering	3.2	2.8
Technical personnel	10.2	9.9
Skilled trades	4.1	3.5
Other manual	3.3	2.9
Transport and communications	2.2	2.1
Clerical and office staff	11.3	11.7
Shop and personal	5.3	5.0
Not working	4.3	6.8
In institutions	.1	.1

The proportion of male/female students has remained
fairly constant at about 58:42, though the gap is beginning to
narrow.

Even these more detailed analyses conceal much that is
below the surface. For example, a longitudinal study of LEA
students over five years conducted in the Metropolitan Borough
of Bury, near Manchester, demonstrated the initial fall-off in
enrollment caused by a sharp increase in fees; and it further
demonstrated the recovery of the total enrollment figures
over the subsequent two years. But it also showed that the
social "pattern" of participating students had changed towards
a norm of more affluent students from more expensive housing
districts of the town.

Another interesting figure is revealed by an Open
University analysis of the occupations of parents of existing
students, demonstrating that although the University does not

appear to attract large proportions of manual working class students as judged by their occupations, there is a very large proportion whose <u>parents</u> were manual workers--a much larger proportion than in conventional universities.

Similarly, analyses of special adult education projects, e.g., for immigrants or the functionally illiterate, demonstrate clearly that many semi-skilled or unskilled workers are attracted to the programmes when the offer is projected skillfully and geared to their particular needs.

Certainly there is sufficent statistical evidence to warrant the statement (p. XI) of the Russell Committee in their 1973 Report:

> Even at the present level of attendance...adult education is by any standards a mass activity. It is growing, has demonstrated its great adaptability to local conditions and proved its responsiveness to local demands. It is popular, voluntary education rooted in a profound sense of need.

Future Trends

One could say, perhaps with over-simplicity but nevertheless with considerable justification, that the main problem for the immediate future of adult education in Great Britain is financial support; and the main tendency is of continuing demand and newly identified need.

If the service is going to be able to develop fully, particularly to meet the needs of the educationally disadvantaged groups of the population, it must receive extra financial support from government, from industry and possibly from other external resources. Whilst it may be possible to promote a rather "high-fee" service for fairly affluent middle-class people, it is clearly impossible to engage in outreach services for areas of urban or rural deprivation, for immigrants or for individuals with relatively low weekly wages on a purely self-sufficiency basis. At the present time, general, personal and community adult education (other than specifically occupationally-related provision) attracts less than one percent of the total national expenditure on education; and the percentage in the present difficult economic situation is falling. The high priority programmes aimed at particular social-educational objectives such as basic education for the underprivileged, the integration of immigrants or the re-education and retraining of redundant employees all gain their very good cost-benefit ratios by using the existing networks of "mainstream" adult education to

maximum advantage. If these mainstream networks become either
so debilitated (or so commercialised) that they cannot satisfactorily carry these special priority programmes, then the
whole structure will become more fragmented, more costly and
much less effective.

This rather stark prospect exemplifies the general
paradox in which British adult educators find themselves. In
one sense, at least conceptually, they are in the forefront of
the universally accepted notions of continuing, life-long
education--of "education permanente"; but at the same time,
whilst lipservice is paid to their work and their immense
efforts, resources to continue the process to a logical
conclusion are denied to them. In personnel terms, too, they
face major readjustments and difficulties: the last few years
have seen a much greater professionalisation of the service,
certainly at the level of field organisers and managers;
but again, to achieve many of the priority goals, they
must recruit and train unpaid volunteers if the programmes
necessarily requiring labour-intensive styles of provision are
to be carried through. Their work increasingly overlaps that
of community and social workers, so further professional
adjustments are needed to ensure effective cooperation
and collaboration with colleagues of different qualification
and background. In short, it will be a testing time over the
next few years to hold on to what has been gained whilst also
trying to change and adapt to the new needs and circumstances
of a rapidly changing society.

However, progress is being made in gaining an understanding of the new educational concepts which inform
our ideas for the future. And although we do not have an
Olaf Palme or a Julius Nyerere to take the political lead
in such matters, the necessary reforms are at least being
tentatively discussed along the "corridors of power."
But it still needs a great deal of educating our colleagues,
particularly in secondary and higher education, and in overcoming the enormous inertia of the formal "front-end" model of
education which really works. Ultimately a new Education Act
will be necessary, which not only spells out the new aims
and concepts, but specifies the organisational requirements
and functions necessary to achieve them.

As an early step in the right direction, the setting up
of a Russell Report recommended National Development Council
for Adult Education would be important. Another important
strategy would be the closer joint working, either by interdepartmental committees or special commissions of central
government ministries such as the Department of Education and
Science, Department of Employment, the Home Office and the
Department of Health and Social Security. At the present
time there is little collaboration at this level, although
at regional and district levels there are often excellent

cooperative relationships in spite of the lack of example from the top.

In all this "education about continuing education" the broadcast media will have an important and highly responsible role. Already, as well as providing an important direct educational element in numerous programmes and fields of study, they are projecting powerful stimuli towards the acceptance of new ideas and new practice. Their duty to promote adult education in all its forms, as well as to provide certain specific programmes, must be accepted even more firmly than is the case at the present time. The legal charter under which all public broadcasting proceeds requires the broadcasting organisations to "...inform, entertain and educate." This latter concept needs to be further extended and carefully delineated in its specification for the general improvement of all education and society.

Thus the tendency is to perceive the need for change, to catch glimpses of the goals towards which the changes should be moving, but to have to struggle to achieve the necessary changes without losing all continuity.

So, although British adult education is passing through difficult and trying times, the general prognosis would suggest that its undoubted flexibility and adaptability will carry it through to better days ahead, when it will finally be accepted and endorsed as the true fourth sector of British education.

ADULT LEARNING OPPORTUNITIES IN THE UNITED STATES

K. Patricia Cross

Harvard Graduate School of Education

Introduction

Perhaps the most distinctive characteristic about adult education in the United States is the fact that there is no national program or sustained coordination or direction of adult education activities. Initiatives for providing learning opportunities for adults may come from almost any source--local, state, or federal governments, private business and industry, colleges and universities, community agencies as varied as museums, churches, and centers for the elderly, and even individuals and groups who volunteer their services or obtain funding grants from governmental agencies or private foundations. Only recently has there even been a systematic attempt on the part of the national government to collect data about participation in adult learning activities. Thus, any description of adult education in the United States is necessarily a loose collection of examples of a great variety of programs and services.

Starting in the 1960s and 1970s, there was a pronounced surge of interest in adult learning under a variety of nomenclatures, among them lifelong learning, continuing education, nontraditional study, and community education. The dramatic increase in the numbers of programs and participants in recent years is sufficient to label the phenomenon the "Lifelong Learning Movement," but it is highly decentralized and varied in both amount and kind of activity. The federal government and most states have no overall public policy concerning the provision or funding of adult educational activities. Rather individual colleges are newly sensitive to the adult "market" for education, and governmental policy is reflected in a number of programs targeted at particular segments of the adult population. The Manpower Development and Training Act of 1962, the Equal Opportunity Act of 1964, and the comprehensive Adult Education Act of 1966 provided funds and leadership to spark substantial activity in the 1960s. Interest also began to accelerate in traditional colleges and universities in the 1970s when the term "nontraditional study" was coined to suggest that traditional academic programs would have to be changed if colleges hoped to attract adult learners to replace the dwindling supply of younger students.

Nontraditional Study in Traditional Colleges

Nontraditional education is concerned largely with the efforts of traditional colleges and universities to attract adults to degree-granting programs through making access easier, rearranging class schedules to meet when working adults could attend, offering off-campus classes in convenient locations, and gearing subject matter to the interests of adult learners. The stimuli for the nontraditional movement were present in a variety of forces for change in higher education, but the movement was sparked into action and given visibility largely through the initiatives of a private foundation--the Carnegie Corporation of New York. A widely quoted speech on the need for an external degree by the president of the Foundation (Pifer, 1970-71) was followed by the creation of the Commission on Non-Traditional Study, funded by the Carnegie Corporation and sponsored by the College Entrance Examination Board and the Educational Testing Service. The Commission brought together a group of national leaders to discuss issues, formulate recommendations, and bring national attention to the need for new flexibility and alternatives in higher education.

Concurrently with the work of the Commission, two widely-read reports stimulated interest and accelerated the growth of the nontraditional movement. The Carnegie Commission on the Future of Higher Education, a study group also funded by the Carnegie Corporation, published a report entitled Less Time, More Options (Carnegie Commission, 1971), and the U.S. Office of Education issued the Report on Higher Education (Newman, 1972) which urged the creation of alternatives to traditional education. At about the same time, the federal government took a position on the need for innovation and change in higher education by creating the Fund for the Improvement of Postsecondary Education to finance assistance to public and private postsecondary institutions interested in a variety of reforms that lay at the heart of nontraditional education (Public Law 92-318, enacted in 1972).

Within a short period of time the nontraditional movement was full blown. The Commission on Non-Traditional Study issued its report containing 57 recommendations in 1973 (Commission on Non-Traditional Study, 1973), and this was quickly followed by two books growing out of the work of the Commission. One was a comprehensive treatment of the external degree (Houle, 1973); the other reported the findings of a national research program which provided information about nontraditional students, programs, and issues (Cross, Valley, and Associates, 1974). Among other things, the research report documented the full reality of the nontraditional movement. Approximately one-third of the 1,185 colleges and universities responding to the survey reported that they offered at least one nontraditional program; most programs were designed specifically for adults, and almost two-thirds had been established since 1970 (Ruyle and Geiselman, 1974). Thus, in an incredibly short time span, hundreds of new programs had been launched in response to the demand for unconventional forms of postsecondary education, free of the time and place limitations of traditional classroom instruction.

While the full fruition of the nontraditional movement burst forth in the 1970s, it had its roots in the confluence of a number of trends and concerns occurring in the 1950s and 1960s. Among the precipitating factors were the following:

(1)   Rising concern for equal educational opportunity focused attention on certain segments of the population that had been denied equal access to college in the past. Among these groups were ethnic minorities, women, and people older than the usual college population.

(2)   In order to accommodate the unusually large youth population coming of college age in the 1960s and 1970s, higher education had more than tripled its capacity between 1950 and 1975. By the late 1970s, however, many colleges were having trouble enrolling enough students to keep their faculties employed. Thus there was considerable motivation on the part of colleges to find new markets for their services. Adult learners constituted a promising new clientele.

(3)   The average adult in the United States now has more than 12 years of formal schooling. Research shows that the more education people have, the more likely they are to seek further educational opportunity. Thus, the rising level of educational attainment of the populace is creating a demand for continuing adult education.

(4)   The escalation of new knowledge and the rising requirements for advanced education in the labor market are

creating an unprecedented demand for job-related education, especially among women who are entering or re-entering the labor force. Added to the desire for job-related education is the legislation that requires professionals and others licensed to serve the public to keep up with new developments in their field through continuing education.

For all of these reasons, adult education is growing faster than any other segment of postsecondary education in the United States. Nationally, more than 40 percent of all college students are part-time students, and approximately one-third are over the age of 25. Public two-year community colleges serve the largest share of adult learners, most of whom live within commuting distance of the campus, are married, and working at full-time jobs.

Current Collegiate Activities

The response of colleges to the rising interest in education for adults can be divided into two segments-- noncredit activities and regular degree programs. Noncredit education has been growing more rapidly than degree programs for adults, largely because noncredit offerings can respond to the market more quickly. They do not require the approval of faculty committees, and they usually operate on their own budgets. Thus, the decision to offer noncredit courses is responsive to demand; a course will be offered if there is enough interest in it to support it financially.

The number of colleges offering noncredit education has more than doubled over the past ten years, going from 1,102 colleges in 1968 to 2,375 in 1978, and the number of students enrolled in noncredit courses sponsored by institutions of higher education now exceeds the number of students enrolled for credit. Noncredit activities come in a variety of forms, ranging from a two-day career development workshop for women wanting to enter the labor market to advanced professional training for tax accountants. Classes are usually taught by teachers from colleges or high schools in the area, but local businessmen, craftsmen, and housewives are also frequently recruited as part-time teachers of noncredit courses.

Among the most spectacular successes in noncredit programs is a college for the elderly called Elderhostel. Elderhostel involves a loose coalition of three hundred colleges that provide special summer programs for adults 60 years of age or older. The elderly students live in college dormitories and attend classes taught by the regular college staff. Elderhostel seems to have found a formula that has great appeal to both students and colleges. To the elderly, it offers an enriching summer vacation at relatively low cost; to financially-strapped colleges, it offers a way to utilize fixed-cost dormitories and campus facilities, while providing educational programs of social value.

Another interesting nontraditional activity that is becoming popular at a wide range of colleges is the course offered as a joint enterprise of higher education and industry. The course may be offered for credit, but more often the employer specifies what kinds of education are needed for employees, and the college provides the instruction. Usually, the classroom is provided by the employer, and the college instructor travels to the plant or business site, but Stanford University has for some years now been using a closed circuit television system which transmits an on-campus class lecture and discussion to engineering firms within a thirty-mile radius of the Stanford campus. Two-way communication systems permit workers to participate in class discussions almost as though they were present on the campus.

Many two-year colleges are actively seeking contracts for instructional services with local business and industrial firms on the grounds that their mission as community colleges requires them to serve the community in whatever ways seem appropriate. The governor of South Carolina, for example, has recently recruited business and industry to the state with the promise that local community colleges will provide whatever training is needed to furnish labor for the incoming business. State and federal agencies also frequently contract for job training designed to put the unemployed to work in local factories and businesses.

Although the literature of lifelong learning is frequently inspirational and somewhat idealistic, its implementation in the United States is highly pragmatic on the part of both colleges and students. Job-related education is the most popular form of continuing education for adults, and it is probable that higher education and industry will become closer partners in the years ahead. Public funds for education are in short supply now, and the recent elections provide no assurance that even public colleges will be able to survive on public funding. Thus, there is a strong motivation for colleges to provide services to those who can pay for them. Industry will almost certainly be one of those new clients.

To most colleges and universities, however, their identity lies largely in degree programs and credit classes. While traditional faculties and curricula are slower to respond to the expanding market of adult learners, there is a great deal of activity in degree as well as nondegree programs for adults. It will be helpful to organize the degree credit activities of colleges under four major responses: (1) administrative arrangements, (2) delivery methods, (3) program content, and (4) noninstructional services. These are not exclusive categories, of course, since some programs designed from the beginning for adult learners may involve all four departures from traditional educational practices.

Administrative Arrangements

Modification in academic scheduling is the oldest and most common administrative arrangement to accommodate the needs of working adults. A national survey sponsored by the Commission on Non-Traditional Study (Ruyle and Geiselman, 1974) showed that 88 percent of the colleges departing from traditional programs in some way offered new flexibilities in scheduling. The options ranged through the standard evening college to block scheduling on weekends or in the summer, to completely self-paced programs permitting people to enter and exit at their own convenience. The largest number of working adult students attend evening classes, but one of the complaints about evening college is that it offers no immersion in the academic experience. To counteract that limitation some programs provide a mix of independent study and residential experience by having adults study independently at home most of the year, coming together on the campus for a week or two in the summer. Other colleges offer programs concentrating on an intensive block schedule. Weekend colleges, for example, typically conduct classes for ten to fifteen hours on Saturday and Sunday, offering adults an intensive experience wherein they can come to know fellow students and teachers better than is possible in the evening colleges.

Next to schedules compatible with the hours of working adults, the most common nontraditional administrative arrangement is the provision of convenient locations. The need for convenient locations was articulated most clearly in the 1960s when the common recommendation of a number of study commissions was to place colleges within commuting distance (typically 45 minutes or 45 miles) of all potential learners. Many states have now achieved that goal and both research and experience give clear evidence that location does make a difference. California, with 106 low-cost open-admissions community colleges, places a college within commuting distance of every citizen and has the highest educational participation rate in the nation for both adults and young people.

The newest model for convenient locations, however, involves making classrooms rather than campuses convenient for learners. Some colleges offer classes in 80 or more separate locations, including shopping centers, church basements, jails, factories and offices, and even commuter trains. One increasingly common model for colleges interested primarily in serving adults is to have no campus at all. The administrative offices of a number of colleges are now located in a downtown office building with administrative matters being handled by mail or decentralized among the various learning sites. Deans of students or career counselors, instead of having offices on a campus, travel from class to class to introduce themselves and their services and then do their counseling by telephone.

The most dramatic departure from the tradition of residential colleges is probably the external degree that places minimal emphasis on campus life and location. Frequently, students in external degree programs put together a program that consists of combinations of classes, independent study, credit for experiential learning, credit by examination, and other learning experiences until they add up to a college degree. In 1976, more than 54,000 adults were enrolled in almost 250 external degree programs in the United States (Sosdian, 1978).

It is impossible to cover the wide range of options with respect to locations that are offered in the United States today. The fact is that colleges have become so flexible and adaptive to work schedules that difficulty in getting to a college campus is no longer a valid excuse for not participating in lifelong learning.

Delivery Methods

New methods for bringing education to adults is more likely to revolutionize education than any other single factor. The new delivery methods offer maximum flexibility in location and scheduling, of course, but they also change the traditional role of teachers and learners. Teams of educational specialists, consisting of experts in content, instructional design, evaluation, and technical procedures, supplement the generalist teacher, and students may have their questions answered by computers, telephones, or audio tapes, as well as by the classroom teacher or study center tutor.

There is nothing in the United States at present to compare with British Open University in England. Because of the decentralized nature of American education, there is no national university with the mission to serve adult learners through television, correspondence, and other delivery systems known as "distance learning" methods. There is, however, a proposal for an American Open University that would offer a wide variety of educational services, including counseling, assessment of prior learning, consolidation of academic credits earned elsewhere, and home delivered courses.

Since there is little hope of full federal funding, the proposal calls for substantial funding from industry, private foundations, tuition fees, and sales of materials and services. It is unlikely, however, that the United States will ever have a single provider emphasizing new delivery mechanisms; growth will no doubt continue to occur in a variety of ways. There are already numerous colleges and consortia offering college instruction via new delivery methods.

Television and its assorted technological cousins, such as video cassettes and video discs, remain the glamour children of new delivery systems in education. Such systems are usually the results of cooperation among groups of colleges. In the beginning, telecourses were produced at reasonable cost because people were content with the so-called "talking head" which was simply a video recording of the standard classroom lecture. Today, however, the cost of telecourses runs into millions of dollars because the industry has grown sophisticated and wants to present the full educational power of television. And so we have historical documentaries, lapsed-time photography for science courses, beautiful color photography for art treasures, and other powerful visual presentations. For the foreseeable future, the use of telecourses will require the combined resources and markets of many colleges.

There no longer seems to be much resistance to the use of telecourses; the problem is the lack of high-quality programs. Although there are nearly 100 distance delivery courses listed in a new catalog, only about 30 are considered adequate for use as college courses. It is estimated, however, that nearly 600,000 students have enrolled in five of the most popular telecourses and have received college credit from some 500 colleges and universities throughout the United States.

A less costly approach to producing telecourses is for colleges to provide "wraparound materials," that is, study guides and textbooks for documentaries or quality cultural programs produced by public or commercial television. "Roots," the documentary on black history, for example, was not originally produced as a college course. However, Miami-Dade Community College in Florida obtained permission to produce wraparound study materials and to promote it to other colleges as a college-level course worthy of credit. Thousands of students received credit from local colleges for their completion of the course materials accompanying "Roots."

Distance-delivery methods need not involve technology. Last year, newspapers throughout the country carried ten adult education courses with lessons prepared by notable scholars. More than 50,000 students received college credit for the courses by reading their newspapers and coming together under the direction of a local college faculty member for group discussion and testing. Uncounted millions more, no doubt, read the material but did not apply for college credit.

Program Content

The national survey of nontraditional practices in higher education in the United States showed that designing special courses was the least likely concession to adult learners. Fewer than half of the college programs tried to attract adult learners through offering content that differed from traditional, discipline-based subject matter. Nevertheless, there are some notable examples of special programs designed for adult interests. The Bachelor of Liberal Studies degree at the University of Oklahoma was designed from the beginning to appeal to adults who wished to be liberally educated, as opposed perhaps to prepared for a job. The program is considered academically rigorous but it is interdisciplinary and it, and others like it, attract primarily older adults who may have reached the point in their careers where the direct relationship between job skills and lessons is no longer so important.

A second increasingly popular program option for adults is illustrated by the learning contract. Because the learning contract is so important to the lifelong learning philosophy, a brief illustration of how it works may be helpful. The student entering Metropolitan State University in Minnesota, to cite one model, develops with the help of a faculty advisor, an Educational Pact setting forth his or her educational goals, the competencies to be mastered, the learning strategy, and the evaluation methods that will be used to determine the attainment of the goals. There is no formal curriculum, but students are encouraged to develop competencies in five areas: basic learning and communication, civic involvement, vocation and career, leisure and recreation, and personal growth and self-assessment. Students may develop these competencies through formal study in university courses, experiential learning, independent study, telecourse or correspondence courses, or any other learning strategy that meets the conditions of the learning contract developed between student and faculty mentor. Such programs offer maximum flexibility to the highly motivated, self-directed adult, but they have not proved especially attractive to the undereducated, the unemployed, or the occupationally disenchanted.

Although modifications in program content to meet the needs of adults who want college degrees, but not traditional discipline-based subject matter, frequently raises questions about quality, research on the characteristics of the students

in such programs generally shows them to be superior learners
with clear goals and high motivation.

Noninstructional Services

The need for noninstructional services to facilitate
student access to educational opportunity has emerged as
a major component in lifelong learning. For discussion
purposes, I shall divide noninstructional services into three
categories--financial aid, information and counseling, and
assessment and evaluation of learning.

Financial Aid. The response to the financial needs of
adults has lagged behind responsiveness to other needs. The
assumption at the level of higher education has been that
adults can pay for their own education, and most financial aid
programs have openly discriminated against part-time learners.
As recently as 1973, only four state student aid programs
offered eligibility to part-time students. There is now a
general awakening to financial needs, but little consensus on
what to do about it. With new financial pressures on state
and federal budgets, it seems unlikely that financial aid
will be generally available to adult learners. However, for
many of the more traditional forms of financial aid offered by
federal and state governments, regulations are being revised
to end discrimination against adult part-time learners. There
is more flexibility in determining who qualifies for assistance and more consideration of the personal and financial
circumstances of "independent" young adults where parental
ability to support education is irrelevant.

Since the lifelong learning movement in the United States
consists largely of the already well educated getting better
educated, the lack of public financial assistance is likely
to increase the gap between the poorly educated and the well
educated. Private sources of funding, such as employers'
and professional associations, will further exacerbate the
problem since employers are most likely to fund executives and
managers, whereas professional associations subsidize the
education of the best educated adults in the nation.

Counseling and Advisory Services. The availability and
adequacy of counseling and information services has a powerful
impact on access to educational opportunity. The foremost
group taking the position that new models of support services
are needed for adult learners is the National Center for
Education Brokering established in 1976. The Center acts
as a central clearing house to coordinate communication
among agencies involved in advising adults about educational
opportunities. The function of "educational brokering" is to

help adults define goals for their personal and working lives, to assist in setting objectives for further education, to help select learning experiences to achieve competencies and certification, and to help adults gain access to appropriate learning opportunities.

Some educational brokers are volunteers with little more than a telephone and a list of educational opportunities; others are counselors with federal and state grants to provide information services to adults; still others may be the human components of extensive computerized systems of information. The earliest counseling and information services for adults were developed by individuals who saw a need and established information centers in downtown stores, community buildings, or any other location convenient to people who lacked easy access to standard information networks. Sometimes the location was simply a telephone number where people could call to request information about educational opportunities. Many early efforts were funded by grants from the federal or state governments, but they also relied heavily on volunteer services. In recent years, governmental agencies are assuming greater responsibility for dissemination of information. For three years now, the federal government has made small grants to each of the 50 states to assist in establishing Education Information Centers. The common finding of research studies is that there are far more opportunities available for adult learners than there are people who know about them. Thus one of the major problems facing the learning society in the United States is the development of efficient and effective methods for getting learners and opportunities together. So far, information centers for adults vary greatly; some adults have good access to information, others have almost none. With the new wave of political conservatism throughout the country, it seems unlikely that there will be much public funding available. Providers of educational services will be left to their own devices to publicize their offerings. Because adults are now seen as an attractive market for educational providers, there is considerable motivation for colleges and other providers to publicize their offerings.

Measures of Educational Accomplishments. The newest and probably the most controversial component in nontraditional programs has to do with the measurement of educational accomplishments. Whereas traditional degree certification depends heavily on process measures, such as documentation of courses taken, credit hours accumulated, residency requirements fulfilled; nontraditional programs are beginning to emphasize outcome measures, such as competencies achieved, skills learned, knowledge demonstrated. The arguments for the new alternative measures of learning are especially important since adults come with such a variety of backgrounds. Some form of collecting, assessing, and certifying learning from a variety of sources is responsive to the needs of many self-educated adults.

There are currently three measures of educational accomplishment that are visible in the lifelong learning movement. One that is accepted by almost all colleges today is credit-by-examination, through which an adult learner may demonstrate on a suitable examination that he or she has achieved the same level of learning as a college student taking the traditional course on campus. A second form of assessment is practiced by fewer than 15 percent of the colleges today, but it seems to be gaining acceptability under the leadership of the Council for the Advancement of Experiential Learning (CAEL), which is a consortium of approximately 350 colleges working together to develop improved methods for assessing experiential learning. This method requires a varied battery of assessment tools and techniques, and it is usually quite expensive to conduct an individual assessment of the college-level learning of an adult. Some colleges, however, have established assessment centers where the applicant's learning from a variety of sources--previous college work, job experience, noncredit learning activities, and self-directed learning projects-- may be considered for college credit. A third measure of educational accomplishment is operated by one of the major professional associations of higher education. The American Council on Education (ACE) has established an Office on Educational Credit (OEC) which has taken on the formidable task of sending a team of subject matter specialists to the site of any organization (usually a noncollege provider of educational services) wishing to nominate a course for college credit recommendations. In its first two years of operation the OEC evaluated more than 800 courses offered by more than 50 organizations in every state in the nation, involving nearly 200,000 students. The OEC publishes a guide with recommendations regarding the amount and category of credit which might legitimately be awarded. The "legitimacy," of course, derives from the national prestige of the ACE and from the rigorous standards established by the OEC for the evaluation of courses. Colleges and universities, however, are free to accept or reject the recommendations.

A Brief Look at Noncollegiate Adult Education

In a brief overview of adult learning in the United States, it is impossible to describe the great variety of programs and opportunities available. It is generally agreed that colleges and universities provide less than half of all "organized instruction" for adult part-time learners, but estimates vary from less than one-fourth (Peterson, 1979) to almost half (National Center for Education Statistics, 1978). Whichever figure is used, it is clear that a majority of adults are pursuing organized learning activities in non-school organizations. It also seems clear that organizations whose major business is not education are becoming increasingly involved in the education of adults. It is estimated that industry spends between 20 and 40 billion dollars per year on the education of employees, and that is more than is spent by the combined state appropriations for higher education in all 50 states (Lynton, 1981). Because of its size and lack of visibility, the educational system operated by industry for its own employees has been called the "shadow educational system." Although the major purpose of such programs is to enhance the productivity of employees, it is increasingly possible to gain college credit for study done in the noncollegiate sector. Some corporations are empowered to grant academic degrees (Cross, 1981), while others may request a review of particular courses by respected educational agencies that may suggest to colleges the kind and amount of course credit that might be awarded. A few of the larger corporations have built substantial campuses, complete with residential and recreational facilities, for workers who may spend anywhere from a few days to several months on "the campus."

Another shadow educational system is operated by professional associations that are becoming increasingly active in developing and distributing educational programs for their members. The American Management Association, for example, has an annual education budget of 50 million dollars and uses 7,500 lecturers and discussion leaders to conduct more than 2,000 workshops, seminars, and institutes each year. Lawyers are increasingly gathering in law offices throughout the country to inform themselves of the latest developments in the legal profession via video cassettes developed by their state bar associations. The tendency of state and licensing agencies to require professionals, managers, and technical and skilled workers to keep up with new developments increases the pressure on professional and trade associations to create educational materials that will help members fulfill mandatory educational requirements.

Still other educational services are offered by a great variety of special interest groups. Examples are water safety for members of the yacht club, leadership training for boy scout leaders, German for the descendants of German immigrants. For the most part, the recognized school and college system and the various shadow educational systems go their own ways, usually quite unaware of the similarity

of their activities.   In recent years, however, the formal
educational system, especially at the postsecondary level, has
become increasingly interested in forming partnerships with
industry, professional associations, the military, and other
major providers of educational services for adults.   The theme
for the 1981 annual convention of the American Association for
Higher Education, for example, was "Promising Frontiers: Five
Partnerships to Offset Decline."   The message delivered in the
more than 75 conference sessions was that through forming
partnerships with other colleges, business, professional
associations, high schools, and telecommunications, the
traditional institutions of higher education could enrich
the educational opportunities available to adults in the
United States while keeping teachers employed and campuses
occupied.

The above examples illustrate the activity and change
that is taking place in the education of adults in the United
States.   It is probably fair to say that adult education today
is an entrepreneurial business.   Most providers have something
to gain by furnishing educational opportunities for adults,
and education has become something more than a service
provided by the collective society.   Although a few people are
concerned about the "quality" of the education offered by the
tremendous range of providers and opportunities available
today, and more are concerned about the lack of coordination
and direction in the far flung educational opportunities, the
majority of people in the United States seem inclined to
encourage individual enterprise and initiative in what appears
to be a healthy and flourishing learning society.

PART IV:

IMPLICATIONS
FOR GOVERNMENT POLICY
IN THE UNITED STATES

Introduction

An important purpose of this project, and of this report, is to set forth possible implications of policies and programs in the eight foreign countries studied, for government policy on adult education and training in the United States. After introductory comments on cultural differences among the countries, as well as on limitations of available adult education statistics, this section first discusses implications for a comprehensive national policy for adult learning in the U.S. It then considers implications for new policy and programs to better meet the learning needs of the five selected subpopulations focused on in the study: workers, older persons, women entering the labor force, parents, and undereducated adults.

As the reader has seen, the study has adopted a broad definition for adult education--to include essentially all opportunities for organized education and training, other than the "regular" full-time progression of secondary and higher education in the respective nations. In some instances, forms of education have been included that some would consider "regular," such as part-time study at the Polytechnics in England, at the community colleges in the U.S., or at the Soviet elementary, secondary, or higher education institutions. When it was difficult to classify what seemed clearly an important adult learning opportunity as either "regular" or "nonregular," we generally included it in the study; that is, in our descriptions of each country's range of adult learning opportunities, we generally were inclusive rather than exclusive. Thus the foregoing pages contain descriptions of a very large number of programs, any of which--or aspects of which-- may be considered for possible application in the United States.

Cultural Differences. It must of course be said immediately that while the nine nations included in the project are all "industrialized" or "developed," that may be close to the limit of their similarity. Perhaps Canada, of the eight foreign countries, shares the most in common with the U.S. In general, the nine countries are substantially different geographically, demographically, in their political and economic systems, and in their national traditions and philosophies concerning education. The existence of a particular adult learning program in one or several countries, but not in others, can be generally explained by particular combinations of social and political circumstances interacting over time (as was indicated in many of the overviews in Part I). The existence, for example, of traditionally strong trade union movements in Sweden, West Germany, and France accounts in large measure for the educational leave programs for workers in those two countries. And without the voluntary associations (also described earlier, and in Part III), for which there is no American counterpart, there would presumably not be the many hundreds of study circles in Sweden and Denmark.

Political Feasibility. Of importance for our present purposes is whether it is "realistic" to suggest that a given foreign practice be adopted in this country when the under-lying and supporting social realities in the two countries are quite different. This type of question is similar to the common question in policy analysis of "feasibility" or "political feasibility." This said, our general stance, when a concept or a program from one of the countries is judged to be a "good" one--that is, potentially capable of meeting important adult learning needs in this country--is to identify it as such, despite the differing political contexts and possible low "political feasibility" in the U.S.

One need not advocate more or less complete importation of some program from one of the countries. In most instances, such wholesale adoption would most certainly not be realistic. Instead, the basic idea or purpose for a given program that deserves serious consideration in this country could be imported, with the prospect that the implementing structure would be designed to fit U.S. circumstances. Or, the imple-menting structure could be imported for a program with similar purposes in the two countries.

In calling attention to new ideas (to this country) for new forms of service, we most certainly recognize that unfamiliar ideas take time to become understood, as well as time to attract the necessary support--the "political feasibility"--for their eventual implementation.

Statistical Comparisons

Another purpose of the project as it was initially conceived was to assemble comparative statistics. In general, this proved to be only partially possible. Several of the countries have no national statistics on adult education whatsoever. In no instances (other than by sex) were national data categorized in comparable ways. In no country is there a tabulation of all participants according to a definition of adult education approximating that used in this study. Likewise, with the exception in several of the countries of reasonably good data on the training of workers, there are no national participation data for the five population categories specified for the project.

An attempt was made, however, to obtain informed estimates from our country consultants of the participation rates for the five subgroups, and for all adults, for each of the countries. Three of the eight consultants returned estimates. One made a concerted attempt (by contacting a number of knowledgeable colleagues). The other four did not respond, presumably because they judged that sufficient data on which to make such judgments were simply not available.

Finally, except for several evaluative studies in Sweden, there are almost no data--even on dropout rates--that assess the effectiveness of programs. Several mostly qualitative evaluations were uncovered, such as the Jones and Charnley (1979) evaluation of the British adult literacy campaign.

Such data on participation in organized adult education activities as do exist are usually limited to total number of participants in major programs. Most of these figures are given in the tables contained in each of the country overviews in Part I of this report. Those statistics, including the total participation rate estimate given at the bottom of each table, ought not to be regarded as definitive. (Indeed it is only with considerable effort and expense that entirely accurate and up-to-date social statistics of any kind can be compiled.)

The figures below, taken from the tables in Part I, however, do provide rough, order-of-magnitude estimates of total adult involvement in organized education and training activities in each of the nine countries. The countries clearly do differ in this regard, often by a factor of two or three.

	Estimated Total Participation Rate in Organized Adult Learning Activities
Australia	13 percent
Canada	23 percent
Denmark	17 percent
The Federal Republic of Germany	11 percent
France	7 percent
The Soviet Union	31 percent
Sweden	29 percent
The United Kingdom	15 percent
The United States	27 percent

Government Policy on Adult Education

Issues and Alternatives

All nine of the countries studied disburse some amount of funds from national sources for the education or training of adults. Thus all the countries could be considered to have policies concerning adult learning, however ill-formed or vaguely stated they may be.

What could be considered a comprehensive national policy, however, seems not to be common. The Swedish Parliament together with other national organizations in Sweden have given as much recent attention to adult education, broadly conceived, as perhaps any country. To the extent the 1971 French Law on Continuing Vocational Training, in fact, covers a broad subject matter range, France can be said to have a comprehensive national policy. Denmark, a small homogeneous nation where national policies can, it is assumed, be more readily agreed upon, has two broadly conceived adult education statutes (the Act on Leisure Time Instruction and the Act on Vocational Training), which more or less cover the range of adult learning content.

Several of the countries have systematic national manpower training policies; those in West Germany, the Soviet Union and the United Kingdom have existed for some time, and a national training system is currently emerging in Canada. Australia and the U.S. have national manpower training programs only for targeted populations.

Interestingly, the nations with the most comprehensive adult education policies are not necessarily those with the highest levels of participation. Sweden and France both have highly rationalized national policies, including financial incentives; participation is relatively high in Sweden, but relatively low in France. (There are, of course, marked differences in the types of opportunities in the two countries; the government-subsidized study circles, for example, thrive in Sweden; there is no counterpart in France.) The U.K. and the U.S. both lack national policies (other than categorical programs in the U.S.): the U.S. has a relatively high level of participation, due mostly to local entrepreneurship; the U.K. has a relatively low rate.

Must the fact of national or federal policies necessarily mean national or centralized control, via guidelines or regulations? With the possible exception of the highly centralized U.S.S.R., where it is difficult to know the realities of local compliance with national mandatory training-for-promotion policies, it is reasonably clear that even in the countries that have comprehensive education and training policies, much discretion is left to local jurisdictions. Thus in Sweden, while certain guidelines must be followed in forming study circles in order to receive government subsidies, the local units of the voluntary associations have wide freedom to set the content of the circles. Somewhat the same arrangement exists in Denmark. And in France, where government in general is usually regarded as highly centralized, the 1971 Law on Continuing Vocational Training was intended to be, and has been, implemented in a relatively (for France) participatory manner; unions, management and the state participate in both national- and regional-level decisions, and those constituencies plus diverse providers of education--operating in a free market situation--are involved at the level of the firm in arranging for specific courses.

Perhaps the most common alternative to a comprehensive national policy is a policy of focusing resources on particular populations or national problems. Most of the countries, as we have seen, have special training programs for the unemployed or marginally employable as well as basic education programs for the poorly educated and for recent immigrants. In general, this is the policy in the United States--a policy which has proved "politically feasible." But is it in some sense the best model, the model that will best serve the interests of all individuals as well as the society more generally?

Purposes of Adult Education Policy

Different countries at different times in their histories have set different goals for their adult education enterprises. For convenience, these may be divided into (1) social (political and economic) goals, and (2) individual- or learner-determined goals. Compared to the latter, the former much more often are the basis for public policy.

Social Goals. Of the essentially social objectives of adult education, perhaps the most widespread national goal in countries throughout the world has been to reduce or "eradicate" adult illiteracy. Thus numerous government-sponsored literacy campaigns have been conducted in the 20th century. Often in nonindustrialized countries they have been mounted in the wake of armed revolutions. The campaigns in the U.S.S.R., China, Cuba, and currently in Nicaragua, are examples. Two recent literacy campaigns that did not follow revolutions were those in Iraq and Great Britain: in Iraq the campaign was tightly directed by the central government; in England, while the government contributed the bulk of the funding, numerous organizations cooperated, and the local educational authorities orchestrated the instructional work in their respective localities much as each saw fit. Adult illiteracy persists in the U.S., as was noted in Part II. Arguably a sizeable literacy effort is needed in this country. The experience of the campaign in Britain would seem to provide a good model.

In industrialized nations, perhaps the predominant general goal--certainly the goal of manpower training policies --has been development of human resources on behalf of economic expansion. Such "investment in human capital" concepts underpinned, for example, the French Law of 1971, the recent Adult Occupational Training Act in Canada, and labor market policy in Sweden until the reforms of the mid-1970s. Such concepts underlay the U.S.'s Comprehensive Employment and Training Act (CETA), although as it has evolved, most of the "investment" is in the marginally employable--probably a reasonable objective in a time of not unlimited revenues.

Most industrialized countries quite explicitly (by law) use their national manpower training systems to meet national economic or labor market needs (shortages). Thus Sweden, France, West Germany, Canada and the U.K., through varying combinations of special subsidies to training institutions (for new or additional courses) and special grants (and sometimes leaves) to individuals, intercede in the normal working of their training systems in order to stimulate provision of additional trained manpower in occupations where shortages either exist or are predicted. This is accepted public policy throughout the industrialized world. In this country, CETA has rarely functioned as a labor market stabilizer.

National manpower training programs can and do have goals other than to operate as a counter-cyclical (anti-recession) instrument and to respond to labor market shortages. The training programs set up in West Germany subsequent to the Labor Promotion Act of 1969, for example, were intended to facilitate (1) upward mobility (job advancement) and (2) continuous adjustment to technological change (Schmid, 1978). Opportunities for adults to shift careers in midlife are explicitly afforded, for example, in both West Germany and the United Kingdom (in the latter, through Britain's Training Opportunities Scheme--TOPS). Goals such as these have not been prominent in manpower planning in the U.S. In Sweden at the present time the dominant adult education goal is related to educational equity; disproportionate resources are directed to the undereducated (as Rubensen points out in his paper in Part III). This is the general goal of the U.S. government's principal adult education initiative, the Adult Basic Education Program.

Other countries, notably Finland, but also the U.S., have sought deliberately to promote economic equity through their national education policies, including adult education

policies. Economic and educational disadvantage, of course,
overlap very considerably. The goal of equity is an appropriate one for the federal government, since when adult
education provision is left up to local organizations, which
is mostly the case, the widely documented result is a pattern
of participation heavily biased in favor of the affluent and
educated classes (see Peterson and Associates, 1979).

In some nations--again, often <u>new</u> nations--an important
purpose for adult education, sometimes attempted in tandem
with literacy work, is <u>ideological</u>--to create support for new
political institutions and processes. This would not be an
acceptable goal for national policy in the U.S.; it might,
however, be an appropriate goal for local or regional adult
education work that seeks to aid impoverished populations in
gaining a larger share of political power. Interestingly, in
European countries employer associations have frequently
opposed government adult education programs--paid educational
leave schemes, for example--out of concern that political and
economic views averse to their interests would be studied
(von Moltke and Schneevoight, 1977).

In other countries, most notably Sweden and Denmark among
the countries in this study, a purpose of adult education
is to help build consensus from the "bottom up" concerning
possible important new national initiatives. In Sweden, for
example, many of the study circles during 1980 were devoted
to issues related to a new energy policy for the country.
Adult education as consensus-building is an interesting idea,
but a somewhat difficult one to imagine in the U.S. In this
country, issues of public policy tend to get politicized;
people take sides. There is little tradition (except in small
New England towns) of authentic individual participation in
shaping public policy. Rank and file Americans seem not
to be in the habit of dispassionately deliberating policy
alternatives.

<u>Individually-Determined Goals</u>. Admittedly, it is not
easy conceptually to separate individual learning goals from
social or economic objectives--job retraining, for example.
Nonetheless, it is less common for national adult education
policy to include goals explicitly related to the personal
development of <u>individuals</u>, with the particular learning
experiences for this purpose chosen by the individual learner.
The Danish Act on Leisure Time Instruction is a notable
example of such legislation. The French Law of 1971 permits
paid leave for "cultural" education, although in practice
leaves have seldom been used for this purpose. In England,
the Education Act of 1944 permits--does not require--use of
government funds for "spiritual, moral, mental and physical
development," "cultural training," and "recreative activities"

(see Stock's essay in Part III). Unquestionably, great
numbers of adults in many countries engage in learning
activities for essentially personal reasons.

In the United States, what was known as the "Lifelong
Learning Act" (Title IB of the Higher Education Act of 1965)
was passed into law in 1976. It contains the following
language:

1) accelerating social and technological changes have
   had impact on the duration and quality of life:

2) the American people need lifelong learning to enable
   them to adjust to social, technological, political
   and economic changes;

3) lifelong learning has a role in developing the
   potential of all persons including improvement of
   their personal well-being, upgrading their workplace
   skills, and preparing them to participate in the
   civic, cultural, and political life of the Nation.

No funds were ever appropriated, however, and Title IB
was never implemented.

In 1980, when the Higher Education Act was once again
revised ("reauthorized"), Title IB was reconceived as
"Education Outreach Programs." Language relevant to the
purpose here was limited to the following:

1) the rapid pace of social, economic, and technological
   change has created pressing needs for postsecondary
   educational opportunities for adults in all stages of
   life.

Funds ($15 million) were appropriated for Title IB, but
in the summer of 1981 they were "rescinded" (eliminated) by
the new Republican-dominated Congress.

Statements of goals from individual colleges or universities or other local or regional providers of adult learning
opportunities do stress personal goals for their programs.
Thus a university extension division, or a local Club des
Anciennes in France, would stress the personal benefits from
lifelong learning.

Such directly personal goals for adult learning, however, seldom find expression in statements of public policy.
Yet certainly learning for reasons such as intellectual
growth, avocational pleasure, and even social and political
awareness are in the interests of individual citizens--and
also of democratic societies.

Finally, what can be said of the idea of comprehensive
lifelong learning policy as an organizational concept that

embraces education at all levels? The general notion is that, instead of organizing a national (or state) education system into a number of component parts or levels, and operating them essentially separately, there would be a single unified and integrated formal education system that provides learning opportunities for people throughout their lifespan. With the possible exception of Spain, no country that we know of in fact has such an arrangement, although it is presently being seriously considered in Sweden.

From all the foregoing, what can we conclude with regard to government policy on adult education and training for the United States? First, it is abundantly clear that there are concepts of service and types of programs in the eight foreign countries studied that do not exist in the U.S., but which have potential for meeting learning needs of individual adults in America and for improving the functioning of its economy and the quality of its culture. Second, it is clear that many industrialized countries have national policies on adult education, with adult education variously conceived but almost always including labor market training. That is, over the years these nations have reached the position that it is indeed appropriate for their national governments to have an important role in orchestrating and financially supporting adult education and training.

In the United States, by law and strong tradition, provision of education is primarily the responsibility of the 50 states. Federal initiatives have generally been limited to programs targeted to special populations, usually economically and educationally disadvantaged students. Vocational education has come to be construed somewhat separately from the rest of education, and is accepted as worthy of fairly extensive federal funding (through the Department of Education)--mostly to the nation's secondary schools pursuant to the federal Vocational Training Act of 1963. Manpower training has in the past ten years come to be quite clearly accepted as a policy area in which the federal government should have a role; CETA's programs, as noted already, have been modest and directed mainly at marginally employable youth and adults.

In sum, at the federal level in the U.S., while there are numerous programs serving particular categories of adults (U.S. Department of Education, 1981), there is no coherent, comprehensive policy for adult education or training, in the sense of measures to encourage provision of meaningful, accessible learning opportunities for all adults.

Furthermore, as this is being written, the Reagan Administration is seeking broad disengagement of the federal government from education at all levels (including dismantling the recently created Department of Education). The Comprehensive Employment and Training Act is scheduled for "reauthorization" in 1982, and there are signals that the new Administration, as part of its general effort to reduce federal spending, will markedly cut back or possibly eliminate CETA. Thus the present time, in short, seems inauspicious for important new federal initiatives in the domain of adult education and training.

If there is to be comprehensive policy on adult learning in the U.S., it may have to come principally at the state, regional or local level.

*

The following, briefly and very generally stated, are implications for government policy in the United States, in the area of adult education and training.

(1) Broad goals for adult education and training—set forth at all levels of government—should be multiple in nature. They would vary from state to state, and would be expected periodically to change. Government-sponsored adult learning programs should seek to serve the self-determined learning interests of individuals, both vocational and non-vocational, as well as the literacy and manpower needs of the society and economy. Special attention still needs to be given to equity considerations, in view of the persisting economic bias in adult education participation rates (Cross, 1979). Procedurally, a general goal of adult learning policy at the state and federal levels should be to stimulate effective local-level initiatives.

(2) If education is to be a domain for federal policy in the U.S., as articulated, for example, by a cabinet-level Department of Education, that policy should strongly affirm the importance of opportunities for continuous learning as in the interests of individuals and the nation. Beyond this philosophic commitment and leadership, the federal government should sponsor program demonstrations, research, and dissemination and clearinghouse work related to adult education and training.

(3) State government, with unquestioned responsibilities for education, should likewise promulgate broad policy that recognizes the importance of wide opportunities for education and training throughout the adult years.*

------

*Concepts for state initiatives in adult education are currently being developed by the Kellogg Foundation-funded "Lifelong Learning Project," which is based at the Education Commission of the States (Denver).

(4) Arguably a <u>nationally</u>-conceived and directed man-power or labor market <u>training</u> program, in addition to or in place of state programs, <u>is</u> needed in the U.S. The realities of regional job market <u>imbalances</u> and worker geographic mobility make a nationally-organized program imperative. National labor market policies exist in almost all industrial-ized countries, and much can be learned from them in designing a program for this country that is efficient, accessible to all, and effective in meeting both the career aspirations of individuals and the manpower needs of the economy.

(5) Since at the federal level diverse programs are likely to be conducted by different agencies--principally by the Department of Education and the Department of Labor (but also by the Departments of Defense, Agriculture, and Health and Human Services)--it is important that there be an interdepartmental mechanism for coordinating federal adult education and training programs.

(6) A similar mechanism is likewise needed at the state level, to coordinate diverse adult learning programs, vocational and nonvocational, administered by and funded through separate state agencies.

(7) Actual implementation of adult education and train-ing programs should be decentralized to the greatest extent feasible, as is the practice in all the countries studied except for the Soviet Union. Funds for adult education could be distributed through local school district adult education offices to diverse local providers of educational services (including two- and four-year colleges as well as non-school agencies such as museums and community organizations).

(8) Local (and/or metropolitan or regional) juris-dictions should establish councils, with members from major area providers, to cooperatively plan, allocate funds for, and coordinate the broad range of education provision in the community to meet the broad range of adult learning needs in the community. (The Local Further Education Councils through-out the Province of Alberta could provide one model.)

Learning Opportunities for the Five Selected Populations

This section considers policies and programs in the eight foreign countries that are judged to have promise for better meeting the learning needs of the five analytic subpopulations designated for the study. Many of the specific implications to be drawn will be set in the context of the broad issues discussed in the previous section.

Workers

Our definition of workers, as indicated in the Introduction to this report, is roughly synonomous with employees-- both blue- and white-collar--in both the public and private sectors. Our interest is in any and all learning opportunities for workers--not just job training.

Much has been written about the necessity for workers at all levels to be suitably trained and periodically retrained. The litany of technological change, information explosion, shifts in occupational structures, changes in life situations, and so forth, is too well known to need recounting here. While some of it is perhaps overblown, the fact of change and the prospect of occupational obsolescence seem undeniable.

In general, most European countries have progressed further than the U.S. (and Australia) in devising education and training programs for workers, particularly blue-collar workers. There are shift schools, extramural (correspondence) schools, evening elementary and secondary schools, and work-site training in the Soviet Union; various kinds of "release" and "sandwich" arrangements in the United Kingdom; the huge employer-based training enterprise in Sweden; West Germany's generous support for retraining under its 1969 Labor Promotion Act, England's Training Opportunities Scheme, which provides "training on demand"; and the various educational leave plans in effect in Denmark, France, Sweden, the U.S.S.R. and West Germany. The range of training models potentially of value to the U.S. is large indeed.

How is one to account for the relative backwardness of manpower training policy in the U.S.? First, as noted earlier, compared to most European nations, the trade union movement in the U.S. has been weak. In Scandinavia especially, the strong trade unions and employee associations, operating in consensual fashion (until the spring of 1980 in Sweden), have been a powerful force for the creation of worker training opportunities--indeed, of adult education programs generally. In America, the unions have tended to limit their concerns to "bread and butter" matters (often in adversarial ways). In general--there are notable exceptions--they have been relatively uninterested in education and training for their members, even in encouraging them to participate in such (paid) programs as are available to them.

Second, compared with most European countries, the higher education system in the U.S. is exceedingly large. Terms like "mass" have been used to describe it. In America, there is a tradition for employers to rely for their trained manpower on the ubiquitous public educational institutions, which--the community colleges, for example--are increasingly used for the retraining of workers.

Third, virtually all the national training systems reviewed rely on levies or contributions from the employing firms--for the obvious reason that they are important beneficiaries of the training. American business and industry is apparently reluctant to accept this model, preferring to rely on the schools and colleges,* their own training programs, and a favorable market for potential employees. Similarly, U.S. employers are reluctant to give their employees time off for education and training.

In sum, the situation in the U.S. is that: (1) there are many convenient educational institutions at which workers can enroll--including two- and four-year colleges and technical institutes, school district adult schools and vocational training centers, as well as hundreds of proprietary schools; and (2) workers must generally enroll during time left over after work and, where there is a fee, at their own expense (although many organizations, public and private, do defray school fees if the schooling is sufficiently job-related).

Labor market policy--the European term for what has usually been called "manpower" policy in the U.S.--can be understood as a complex of measures or interventions intended to meet labor market needs and minimize unemployment. Specific measures in use in various industrialized countries include: incentives for industries to conduct in-house training, paid educational leave, wage subsidies to firms for hiring or retaining certain categories of workers, work sharing, public works programs, publicly subsidized training (for skill upgrading or new jobs) with associated aptitude testing and counseling, and development and dissemination of up-to-date labor market information.

---

*South Carolina over the past two decades, for example, has successfully attracted much new industry, after establishing a system of two-year technical institutions throughout the state (Bushnell, 1981).

The practice of industry-conducted in-plant training for employees is widely accepted in Europe, particularly in West Germany, Sweden, the Soviet Union and the United Kingdom among the countries studied. It is regarded as in the long-term interests of the firm, and in some countries--West Germany, for example--as a reflection simply of good corporate citizenship.

Paid educational leave (PEL) plans are also widely in effect in Europe, as we have seen. The International Labor Organization (of which the U.S. is once again a member), after eight years of study, endorsed the principle of paid educational leave as national policy (OECD, 1976, Annex 1). PEL was recently advocated for Canada by the prestigious Adams Commission (1979). There are unresolved issues in PEL policy to be sure, even in the European countries that accept the general concept (von Moltke and Schneevoight, 1977): Should PEL be available at regular intervals, for perhaps limited time periods, or on an irregular basis for possibly longer periods? How long should the PEL be? Should employees be able to study general (nonvocational) subjects as well as vocational ones under PEL? Should PEL be viewed in the context of (adult) education policy or labor market policy (the latter is the more common pattern)?

In the U.S., labor market programs have tended to be divided between the federal government and the states. All of the states operate employment services that aid the unemployed in finding jobs; a handful (e.g., South Carolina, Georgia, Oklahoma) administer fairly systematic training programs. The federal government, through the Comprehensive Employment and Training Act, sponsors very limited training and "public works" programs, mostly for a population of economically disadvantaged "CETA eligibles." U.S. corporations, with limited federal and state tax incentives, are increasingly providing in-plant training for employees. Relatively small firms, however, seldom provide training for improved or new skills for employees. Government-subsidized opportunities for adults to obtain training in new fields are essentially nonexistent in the U.S. (although fees for vocational studies may be quite low at many public schools and colleges). Except for college professors' sabbaticals, paid educational leave is unheard of in the U.S.

In view of the Republican Administration's commitment to reduce federal (nonmilitary) spending, the task of drawing feasible implications is somewhat difficult, since, from the perspective of the countries surveyed in this study, the federal government in the U.S. should be doing much more than it currently is in providing for job training. Consequently, several of the implications below are phrased to speak to both federal and state government, in recognition of the Administration's "new federalism" approach to government.

*

With this backdrop, we note--mostly on the basis of European experiences--the following implications:

(9) Agencies reponsible for national and state manpower and employment policies should consider designing a mechanism, national in purpose and scope, but local in implementation, by which government can intervene in the on-going training systems in a locality, to provide additional trained adults for critical occupations in which there are regional employee shortages.* Local cooperative councils, discussed under No. 8 above, could help identify skill shortages as well as the institutions to provide the new or expanded training.

(10) Federal and state manpower agencies should likewise consider plans for creating programs through which individual adults of any age may on their own volition, or if their jobs are threatened by technological obsolescence, obtain up to a year of full-time training in a new occupation for which there is a known labor market shortage. Training should be free, and trainees could receive a stipend equal to the current minimum wage. (A program of this kind could be modeled in the large part on elements of the Training Opportunities Scheme--TOPS--in Great Britain and the training system created under West Germany's 1969 Labor Promotion Act.)

(11) Federal and state policy makers need to consider substantially expanding tax incentives to businesses of all sizes for in-house training of employees.

(12) Federal and state agencies responsible for manpower policy should give consideration to plans for a system of paid educational leaves for employees at all levels in the U.S.,

---

*Specifically with regard to CETA, we cannot say whether the Act should be extensively revamped when it comes up for reauthorization in 1982, or whether it should be set aside and a fresh attempt made to devise an entirely new national (or federal-state-local) training policy for the country. It does seem unreasonable for there not to be some federal role, even if it is limited to coordination and information dissemination. Undoubtedly these are matters currently being deliberated by the Senate Subcommittee on Employment and Productivity and the National Commission for Employment Policy.

possibly to be financed jointly from federal, state, employer and employee sources. Manpower planners should study the analyses and recommendations of the (Canadian) Commission on Paid Educational Leave and Productivity (the Adams Commission). Of the countries studied, Canada, in its social and economic characteristics as well as level of development of labor market policies, is most similar to the U.S.

(13) Schools and colleges should act to create special educational opportunities for workers--to be conducted on campuses, at workplaces, or elsewhere, at times and in formats tailored to identified groups of workers. Planning and coordination could occur through the aforementioned co-operative councils.

(14) While training opportunities for government workers in the U.S. are extensive, and extensively used, adoption of new approaches could conceivably lead to more effective training and eventually to better performance. Denmark, for example, has a residential College of Municipal Administrators. The Federal Republic of Germany has a civil service paid educational leave arrangement.

Older People

As all the statistics show, both the numbers and the proportion of older persons in the U.S. are increasing--the result of declining birth rates and medical advances. As was shown in Part II, numerous new social services for older people, including some that are explicitly educational, are springing up in local jurisdictions--both here and abroad--due mostly to the ingenuity of local people.
There are no national policies on education for older people in any of the countries studied. One fairly common state policy in the U.S. is for state higher education systems to allow people over a certain age to enroll at substantially reduced fees.
It appears from our review that the present is a time for local experimentation with diverse modes of educational service for older citizens. The U.S., with successful models such as the Elderhostels and numerous community college special programs, seems to be progressing as fast as any of the nine countries in extending learning opportunities to older people.
One model that does not exist in the U.S. is that of the multi-purpose or multiservice Universites du Troisieme Age (Universities for the Third Age) in France, which were described in some detail in Part II.

National surveys (Okes, 1976; Boaz, 1978) make it clear
that older persons are substantially under-represented in
adult learning activities generally in the U.S. Conceivably,
many do not see the possibility of personal benefit from
continued learning; many feel intimidated by colleges; often
schools and colleges simply do not arrange courses or other
activities in ways that older people find convenient.

Finally, it seems the case that older people in America
do not join national organizations (in fact there are not
very many) set up to promote member interests, to the extent
seen in other countries. The Pensioners Associations in
Scandinavia, for example, exercise considerable political
influence in their respective countries. Perhaps their
closest counterpart in the U.S. is the National Association of
Retired Persons/ American Association of Retired Teachers
(NARP/AART) combination, which sponsors educational activities
throughout the country for their members.

*

Four general implications:

(15) Local cooperative adult education councils and their
member organizations need to analyze systematically the
learning needs of older people in their communities, and then
devise means for meeting them. One kind of activity, which
could be carried out in churches and other community organizations, might consist essentially of consciousness-raising
about personal benefits from lifelong learning, and about how
to bring influence on provider institutions to offer suitable
learning opportunities.

(16) Older persons should be encouraged to join existing
national organizations for older people, or to help form new
ones. High on the agenda of such organizations, then, should
be provision of suitable learning experiences for all older
people in the country.

(17) Various federal funding agencies should consider
special efforts--perhaps through special competitions--to
support innovative, promising educational programs for older
people.

(18) Experiments or demonstration projects should be
carried out in the U.S. with the University for the Third Age
multiple-service model. The NARP/AART would be a likely
prime contractor, as would one of the national Ys or church
organizations, or a university located in a metropolitan
area.

Women Entering the Labor Force

Entry of large numbers of women into the work force is surely one of the most significant contemporary social and economic trends in the U.S., with ramifications throughout the fabric of American life. Fifty-one percent of all adult women are now gainfully employed, accounting for about 45 percent of the civilian work force. Interest on the part of women to enter or re-enter the job market seems certain to continue; basic principles of equality bid the nation to facilitate this intention.

Several of the countries studied have special training programs or categorical implementation arrangements for women, although, with the exception of Canada, they are not especially large or innovative in comparison with the U.S. Canada's National Plan of Action on the Status of Women was announced in 1979; its many components are in various stages of initial implementation. Sweden has a system of training stipends for (the few remaining) women who wish to join the work force. France has called attention to the special needs of women through creation of the posts of Secretary of State for the Feminine Condition and Assistant Secretary of Labor for Women's Employment, but women are still underrepresented in training under the Law of 1971. Britain's government has recently launched a limited program of job exploration and counseling courses for women.

Somewhat in contrast, despite the absence of major federal initiatives and funding, a wide range of learning opportunities for women seeking to enter the work force exists in the U.S., largely due to local efforts. There are many hundreds of women's centers which provide personal assessment and career exploration services; many are based at colleges and universities, others are sponsored by churches and other community organizations (such as YWCAs). Colleges and universities, especially the many community colleges, have set up occupational training programs in formats convenient to women with family and other responsibilities.

Federal programs--CETA, the Work Incentive Program (for welfare recipients), the Minority Women's Employment Program, and the training conducted under the Vocational Education Act--do have special provisions for adult women, particularly displaced homemakers, but in practice they serve mainly economically disadvantaged women.

Women (and men) in the U.S. need a service through which they can receive "training on demand" for jobs that are known to exist (perhaps designed along the lines of TOPS in the U.K.)

Arguably, however, the most important structural barrier to job training (and employment) for women in the U.S. is the absence of a comprehensive system of childcare. Numerous, perhaps most, developed countries, as well as many less developed nations (Mainland China, for example), have national childcare policies.   Among the countries in our study, Denmark, France, the U.S.S.R., and Sweden, have such policies. Denmark's has existed for almost 90 years.   France's national childcare network is run by the PMI (La Protection Maternelle et Infantile en France); others are operated by municipal authorities and private organizations.   Sweden's, conducted through its barnstuga--local multi-service childcare houses-- is judged by some experts to be the most effective of all the national childcare systems (Evans and Saia, 1972).   Also well-known are the arrangements in Israel and Yugoslavia.

*

Mindful of the Reagan commitment to reduce federal spending, we nonetheless put forth the following implications:

(19)   As is the policy in almost all industrialized countries, the United States should have a national (or national-state-local) childcare system.

(20)   As noted earlier, the U.S. needs a federally-coordinated training program through which adults of any age may receive short-term training in fields of their choice (in which jobs are available).   Such a program would be particularly useful to women seeking to enter or reenter the labor force.

(21)   There needs to be improved enforcement of sex discrimination laws in registered apprenticeship programs.

(22)   Schools and colleges should continue to improve their educational programs for older women.   Instructional programs in flexible and convenient formats, part-time opportunities without fee discrimination, granting of credit for prior learning, and childcare services are among the numerous services that colleges should consider in accom-modating women preparing to join the work force.

Parents

Education for effective parenting is a relatively recent adult education emphasis in the U.S.   Conceivably in part it was a consequence of the general breakdown in authority that characterized the late 1960's in the U.S. (and in other countries); parents were dismayed by their children who seemed unwilling to abide by many accepted conventions, including traditional family ties.   It was also a consequence of the realization that parenting is a demanding task, the knowledge and skills for which could no longer be taken for granted.

Parent education, of course, means much more than trying to understand how to live with obstreperous teenagers, as can be seen from the numerous descriptions of programs given in Part II. It may include topics from preparing for childbirth to arranging for a daughter's wedding.

Perhaps not surprisingly, there are no government policies on parent education as such in the nine countries studied, nor statistics that give evidence of its extent under any sponsorship. Parents for the most part, one surmises, must believe (at the outset, at least) that they know how to raise children; they learn from their parents. Nonetheless, various kinds of educational opportunities for parents under government sponsorship are provided through national health services, diverse government services for families (the best examples probably being in Scandinavia and France), various welfare programs, and national educational programs (Headstart and programs under Title I of the Elementary and Secondary Education Act in the United States have called for parental participation in their children's education).

Beyond such modest and somewhat indirect government-sponsored parent education opportunities, in most of the countries--the United States included--there are numerous non-governmental organizations that offer informal parent education opportunities (or provide facilities in which groups can form and meet); the churches, Ys, women's organizations, and the PTA (and its foreign equivalents) would be examples. As outlined in Part II, instructional materials for various approaches to parent effectiveness training are published in the U.S. The Open University in Britain has an excellent multi-media course for new parents, which may be particularly appropriate for parents who prefer not to discuss family problems in groups.

One can imagine that the idea of government policy on parent education would not be widely accepted in America. The U.S. is a distinctly pluralist nation; for better or worse, its social fabric is a patchwork quilt of religious, ethnic, national origin, and economic class differences, many of which are linked to parenting practices and family life in general.* Furthermore, at the time of this writing "family issues"

---

*A counter-case can be made that a national parent education program could help weld together diverse cultural strains, with the potential of greater social harmony. This, needless to say, is a common argument for the existence of the public school system in America.

have become sharply politicized; the issue of abortion, especially, together with other issues brought to last year's White House Conference on the Families are potentially highly divisive.

*

The two implications are somewhat modest and narrow.

(23)   Individuals and agencies engaged in framing national health care plans for the U.S. should consider including provisions for (1) parent education, and (2) therapy for parents and/or families perceiving themselves to be in trouble and in need of professional assistance.

(24)   A television network or station--public or private-- possibly in collaboration with a college or college system, should give consideration to presenting experimentally the (British) Open University's course on parenting, for an audience of parents who presumably would prefer such learning to be mainly in "distance education" terms rather than face to face.

Undereducated Adults

As noted in Part II, undereducated adults are defined in the U.S. as all those who failed to complete secondary school. Totaling over 50 million adults, this is the so-called "target population" for the federal Adult Basic Education program, conducted under the Adult Education Act of 1966.   This Act embodies the federal government's basic policy with respect to undereducated adults in America.   Currently funded at $100 million, and expanded in 1978 to allow non-school organizations to receive funding for ABE work, it looks on paper to be a quite comprehensive policy.

However, the population served in practice by ABE are the "better students"--the "cream" (Hunter and Harman, 1979)-- mostly adults who are in fact able to prepare themselves over several years to pass the GED examination. Populations of somewhat this same ability level are served by basic skill programs in the military, in many prisons, in many community colleges (where students have graduated from high school), and, for their employees, in an increasing number of corporations and government agencies.

Undereducated adults who are illiterates, or essentially so, are served largely by the voluntary literacy organizations --chiefly the National Affiliation for Literacy Advance and the Literacy Volunteers of America.

A third category of Americans needing basic skills training are the non-English speaking immigrants and refugees who continue to arrive in this country. Many are learning English through ABE/ESL (English-as-a-second-language) classes, or through one of the voluntary literacy organizations, where instruction generally takes the form of one-to-one tutoring.

At the federal level, the situation is confused somewhat by the existence of the Basic Skills Program, which funds diverse projects throughout the country, mostly at the elementary and secondary level, but with some activities focused on adults (such as the Reading Academies).

With Denmark and Australia somewhat as exceptions, all the countries in the study have policies affecting under-educated adults, in the sense that resources are targeted for this purpose. In a majority of the countries--Canada, Sweden, the U.S.S.R., the U.K. and West Germany--national manpower or labor market training programs require or strongly encourage basic skills training along with vocational training. The U.S.S.R., in addition, appears to require workers (under age 30) who do not have a complete secondary education to enroll in elementary or secondary evening or correspondence schools.

For immigrants, the German "Folk High Schools" conduct scores of "German-as-a-second language" courses for guest workers. France's Friends for Education of Foreigners--a voluntary organization--does likewise, with funding from the national government's Social Action Fund.

Literacy work in the U.K. is carried out by many of the Local Education Authorities, as well as by several of the voluntary associations, also with government funding in accord with the "Russell (Report) priorities." Voluntary literacy organizations exist in France (with some government funding, as said) and in Canada (The Movement for Canadian Literacy) without government funding.

It is the Swedish government, however, that has made the most concerted efforts on behalf of its "undereducated" population. National policy on adult education has been refocused in the 1970s on this population. The general goal is to provide all in this group with "bridging education" to bring them up to a level comparable to graduates of the contemporary comprehensive school (nine years). Special Municipal Adult Schools are the main providers of bridging education. "Bridging" study circles are 100 percent government subsidized. Highly significant--and innovative--are the government's (The Swedish Board of Education's) "outreaching" efforts, conducted in work places and housing areas, designed to recruit through personal contact educationally disadvantaged adults into instructional programs.

*

Seven implications:

(25) Needed is a program of grants to private firms to help them finance basic skills instruction for employees in need of such education.

(26) Government agencies at all levels need to expand opportunities for basic skills training for their employees.

(27) CETA (or its successor) should expand and improve the instruction in basic skills given in conjunction with the job training it sponsors. (The basic skills programs used by the Canada Manpower Training Program may provide useful models.)

(28) Major employers should facilitate recruiting activities among employees at the work site by local ABE staff. Churches and other community organizations should publicize local ABE opportunities. (A critical problem is that the great majority of undereducated adults in the U.S. is not being reached by existing ABE and literacy programs.)

(29) Churches and other community organizations which do not already do so should consider becoming active providers of basic skills and literacy training. (Churches in the Federal Republic of Germany receive public funds for general education work.)

(30) The major voluntary literacy organizations in the U.S. should receive continuing federal funding to partially support their on-going progams. (Their current work with immigrants and refugees, for example, is clearly in response to a federal government-created need.)

(31) A literacy campaign--multi-organizational, multi-media and tutorially-based along the lines of the British adult literacy campaign--needs to mounted in the U.S., first on a pilot basis in one metropolitan area, and then nationwide.

These then are the implications for government policy on adult education in the U.S. drawn from our review of policies and practices in eight industrialized countries. In particular, we noted types of services to adult learners that exist in some number of the nations studied, but not in the United States. Briefly outlined were 31 implications for both national adult education policy and for improved learning opportunities for the five population groups designated for the study. We trust that our observations will become part of the grist for deliberations in the years ahead, as the U.S. moves ever closer to becoming a genuine learning society.

PART V:
REFERENCES

AUSTRALIA

Aboriginal Training and Cultural Institute (ACTI). 1979.

Adult Aboriginal Education. 1977 Annual Report. West Perth: Technical Education Division, Education Department of West Australia, 1977.

Australian Bureau of Statistics. Labor Force Experience During 1978, Preliminary. Canberra: May 14, 1979.

Australian Committee on Technical and Further Education. TAFE in Australia, Report on Needs in Technical and Further Education. Volume I. Canberra: ACTFE, 1974.

Australian Committee on Technical and Further Education. TAFE in Australia, Second Report on Needs in Technical and Further Education. Canberra: ACTFE, 1975.

Darwin Community College. Annual Report: 1977. Casuarina: Darwin Community College, 1977.

D'Cruz, J. V., and Sheehan, P. J. The Renewal of Australian Schools: A Changing Perspective in Educational Planning. Hawthorne, Victoria: Australian Council for Educational Research, Limited, Second and enlarged edition, 1978.

Deakin University. Guide to Open Campus Studies. Geelong: Deakin University, 1980.

Department of Employment and Youth Affairs. Facts on Women at Work in Australia 1978. Canberra: DEYA, 1979.

Department of Immigration and Ethnic Affairs. Courses in Industry Scheme. Canberra: DIEA, 1980 (Mimeo).

Duke C. "Australian Perspectives on Lifelong Education." Australian Education Review, No. 6, 1976a.

Duke, C. (Ed.) Continuing Education in the CAES: Proceedings of a Search Conference on the Finance and Administration of Continuing Education in Colleges of Advanced Education. Canberra: Australian National University, 1976b.

Finnegan, D. M. Outreach: Awareness of and Access to Adult
    Education. Adelaide: Department of Further Education,
    1977.

Galbally, F. Migrant Services and Programs, Report of the
    Review of Post-Arrival Programs and Services for Migrants.
    Canberra: Australian Government Publishing Service,
    May 1978.

Goyen, J. D. "Incidence of Adult Literacy in the Sidney
    Metropolitan Area." Literacy Discussion, Autumn 1976, VII
    (3), 63-69.

Haines, B. J., and Collins, J. M. "Return to Study: The
    Mount Lawley Experience." Australian Journal of Adult
    Education, April 1979, 3-11.

Hooper, W. "Towards A Survey of Post-school Education in the
    Wollongong Area of N.S.W." In C. Duke and A. Davies, Adult
    Education In Australia, Regional Case Studies. Canberra:
    Australian Association of Adult Education, 1978, 1-71.

Houston J., and Wesson, G. "On the Outside Looking In: Adult
    Education and Immigrants." In C. Duke and A. Davies, Adult
    Education In Australia, Special Group Needs. Canberra:
    Australian Association of Adult Education, 1978, 18-41.

Interdepartmental Working Party, Report of the Interdepart-
    mental Working Party. Canberra: Commonwealth Department of
    Education, May 1979.

Lovering, K. "Australian Women Workers in a Changing
    Society." Address to the Biennial Conference of Australian
    Federation of Business and Professional Women, 1978.

Mackellar, M. J. R. Adult Migrant Education Program Financial
    Year 1977-78. Canberra: Department of Immigration and
    Ethnic Affairs, 1978.

Nelson, A. J. A. "Adult Education and Adult Literacy."
    Literacy Discussion, Autumn 1976, VII (3), 1-97.

Newling, K. N. "The YMCA--A Social Education Agency."
    Australian Journal of Adult Education, July 1974, 14 (2),
    57-59.

New South Wales Workers' Educational Association. Annual
    Report 1978.

Potter, R. E. "The External Graduate Degree in Australia." Phi Delta Kappa, June 1981, 62 (10), 715-717.

Trade Union Training Authority, Annual Report 1977-78. Wondonga: TUTA, 1978.

Universities Commission. 6th Report: 1975 (extracts). Canberra: Universities Commission, 1975.

Victoria Council of Adult Education. Adult Education in Victoria, 1976-77, Including the Thirtieth Annual Report. Melbourne: VCAE, 1977.

Victoria Council of Adult Education. Thirty Second Annual Report, 1978-79. Melbourne: VCAE, 1979.

Williams, B. Education, Training, and Employment. Report of the Committee of Inquiry Into Education and Training. Volume I. Canberra: Australian Government Publishing Service, 1979.

Workers' Educational Association of South Australia. Sixty-Second Annual Report, 1978. Adelaide: WEASA, 1979.

CANADA

Adams Commission. See Report of the Commission of Inquiry on Paid Educational Leave and Productivity, June 1979.

Alberta Commission on Educational Planning. A Choice of Futures. Edmonton: Queen's Printer, 1972.

Alberta Department of Advanced Education and Manpower. Further Education Participation Statistics 1971-72 to December 31, 1978 (Mimeo).

Anderson, E., Thomas, A., and Yousef, C. Directory of Adult Basic Education Programs in Canada. Toronto: Movement for Canadian Literacy, April 1978.

Armitage, W. "The Family and Canadian Social Policy." In Canadian Council on Social Development Conference on Family Policy Proceedings, Ottawa, April 22-26, 1977.

Assemblee Nationale du Quebec. Projet de loi #5. Loi modifant la loi de l'Office de radio-television du Quebec. Juin 22, 1979.

Assemblee Nationale du Quebec. Projet de loi #4. Loi sur la programmation educative. Novembre 27, 1979.

Cairns, J. C. "Adult Functional Illiteracy in Canada." Convergence, 1977, X (1), 43-51.

Canada Employment and Immigration Commission. The Canada Manpower Training Program. A Policy Review. Manpower Training Branch, September 1977.

Canada Employment and Immigration Commission. Women's Employment Program. Ontario Region 1979-80.

Canada Manpower Training Program. Annual Statistical Bulletin, 1977-78, p. 36. Quoted in Adams, p. 123.

Canadian Association for Adult Education. A White Paper on the Education of Adults in Canada. Toronto: CAAE, 1964.

416

Canadian Association for Adult Education. "Conference Report: Manpower Training at the Crossroads". CAAE Learning, Summer 1977, 1, (2), 17-19.

Canadian Commission for UNESCO. Adult Education in Canada, Occasional Paper #6. Ottawa: Canadian Commission for UNESCO, 1972.

Clark, R. and Draper, J. "Major Issues in College Adult Basic Education in Canada." CAAE Learning, Fall-Winter, 1979-80, 3, (1), 48-59.

Cook, G. (Ed). Opportunity for Choice: A Goal for Women in Canada. Ottawa: Statistics Canada and the C.D. Howe Research Institute, 1976.

Daniel, J. S., and Smith, W. A. S. "Open Universities-The Canadian Experience." Higher Education in Europe, October-December 1979, 14-17.

Directory of Adult Basic Education in Canada. Movement for Canadian Literacy, April 1978.

Duquet, D., and Field, J. In Manpower Training at the Crossroads; Conference Report. Toronto: CAAE/ICEA, 1976.

Employment and Immigration Canada. Annual Report, 1978-79. Ottawa: EIC, 1979.

Employment and Immigration Canada. Interdepartmental Evaluation Study of the Canada Manpower Training Program, Technical Report. Ottawa: EIC, 1977.

Employment and Immigration Canada. Interdepartmental Evaluation Study of the Canadian Manpower Training Program, Technical Report. Ottawa: EIC, 1977, 32. Table adapted.

Employment and Immigration Canada. The Canadian Manpower Training Program: A Policy Review. September 1977, 6 ff.

Fales, A., and Nusyna, R. The Learning Needs and Interests of Senior Citizens in Hamilton; Report of a Study for the Hamilton Board of Education. Toronto: OISE, Department of Adult Education, 1975.

Falkenberg, E. "An Analysis of Alberta's Further Education Policy." CAAE Learning, Fall 1976, 1 (1), 36-37.

Faris, R. The Passionate Educators; Voluntary Associations and the Struggle for Control of Adult Educational Broadcasting in Canada, 1912-1952. Toronto: P. Martin, 1975.

Frontier College. Annual Report, 1977-78. Toronto: Frontier College, 1979.

Gouvernement du Quebec. Conseil Superieur de l'education. L'etat et les besoins de l'education: Rapport 1978-79. Quebec: Gouvernement du Quebec, 1979.

Gouvernement du Quebec. Ministere de l'Education, Direction generale de l'education des adultes. Presentation de la Direction generale de l'education des adultes. Quebec: Ministere de l'Education, 1978a, 6.

Gouvernement du Quebec, Ministere de l'Education, Direction generale de l'education des adultes. Statistiques de l'education des adultes. Quebec: Ministere de l' education, 1978b.

Gunderson, M. "Evaluation of Government Supported Training in Canada." In Manpower Training at the Crossroads; Conference Report. Toronto: CAAE/ICEA, 1976.

Hautecoueur, J. P. Analphabetisme et alphabetisation au Quebec. Quebec: Gouvernement du Quebec, 1978.

Hepworth, B. "Workers' Education in Canada: Selected Programs and Experiences." Toronto: CAAE Learning, Winter 1979, 2 (2), 16-18.

Kidd, J. R., and Selman, G. Coming of Age: Canadian Adult Education in the 1960's. Toronto: Canadian Association for Adult Education, 1978.

Kutarna, J. "Saskatchewan Community Colleges: A Statement of Basic Concepts," Quoted from Province of Saskatchewan, Department of Continuing Education, Report of the Minister's Advisory Committee on Community Colleges, 1972.

Labor Canada, Women's Bureau. Women in the Labor Force: Facts and Figures. 1977.

Lachine, L. La Lecon des Faits: Programme de formation des educateurs d'adultes (SESAME). Quebec: l'Editeur official du Quebec, 1974.

Lallez, R. The TEVEC casi: An Experiment in Adult Education Using the Multi-Media System. Paris: UNESCO-IBE, 1973.

MacKeracher, D. A Report to the Canadian Committee on Learning Opportunities for Women: Background to Policy Development. November 1978 (Mimeo).

Ministere de l'Education. Direction Generale de l'Education Permanente. l'Operation Depart: Synthese des rapports regionaux. 1970.

Ministere de l'Education. Rapport des Activities L'Education au Quebec. Quebec: Ministere de l'Education, 1979a.

Ministere de l'Education. Revue de programmes 1980-81: Objectif general et infrastructure. Quebec: Direction generale de l'education des adultes, 1979b.

Munroe, D. Case Studies on Alternative University Structures in Canada. Paris: UNESCO, June 1975.

Newsletter IQRT. "Leadership in Learning Opportunities for Older People." 1980, p. 19.

Organisation for Economic Co-operation and Development. Reviews of National Policies for Education: Canada. Paris: OECD, 1976.

Organisation for Economic Co-operation and Development. Equal Opportunities for Women. Paris: OECD, 1979.

Ontario Educational Communications Authority. TV Ontario and the Family. Toronto: OECA, undated brochure.

Ontario Ministry of Colleges and Universities. Training for Ontario's Future. Report of the Task Force on Industrial Training. 1973.

Ontario Ministry of Community and Social Services, Senior Citizens' Branch, Office on Aging. Report of the National Symposium on Aging. Ottawa: October 25-27, 1978.

Ontario Provincial Secretariat for Social Development. Compendium to the Family as a Focus for Social Policy. September 1979.

Pearl, B. (Ed.) Labor Education In Canada, Report of the National Conference on Labor Education. Ottawa: Labor Canada, 1975.

Province of Alberta. Further Education: Policy Guidelines, and Procedures. Edmonton: Ministry of Advanced Education and Manpower, 1975.

Province of British Columbia, Ministry Advisory Committee on Continuing Education. A Draft Policy on the Provision of Community Education and General Interest Education Programs. January 1980; and A Draft Policy on the Provision of Continuing Education in the Public Educational System of British Columbia. November 1979.

Province of British Columbia, Ministry of Education. Report of the Committee on Continuing and Community Education in B.C. December 1976.

Province of British Columbia, Ministry of Education. B.C. Post-Secondary Statistics 1976-77. Continuing Education Data. Victoria: Ministry of Education, Educational Data Services, 1978a.

Province of British Columbia, Ministry of Education. Report of the Committee on Assessment of the Continuing Education System of the Continuing Education Division, Ministry of Education, Government of British Columbia. December 1978b.

Province of British Columbia, Ministry of Education. Report of the Distance Education Planning Group on a Delivery System For Distance Education in British Columbia. March 1978c.

Province of British Columbia, Ministry of Education. English as a Second Language for Adults. Discussion Paper 04/79. February 1979a.

Province of British Columbia, Ministry of Education, Science, and Technology. Report of the Committee on Adult Basic Education; Discussion Paper. January, 1979b.

Province of British Columbia, Ministry of Education. Women's Access Centers: A Proposal. Discussion Paper, 03/79. February 1979c.

Report of the Commission of Inquiry on Paid Educational Leave and Productivity: Education and Working Canadians (Adams Commission), R. J. Adams, Chairman. Ottawa: Labor Canada, June 1979.

Riddell, C. "Gerontology in Canada" Toronto: CAAE Learning, Spring 1978, 1 (4), 15-29.

Robertson, Nickerson, Group Associates, Ltd. Case Studies on Aspects of Training Upper Skilled Blue-Collar Industrial Workers. Report to the Department of Employment and Immigration. Ottawa: 1972.

Sandiford, P. Adult Education in Canada: A Survey. Toronto: University Press, 1935.

Shore, V. "Enrollment Double Most Optimistic Estimates." University Affairs, January 1980, 2-3.

Sissons, E. "Future of an Illusion," CAAE Learning, Summer 1977, 1 (2), 15-16.

Sloan, E. P. "The Canada New Start Program: An Overview". In J. R. Kidd and G. Selman, Coming of Age: Canadian Adult Education in the 1960's. Toronto: Canadian Association for Adult Education, 1978. 241-250.

Statistics Canada. Continuing Education: Community Colleges, 1976-77. Ottawa: August 1978.

Statistics Canada. Canada's Elderly. Ottawa: Statistics Canada, March 1979a.

Statistics Canada. Vocational and Technical Training, 1976-77. Ottawa: Statistics Canada, March 1979b.

Statistics Canada. Continuing Education, Participation in Programs of Educational Institutions 1976-77. Ottawa: Education, Science, and Culture Division, Vocational-Continuing Education Section, Statistics Canada, May 1979c.

Statistics Canada. Education In Canada: A Statistical Review for 1977-78. Ottawa: Statistics Canada, Education Science and Cultural Division, May 1979d.

Statistics Canada. The Labor Force. Ottawa: Statistics Canada, May 1979e.

Statistics Canada. Publicly-Supported Vocational Training Involving the Private Sector, 1977-78. Ottawa: Statistics Canada, June 1979f.

Swan, J. Continuing Education and Continuing Competence, Working Paper Prepared for the Professional Organizations Committee, 1979. See Appendix A, S. N. Colvin, "On Continuing Education."

Third Career Research Society. Retirement in Alberta. Edmonton: Career Research Society, 1976.

Thomas, A. A Brief on the Concept of Continuing Education. Washington, DC, ERIC Reports, 1970. Also Canadian Commission for UNESCO, Adult Education in Canada Occasional Paper #6. Ottawa: Canadian Commission for UNESCO, 1972.

Thomas, A. Adult Basic Education and Literacy Activities in Canada, 1975-76. Toronto: World History of Canada, April 1976.

Thomas, A. Canadian Adult Basic Literacy Resource Kit. Toronto: Movement for Canadian Literacy, July 1979a.

Thomas, A., et. al. OISE Review of Penitentiary Education and Training 1978-79. Ottawa: Department of Solicitor General, Canadian Penitentiary Service, Education and Training, 1979b.

Vanier Institute of the Family. Report of the Family Life Education Survey. Part I: Family Life Education in the Media of Mass Communication. Ottawa: Vanier Institute of the Family, 1970.

Vanier Institute of the Family. Report of the Family Life Education Survey. Part III: Family Life Education in Voluntary Associations. Ottawa: Vanier Institute of the Family, 1973.

Verner, C., and Dickenson, G. Union Education in Canada: A Report of the Educational Activities of Labor Organizations. Vancouver: University of British Columbia, Adult Education Research Center, 1974.

Vigoda, D., and Ellis, D. "Some Factors Influencing Participation in Educational Activities of Older Ontario Men." Paper presented at the Eighth Annual Scientific and Educational Meeting of the Canadian Association of Gerontology, Halifax, November 2, 1979.

Waniewicz, I. Demand for Part-Time Learning in Ontario. Toronto: Ontario Institute for Studies in Education , 1976.

Willis, J. "Learning Opportunities for Women." CAAE Learning, Spring 1978, 1 (4), 8-19.

DENMARK

Baunsbak-Jensen, A. "Danes Flock to Adult-Education Classes."
    In Fact Sheet/Denmark. Copenhagen: The Press and Cultural
    Relations Department, Ministry of Foreign Affairs of
    Denmark, 1979.

Bjorn, L. Th. "Denmark." In Learning Opportunities for
    Adults, Vol. III, The Non-Participation Issue. Paris:
    Organisation for Economic Co-Operation and Development,
    1979.

Central Council of Education, Ministry of Education. U90,
    Danish Educational Planning and Policy in a Social Context
    at the End of the 20th Century. Copenhagen: Schultz
    Forlag, 1978.

Gage, G. G. "The Nordic Example." Saturday Review, Septem-
    ber 20, 1975.

Hansen, B. Recurrent Education, Policy and Development in
    OECD Member Countries, Denmark. Paris: Organisation for
    Economic Co-Operation and Development, 1976.

Himmelstrup, P. "Denmark." In Learning Opportunities for
    Adults, Vol. IV. Paris: Organisation for Economic Co-
    Operation and Development, 1979.

International Labour Office. Residential Workers' Education.
    Geneva: International Labour Office, 1971.

Kurland, N. D. "The Scandinavian Study Circle: An Idea for
    the U.S.?" The College Board Review, Winter, 1979-80 (114),
    20-25.

Levine, H. A. "Paid Educational Leave." In NIE Papers in
    Education and Work. Washington, D.C.: National Institute
    of Education, 1977.

Nordic Council and the Secretariat for Nordic Cultural Co-
    Operation. Adult Education in the Nordic Countries.
    Stockholm: Gotab, 1976.

Organisation for Economic Co-Operation and Development. Youth Unemployment, Vol. II, Inventory of Measures Concerning the Employment and Unemployment of Young People. Paris: Organisation for Economic Co-Operation and Development, 1978.

Prial, F. J. "Danish Folk Schools: Live In and Learn." The New York Times, September 7, 1980, Section 12, p. 24.

Rasmussen, W. "Case Study: Denmark, Experimental Vocational Courses with a Component of General Subjects." Conference on Developments in Recurrent Education. Paris: Organisation for Economic Co-Operation and Development, 1977.

Rordam, T. The Danish Folk High Schools. Denmark: Det Danske Selskab, 1965.

Secretariat for Nordic Cultural Cooperation, The Nordic Council of Ministers. Recurrent Education in the Nordic Countries. Stockholm: Gotab, 1977.

Severinsen, H. "A New Approach in Danish Adult Education." In Learning Opportunities for Adults, Vol. II. Paris: Organisation for Economic Co-Operation and Development, 1979.

Andrews, P., et al. The German Vocational Educational System. Comparative Papers in Further Education. Bristol, England: The Further Education Staff College, 1979.

Center for Educational Research and Innovation. Developments in Educational Leave of Absence. Paris: Organisation for Economic Co-Operation and Development, 1976.

Clyne, P. "Adult Education for Underprivileged Groups." Strasbourg: Council of Europe, November 1979.

Deutscher Volkshochschul-Verband. Statistische Mitteilungen, Arbeitsjahr, 1978. Frankfurt: 1978.

Dolff, H. "West German Experience of 'Popular' Higher Education." In T. Schuller and J. Megarry (Eds.), Recurrent Education and Lifelong Learning. New York: Kogan Page, 1979.

European Bureau of Adult Education. "Paid Educational Leave in the Federal Republic of Germany." In News Letter. Amersfoort, The Netherlands: European Bureau of Adult Education, September 1979.

Knoll, J. "New Approaches in Post-Secondary Education in Germany." In Learning Opportunities for Adults, Vol. II, New Structures, Programmes and Methods. Paris: Organisation for Economic Co-Operation and Development, 1979.

Mueller-Maerki, F. F. "Workers Codetermination: Should the U.S. Follow Germany's Lead?" German-American Trade News, July/August 1980, 34 (4), 15-17.

National Broadcasting Company. America Works when America Works. NBC White Paper (Part III: West Germany). New York: National Broadcasting Company, 1981.

Nollen, S. D. "The Current State of Recurrent Education." In D. W. Vermilye (Ed.), Education and Work. San Francisco: Jossey-Bass, 1977.

Organisation for Economic Co-Operation and Development. Alternation Between Work and Education, A Study of Educational Leave of Absence at Enterprise Level. Paris: OECD, 1978.

Organisation for Economic Co-Operation and Development. Beyond Compulsory Schooling, Options and Changes in Upper Secondary Education. Paris: OECD, 1976.

Organisation for Economic Co-Operation and Development. Learning Opportunities for Adults, Vol. III, The Non-Participation Issue. Paris: OECD, 1979.

Organisation for Economic Co-Operation and Development. Recurrent Education, Policy and Development in OECD Countries, Germany. Paris: OECD, 1972.

Pfluger, A. "Lifelong Education and Adult Education: Reflections on Four Current Problem Areas." In A. J. Cropley (Ed.), Lifelong Education: A Stocktaking. Hamburg: UNESCO Institute for Education, 1979.

Rudolph, H. "Germany." In Learning Opportunities for Adults, Vol. IV. Paris: Organisation for Economic Co-Operation and Development, 1979.

Schmid, G. "Selective Employment Policy in West Germany: Some Evidence of its Development and Impact." In National Commission for Manpower Policy, European Labor Market Policies. Special Report No. 27. Washington, D.C.: National Commission for Manpower Policy, 1978.

Secretariat of the Standing Conference of Ministers of Education of the States of the Federal Republic of Germany. The Educational System in the Federal Republic of Germany. New York: College Entrance Examination Board, 1979.

Trimborn, H. "W. German Effort; Apprentice Plan: Steady Talent Pool." Los Angeles Times, April 17 1981, 1.

FRANCE

Association du Centre Universitaire de Cooperation Economique et Sociale. Presentation du Systeme des Unites. Nancy: ACUCES, n.d.

Association du Centre Universitaire de Cooperation Economique et Sociale. Rapport d'Activite, 1978. Nancy: ACUCES, 1979.

Association pour la Formation Professionnelle des Adultes. Rapport Annuel, 1978. Montreuil: AFPA, 1979.

Bekombo-Priso, M. Parent Education: Selective Annotated Bibliography. Paris: United Nations Educational, Scientific and Cultural Organization, n.d.

Belorgey, J. M. Recurrent Education Policy and Development in OECD Member Countries: France. Paris: Centre for Educational Research and Innovation, Organisation for Economic Co-Operation and Development, 1976.

Besnard, P. "La Sacralisation de l'Etate-Ogre." Education Permanente, No. 31, 1977.

Besnard, P. L'Animation Socio-Culturelle. "Que Sais-Je?" Series. Paris: Presses Universitaires de France, 1980.

Besnard, P. Socio-Pedagogie de Formation des Adultes. Paris: ESF, 1980.

Besnard, P. L'Animateur Socio-Culturel: Une Profession Differente. Paris, ESF, in press.

Besnard, P., and Lietard, B. Adult Education in Europe, No. 2. Prague: European Centre for Leisure and Education, 1977.

Besnard, P., and Lietard, B. La Formation Continue. Que Sais-Je? Series 1955. Paris: Presses Universitaires de France, 1976.

Besnard, P., Poujol, G., and Labourie, R. Traite des Sciences Pedagogiques, Tome 8. Paris: ESF, 1978.

Brasseul, P. "Inauguration des Nouveaux Locaux du Club Des Retraites MGEN de la Region Parisienne." Troisieme Age, May/June 1978, 9-15.

Callet, C. and du Granrut, C. Place Aux Femmes: Collection Les Francais Qui Changent La France. Paris: Stock, 1973.

Caspar, P. "Paid Educational Leave in France." In T. Schuller and J. Megarry (Eds.), World Yearbook of Education, 1979: Recurrent Education and Lifelong Learning. London: Kogan Page, 1979.

Centre d'Information Feminin. En cas de... Reinsertion Professionnelle: Flash d'Information. Paris: C.I.F., September 1979.

Centre Universite Economie d'Education Permanente. Formations en Informatique, Automatique, Electronique. Lille: Universite des Sciences et Techniques de Lille, 1979.

Centre INFFO. Centre pour le Developpement de l'Information sur la Formation Permanente. Paris: Centre INFFO, October 1979.

Centre National de Documentation Pedagogique. Les Personnes Agees: Bibliographie Analytique. Paris: Ministere de l'Education, May 1977.

Clermont, J. Une Universite du IIIe Age. SHP Vie Culturelle. Annees--Documents Cleirppa, October 1977, 66, 13-15.

Comite du Travail Feminin. Equipements et Services Collectifs Necessaires Aux Femmes Qui Travaillent: Rapport, Actualites du Travail Feminin. Paris: Ministere du Travail, March 1977.

Council of Europe. Preparation for Retirement. Strasbourg: Council of Europe, 1977.

Council of Europe. Recent Demographic Developments in the Member States of the Council of Europe. Strasbourg: Council of Europe, 1979.

Debeauvais, M. Elaboration d'un Modele d'Universite Ouverte Sur la Base de l'Experience de Vincennes (First Conference of Member Institutions Program on Institutional Management in Higher Education). Paris: Centre for Educational Research and Innovation, Organisation for Economic Co-Operation and Development, 8-10 January 1973.

Dimnet, J. Adequation et Fonction des Media dans la Formation des Adultes. Paris: Ministere de l'Education Centre National de Documentation Pedagogique, March 1979.

Dubar, C. Le Public de L'Examen Special d'Entree a l'Universite dans le Nord-Pas-de-Calais. Lille: Universite Lille I, Institut de Sociologie, June 1979.

Dubar, C., Feutrie, M., and Mlekuz, G. Second Rapport: La Volonte de Former. Lille: Universite de Lille I, CUEEP--Institut de Sociologie, January 1978.

"Education and the Elderly: The Integration of Elderly Persons into the Student Population at Paris University X." Aging, III 2, 1978.

"Education: France." Ageing International, Summer 1979, VI (2), 5.

Federation Nationale des Associations Familiales Rurales. Actions de Formation Conduites par la F.N.A.F.R. September 1979-Juin 1980. Paris: FNAFR, September 1979.

Feutrie, M. La Demande de Formation en Milieu Ouvrier: l'Action de Formation Collective de Sallaumines-Noyelles. Paris: Universite Rene Descartes: U.E.R. de Sciences de l'Education, n.d.

Feutrie, M. Le Public des Actions Collectives de Formation dans le Region Nord Pas-de-Calais. Lille: Office Regional d'Information et de Coordination d'Education Permanente, March 1979.

Gehmacher, E. On the Elderly I: Educational Questions Concerning the Elderly. Paris: UNESCO, Adult Education Section, Literacy, Adult Education and Rural Development Division, December 1978.

INFOSUP. "Faire Carriere au Feminin." Formation Professionnelle, No. 23, May, 1977, 3-5.

Labourie, R. Les Institutions Socio-Culturelles. Paris: Presses Universitaires de France, 1978.

Legave, C. La Formation Professionnelle Continue en France.
Paris: Centre pour le Developpement de l'Information sur la
Formation Permanente, January 1979.

Legendre, J. La Formation Professionnelle Continue en Quel-
ques Chiffres. Paris: Centre Pour le Developpement de
l'Information sur la Formation Permanente, 1979.

Martin, Y. Pratiques de Formation: La Formation Permanente a
l'Universite de Paris VIII-Vincennes, Lahier No. 1.
Paris: Universite Paris VIII, Group de Travail Formation
Permanente, June 1977.

Ministere du Travail et de la Participation. Statistics du
Travail: Les Problemes Specifiques du Chomage Feminin,
Supplement 66. Paris: Ministere du Travail et de la
Participation, 1979.

Nallet, J. F. Evolution dans les Mesures pour l'Emploi des
Jeunes (1977 et 1978). Paris: Centre INFFO, 1979.

Parkes, D. Craft Apprenticeship in Europe: Comparative Papers
in Further Education, No. 5. Coombe Lodge, Blagdon,
Bristol: The Further Education Staff College, 1979.

Pasquier, B. Further Vocational Training in France.
Brussels: Commission on the European Communities, 1977.

Poujol, G. Pour. No. 59, 1978.

Poujol, R. "Quelle Universite Pour les Retraites?" Notre
Temps, September 1975, 20-24.

Project de Loi de Finances pour 1980: Document Annexe,
Formation Professionnelle et Promotion Sociale. Paris:
Imprimerie Nationale, 1979.

Rey, V., and Brocard, M. "Recent Developments in French
Higher Education Regarding Access to Lifelong Education."
In European Centre for Higher Education, Higher Education
in Europe. Bucharest: October-December 1979, IV (4),
27-28.

Ruet, Senator. Cultural Affairs Committee. National Assembly
Budget, 1976.

Scheffnecht, J. J. "Introduction to the French Law on Continuous Vocational Training." Presentation to the Salzburg
Seminar in Continuing Education, Salzburg, Austria, Seminar
in American Studies, August 6-26, 1978. (Audiotape Tran-
script).

Schuller, T., and Megarry, J. World Yearbook of Education 1979: Recurrent Education and Lifelong Learning. London: Kogan Page, 1979.

Secretariat d'Etat Charge de l'Emploi Feminin. Travail Informations, 27 Novembre-3 Decembre 1978, 31. Paris: Ministre du Travail et de la Participation, 1978.

Secretariat d'Etat a la Formation Professionnelle. La Formation Professionnelle Continue des Salaries et le Conge de Formation, Loi du 16 Juillet 1971, Loi du 17 Juillet 1978: Dossier Technique. Paris: Ministre du Travail et de la Participation, 1979.

Secretariat d'Etat Charge de la Formation Professionnelle. Measures pour l'Emploi, Loi du 10 Juillet, 1979: Dossier Technique, Pacte Nationale pour l'Emploi. Paris: Ministere du Travail et de la Participation, 1979.

Secretariat General de la Formation Professionnelle. Bilan des Stages de Formation et des Stages Pratiques en Entreprise Menes dans le Cadre du Pacte pour l'Emploi des Jeunes. Paris: Secretariat d'Etat aupres du Ministre du Travail charge de la Formation Professionnelle, 1978.

Secretariat General de la Formation Professionnelle. Bilan des Actions de Formation Professionnelle Organisees en Faveur de l'Emploi des Femmes. Paris: Secretariat d'Etat aupres du Ministre du Travail et de la Participation, 1979.

"Sexology, Squalor and No 'Bac:' The Perils of 'Openness' at France's Vincennes Campus." Time, March 31, 1980, 39.

THE SOVIET UNION

Chebotarev, D. R., and Sachuk, N. N. "A Social Policy Directed Toward the Health and Welfare of the Aged in the Soviet Union." Journal of the American Geriatrics Society, February 1979, 27, 49-57.

Darinski, A. V. "The Role of Tertiary Institutions in Adult Education in the Soviet Union." Journal of the International Congress of University Adult Education, May 1972, 11 (1-2), 24-35.

Darinsky, A. "People's Universities in the USSR." Convergence, 1974, 7 (1), 51-57.

Darinsky, A. V. "The System of Education in the U.S.S.R." Literacy Discussion, Spring 1976a, 8 (1), 3-24.

Darinsky, A. V. "The Development of Schools for Adults in the Soviet Union." Literacy Discussion, Spring 1976b, 8 (1), 73-108.

Ek'golm, I. K. "Problems of Continuing Education under Modern Conditions of Social Progress and the Scientific-Technological Revolution." Soviet Education, March 1979, 21, 26-69. (Translation of "Problemy Nepreryvnogo Obrazovaniia v Sovremennykh Usloviiakh Sotsial'nogo Progressa i Nauchno-Tekhnologicheskoi Revoliutsii." Sovetskaia Pedagogika, 1978 (7).)

Feldmesser, R. A. (Ed.). Report of an Exchange between the United States and the Soviet Union in the Area of Higher Education. Princeton, N.J.: Educational Testing Service, 1979. (ERIC document no. ED 177 180)

Grebennikov, I. V. "Increasing the Pedagogical Sophistication of Parents: The Basis for Improving the Education of School Pupils in the Family Setting." Soviet Education, July 1978, 20 (9), 54-67.

Kashin, M. P., and Chekharin, E. M. (Eds.). Narodnoe Obrazovanie v RSFSR (Public Education in the RSFSR). Moscow: Izdatel'stvo Prosveshcheniia, 1970.

Kokorev, I., and Liubashevskii, Iu. "Svobodnoe Vremia i Obrazovanie Vzroslykh" (Free Time and the Education of Adults). Convergence, 1970, 3 (2), 64-71.

Lapidus, G. W. "The Female Industrial Labor Force: Dilemmas, Reassessments, and Options." In A. Kahan and B. A. Ruble (Eds.), Industrial Labor in the U.S.S.R. New York: Pergamon, 1979.

Maksimov, G. "The Educational Level of the Population of the U.S.S.R." Soviet Education, September-October 1974, 16, 46-59.

Malakhov, N. D. "Vecherniaia Shkola v Sisteme Nepreryvnogo Obrazovaniia" (The Evening School in the System of Continuous Education). Sovetskaia Pedagogika, 1979, 10, 42-46.

Matthews, M. Class and Society in Soviet Russia. London: The Penguin Press, 1972.

Matthews, M. "The Soviet Worker at Home." In A. Kahan and B. A. Ruble (Eds.), Industrial Labor in the U.S.S.R. New York: Pergamon, 1979.

Mickiewicz, E. P. Soviet Political Schools: The Communist Party Adult Instruction System. New Haven: Yale University Press, 1967.

Narodnoe Khozyaistvo SSSR v 1978 G.: Statisticheskii Ezhegodnik (The National Economy of the USSR in 1978: A Statistical Yearbook). Moscow: Central Statistical Administration of the USSR, 1979.

Narodnoe Obrazovanie, Nauka i Kul'tura v SSSR: Statisticheskii Sbornik (Public Education, Science and Culture in the USSR: A Statistical Collection). Moscow: Central Statistical Administration of the Council of Ministers of the USSR, 1977.

Naselenie SSSR Po Dannym Vsesoiuznoi Perepisi Naseleniia 1979 Goda (The Population of the USSR According to the Data of the 1979 National Census of the Population). Moscow: Izdatel'stvo Politicheskoi Literatury, 1980.

Onushkin, V. G., and Tonkonogaja, E. P. "Adult Education as Part of the System of Lifelong Education in the U.S.S.R." Prospects, 1978, 8 (2), 211-219.

"Otvety na Voprosnik Iunesko po Obrazovaniiu Vzroslykh" (Answers to the UNESCO Questionnaire on the Education of Adults). Convergence, 1972, 5 (1), 44-53.

Popkov, V. "Popular Education in the U.S.S.R." International Journal of Adult and Youth Education, 1964, 16 (1), 33-39.

Rosen, S. M. Part-Time Education in the U.S.S.R.: Evening and Correspondence Study. Washington: U.S. Government Printing Office, 1965.

Rosen, S. M. Education in the U.S.S.R.: Recent Legislation and Statistics. Washington: U.S. Government Printing Office, 1975.

Severtsev, V. "Case Study of the Development of Higher Education in the USSR." Paris: UNESCO, 1976.

Soviet Education, November 1972, 15 (1).

"Statistical Profile of Soviet Education." Soviet Education, September-October, 1974, 16 (11-12) (entire issue).

Swafford, M. "The Socialization and Training of the Soviet Industrial Labor Force." In A. Kahan and B. Ruble (Eds.), Industrial Labor in the U.S.S.R. New York: Pergamon, 1979.

Tymowski, J., and Januszkiewicz, F. Post-Secondary Education of Persons Already Gainfully Employed in Several European Socialist Countries. Paris: UNESCO, 1976.

"USSR Economic Development Plan for 1976-1980." Daily Report: Soviet Union, 12 March 1976, 3 (50, supp. 27). Washington: Foreign Broadcast Information Service. (Translation from Pravda, March 7, 1976.)

Vasilyev, D. "USSR: Upgrading as a Part of Lifelong Education and Its Contribution to Democratization of Higher Education." Higher Education in Europe, October-December 1979, 4, 23-26.

Vladislavlev, A. P. "Continuing Education in Developed Socialist Society." Soviet Education, March 1979, 21, 6-25. (Translation of "Problema Nepreryvnogo Obrazovaniia v Usloviiakh Razvitogo Sotsialistichekogo Obshchestva," Voprosy Filosofii, 1978 (3).)

SWEDEN

Ahlqvist, E-L. Manpower Training in Sweden. Stockholm: The
Swedish Institute, 1977.

Arbetarnas Bildningsforbund. Workers' Education in Sweden.
Stockholm: 1973.

Borgstrom, L., et al. Elementary School Studies for Adults.
Stockholm: Pedagogical Centre of the Stockholm L.E.A.,
1979.

Brostrom, A., and Ekeroth, G. Outreaching Activities in Adult
Education in View of Allocation Policy. Uppsala: Department of Sociology, University of Uppsala, 1976.

Brostrom, A., and Ekeroth, G. Adult Education and Allocation
Policy. Uppsala: Department of Sociology, University of
Uppsala, 1977.

Centre for Educational Research and Innovation. Developments
in Educational Leave of Absence. Paris: Organisation for
Economic Co-operation and Development, 1976.

Cohen, D., and Garet, M. "Reforming Educational Policy with
Applied Research." Harvard Educational Review, 1975, 45(1),
17-43.

The Committee on Methods Testing in Adult Education. Extended
Adult Education: Outreaching Work and Study Circles--
Experiences and Proposals. Stockholm: LiberTryck, 1974.

Denison, E. The Sources of Economic Growth in the United
States and the Alternatives Before Us. Paper No. 13.
New York: Committee for Economic Development, 1962.

Eckberg, V. Pensioners' Organizations: An Active Part of
Swedish Society. Stockholm: The Swedish Institute, 1978.

Folkbildningsarbeter. Special Issue: The Study Associations
in Sweden. No. 6-7. Stockholm: 1976.

435

Folkbildningsarbeter. Special Issue: The Swedish "Folk-
hogskala"/"Folk High School." No. 8-9. Stockholm: 1977.

Government Bill 1967:85.

Government Bill 1970:35.

Government Bill 1975:23.

Gustafsson, S. "Women and Work in Sweden." In Working Life
in Sweden. New York: Swedish Information Service, 1979.

Harnqvist, K. "Recent Trends and Changes in Individual
Demand: The Case of Sweden." Individual Demand for Educa-
tion: Analytical Report. Paris: Organization for Economic
Co-Operation and Development, 1978.

Hoghielm, R. "The Teaching Process in Municipal Adult
Education in View of Allocation Policy". In R. Hoghielm and
K. Rubenson (Eds.), Research in Adult Education and Alloca-
tion Policy in Sweden. Stockholm: Stockholm Institute of
Education, 1980.

Jakobbson, I. The Swedish Folk High School. Stockholm: The
Swedish Institute, 1977.

Johansson, S. "The Living Survey." In Report on the Swedes
Living Conditions. Stockholm: Allmanna Forlaget, 1970.

Kurland, N. D. "The Scandinavian Study Circle: An Idea for
the U.S.?" The College Board Review, Winter 1979-80, 114,
20-25.

National Board of Universities and Colleges. The 25/4 Scheme
During the Period 1969-1976. Stockholm: National Board of
Universities and Colleges, 1978.

The National Labour Market Board. "Swedish Employment
Policy." The National Labour Market Board's Annual Report,
1978/79. Stockholm: 1979.

National Swedish Board of Education. Adult Education on the
Threshold of the 1980s--Some Guidelines for the Work of the
NBE." Stockholm: 1977.

Organization for Economic Co-Operation and Development. Equal
Opportunities for Women. Paris: OECD, 1979.

Ostlund, H. E. "Strategic Planning on a Recurrent Basis." In T. Schuller (Ed.), World Yearbook of Education 1979: Recurrent Education and Lifelong Learning. London: Kogan Page, 1979.

Rubenson, K. Adult Education and Undereducated Young Men. Stockholm: Stockholm Institute of Education, 1976a.

Rubenson, K. Recruitment in Adult Education: A Research Strategy. Stockholm: Stockholm Institute of Education, 1976b.

Rubenson, K. "Recruitment to Adult Education in the Nordic Countries--Research and Outreaching Activities." Reports on Education and Psychology, No. 3. Stockholm: Stockholm Institute of Education, 1979.

Rubenson, K. "Background and Theoretical Context." In R. Hoghielm and K. Rubenson (Eds.), Research in Adult Education and Allocation Policy in Sweden. Stockholm: Stockholm Institute of Education, 1980a.

Rubenson, K. Dropout in Municipal Adult Schools. Stockholm: Stockholm Institute of Education, 1980b.

Rubenson, K., Bergsten, U. and Bromsjo, B. The Attitudes of Under-educated Adults toward Adult Education. Stockholm: Utbildningsforskning, Liber Laromede Utbildnings forlaget, 1976.

Stockholms Skolforvaltnings Utvarderingsbyra Pedagogiskt Centrum. Report No. 27, Elementary School Studies for Adults: A Summary Report from the GRUV Project. Stockholm: 1979.

Strawn, W. Sweden's Study Associations. Stockholm: The Swedish Institute, 1977.

Swedish Central Bureau of Statistics. The Survey of Living Conditions: Education, Adult Education and Wage-Earning. Stockholm: SCB, 1978.

Swedish Central Bureau of Statistics. The Survey of Living Conditions: Education, Adult Education and Wage Earning. Stockholm: SCB, 1979.

Swedish Government Official Reports. Expanded Adult Education. Stockholm: SOU, 1974.

Swedish Government Official Reports. <u>Municipal Adult Schools and the Voluntary Educational Associations</u>. Stockholm: SOU, 1979a.

Swedish Government Official Reports. <u>Popular Adult Education for the 80's</u>. Stockholm: SOU, 1979b.

The Swedish Institute. <u>Sweden in Brief</u>. Stockholm: 1977.

The Swedish Institute. "Adult Education in Sweden." <u>Fact Sheets on Sweden</u>. Stockholm: 1979a.

The Swedish Institute. "Equality Between Women and Men in Sweden." <u>Fact Sheets on Sweden</u>. Stockholm: 1979b.

The Swedish Institute. "Swedish Labor Market Policy." <u>Fact Sheets on Sweden</u>. Stockholm: 1979c.

Viklund, B. <u>Rising with One's Class, Not above It: Adult Education</u>. Stockholm: The Swedish Institute, 1977.

THE UNITED KINGDOM

Adamson, C. Case Study on Alternative University Structures
   in the United Kingdom. Paris: United Nations Educational,
   Scientific and Cultural Organization, 1978.

Adult Literacy Unit. Adult Literacy: 1978/79. Leicester:
   National Institute of Adult Education, 1979.

Advisory Council for Adult and Continuing Education. Response
   to "Higher Education into the 1900s." London: ACACE, 1978.

Advisory Council for Adult and Continuing Education. Links to
   Learning. Leicester: ACACE, 1979a.

Advisory Council for Adult and Continuing Education. A
   Strategy for the Basic Education of Adults. Leicester:
   ACACE, 1979b.

Advisory Council for Adult and Continuing Education. Towards
   Continuing Education. Leicester: ACACE, 1979c.

Advisory Council for Adult and Continuing Education. Present
   Imperfect. Leicester: ACACE, 1980.

BBC Education. A Guide to BBC Educational Broadcasting.
   London: The British Broadcasting Corporation, 1979.

Becher, T., Embling, J., and Kogan, M. Systems of Higher
   Education: United Kingdom. New York: International
   Council for Educational Development, 1978.

British Association of Settlements. A Right to Read: Action
   for a Literate Britain. London: British Association of
   Settlements, 1974.

British Association of Settlements. Adult Literacy: A
   Continuing Need. The Final Report of the BAS Adult Literacy
   Project 1975-1977. London: BAS, 1978.

Cantor, L. M. Recurrent Education: United Kingdom. Paris:
   Organization for Economic Co-operation and Development,
   1974.

Charnley, A. "Education in Retirement." Age Concern (Manifesto Series Number 15), June 1974.

Charnley, A. H. The Concept of Success in Adult Literacy. London: Huntingdon Publishers, 1979.

Clyne, P. The Disadvantaged Adult: Educational and Social Needs of Minority Groups. London: Longman Group Ltd., 1972.

Committee on Continuing Education, The Open University. Report of the Committee on Continuing Education. Milton Keynes: The Open University, 1976.

Committee of Directors of Polytechnics. The Polytechnics: Vision into Reality. London: CDP, 1979.

Council for Continuing Education, Department of Education for Northern Ireland. Continuing Education in Socially Disadvantaged Areas of Northern Ireland. Belfast: Her Majesty's Stationery Office, 1978.

Council for Cultural Co-Operation, Committee for Out-of-School Education and Cultural Development. Adult Literacy Resource Agency of the United Kingdom. Strasbourg: Council of Europe, 1978.

Department of Education and Science. Adult Education: A Plan for Development (The Russell Report). London: Her Majesty's Stationery Office, 1973.

Department of Education and Science. Statistics of Education: 1975, Vol. 3, Further Education. London: Her Majesty's Stationery Office, 1977.

Department of Education and Science. Adult Literacy in 1977-78: A Remarkable Educational Advance. London: Her Majesty's Stationery Office, 1978.

Department of Education and Science. Statistics of Education: 1976, Vol. 3, Further Education. London: Her Majesty's Stationery Office, 1979.

Department of Education and Science and the Scottish Education Department. Higher Education into the 1990s. London and Edinburgh: Her Majesty's Stationery Office, 1978.

Fairbairns, J. Evaluation of Wider Opportunities for Women ("WOW") Courses: Final Report: London: Psychological Services, Manpower Services Commission, 1979.

Flude, R., and Parrott, A. Education and the Challenge of Change: A Recurrent Education Strategy for Britain. Milton Keynes: The Open University Press, 1979.

Fowler, G. Unit 13: Higher Education. Milton Keynes: The Open University, 1979.

Glatter, R., and Wedell, E. G. Study by Correspondence. Manchester: Longman, 1971.

Hall, J. "Parent Education--An Integral Part of Adult Education." Adult Education (Journal of the National Institute of Adult Education--England and Wales), March 1974, 46 (6), 387-390.

Hargreaves, D. On the Move: The BBC's Contribution to the Adult Literacy Campaign between 1972 and 1976. London: The British Broadcasting Corporation, 1977.

Hargreaves, D. Adult Literacy and Broadcasting. London: Pinter, 1980.

Hay, W. Adult Literacy in Britain: An Annotated Bibliography. London: The Library Association, 1978.

Hoggart, R. After Expansion: A Time for Diversity. Leicester: Advisory Council for Adult and Continuing Education, 1978.

Hutchinson, E., and Hutchinson, E. Fresh Horizons in English Adult Education. London: R.K.P., 1978.

Harvis, P. "Pre-Retirement Education: Design and Analysis." Adult Education, 1980 (in press).

Jones, H. A. Education and Disadvantage. Leicester: University of Leicester, Department of Adult Education, 1977.

Jones, H. A., and Charnley, A. H. (Eds.). Literacy and Adult Education: The U. K. Experience. Special issue of Literacy Discussion, Winter 1978, 9 (4).

Jones, H. A., and Charnley, A. H. Adult Literacy: A Study of Its Impact. Leicester: National Institute of Adult Education, 1979.

Jones, H. A., and Williams K. E. Adult Students and Higher Education. Leicester: ACACE, 1979.

Lowe, J. Adult Education in England and Wales. London: Michael Joseph, 1970.

Manpower Services Commission. MSC Review and Plan, 1978. London: MSC, 1978.

Manpower Services Commission. Annual Report 1978-79. London: MSC, 1979.

Mee, G., and Wiltshire, H. Structure and Performance in Adult Education. London: Longman Group Ltd., 1978.

Morgan, C., and Turner, C. Unit 12: The Colleges and Schools: Provision for the 16-19 Year Olds. Milton Keynes: The Open University, 1979.

McIntosh, N. E., and Woodley, A. Excellence, Equality, and the Open University. Milton Keynes: Survey Research Department, the Open University, 1975.

McIntosh, N. E. "A Comprehensive System of Education for Adults." In T. Schuller and J. Megarry (Eds.), World Yearbook of Education, 1979: Recurrent Education and Lifelong Learning. London: Kogan Page Ltd., 1979a.

McIntosh, N. E. To Make Continuing Education a Reality. Leicester: Advisory Council for Adult and Continuing Education, 1979b.

The National Institute of Adult Education. The Yearbook of Adult Education, 1979-80. Leicester: NIAE, 1979.

Newman, M. The Poor Cousin: A Study of Adult Education. London: George Allen and Unwin, 1979.

The Open University. The First Years of Life, Book 1, A New Life. Milton Keynes: The Open University, 1977.

The Open University, Information Services Department. An Introduction to the Open University. Milton Keynes: The Open University, 1978.

The Open University. Associate Student Handbook, 1980. Milton Keynes: The Open University, 1979.

The Open University and the Confederation of British Industry. Education and Industry. Milton Keynes: The Open University, 1978.

The Open University and Trades Union Congress. Education for Adults. Milton Keynes: The Open University, 1978.

Pre-Retirement Association of Great Britain and Northern Ireland. The Challenge of Retirement: A Handbook for Pre-Retirement Course Organisers and Tutors. London: PRAGBNL, 1977.

Roderick, G., and Stephens, M. (Eds.). Higher Education for All? London: Lewes, Falmer Press, 1979.

Russell, R. The FE (Further Education) System of England and Wales. Coombe Lodge, Blagdon, Bristol: The Further Education Staff College, 1979.

Scottish Adult Literacy Agency. Adult Literacy in Scotland: The Work of the Scottish Adult Literacy Agency. 1976-1979. Edinburgh: Scottish Adult Literacy Agency, 1979.

Scottish Education Department. Adult Education: The Challenge of Change (The Alexander Report). Edinburgh: Her Majesty's Stationery Office, 1975.

Scottish Education Department. Professional Education and Training for Community Education (The Carnegy Report). Edinburgh: Her Majesty's Stationery Office, 1977.

Scottish Institute of Adult Education. Yearbook of Adult Education in Scotland. Edinburgh: SIAE, 1978.

Small, N. Unit 14: Adults and Education. Milton Keynes: The Open University, 1979.

Smith, A. E. "An Adult Literacy Campaign in Great Britain." Reading World, December 1980, 20 (2), 119-122.

Smith, V. Opportunities for Women. Edinburgh: Scottish Institute of Adult Education, 1979.

Stephens, M. Living Decisions in Family and Community. A Retrospective Impression of an Experimental "Open Learning" Project for Adults. London: The British Broadcasting Corporation, 1976.

Tidmarsh, W. M. "Objectives in Pre-Retirement Education." Adult Education, May 1975, 48 (1), 251-256.

TOPS SP1. TOPS Completions (April 1978 - March 1979). London: Manpower Services Commission, 1980a (Mimeo).

TOPS SP1. The Training Opportunities Scheme. London: Manpower Services Commission, 1980b (Mimeo).

TPFU. TOPS 1 in 6 Follow-up Survey of Trainees; Results for the 1978/79 Financial Year. London: Manpower Services Commission, 1979 (Mimeo).

Training Services Division. Training for Skills: A Programme for Action. London: Manpower Services Commission, 1977.

Training Services Division. TOPS Review, 1978. London: Manpower Services Commission, 1978.

Williams, G., and Woodhall, M. Independent Further Education. London: Policy Studies Institute, 1979.

Wiseman, J. "United Kingdom: Proprietary Schools." In Organisation for Economic Co-Operation and Development, Learning Opportunities for Adults, Volume IV, Participation in Adult Education. Paris: OECD, 1977.

Woodhall, M. "United Kingdom: Adult Education and Training." In Organisation for Economic Co-Operation and Development, Learning Opportunities for Adults, Volume IV, Participation in Adult Education. Paris: OECD, 1977.

Workers' Educational Association. Report of the National Committee of the Workers' Educational Association for 1975-77. London: WEA, 1977.

Wynne, R. The Adult Student and British Higher Education. Brussels: Institute of Education, European Cultural Foundation, 1979.

THE UNITED STATES

Administration on Aging. HEW Fact Sheet AoA: Educational Opportunities for Older Persons. Washington, D.C.: U.S. Department of Health, Education and Welfare, Office of Human Development, National Clearinghouse on Aging, January 1978.

Administration on Aging. Facts About Older Americans 1978. Washington, D.C.: U.S. Department of Health, Education and Welfare, Office of Human Development Services, National Clearinghouse on Aging, 1979.

American Institute of Banking. American Institute of Banking Student Catalog. Washington, D.C.: American Bankers Association, 1980.

American Society for Training and Development. "Professional Societies Do More Continuing Education." ASTD National Report for Training and Development, January 16, 1978.

Arns, K. F. (Ed.). Occupational Education Today. New Directions for Community Colleges, No. 33. San Francisco: Jossey-Bass, 1981.

Atchley, R. C. The Social Forces in Later Life. Belmont, CA: Wadsworth Publishing Co., 1977.

Atelsek, F. J., and Gomberg, I. L. College and University Services for Older Adults. Washington, D.C. American Council on Education, 1977.

Benjamin, E. Barriers to Academic Re-Entry Women and How to Overcome Them: A Review Article. Evanston, Ill.: Program on Women, Northwestern University, 1980.

Benjamin, E., and Levy, J. Barriers to Educational Opportunities for Re-Entry Women in Private Universities. Evanston, Ill.: Program on Women, Northwestern University, 1980.

Boaz, R. L. Participation in Adult Education, Final Report, 1975. Washington, D.C.: National Center for Education Statistics, 1978.

Boaz, R. L.   Participation in Adult Education 1978.   Preliminary Tables.   Washington, D.C.:   National Center for
Education Statistics, 1980.

Bolton, N. H.   "The Older Wiser Learner in the Long Term Care
Facility."   Paper presented at the 32nd. Annual Scientific
Meeting of the Gerontological Society, Washington, D.C.,
November 28, 1979.

Brown, C. A. "Municipal Training Programs: 1975."   In Urban
Data Service Reports #8.   Washington, D.C.:   International
City Management Association, 1976.

Bushnell, D.   "Articulating with Industry in Economic
Development."   In K. F. Arns (Ed.), Occupational Education
Today.   New Directions for Community Colleges, No. 33.
San Francisco: Jossey-Bass, 1981.

Cahn, A. F.   (Ed.).   Women in Midlife--Security and Fulfill-
ment (Part I).   Washington, D.C.:   U.S. House of Representatives, Ninety-Fifth Congress, Select Committee on Aging and
Subcommittee on Retirement Income and Employment, Comm. Pub.
95-170, December 1978.

Calvert R., and Draves, C.   Free Universities and Learning
Referral Centers.   Washington, D.C.:   National Center for
Education Statistics, 1978.

Carnegie Commission on Higher Education.   Less Time, More
Options: Education Beyond the High School.   New York:
McGraw-Hill, 1971.

Carp, A., Peterson, R. E., and Roelfs, P. J.   "Adult Learning
Interests and Experiences."   In K. P. Cross, J. R. Valley,
and Associates, Planning Non-Traditional Programs.
San Francisco: Jossey-Bass, 1974.

Carr, T. W., and Ripley, R. M.   "Armed Forces and Veteran's
Education."   In E. J. Boone, R. W. Shearon, E. E. White, and
Associates, Serving Personal and Community Needs Through
Adult Education.   San Francisco: Jossey-Bass, 1980.

Catalyst.   General Information for the Returning Student:
Education Opportunities Series New York: Catalyst, 1979.

Cerra, F.   "Study Finds College Women Still Aim for Traditional Jobs."   The New York Times, May 11, 1980.

Charner, I., et al. An Untapped Resource: Negotiated Tuition Aid in the Private Sector. Washington, D.C.: National Manpower Institute, 1978.

Charner, I. Worker's Educational Benefits: An Exploration into the Non-use of Tuition Aid Programs. Washington, D.C.: National Institute for Work and Learning, 1979.

Charner, I. Patterns of Adult Participation in Learning Activities. Washington, D.C.: National Institute for Work and Learning, 1980.

Chase, B. (Ed.). The Single Parent: Journal of Parents Without Partners, April 1980, XXIII (3).

Christoffel, P. H. "Current Federal Programs for Lifelong Learning." School Review, 1978, 86 (3), 348-359.

Commission on Non-Traditional Study. Diversity by Design. San Francisco: Jossey-Bass, 1973.

Committee on Executive Management and Fiscal Affairs. State Government Training: State of the Art. Washington, D.C.: National Governors' Association, 1981.

Creange, R. "Campus Child Care: A Challenge for the 80's" (Field Evaluation Draft). Washington, D.C.: Project on the Status and Education of Women, Women's Re-entry Project, Association of American Colleges, 1980.

Cross, K. P. "Adult Learners: Characteristics, Needs, and Interests." In R. E. Peterson and Associates, Lifelong Learning in America. San Francisco: Jossey-Bass, 1979.

Cross, K. P. "Exploring New Frontiers in Higher Education." Delta Epsilon Sigma Lecture at the 1981 National conference of the American Association for Higher Education, Washington, D.C., March 1981.

Cross, K. P., Valley, J. R. and Associates. Planning Non-Traditional Programs. San Francisco: Jossey-Bass, 1974.

Cross, W., and Florio, C. You Are Never Too Old To Learn. New York: McGraw-Hill, 1978.

Delaloye, J. E. "Extending Continuing Education to the Elderly Homebound." Update/Interface, Center for Community Education/Older Americans Program, American Association of Community and Junior Colleges, January/February 1980, 1.

Dinkmeyer, D., and McKay, G. D. Systematic Training for Effective Parenting (STEP) Leader's Manual. Circle Pine, MN: American Guidance Service, Inc., n.d.

Education Commission of the States. Families and Schools: Implementing Parent Education, Report 121. Denver: Education Commission of the States, 1979.

Ekstrom, R. "Credentialing Women's Life Experiences." Paper presented at the American Association for Higher Education Annual Conference, Washington, D.C., March 1980.

Eliason, C. "It's (Past) Time to'Unstereotype'!" School Shop, June 1977a, 13-14.

Eliason, C. Women in Community and Junior Colleges: Report of a Study on Access to Occupational Education. Washington, D.C.: American Association of Community and Junior Colleges/American Association of Women in Community and Junior Colleges, 1977b.

Eliason, C. Neglected Women: The Educational Needs of Displaced Homemakers, Single Mothers and Older Women. Washington, D.C.: National Advisory Council on Women's Educational Programs, 1978.

Eliason, C. "Adult Assessment." Paper presented at American Association for Higher Education Annual Conference, Washington, D.C., March 1980.

Engelberg, S., Langley, P., and Warden, B. (Eds.). The Washington COFO Memo. Washington, D.C.: Coalition of Family Organizations, Spring 1979, 11 (2).

Family Network News. Menlo Park, Calif.: National YMCA Family Communication Skills Center, Fall 1979.

Feeney, H. M. "Women's Education." In E. J. Boone, R. W. Shearon, E. E. White, and Associates, Serving Personal and Community Needs Through Adult Education. San Francisco: Jossey-Bass Publishers, 1980.

Fisher-Thompson, J. "Barriers to Re-entry Women: College Tranfer Policies, Residency and Graduation Requirements" (Field Evaluation Draft). Washington, D.C.: Project on the Status and Education of Women, Women's Re-entry Project, Association of American Colleges, 1980.

Florio, C. "Education and Work Training Programs for Older Persons." Paper prepared for the HEW Lifelong Learning Project, Washington, D.C., 1978.

Frandson, P. E. "Continuing Education for the Professions." In E. J. Boone, R. W. Shearon, E. E. White, and Associates, Serving Personal and Community Needs Through Adult Education. San Francisco: Jossey-Bass, 1980.

Fraser, B. S. The Structure of Adult Learning, Education and Training in the United States. Washington, D.C.: National Institute for Work and Learning, 1980.

French, J. Education and Training for Middle-Aged and Older Workers: Policy Issues and Options. Washington, D.C.: National Institute for Work and Learning, 1980.

Gappa, J. M., and Uehling, B. S. Women in Academe: Steps to Greater Equality. AAHE-ERIC/Higher Education Research Report No. 1. Washington, D.C.: American Association for Higher Education, 1979.

Goldstein, H. Training and Education in Industry. Washington, D.C.: National Institute for Work and Learning, 1980.

Greenwald, S. Survey of Professional Society Continuing Education Programs. New York: Society of Mechanical Engineers, 1977.

Gordon, T. Parent Effectiveness Training. New York: Prentice-Hall, 1970.

Grosgebauer, C. "The Little Courses that Grew." American Education, U.S. Department of Health, Education and Welfare, June 1977, 13 (5).

Gross, R. The Lifelong Learner: A Guide to Self-Development. New York: Simon & Schuster, 1977.

Hansen, H. S., and Rapoza, R. S. (Eds.). Career Develoment and Counseling of Women. Springfield, IL: Charles C. Thomas Publishers, 1978.

Harrison, C. Working Women Speak: Education, Training, Counseling Needs. Washington, D.C.: National Advisory Council on Women's Educational Programs, July 1979.

Houle, C. O. The External Degree. San Francisco: Jossey-Bass, 1973.

Howe, L. K. Pink Collar Worker: Inside the World of Women's Work. New York: G.P. Putnam's Sons, 1977.

Hunter, C. S. J., and Harman, D. Adult Illiteracy in the United States. New York: McGraw-Hill, 1979.

Institute for Retired Professionals. Institute for Retired Professionals Bulletin, 1979-80. New York: New School for Social Research, 1979.

Institute of Lifetime Learning. Learning Opportunities for Older Persons. Washington, D.C.: National Retired Teachers Association/American Association of Retired Persons, 1979.

Jacobson, C. I. "New Challenges for Women Workers." The AFL-CIO American Federationist, April 1980, 87 (4), 1-8.

Johns, Y. A Survey of Older Women as Candidates for Re-Entry at Northwestern University. Evanston, IL.: Program on Women, Northwestern University, 1980.

Johnstone, J. W. C., and Rivera, R. J. Volunteers for Learning. Chicago: Aldine, 1965.

Jones, C. "Returning to Campus Careers for Older Americans." The Christian Science Monitor, December 6, 1979.

Kane, R. D., and Frazee, P. Adult Women in Vocational Education: Reentrants and Career Changers. Arlington, VA.: RJ Associates, Inc., May 1979.

Kanun, C., and Swanson, R. H. (Eds.). Programs and Registrations: 1976-77 Joint Report of the Association of Continuing Higher Education and the National University Extension Association. Washington, D.C. and Norman, OK.: Joint ACHE-NUEA Committee on Data and Definitions, 1977.

Kay, E. R. Adult Education in Community Organizations, 1972. Washington, D.C.: National Center for Education Statistics, 1974.

Kay, E. R. Program and Enrollments in Non-Collegiate Post-secondary School: 1973-74. Washington, D.C.: National Center for Education Statistics, 1976.

Kemp, F. B. Noncredit Activities in Institutions of Higher Education for the Year Ending June 30, 1976. Washington, D.C.: National Center for Education Statistics, 1978.

Kenny, W. R., and Grotelueschen, A.D. Educational Opportunity for American Workers: A Responsibility and Challenge for Adult Educators. College of Education Occasional Paper No. 8. Urbana-Champaign: University of Illinois, 1979.

Kerr, C. K. "Forward." In K. von Moltke, and N. Schneevoigt, Education Leaves for Employees. San Francisco: Jossey-Bass, 1977.

Kieffer, J. A. "What About Those Potential Students Over 50?" The Chronicle of Higher Education, February 19, 1980.

Kirschner Associates Inc. An Analysis of Selected Issues in Adult Education. Washington D.C.: Kirschner Associates Inc., 1976.

Klus, J. P., and Jones, J. A. Continuing Education Activities for Scientists and Engineers. Washington, D.C.: American Society for Engineering Education, 1979.

Kopelov, C. (Ed.). Summary Report: Developing University and Union Workers Education Programs for Women. A National Invitational Conference, June 15, 1979. Ithaca, N.Y.: Institute for Education and Research on Women and Work, New York State School of Industrial and Labor Relations, Cornell University, 1979.

Korim, A. S. Older Americans and Community Colleges: A Guide for Program Implementation. Washington, D.C.: American Association of Community and Junior Colleges, 1974.

Lane Community College Women's Program Newsletter. Eugene, OR: Lane Community College, February 1980.

Levine, H. A. Strategies for the Application of Foreign Legislation on Paid Educational Leave to the United States Scene. New Brunswick, N.J.: Rutgers University Labor Education Center, 1975.

Lifelong Learning Project, U.S. Department of Health, Education, and Welfare. Lifelong Learning and Public Policy. Washington, D.C.: U.S. Government Printing Office, 1978.

Lusterman, S. Education in Industry. New York: The Conference Board, 1977.

Lynton, E. A. The Role of Colleges and Universities in Corporate Education. Boston: Center for Studies in Policy and the Public Interest, University of Massachusetts, 1981.

MacKenzie, J. R.   "Labor Education."   In E. J. Boone, R. W. Shearon, E. E. White, and Associates, Serving Personal and Community Needs Through Adult Education. San Francisco: Jossey-Bass, 1980.

Maes, N.   Re-Entry: A Handbook for Adult Women Students. Evanston, IL: Program on Women, Northwestern University, 1980.

Marano, C.   Displaced Homemakers: Program Options...An Evolving Guide   Baltimore: Older Women's League Educational Fund, 1978.

March, G. B., Hooper J. O., and Baum, J.   "Life-Span Education and the Older Adult: Living Is Learning." Educational Gerontology, 1977, 2, 163-172.

McGuigan, D. (Ed.).   "Researchers Talk About Problems of Women's Continuing Education." Newsletter: Center for Continuing Education of Women, The University of Michigan, Summer 1977, (1).

Mezirow, J., Darkenwald, G. G., and Knox, A. B. Last Gamble on Education. Washington, D.C.: Adult Education Association of the USA, 1975.

Miller, H.   "Adult and Continuing Education in the Armed Services."   Carbondale, Ill.: University of Southern Illinois, 1980 (Mimeo).

Momeni, J.   Adult Participation in Education: Past Trends and Some Projections for the 1980's. Washington, D.C.: National Center for Work and Learning, 1980.

Moses, S. The Learning Force: A More Comprehensive Framework for Educational Policy. Syracuse, N.Y.: Education Policy Research Center, Syracuse University, 1971.

Murphy, J., and Florio, C. Never Too Old To Teach. New York: Academy for Educational Development, 1978.

National Advisory Council on Adult Education. 1975 Annual Report: A Target Population in Adult Education. Washington, D.C.: U.S. Government Printing Office, 1976.

National Advisory Council on Extension and Continuing Education. A Special Report to the President and to the Congress of the United States by the National Advisory Council on Extension and Continuing Education. Washington, D.C.: Government Printing Office, September 1979.

National Association for Public Continuing & Adult Education. The Public Continuing and Adult Education Almanac, 1980. Washington, D.C.: NAPCAE, 1980.

National Center for Education Statistics. Enrollments and Programs in Noncollegiate Postsecondary Schools, 1978. Washington, D.C.: NCES, 1979a.

National Center for Education Statistics. Fall Enrollment in Higher Education 1978. Washington, D.C.: NCES, 1979b.

National Center for Education Statistics. The Condition of Education: 1980 Edition. Washington, D.C.: NCES, 1980.

National Commission on Working Women. A Step Toward Equality: A Progress Report. Washington, D.C.: Center for Women and Work, National Manpower Institute, 1978.

National Commission on Working Women. National Survey of Working Women: Perceptions, Problems and Prospects. Washington, D.C.: Center for Women and Work, National Manpower Institute, June 1979.

National Home Study Council. "Over Four Million Studying by Correspondence." News Release. Washington, D.C.: NHSC, 1973.

National Manpower Institute. Negotiated Education: Tuition Assistance in Collective Bargaining Agreements. Washington, D.C.: National Manpower Institute, 1977.

National Recreation and Park Association. "Local Parks and Recreation." Parks and Recreation, August 1971, 6, 17-31.

National University Extension Association/ Peterson's Guides. 1977-1979 Guide to Independent Study Through Correspondence Instruction. Washington, D.C.: National University Extension Association, 1977.

Newman, F. Report on Higher Education. Washington, D.C.: U.S. Office of Education Department of Health, Education and Welfare, 1971.

North American Society of Adlerian Psychology. The International Directory of Adlerian Family Education Centers. Chicago: North American Society of Adlerian Psychology, 1979.

Northcutt, N. Adult Functional Competency: A Summary. Austin: University of Texas, 1975.

Office of Personnel Management. National Independent Study Center; Fiscal Year 1980 Course Catalog. Washington, D.C.: OPM, 1980.

O'Keefe, M. The Adult, Education, and Public Policy. Aspen, CO: Aspen Institute for Humanistic Studies, 1977.

Okes, I. E. Adult Education in the Public School Systems: 1968-69 and 1969-70. Washington, D.C.: F. Loyal Greer, 1976.

Okes, I. E. Participation in Adult Education, Final Report, 1969. Washington, D.C.: National Center for Education Statistics, 1974.

Okes, I. E. Participation in Adult Education, Final Report, 1972. Washington, D.C.: National Center for Education Statistics, 1976.

Palmer, P. M., and Grant, S. L. The Status of Clerical Workers: A Summary Analysis of Research Findings and Trends. Washington, D.C.: Women's Studies Program, George Washington University and Business and Professional Women's Foundation, 1979.

Parents Without Partners, Inc. The First Twenty Years, 1957-1977. Washington, D.C.: Parents Without Partners, Inc. International, 1978.

Parker, F., and Parker, B. J. Women's Education--A World View. Westport, CT.: Greenwood Press, 1979.

Parks, A. "Children and Youth of Divorce in Parents Without Partners, Inc." Journal of Clinical Child Psychology, Summer 1977, 23, 44-48.

Pascal, A. H., Bell, D., Dougharty, L. A., Dunn, W. L., Thompson, V. M., and others. An Evaluation of Policy Related Research on Programs for Mid-Life Career Redirection: Vol. II--Major Findings. Santa Monica, Calif.: The Rand Corporation, 1975.

Peterson, R. E., and Associates. Lifelong Learning in America: An Overview of Current Practices, Available Resources, and Future Prospects. San Francisco: Jossey-Bass, 1979.

Pifer, A. "Is it Time for an External Degree?" College Board Review, Winter, 1970-71, 78, 5.

Pifer, A. Women Working: Toward a New Society. New York:
Carnegie Corporation of New York, 1976.

Pitchell, R. J. Financing Part-Time Students: The New
Majority in Postsecondary Education. Washington, D.C.:
American Council on Education .

Project on Equal Education Rights. "Summary of the Regu-
lations for Title IX, Education Amendments of 1972."
Washington, D.C.: PEER, NOW Legal Defense and Education
Fund, n.d.

Project on the Status and Education of Women. "Women's
Centers: Survey Identifies Typical Traits." PSEW News-
letter, Association of American Colleges, Washington, D.C.,
Fall 1979.

Purdue University, Office of the Dean of Students. "Span Plan
Program." West Lafayette, Indiana: Purdue University,
1979.

Raspberry, W. "A Warning Behind Cold statistics. Chicago
Tribune, February 12, 1980.

Resident Associate Program. Smithsonian Resident Associate
Program. Washington, D.C.: Smithsonian Institution,
1980.

Rich, D., Mattox, B., and Van Dien, J. "Building on Family
Strengths: The 'Nondeficit' Model for Teaming Home and
School." Educational Leadership, April 1979, 36 (7),
13-27.

Roark, A. C. "Senate Panel Would Spend $23-Million to En-
courage Women to Go into Science." The Chronicle of Higher
Education, May 5, 1980, 15.

Robinson, D. "Control Data's Selby Bindery Plant Employs 100%
Part-Time Staff of Mothers and Students." World of Work
Report, September 1977a, 2 (9).

Robinson, D. "New Jobs, Work Arrangements Needed for Older
People as Right to Work to Age 70 Wins Support in Congress."
World of Work Report, December 1977b, 2 (12).

Roth, E. B. "Education's Gray Boom." American Education,
July 1978, 14, 6-11.

Rowan, C. T. "Some Sad Facts About America's Children."
The Washington Star, May 5, 1980, A-11.

Ruyle, J. and Geiselman, L. A. "Non-Traditional Opportunities and Programs." In K. P. Cross and J. R. Valley, Planning Non-Traditional Programs. San Francisco: Jossey-Bass, 1974.

Safilios-Rothschild, C. Sex Role Socialization and Sex Discrimination: A Synthesis and Critique of the Literature. Washington, D.C.: The National Institute of Education, 1979.

Schecter, I. 1980 Chartbook of Federal Programs in Aging: Services, Research, Training. Washington, D.C.: Care Reports, Inc., 1980.

Servicemen's Opportunity Colleges. Servicemen's Opportunity Colleges, 1979 Directory. Washington, D.C.: American Association of State College and Universities and American Association of Community and Junior Colleges, 1979.

Sexton, R. F. Barriers to the Older Student: The Limits of Federal Financial Aid Benefits. Washington, D.C.: National Institute for Work and Learning, 1980.

Shoup, M. "Uplifting Elderhostel." The Washington Post, May 11, 1980.

Smith, S. "New Law Offers Teachers Opportunity for Job Sharing, Phased Retirement." World of Work Report, January 1980, 5 (1).

Smith, D. A. An Overview of Training in the Public Sector. Arlington, VA: The Analytic Sciences Corporation, 1979.

Smithsonian Resident Associate Program. 1980 Membership Survey. Washington, D.C.: Smithsonian Institution 1980 (Mimeo).

Sosdian, C. P. External Degrees: Program and Student Characteristics. Washington, D.C.: National Institute of Education, 1978.

Sticht, T. G. (Ed.). Reading for Working: A Functional Literacy Anthology. Washington, D.C.: Human Resources Research Organization, 1975.

Timmermann, S. "Lifelong Learning and the Older Adult." The Journal of the Institute for Socioeconomic Studies, Winter 1978, III (4), 19-27.

Timmermann, S., and Chelsvig, K. (Eds.). Tuition Opportunities for Older Persons. Washington, D.C.: Institute of Lifetime Learning, National Retired Teachers Association/ American Association of Retired Persons, 1980.

Tough, A. The Adults Learning Projects: A Fresh Approach to Theory and Practice in Adult Learning. Toronto: Ontario Institute for Studies in Education, 1971.

Tough A. "Major Learning Efforts: Recent Research and Future Directions." Adult Education, Summer 1978, 28 (4), 250-263.

Turner, J. C. "Labor and Continuing Education." In Proceedings of the Invitational Conference on Continuing Education, Manpower Policy, and Lifelong Learning. Washington, D.C.: National Advisory Council on Extension and Continuing Education, 1977.

University of California. Innovative Developments in Aging: Area Agencies on Aging. A Directory. Comm. Pub. No. 96-197. Washington, D.C.: Select Committee on Aging, U.S. House of Representatives, Ninety-Sixth Congress, December 1979.

U.S. Bureau of Labor Statistics. Women in the Labor Force: Some New Data. Washington, D.C.: U.S. Department of Labor, October 1979a.

U.S. Bureau of Labor Statistics. Young Workers and Families: A Special Section. Special Labor Force Report 233. Washington, D.C.: U.S. Department of Labor, 1979b.

U.S. Bureau of the Census. Divorce, Child Custody and Child Support, Current Population Reports: Special Studies. Series P-23, No. 84. Washington, D.C.: U.S. Department of Commerce, 1979a.

U.S. Bureau of the Census. Social and Economic Characteristics of the Older Population: 1978. Special Series P-23, No. 85. Washington, D.C.: U.S. Department of Commerce, 1979b.

U.S. Bureau of the Census. Marital Status and Living Arrangements: March, 1979, Current Population Reports: Population Characteristics. Series P-20, No. 349. Washington, D.C.: U.S. Department of Commerce, 1980.

U.S. Department of Defense. Graduate Education in the Department of Defense: A Report to the House Appropriations Committee. Washington, D.C.: U.S. Department of Defense, March 1979.

U.S. Department of Education. Directory of Adult-Serving Programs. Washington, D.C.: Office of Adult Learning and Community Education, U.S. Department of Education, 1981.

U.S. Department of Labor, Employment and Training Administration, and Office of Human Services, U.S. Department of Health, Education and Welfare. Employment and Training Report of the President. Washington, D.C.: U.S. Department of Labor and U.S. Department of Health, Education and Welfare, 1979.

U.S. Military Enlistment Processing Command. Military-Civilian Occupational Source Book, Second Edition. Washington, D.C.: U.S. Department of Defense, January 1978.

U.S. Office of Personnel Management, Workforce Effectiveness and Development. Employee Training in the Federal Service; Fiscal Year 1979. Washington, D.C.: OPM, 1980.

U.S. Senate Special Committee on Aging. Part I, Developments in Aging: 1979. 96th Congress, 2nd Session, Senate Report No. 96-613. Washington, D.C.: U.S. Senate Special Committee on Aging, 1980a.

U.S. Senate Special Committee on Aging. Part 2, Appendixes, Developments in Aging: 1979. 96th Congress, 2nd Session, Senate Report No. 96-613. Washington, D.C.: U.S. Senate Special Committee on Aging, 1980b.

Von Eckardt, W. "Museums as Schools." The Washington Post, April 12, 1980.

Wakefield, R., and Wakefield, D. (Eds.). "Federally Sponsored Family Research: Current Priorities and Programs." The American Family: National Action Overview, Special Report No. 2. Washington, D.C.: Wakefield Associates, July 1979.

Watfish, B. "Displaced Homemakers the Focus of State Legislation, CETA Amendments; Education, Job Opportunities Offered." World of Work Report, August 1979, 4 (8).

Weinstein, M. "Women and Work." Occupational Outlook Quarterly, Bureau of Labor Statistics, U.S. Department of Labor, Summer 1979, 24-26.

Weinstock, R. The Graying of the Campus. New York: Educational Facilities Laboratories, 1978.

Westervelt, E. M. Barriers to Women's Participation in Post-secondary Education. Washington, D.C.: National Center for Education Statistics, 1975.

Westoff, L. A. (Ed.). Women in Search of Equality: Focus 6. Princeton, N.J.: Educational Testing Service, 1979.

White House Conference on Families. "Major Concerns of Hearing Participants." Washington, D.C.: White House Conference on Families, April 1980 (Mimeo).

"Who's Working Part-Time These Days?" Occupational Outlook Quarterly, Bureau of Labor Statistics, U.S. Department of Labor, Summer 1979, 14-17.

Wilder, B. Issues in Education and Training for Working Women. Washington, D.C.: National Institute for Work and Learning, 1980.

Women's Bureau, U.S. Department of Labor. Women Workers Today. Washington, D.C.: U.S. Department of Labor, October 1976.

Women's Bureau, U.S. Department of Labor. Facts About Women Heads of Household and Heads of Families. Washington, D.C.: U.S. Department of Labor, December 1979a.

Women's Bureau, U.S. Department of Labor. The Earnings Gap Between Women and Men. Washington, D.C.: U.S. Department of Labor, 1979b.

Women's Bureau, U.S. Department of Labor. Women in the Labor Force, January 1979-1980. Washington, D.C.: U.S. Department of Labor, February 1980.

Work Incentive Program. WIN: 1968-1978. A Report at 10 Years. Washington, D.C.: U.S. Department of Labor, U.S. Department of Health, Education and Welfare, 1979.

World of Work. "Around the World of Work: News Items and Updates of General Interest." World of Work Report, November 1979, 5 (1).

World of Work. "Preretirement Education Programs Gain as Business Eyes Effect of Inflation on Retirement Plans of Older Workers." World of Work Report, March 1980, 5 (3).

Yankelovich, Skelly, and White, Inc. Raising Children in a Changing Society: The General Mills American Family Report, 1976-77. Minneapolis: General Mills, Inc., 1977.

MULTINATIONAL ANALYSES

Adult Education Section. <u>National Adult Education Boards,</u>
<u>Councils and Other Co-Ordinating Bodies</u>. Paris: United
Nations Educational, Scientific and Cultural Organization,
1979.

Bureau of International Labor Affairs. <u>One World of Working</u>
<u>Women</u>. Washington, D.C.: U.S. Department of Labor, 1980.

Centre for Educational Research and Innovation. <u>Developments</u>
<u>in Educational Leave of Absence</u>. Paris: Organization for
Economic Co-Operation and Development, 1976.

Centre for Educational Research and Innovation. <u>Alternation</u>
<u>between Work and Education: A Study of Educational Leave</u>
<u>of Absence at Enterprise Level</u>. Paris: Organization for
Economic Co-Operation and Development, 1978.

Charnley, A. <u>Paid Educational Leave in France, Sweden, and</u>
<u>West Germany</u>. London: Hart Davis Educational, 1975.

Charters, A. N., and Associates. <u>Comparing Adult Education</u>
<u>Worldwide</u>. San Francisco: Jossey-Bass, 1981.

Charters, A. N. (Ed.). <u>International Handbook of Resources</u>
<u>for Educators of Adults</u>. Syracuse: School of Education,
Syracuse University, 1977.

Clearinghouse on Development Communication. <u>Development</u>
<u>Communication Report. Special Issue on World Literacy</u>.
Washington, D.C.: Clearinghouse on Development Communication, April 1980.

Council for Cultural Co-Operation, Committee for Out-of-School
Education and Cultural Development. <u>Colloquy on the Inte-</u>
<u>gration of Adult Education Within a Framework of Permanent</u>
<u>Education: Trends towards the Self-Management of Education</u>.
Strasbourg: Council of Europe, 1975.

Council for Cultural Co-Operation, Committee for Out-of School
Education and Cultural Development. <u>Organisation, Content</u>
<u>and Methods of Adult Education</u>. Strasbourg: Council of
Europe, 1977.

Council of Europe. <u>Developments in Adult Education Struc-</u>
<u>tures</u>. Strasbourg: Council of Europe, 1976.

Council of Europe. <u>Preparation for Retirement</u>. Strasbourg:
Council of Europe, 1977.

Council of Europe. <u>Recent Demographic Developments in the</u>
<u>Member States of the Council of Europe</u>. Strasbourg:
Council of Europe, 1979.

Cropley, A. J. (Ed.). <u>Lifelong Education: A Stocktaking</u>.
Hamburg: UNESCO Institute for Education, 1979.

Division of Statistics on Education United Nations Education,
Scientific and Cultural Organization. <u>Manual for the</u>
<u>Collection of Adult Education Statistics</u>. Paris: UNESCO,
1975.

Division of Statistics on Education, United Nations Educational, Scientific nd Cultural Organization. <u>International</u>
<u>Standard Classification of Education</u>. Paris: UNESCO, 1976.

Employment and Training Administration. <u>From Learning to</u>
<u>Earning: A Transnational Comparison of Transition Services</u>.
Washington, D.C.: U.S. Department of Labor, 1979.

European Bureau of Adult Education. <u>Adult Education Legis-</u>
<u>lation in Ten Countries of Europe</u>. Bergen, Netherlands:
European Bureau of Adult Education, 1974.

European Bureau of Adult Education and the International
Council of Adult Education. "European-American Conference
on Facilitating the Re-Entry of Women to the Labor Force."
Newsletter, March 1980, 35-36.

European Centre for the Development of Vocational Training.
<u>Continuing Education and Training: File of Innovations in</u>
<u>the E.C. Member States</u>. Berlin: CEDEFOP, 1979.

European Centre for Higher Education. <u>New Forms of Higher</u>
<u>Education in Europe</u>. Bucarest: European Centre for Higher
Education, 1976.

European Centre for Higher Education. <u>Statistical Study on</u>
<u>Higher Education in Europe 1970-1975</u>. Bucarest: European
Centre for Higher Education, 1978.

Evans, E.B., and Saia, L.S. <u>Day Care for Infants</u>. Boston:
Beacon, 1972.

Fersh, S. (Ed.). International Developments in Post-Secondary Short-Cycle Education. Washington, D.C.: American Association of Community and Junior Colleges, 1978.

Fragniere, G. (Ed.). Education Without Frontiers. London: Duckworth, 1976.

Further Education Staff College. Craft Apprenticeship in Europe. Comparative Papers in Further Education, Number Five. Coombe Lodge, Blagdon, Bristol: The Further Education Staff College, 1979.

Gelpi, E. A Future for Lifelong Education, Volume One, Lifelong Education: Principles, Policies and Practices. Dorset: Direct Design Ltd., 1979.

Ginzberg, E. (Conference Chairman). Facilitating the Reentry of Women to the Labor Force: Summary of Conference Proceedings. Paris: The German Marshall Fund of the United States and the Assistant Secretary of Labor for Women's Employment in France, November 28-30, 1979.

Harnqvist, K. Individual Demand for Education. Paris: Organisation for Economic Co-Operation and Development, 1978.

Holmberg, B. Distance Education, A Short Handbook. Malmo, Sweden: Hermods, 1974.

International Bureau of Education. Directory of Documentation and Information Services in Adult Education. Paris: United Nations Educational, Scientific and Cultural Organization, 1977.

International Bureau of Education. Terminology of Adult Education. Paris: United Nations Educational, Scientific and Cultural Organization, 1979.

International Council for Adult Education. National Organizations for Co-Operation in Adult Education. Essex, England: ICAE, 1974.

International Labor Organization. 59th Session. Geneva, 1974. Texts of the "Convention Concerning Paid Educational Leave" and "Recommendation Concerning Paid Educational Leave." In Centre for Educational Research and Innovation, Developments in Educational Leave of Absence. Paris: Organization for Economic Co-Operation and Development, 1976.

International Labour Office. Ten Years of Training; Developments in France, Federal Republic of Germany and United Kingdom, 1968-1978. Geneva: International Labour Organisation, 1977a.

International Labour Office. Training Systems in Eastern Europe; A Study of Change in the Organisation of Training in the USSR, Poland and the German Democratic Republic. Geneva: International Labour Organisation, 1979b.

Janne, H., and Schwartz, B. Le Developpement Europeen de l'Education Permanente, Collection Etudes, Serie Education No. 3. Brussels: Commission Des Communautes Europeennes, 1977.

Levine, H. A. Paid Educational Leave: NIE Papers in Education and Work, Number Six. Washington, D.C.: National Institute of Education, 1977.

Lowe, J. The Education of Adults: a World Perspective. Paris: The United Nations Educational, Scientific and Cultural Organization, 1975.

MacKenzie, N., Postgate, R., and Scupham, J. Opening Learning: Systems and Problems in Post-Secondary Education. Paris: United Nations Educational, Scientific and Cultural Organization Press, 1975.

Mushkin, S. J. (Ed.). Recurrent Education. Washington, D.C.: National Institute of Education, 1974.

National Center for Higher Education Management Systems. Using ISCED for Reporting NCES Data to UNESCO: A Feasiblity Study; Final Report. Boulder, Colo.: NCHEMS, 1978.

National Commission for Manpower Policy. European Labor Market Policies. Special Report No. 27. Washington, D.C.: National Commission for Manpower Policy, 1978.

Nollen, S. D. "The Current State of Recurrent Education." In D. W. Vermilye (Ed.), Education and Work. San Francisco: Jossey-Bass, 1977.

Organisation for Economic Co-Operation and Development. Beyond Compulsory Schooling: Options and Changes in Upper Secondary Education. Paris: OECD, 1976.

Organisation for Economic Co-Operation and Development. Education and Working Life. Paris: OECD, 1977a.

Organisation for Economic Co-Operation and Development. Learning Opportunities for Adults, Volume I, General Report. Paris: OECD, 1977b.

Organisation for Economic Co-Operation and Development. Equal Opportunities for Adults, Volume IV, Participation in Adult Education. Paris: OECD, 1977c.

Organisation for Economic Co-Operation and Development. Equal Opportunities for Women. Paris: OECD, 1979a.

Organisation for Economic Co-Operation and Development. Learning Opportunities for Adults, Volume II, New Structures, Programmes and Methods. Paris: OECD, 1979b.

Organisation for Economic Co-Operation and Development. Learning Opportunities for Adults, Volume III, The Non-Participation Issue. Paris: OECD, 1979c.

Ridell, L. (Ed.). Nordisk Vuxenutbildning 78/79 (Nordic Adult Education Yearbook). Malmo, Sweden: Liber Laromedel, 1978.

Rubenson, K. Participation in Recurrent Education. Paris: Organization for Economic Co-Operation and Development, 1977.

Schuller, T. "Lifelong Learning: Foreign Experiences." Paper prepared for the HEW Lifelong Learning Project, Washington, D.C., 1978.

Schuller, T., and Megarry, J. (Eds.). World Yearbook of Education, 1979: Recurrent Education and Lifelong Learning. London: Kogan Page Ltd., 1979.

Schwartz, B., and de Blignieres, A. (For the Steering Group on Permanent Education). Draft Final Report. Strasbourg: Council of Europe, Council for Cultural Co-Operation, 1977.

Strub, M. A Selected Bibliography on Paid Educational Leave: Tuition Assistance and Union-Company Educational Opportunity Programs. New Brunswick, N.J: Rutgers Labor Education Center, 1977.

Titmus, C. "Proposed Theoretical Model for the Comparative Study of National Adult Education Systems in Europe." Society and Leisure, 1976, 2, 39-54.

United Nations Educational, Scientific and Cultural Organization. Recommendations on the Development of Adult Education. Paris: UNESCO, 1976.

United Nations Educational, Scientific and Cultural Organization. Report of the Committee of Experts Convened on Making Lifelong Education A Normal Part of University Life: Final Report. Paris: UNESCO, 1977a.

United Nations Educational, Scientific and Cultural Organization. Report of the Committee of Experts Convened on Making Lifelong Education A Normal Part of University Life: Supplement to the Final Report. Paris: UNESCO, 1977b.

United Nations Educational Scientific and Cultural Organization. "Education and the Elderly." UNESCO Adult Education Information Notes, No. 1 1980, 1-6.

von Moltke, K., and Schneevoight, N. Educational Leaves for Employees: European Experience for American Consideration. San Fransicso: Jossey-Bass, 1977.

Williams, G. Towards Lifelong Education: A New Role for Higher Education Institutions. Paris: United Nations Educational, Scientific and Cultural Organization, 1977.

Workers' Education Programme. International Seminar on the Role of Trade Unions in Educational Reform. Geneva: International Labour Office, 1976.

NAME INDEX

SUBJECT INDEX

ABOUT THE AUTHORS

RICHARD E. PETERSON is Senior Research Psychologist in the Berkeley Office of Educational Testing Service.

He has published on the topics of lifelong learning as public policy, adult education interests and participation patterns, community educational needs assessment, college and university enrollment trends, institutional goals, program evaluation, college student subcultures, and student activism. While in the Princeton Office of ETS, he directed development of several instruments for college self-study.

ROBERT A. FELDMESSER is Senior Research Sociologist at Educational Testing Service. Previously he taught sociology at Harvard and Brandeis Universities and Dartmouth College.

He has published in the areas of both Soviet social structure and the sociology of education. His work has appeared in the American Journal of Sociology, Harvard Educational Review, and Educational Record, as chapters in several books, and in monographs published by ETS. In 1976, he directed an exchange of U.S. and Soviet scholars and administrators in the area of higher education.

SALLY SHAKE GAFF is on the staff of the National Association of State Boards of Education. Before this she worked as an independent consultant in Washington, D.C. In Stockton, California, she was an administrator and trainer in public school compensatory education programs.

She has written about faculty development and community needs for adult learning services, co-authoring Professional Development: A Guide to Resources (1978) and Community Needs for Postsecondary Alternatives (1975), for the California Legislature.

JOHN S. HELMICK is presently a Senior Staff Associate at Educational Testing Service. He has been with ETS since 1952 in a variety of roles including administration of testing programs and Director of the Berkeley Office of ETS. Before joining ETS he taught psychology at the University of California at Los Angeles and at the University of Hawaii.

Dr. Helmick has written on various aspects of educational testing and measurement and has consulted on the use of tests and the organization of testing agencies in a number of countries.

H. DEAN NIELSEN is a Senior Research Scientist for the Institute for International Research. He is currently Chief of Party for a USAID-sponsored educational development project in Indonesia. In 1978 and 1979 he was a staff member of ETS' International Office. In 1974 and 1975 he was a Spencer Foundation Research Fellow at the University of Stockholm.

Dr. Nielsen has published on the economics of nonformal education, school social climates, and student-environment interaction.

JOHN R. VALLEY has been at Educational Testing Service for more than twenty-five years where he is currently Area Director for Program Development in the College Board division.

Mr. Valley has published widely on nontraditional education, external degrees, and the education of adults. His "Local Programs: Innovations and Problems" appears in Lifelong Learning in America (Peterson and Associates) and his "External Degree Program" is in Explorations in Nontraditional Study (Gould and Cross).

Northern Michigan University

3 1854 003 374 470

EZNO
LC5215 A38
Adult education and training in industri